Securing Social Networks in Cyberspace

Securing Social Networks in Cyberspace

Edited by
Al-Sakib Khan Pathan

CRC Press
Taylor & Francis Group
Boca Raton London New York

CRC Press is an imprint of the
Taylor & Francis Group, an **informa** business

First edition published 2022
by CRC Press
6000 Broken Sound Parkway NW, Suite 300, Boca Raton, FL 33487-2742

and by CRC Press
2 Park Square, Milton Park, Abingdon, Oxon, OX14 4RN

CRC Press is an imprint of Taylor & Francis Group, LLC

ISBN: 978-0-367-68173-9 (hbk)
ISBN: 978-0-367-68175-3 (pbk)
ISBN: 978-1-003-13452-7 (ebk)

DOI: 10.1201/9781003134527

Typeset in Times
by SPi Technologies India Pvt Ltd (Straive)

To my family

Contents

PART I Protection of Personal Information in Social Networks

Part II Securing Multimedia Contents

Part III Cyberbullying, Cyberstalking, and Related Issues

Part IV   Other Issues for Securing Social Networks and Online Profiles

Preface

Today's world is unimaginable without online social networks. Nowadays, millions of people connect with their friends and families by sharing their personal information with the help of different forms of social media. Using social media is often more convenient than meeting with one another in person but sometimes individuals face different types of issues while maintaining the multimedia contents. For instance, managing audios, videos, photos could be complicated because it is difficult to maintain the security and privacy of these multimedia contents uploaded on a daily basis and often, without enough care of privacy. Simple video can provide a lot of information about a person, about his/her food habit, surroundings, home setting, products used, etc. In fact, sometimes even personal or sensitive information could get viral if that leaks out unintentionally. Any leaked content can be shared and made a topic of popular talk all over the world within few seconds with the help of the social networking sites. In the setting of Internet of Things (IoT) that is supposed to connect millions of devices, such contents could be shared from anywhere anytime.

Considering such a setting, this book aimed to collate the key security and privacy concerns faced by individuals and organizations who use various social networking sites differently for different reasons. Current state-of-the-art defense mechanisms that can bring somewhat long-term solutions to tackling these threats, were also be considered.

As the call for chapters were disseminated, we got a great response from the authors, based all around the globe. After a rigorous selection process, we could accept and include a total of 13 chapters in this book. A total of 40 authors represent at least 12 countries: Algeria, Australia, Bangladesh, Canada, Greece, India, Italy, Malaysia, Saudi Arabia, Turkey, UK, and USA. This shows the diversity of geographical locations for the contributors to this book.

The book has four parts, and each part has similarly themed chapters. The first three parts contain three chapters each and the last one contains four chapters. The parts are labeled as follows:

Part I: Protection of Personal Information in Social Networks
Part II: Securing Multimedia Contents
Part III: Cyberbullying, Cyberstalking, and Related Issues
Part IV: Other Issues for Securing Social Networks and Online Profiles

Each chapter is written in a way that should be easily accessible to the general readers as well as to the experts working in this domain. We hope that the chapters would provide a sufficient amount of beneficial information for research works for the graduate students at the PhD and master's levels, for the academics, researchers in the laboratories, and the people related to the industry.

Al-Sakib Khan Pathan
Independent University, Bangladesh

Acknowledgment

Like all other works in my life, I will first of all give sincere thanks to the Almighty Allah for giving me this stamina and time to complete this work. During the COVID-19 pandemic period, starting this work and completing has proven to be quite difficult indeed. In the usual time (before the pandemic), I would often spend time in the office with full concentration and sometimes would work at night; but during this period, with all family members' educational and other activities online and from home (with periodic lockdown phases), this task became complicated. Interestingly, top-quality chapters still came in from all over the globe, which made the selection process relatively easy. I express my sincere gratitude to all the authors who contributed to this book project. Special thanks to the publishing staff and the publishing editor for giving me this opportunity.

Al-Sakib Khan Pathan
Independent University, Bangladesh

Editor

Al-Sakib Khan Pathan, PhD, is a professor of Computer Science and Engineering. Currently, he is with the Independent University, Bangladesh as an adjunct professor. He received his PhD degree in Computer Engineering in 2009 from Kyung Hee University, South Korea and BSc degree in Computer Science and Information Technology from Islamic University of Technology (IUT), Bangladesh in 2003. In his academic career so far, he worked as a faculty member at the CSE Department of Southeast University, Bangladesh during 2015–2020, Computer Science department, International Islamic University Malaysia (IIUM), Malaysia during 2010–2015; at BRACU, Bangladesh during 2009–2010, and at NSU, Bangladesh during 2004–2005. He serves as a guest professor at the Department of Technical and Vocational Education, Islamic University of Technology, Bangladesh since 2018. He also worked as a researcher at Networking Lab, Kyung Hee University, South Korea from September 2005 to August 2009 where he completed his MS leading to PhD. His research interests include wireless sensor networks, network security, cloud computing, and e-services technologies. Currently he is also working on some multidisciplinary issues. He is a recipient of several awards/best paper awards, and has several notable publications in these areas. So far, he has delivered over 23 Keynotes and Invited speeches at various international conferences and events. He was named on the list of Top 2% Scientists of the World, 2019 by Stanford University, USA in 2020. He has served as a general chair, organizing committee member, and technical program committee (TPC) member in numerous top-ranked international conferences/workshops like INFOCOM, GLOBECOM, ICC, LCN, GreenCom, AINA, WCNC, HPCS, ICA3PP, IWCMC, VTC, HPCC, SGIoT, etc. He was awarded the IEEE Outstanding Leadership Award for his role in IEEE GreenCom's13 conference and IEEE Outstanding Service Award in recognition for the service and contribution to the IEEE 21st IRI 2020 conference. He is currently serving as the editor-in-chief of *International Journal of Computers and Applications* (Taylor & Francis, UK), editor of *Ad Hoc and Sensor Wireless Networks* (Old City Publishing), *International Journal of Sensor Networks* (Inderscience Publishers), and *Malaysian Journal of Computer Science*, associate editor of *Connection Science* (Taylor & Francis, UK), *International Journal of Computational Science and Engineering* (Inderscience), area editor of *International Journal of Communication Networks and Information Security*, guest editor of many special issues of top-ranked journals, and editor/author of 26 books. One of his books has been included twice in Intel Corporation's Recommended Reading List for Developers, second half of 2013 and first half of 2014; three books were included in IEEE Communications Society's (IEEE ComSoc) Best Readings in Communications and Information Systems Security, 2013; several other books were indexed with all the titles (chapters) in Elsevier's acclaimed abstract and citation database, Scopus and in Web of Science (WoS), Book Citation Index, Clarivate Analytics, at least one has been approved as a textbook at NJCU, USA in 2020; one is among the Top Used resources on SpringerLink in 2020 for UN's Sustainable Development Goal 7 (SDG7) (Affordable and Clean Energy), and another has been translated to simplified Chinese language from the English version. Also, two of his journal papers and one conference paper were included under different categories in IEEE Communications Society's (IEEE ComSoc) Best Readings Topics on Communications and Information Systems Security, 2013. He also serves as a referee of many prestigious journals. He received some awards for his reviewing activities: one of the most active reviewers of IAJIT several times; Elsevier Outstanding Reviewer for Computer Networks, Ad Hoc Networks, FGCS, and JNCA in multiple years. He is a senior member of the Institute of Electrical and Electronics Engineers (IEEE), USA.

Contributors

Basant Agarwal
Department of Computer Science and
    Engineering
Indian Institute of Information Technology,
    Kota
Jaipur, India

Mohiuddin Ahmed
Computing and Security Discipline in the
    School of Science
Edith Cowan University
Perth, Australia

Sherif Saad Ahmed
School of Computer Science
University of Windsor
Windsor, Canada

Bilal Alatas
Software Engineering Department
Firat University
Elazig, Turkey

Muhammad Al-Digeil
National Research Council Canada
Ottawa, Canada

Zian Md. Afique Amin
Department of Computer Science
Kulliyyah of Information and Communication
    Technology
International Islamic University Malaysia
Kuala Lumpur, Malaysia

Adnan Anwar
School of Information Technology and
    Strategic Centre for Cyber Security
    Research and Innovation
Deakin University
Geelong, Australia

Saiful Azad
Faculty of Science and Engineering
Department of Computer Science and
    Engineering
Green University
Dhaka, Bangladesh

Alice Baroni
SPGI Department
University of Padova
Padova, Italy

Abhijit Bhowmik
Computer Science
American International University-Bangladesh
Dhaka, Bangladesh

Francesco Buccafurri
Department of Computer Science, Electronics,
    Mathematics and Transportation (DIMET)
University of Reggio Calabria
Reggio Calabria, Italy

Umit Can
Computer Engineering Department
Munzur University
Tunceli, Turkey

Thomas M. Chen
School of Mathematics, Computer Science and
    Engineering
City University of London
London, UK

Vincenzo De Angelis
Department of Information Engineering,
    Infrastructure and Sustainable Energy
    (DIIES) University of Reggio Calabria
Reggio Calabria, Italy

K. A. Dhanya
Department of Computer Science and
    Engineering
SCMS School of Engineering and Technology
Ernakulam, India

Ahmed Falah
School of Information Technology
Deakin University
Geelong, Australia

Eima Fatima
Department of Pharmacology
School of Pharmaceutical Education and
    Research (SPER)
Jamia Hamdard
New Delhi, India

Mohamed Amine Ferrag
Department of Computer Science
Guelma University
Guelma, Algeria

S. M. Raihan Gafur
Computer Science
American International University-Bangladesh
Dhaka, Bangladesh

Robert Gordon
Reverse Logistics Management
American Public University System
Hollywood, California, USA

Yonis Gulzar
Department of Management Information
    Systems
College of Business Administration
King Faisal University
Al-Ahsa, Saudi Arabia

Md. Tanvir Hasan
Department of Computer Science and
    Engineering
Southeast University
Dhaka, Bangladesh

Md. Redwan Hossain
Department of Computer Science and
    Engineering
Southeast University
Dhaka, Bangladesh

Mohammad Husain
Department of Computer Science
California State Polytechnic University,
    Pomona
Pomona, California, USA

Maria Francesca Idone
Department of Information Engineering,
    Infrastructure and Sustainable Energy
    (DIIES)
University of Reggio Calabria
Reggio Calabria, Italy

Rishabh Jindal
School of Information Technology
Deakin University
Geelong, Australia

M. Shamim Kaiser
Institute of Information Technology
Jahangirnagar University
Dhaka, Bangladesh

Mohammad Shadab Khan
Department of Information Systems
Kulliyyah of Information and Communication
    Technology
International Islamic University Malaysia
Kuala Lumpur, Malaysia

Cecilia Labrini
Department of Information Engineering,
    Infrastructure and Sustainable Energy
    (DIIES)
University of Reggio Calabria
Reggio Calabria, Italy

Leandros Maglaras
School of Computer Science and Informatics
De Montfort University
Leicester, UK

Mufti Mahmud
Department of Computer Science
Nottingham Trent University
Nottingham, UK

Mohammad Mamun
National Research Council Canada
Ottawa, Canada

Nicholas Pantic
Department of Computer Science
California State Polytechnic University,
 Pomona
Pomona, California, USA

Vassilis Papaspirou
Department of Electrical and Computer
 Engineering
University of Thessaly
Lamia, Greece

Al-Sakib Khan Pathan
Department of Computer Science and
 Engineering
Independent University, Bangladesh
Dhaka, Bangladesh

Abrar Rafid
Department of Computer Science
American International University-Bangladesh
Dhaka, Bangladesh

Khan Nasik Sami
Department of Computer Science
Kulliyyah of Information and Communication
 Technology
International Islamic University Malaysia
Kuala Lumpur, Malaysia

P. Vinod
Department of Computer Applications
Cochin University of Science and Technology
Cochin, India

P. R. Vishnu
Department of Computer Science and
 Engineering
SCMS School of Engineering and Technology
Ernakulam, India

Sharyar Wani
Department of Computer Science
Kulliyyah of Information and Communication
 Technology
International Islamic University Malaysia
Kuala Lumpur, Malaysia

Part I

Protection of Personal Information in Social Networks

1 User Awareness for Securing Social Networks

Abhijit Bhowmik, S. M. Raihan Gafur, and Abrar Rafid
American International University-Bangladesh, Dhaka, Bangladesh

Saiful Azad
Green University, Dhaka, Bangladesh

Mufti Mahmud
Nottingham Trent University, Nottingham, UK

M. Shamim Kaiser
Jahangirnagar University, Dhaka, Bangladesh

CONTENTS

1.1 INTRODUCTION

Since the invention of the internet in the mid-twentieth century, the internet has grown into one of the most important technologies in the modern world. According to the report by Internet World Stats, 4,833 million people had access to the internet in June 2020, which is 62% of the entire world population and this percentage has increased by 61.6% since 1995 [1]. These data suggest how quickly this technology has grown in such a short period. From education to controlling home appliances from thousands of miles away, the internet is used in every aspect of our life. This rapid increase of the internet has also highly impacted the daily activities of human life [2]. Human interaction has changed significantly over the last two decades. One of these changes is due to the upsurge of social networking sites' usage in recent years. Social networking can be defined as a medium of modern human communication with the help of internet-based services [3]. There are plenty of social networking sites that are different in terms of their features, privacy, users. Still, all of these

DOI: 10.1201/9781003134527-2

websites have a similar goal to ensure a medium where their users can communicate with each other. Some of the most famous social networking websites are Facebook, Twitter, WhatsApp, LinkedIn, WeChat, TikTok, etc. [4]. These websites provide features like creating a profile, post sharing, messaging, commenting, audio and video calling, and group chatting [5]. The emergence of these features has completely revolutionized human interaction as they are easier and less time-consuming. However, the increasing use of social media has raised some serious security concerns [6].

Social networking sites are usually more user-friendly than other websites on the internet, which helps them to attract new users [2]. However, a considerable amount of user knowledge is essential to use these sites responsibly. While signing up for social media sites, users are prompted to provide their personal information such as name, age, address, email id, password, and job information. Most of these data are usually kept private, but many people do not understand the consequence of publicly sharing this data, leading to many security concerns. Another concerning fact is the use of these data by different advertising firms [7]. As social media platforms do not charge any money for their services, they instead show different advertisements based on the interests of their user. Most of users are not aware of this information, while others are concerned about their privacy. A survey in 2014 gathered some interesting facts about the control of personal data collected by these sites. A total 91% of Americans surveyed agreed that they have no control over their shared data on the internet. The survey results also showed that 80% of social media users were concerned about advertisers [8]. Recent stories like the Cambridge Analytica conspiracy have raised more concerns. This agency has used the personal information of more than 50 million Facebook users and used them to influence the 2016 American presidential election. This incident shows the extent of incidents that might occur due to a data breach of social media profiles [9].

Data mining, phishing attempts, botnet attack, malware share – these are some of the major privacy concerns of social networking [10]. The solution to most of these concerns is not possible by the users, but they can secure their accounts by taking some security measures. In this chapter, different steps for securing social networks are discussed in detail. The rest of the chapter is structured as follows: Section 1.2 will discuss the evolution of social networking websites. Section 1.3 will discuss the emergence of different social networking sites and their growth. Different incidents that raise concern about social media are discussed in Section 1.4. In Section 1.5, the finding from different social media related incidents has been presented. In Section 1.6, the discussion and conclusion are provided.

1.2   EVOLUTION OF SOCIAL NETWORKING WEBSITES

It took around three decades for the social networking websites to reach today's position. In earlier days, these websites were only used for networking. But now, most of these websites have expanded beyond our imagination. Social networking sites are now being used for networking, job-searching, online marketing, and advertising [11, 12]. With the addition of numerous features, these sites also have tremendous growth in terms of users. At present, billions of people are using social networking websites on a daily basis.

1.2.1   History

1997–2002: The creation of the first social networking website took place around 1997. With the emergence of SixDegrees.com and AOL Instant Messenger (AIM), we got the our first experience of social networking [13]. AOL created AIM to allow their registered users to communicate in real time. It was highly popular in America during the late 1990s with many interesting features, including chat robots, which could receive texts and send replies. The popularity of this service lasted until the late 2000s until the arrival of other social networking websites. SixDegrees.com was created by Andrew Weinreich in 1997. Using this website, people could receive updates about a SixDegree user, after confirming their relationship with him or her. It had around 3,500,000 registered users. These two social networks introduced many features that are still used in this generation's social networks, like making lists among friends, families, and other members. However, different privacy concerns and lucrative features of other competitors have declined their popularity. Friendster, which was one of the most popular social networking sites of the early 2000s, was founded in 2002 [14]. Although the site was focused on dating, it is considered one of the first original social networks. Like today's social networks, Friendster allowed its users to contact each other, and they could also share posts among them. Sharing of media, finding new events, hobbies – Friendster came up with many features we are still using through other social networks. Before the number of users started to decline, Friendster had around 8.2 million worldwide users in 2008. In 2002, another social networking website, LinkedIn, was launched, which is still widely popular. The website was primarily launched in December 2002 by Reid Hoffman [15]. Unlike other social networks, LinkedIn has been more niche-driven to ensure a professional social network for its users. It is mainly used for networking between professional people. Users can open profiles, share their CV, work experience, skills, achievements, and picture. Different companies can check their potential job candidates by checking their LinkedIn profile beforehand. Users can also follow different companies to keep updated about them. To keep updated about other users and view their profile, users often need to send connection requests. After getting connected, one can get updates about his or her connections on their homepage. There is also a job section on the site, where the users can search for jobs based on their skills and preferences. LinkedIn also provides recommendations based on a user's profile and his skills. Users can also save jobs they would like to apply for later. Nowadays, companies are recruiting their employees directly through LinkedIn. Users are prompted to submit their CVs and resume while applying through their LinkedIn profile. Based on that, companies can then connect with them for further discussion. It has changed the classic concept of job search and recruitment. There is also a feature to invite non-users to join LinkedIn and become a connection. The invitee can accept the request or can choose to decline it. A user can use his/her connection in many ways. (S)he can introduce him/herself to a hiring manager through one of his/her connections. This improves the chance of employment by a huge margin. People also often share their achievements, works, and interests on their homepage with their connections, and others can choose to "like" or give other reactions to that post. These dynamic features have made LinkedIn one of the most popular social networks of the modern era. Currently, there are more than 700 million LinkedIn users worldwide [16].

2003–2006: MySpace was launched in 2003 to share the social networking market beside other websites like Friendster. MySpace cloned many features of the Friendster, but they managed to provide more freedom to the users. The basic version of MySpace was launched with only 10 days of coding by the eUniverse employees. The project gained huge popularity among young users due to its simplicity and attractive user interface. They were different from other social networks by providing options to the users to customize their channel, and their partnership with different bands and musicians also attracted many users. In July 2005, MySpace was purchased for $580 milllion by News Corporation, which attracted huge media attraction. The site reached its visitor peak in 2008, when more than 75.9 million users visited the site per month.

Another social media platform from 2003 is Facebook, which started as a project of Mark Zuckerberg in 2003 while studying at Harvard University. Zuckerberg got the inspiration from the "facebook," a student directory in Harvard University containing students' pictures and personal information. He created an online version of the student directory that allowed only the students at Harvard College to register. The success of this website led Zuckerberg to expand this project for other universities in the USA. The approach of registering university students helped Facebook to show early growth and share acquisition from tech tycoons like Microsoft has helped Facebook gain global exposure. Facebook also launched at a time when the number of people worldwide with internet access was rising at a rapid pace. Despite rising on the top of social networks, Facebook often faced different allegations of data breaching of its users. There were numerous controversies on Facebook's use of their user data. In 2010, US NSA started to take profile information from

Facebook [17]. In April 2018, a report published by Arch Technica showed how the official Facebook app has been breaching user privacy since 2015, which includes phone calls and text messages [3]. However, these controversies did not stop the growth of Facebook. A report by Statista shows that Facebook had 2.701 million users worldwide in the second quarter of 2020 [18].

2007–2010: During these years, Facebook became open and wide. There was a new trend which was about sending friend requests. People all over the world were sending friend requests to everyone all around the world. Afterward, it became famous on the brink. People started doing business on Facebook and started doing publicity for their business. It was a huge evolution for online business. It has grown quite impressively and now it has approximately 1.2 million users. Twitter was also a renowned social networking site at that time. The hashtag (#) debuted at that time. It became a huge success at that time. Another huge breakthrough was when Spotify went live. The music industry thrives within it. Anyone is able to use the app for listening to music. People can stream songs online and can play music on any device. The world moves onto social media, and Facebook introduces the "like" button – people can click "like" on those that they like. Pinterest also goes live and the world takes a holiday from the safety of its armchair, while craft enthusiasts rejoice. Then at the end of 2010, Instagram launches and people begin to understand how to tell stories via photography and images.

2011–2014: Snapchat launched in time as a new app for young people. But slowly, many users got used to it. Then slowly, this app became huge. People started using this app all over the world. Facebook acquired Instagram for $1 billion as a potential competitor to Snapchat. Snapchat was sending 60 million snaps daily in 2013 [19, 20]. Sadly, about 58.5 million of them are posted for the sake of posting, which means more meaningless photos [20]. MySpace relaunched with an endorsement from Justin Timberlake, but nobody cared. Instagram reaches 200 million active users. It became famous among photo-centric people. Ultimately all of them became addicted to photo. Instagram became a huge success.

2015–2020: Facebook enables gifs and became fun. Snapchat also introduces a filter that became popular. All the time, social media apps are trying to do something new. In 2016 Snapchat rebranded itself to "Snapchat Inc." In 2018 Cambridge Analytica harvested troves of user data without their consent and used that for political purposes. Until now, social media has not changed that much. No new revolutionary came. All the social networking sites are introducing some sort of funky features that lure people for a while.

1.3   EMERGENCE OF SOCIAL NETWORKING SITES

People want to communicate with each other. But long distances made it very tough to communicate. As we see, there were lots of mediums of communication systems, i.e., pigeons, telegraph, fax, letter, and many others. All these were time-consuming and might take weeks, months, or even years. We are lucky enough that we are born in the era of the internet, which we use today as part of daily life [21].

In previous eras, people used to depend on those mediums of communications. In the twentieth century, communication is so fast that we can connect with anyone throughout the world. Important data is passed through our social networking sites, which have brought many business opportunities. People conduct their business through these sites. The world is vast; people can easily access the international market through these social networking sites. Many businesses are moving online, and social networking sites play a major role in boosting their sales [11, 16]. In this century, almost everyone has a smartphone in their hands. Businesses get their targeted audience or buyer. These social network sites use ad algorithms, which help other sellers to reach their targeted buyers [22].

At the beginning, there were lots of businesses shutting down and the economy was suffering. People were getting fired from their jobs. After the evolution of the internet and social networking sites, the economic boom was ready to start [23]. After a time, everyone has become dependent on social networking sites to know the daily news. No one thought that social networking sites could manage to enter the share markets, and people would be buying shares of the social networking sites. Eventually, they were expecting a high margin profit.

Facebook has the largest user base in the world, with around 2.4 billion users. Other web-based media platforms include YouTube and WhatsApp, which have more than one billion clients each.

These numbers are enormous – there are 7.7 billion individuals on the planet, with 3.5 billion of us on the internet. This implies online media platforms are utilized by at least one in three individuals on the planet, and more than 66% of all web clients [24].

Social media has changed the world and turned world communication into a global village. TikTok just launched its app in 2016 and reached half a billion users by 2018. And in 2020, this app has been adding 20 million new users per month [19].

But Facebook has dominated the market for a decade. Facebook has always been a people's choice for business. Facebook just doesn't have a good number of users, but also it attracts people to share their good times. Facebook also plays some mind games. In 2018 Mark Zuckerberg tweeted that their motto is to make Facebook for people to share their good times together. Thus people share their thoughts and choices on Facebook. For this reason, Facebook wins the market on the aspects of users, and people are expected to stick with Facebook for a while yet. Facebook always attracts people for content and entertainment. If we talk about communication, Facebook has it all. Facebook now has 2.4 billion clients and is the most famous online media platform today. YouTube, Instagram, and WeChat follow, with more than a billion clients. Tumblr and TikTok follow straight after, with over a large portion of a billion clients [4].

Already Facebook has obtained all information from its users and access to their activities. So it can easily send any sort of advertisement to them according to the user [25].

Social media sites are popular among teenagers. Snapchat and Instagram are famous among them. Most teenagers use Snapchat and Instagram as their daily social networking sites, and they often share their thoughts and feelings through these sites. Even Facebook has bought Instagram. And on a user basis, many young people are using these sites mostly as a daily ritual. Influencers find these sites great places for product branding. They can gain popularity as well as money. So both these sites are hyped up with young kids from all around the globe.

Snapchat has 238 million active users daily; 70% are female and 30% are male. All over 24% are adults [19], which means young people are more likely to use the app. But most people use this app right now as a source of entertainment and have less productive uses. But those who want to make money out of it can really take advantage of people and lure them into buying or viewing their product and making money out of it. So in the next few decades, it might be the case that people are more dependent on many other social networking apps, which are yet to be launched.

At the time of writing, Instagram has a total number of 1 billion active users. Instagram was started by Kevin Systrom and Mike Krieger in San Francisco, who at first had a go at creating a stage like Foursquare, but then turned their attention only to picture sharing. The word Instagram is a combination of "moment camera" and "wire."

The iOS variant was delivered through the iTunes App Store on October 6, 2010, and the Android app was delivered on April 3, 2012. The prevalence of the platform soars, with the company reporting more than 40 million diverse customers just two years after dispatch. This grabbed the eye of Facebook, which authoritatively bought Instagram for $1 billion in the mid of 2012 [26]. In the near future, Instagram likely overtake Facebook – it's clear that Instagram is adding many users every day. It's already one of the most popular social networking apps among younger people. The total number of businesses on Instagram is 25 million plus. So we can imagine there are lots of businesses going on Instagram. Instagram ranks as number six worldwide among social networking apps.

Twitter is also one of the popular news feed-related apps among people. Despite that, Twitter has 325 million active users in different countries around the world [27]. Twitter has been published using Ruby on Rails, a particular Ruby PC programming language in the web application framework. Its interface allows for open variety and combination with other online administrations. The administration was organized for 2006 by Evan Williams and Biz Stone, both of whom worked at

Google before leaving to dispatch Odeo's podcasting adventure. Williams, who recently developed the mainstream web composing apparatus Blogger, began pursuing various avenues for one of Odeo's side tasks – a short message administration (SMS), which at that point was called Twttr. Seeing the future of the item, Williams bought Odeo and started to create Obvious Corp. as well. Specialist Jack Dorsey joined the supervisory crew, and the finished version of Twitter appeared at the Southwest Music Meeting in Austin, Texas, in March 2007. Twitter, Inc., was made as a corporate company the following month, due to an investment imbuement.

From its commencement, Twitter was principally a free SMS with an informal communication component. All things considered, it came up short on the reasonable income stream that one could discover on locales that got pay from pennant promoting or enrollment expenses. With the quantity of one-of-a-kind guests expanding somewhere in the range of 1,300% in 2009, clearly Twitter was more than a specialty interest. Notwithstanding, in a year that saw the person-to-person communication juggernaut Facebook make money for the first time, it was not clear whether Twitter could accomplish monetary autonomy from its funding financial specialists. In April 2010, Twitter uncovered "Advanced Tweets" – promotions that would show up in indexed lists – as its planned essential income source [28].

As we are dependent on the internet, we need to use it daily. More social networking platforms are going to emerge for the need.

1.4　THE DARK SIDE OF SOCIAL NETWORKING

Social networking has a big dark side, of which we aren't fully aware. We are just simply coming to understand the role online media plays throughout everyday life and in business. The bright side of web-based media is broadly noted. Numerous individuals, brands, and associations have profited from web-based media as it interfaces individuals with each other and regularly with sponsors. But there are many disadvantages of social networking platforms [6, 29–31].

There is a dark side to online media that more individuals should talk about – computerized dramatization and unintended ramifications for shoppers, brands, or businesses. What's more, each brings new security considerations, difficulties, and opportunities for customers and promoters. Mindfulness is the initial segment of tending to the dark side of web-based media. At that point, we need to address the risky unintended results of online media use. The unintended outcomes of web-based media are first for customers. The saddest episodes incorporate suicides and murders broadcast through Facebook Live. Web-based media was the stage for these misfortunes, and web-based media made another sort of crowd of live conduct that can circulate around the web rapidly. There are social dangers inherent with live online media, and our age is amidst this exceptional social test. Advanced dramatization is the event of and responses to negative online customer practices, for example, cyberbullying, vengeance, sexual entertainment, assault, and related online happenings [24].

Advanced dramatization can happen with different types of innovation, for example, through messaging; however, web-based media is a ready setting and stage for it on account of the audience, intuitive nature, and now the ability to stream live. Other unintended results of online media are for brands, organizations, and associations. Fired-up buyers have taken to Pepsi, New Balance, Nordstrom, and American Air's online media pages with a barrage of complaints and abuse. The Age of Social Media offers capacity to shoppers, who utilize web-based media for customer activism. Computerized dramatization is additionally intrinsic when customers depict an ideal self as opposed to a more credible self. This creates identity clashes as upward self-correlations conflict with an unauthentic picture. Regular posting of costly material belongings or luxurious excursions can also create negative sentiments to other online media users, such as envy or dread of passing up some major opportunity, i.e., "fear of missing out," or "FOMO."

After some time, an observed outcome is abuse, overconsumption, and web-based media fixations or addictions. Individuals can feel associated, in any event, when they truly are not. A consistent theme in the entirety of this is protection. Since the introduction of the Information Age, the sharing, assortment, and utilization of individual information have developed exponentially, with an ever-expanding sum gathered from various new and advancing sources. For advertisers, the estimation of this information lies in the capacity to all the more likely comprehend and collate purchasers' needs, empowering a more engaged comprehension of crowds and division. What can web-based media organizations or potential advertisers do to address the dark side of online media use? Versatile innovation, and the enormous information insurgency it is assisting with driving, have achieved a requirement for another perspective just as new strategies for overseeing information in a moral way. As opposed to depending on legitimate rules for reasonable data practices and customer information assurance set by legislative controllers, it is significant for a business to set up important self-administrative rules dependent on intensive comprehension of future advantages and disadvantages, why they matter, and how they will affect buyers, the economy, and society. More advanced tactics to deal with cyberbullying include instructive assets, protection settings, and mindfulness crusades from web-based media organizations, which are sure strides forward. For advertisers and industry experts, contemplations of information assortment settings and data sensitivities must be perceived and tended to morally. For instance, recognizing the changing conditions where purchasers invite promotion personalization and information-driven informing methodologies requires progressive, ongoing exploration as innovations rise, gadgets become more associated, and protection observations develop [29].

Such an examination plan would improve strategy suggestions for industry to consider before strict government guidelines lessen these chances. Doing so won't just secure their notorieties and estimate their plans of action but will, however, increase their upper hand by defining themselves as shopper backers and trailblazers of new network norms that honor the aspects of individual protection rights generally essential to versatile web-based media clients.

Facebook and different types of online media have assumed control over the web. Clearly, individuals are using online media because they think it improves their lives. However, does it truly? Are individuals truly jumping on Facebook to mingle or would they say they are studying others and their lives to observe what goes on? Is it true that they are venting about their abhorrence of legislative issues or government substances on the planet all in all? Are individuals battling on Facebook or different types of online media and annihilating connections instead of upgrading them or improving individuals' lives?

In 2014, an examination was distributed in "PCs in Human Behaviors" that uncovered that most individuals using web-based media are not utilizing it to be social. Rather it was uncovered that the dominant parts utilize it as a method for devouring data, which analysts discovered leaves them unfilled and unsatisfied. In 2016, another examination was published in *Current Opinion in Psychology* that said that begrudging others via web-based media prompts sorrow. At the point when you are looking through photographs of somebody's ongoing outing to Hawaii, cheerful relationship statuses, gatherings, or individuals making some great memories as a rule and you are sick, tragic, or alone, it just causes you to feel even more forlorn and discouraged [30].

Nowadays, we see that people's happiness depends on social media. Yet people often get depressed and have feelings of emptiness when they see people are buying expensive things and flaunting them on social networking sites. Many people put on a false face, showing that they are happy on social media, but they are not in real life.

Another important topic is that our social life on the internet is not personal anymore. Many hackers depend on the chance of gaining access to our personal information for their own interests. At anytime and in any situation, it might fall into the wrong hands. There is a huge problem; just because everybody uses a site doesn't mean it is 100% safe. This previous year was one of the most terrible in information breaches yet, with 6,000,000 Facebook individuals influenced by a bug that sent clients' private data to outside sources. 8,000,000 LinkedIn, eHarmony, and Last.fm passwords were taken and transferred to a Russian programmer gathering, and 250,000 Twitter clients' data were hacked. We've all observed the phony tweets by individuals claiming to be anecdotal characters, or in any event, emulating famous people [31].

I was doing some research on hacking. While researching the hacking, there were some people who faced serious problems that ruined their reputation and life. Hackers always try to find a way to interfere with their network and then blackmail them. Basically, what do hackers do? They take recognizable data (PII – Personally Identifiable Information) like names, locations, and government-backed retirement numbers to break into somebody's records and use them. Organizations are especially helpless because they handle and store colossal measures of this sort of information. What's more, the more information they store, the more prominent the dangers. There is a term known as identity theft. There are various reasons why hackers take information. The most famous and most evident explanation is monetary benefit. Most hackers need to benefit, and they can undoubtedly do this by taking data like bank or login subtleties. They can take your cash from your records, apply for a MasterCard, or advance under your name, or they can likewise exchange your data to another criminal on the web. The dark web is loaded with criminals purchasing and selling taken individual data. In the previous scarcely of all those years, there has been another improvement in hacking for monetary profit. It has gotten progressively mainstream for hackers to break into your gadget and encode the information on it. It's called ransomware, and its pernicious entertainers hold your records prisoner until you make the requested payment within a specific timeframe. On the off chance that you don't pay, the information is normally annihilated by the hacker.

Shockingly, not all programmers are in it for the cash; some take data and go about as shadowy vigilantes. Known as "hacktivism," gatherings or people cooperate to bring down fear-monger gatherings, severe systems, governments, and dealing rings. We've all known about Edward Snowden, presumably one of the most notable hacktivists, who leaked information from the National Security Agency. There's also the Anonymous organization, which has been behind 45% of hacktivism in the previous four years. Nonetheless, the gathering presently is by all accounts outdated, or possibly just extremely quiet. An extremely modest number of programmers simply need to flaunt what they can do, and they have no expectation of taking data or making a benefit. Some of the time, they dispatch a hack to show how poor an enterprise's network protection is. A case of this is the scandalous Ashley Madison information leak, where the profiles of 32 million clients were made freely accessible. The programmers didn't need cash; they simply needed the site brought down. Ashley Madison is a dating stage for individuals looking for extramarital undertakings, and the hole, in a real sense, destroyed a few families.

We should always concentrate on our usage of the internet and try to help our family members, so they don't face such difficult problems.

There are various ways to obtain someone's private or personal information. Malware is one of the easiest ways to get into someone's device. There are numerous sorts of malware that can be utilized to take your own data, including key loggers, information stealers, banking malware – and that's only the tip of the iceberg. Most strains ordinarily center on login qualifications, charge card data, program autofill information, and cryptographic money wallets. Certain varieties, for example, the scandalous Vega Stealer, track down explicit document types, for example, PDF, Word, Excel, and text records and exhilarate (move the information without approval) them to a distant order and control worker. Malware normally spreads through malevolent email connections, advertising, drive-by downloads, and pilfered programming.

Another method is phishing. Phishing is a type of low-tech social design in which cybercriminals endeavor to remove sensitive data, for example, login accreditations, credit or debit card data, and recognizable data (PII). In an ordinary phishing trick, assailants act like a legitimate organization, for example, Microsoft, Amazon, or Netflix and guarantee there's an issue with your record. The message urges you to tap on a connection where you can probably resolve the issue by affirming your secret key or entering your charge card data. This information is sent straightforwardly to the hackers, who would then be able to access your genuine record and the data inside.

Phishing assaults are normally conveyed through email, yet they can likewise be executed through web-based media, instant messages, and calls.

Weak passwords are another way private identities can be accessed. A password is key to ensuring full access to all of our computers and smartphones, from email to internet banking. A JanRain Software Company survey showed that 50% of adults use five or more passwords, and while the situation seems positive, multiple passwords may cause problems when people noted that they prefer to take the simplest concept in several different codes. What are the 25 worst-used passwords of the year 2019? The words "123456," "Password." It's funny that these passwords are still in use. We should use strong passwords that are difficult to guess.

There are lots of other side effects of using online platforms. Everything we share online remains on the internet. So anyone can have access to our privacy. But the thing is, social media or networking platforms are working for user security; they always say that their first priority is always their users' security. Still, there is always a chance of getting hacked.

1.5 FINDINGS AND WAYS TO RAISE USER AWARENESS

Social media has its flaws. And while there are also negative aspects to it, we also see that individuals don't always take the best precautions. The online media stages are ubiquitous these days, and we have linked ourselves in ways that we never imagined 10 years ago. We instantly exchange details and updates with the association organizations we have assembled and are thus overflowed with updates from these corresponding organizations. While it is beneficial to exchange data as such, it brings with it a range of risks. The riskiest method of using online media is apparently to exchange data and different ways in which this data appears to be harmful. Potential offenders search for individuals in the middle of a journey; hackers look for data they can use to browse their records; tricksters look for poor people to exploit; and personality hoodlums pursue appropriate goals. The root problem is the same – there are many data available to people who do not even know it. There are many different models.

Cyberbullying is another concern that has come to the fore due to the increased use of web-based media. The web has shown itself to be where individuals feel good making comments that they will possibly never say face to face. Frequently, the problem is compounded by the posting of individuals without understanding the actual factors in a given situation. It's imperative to be mindful of your web operations, so you don't add to such an issue or become a casualty. Instruct yourself about every platform's abilities for managing oppressive, hostile, or unlawful materials and communications, and with the policy that you set up in circumstances of cyberbullying, provocation, or following. Try not to comment unnecessarily or post disturbing content on Facebook or any other networking site. Be mindful about the applications (tests, games, and so on) that you permit to connect to your web-based media profiles. These applications might be gathering individual data about you beyond your email address. There are some tips to help us maintain best practices while using social media. They are:

- Don't use slang or swear words on any platforms.
- Educate yourself before using any platforms of social networking sites. Always be prepared for something unusual.
- Be careful giving quizzes, installing apps, playing online games because they may cause harm to your device and claim access to your personal information, gallery, or other bank credentials.
- Don't automatically believe that somebody is who they indicate to be – confirm. Fake profiles are an enormous issue for web-based media platforms, identified with fraud and online harassment.
- Utilize two-factor validation and solid passwords to make sure about your logins to web-based media. Specifically, two-factor confirmation will make it considerably harder for programmers to assume control over your records, regardless of whether your secret word is taken. The majority of the bigger, notable locales offer this component.

- Don't accept cookies from every site, because who knows what site will take intrusive data.
- Keep your profile private and try to keep your information private. Many people don't give a second thought about giving their personal data, a major aspect of their profile. When the client gives any recognizable data, for example, address and date of birth, the expectation is that it helps their friends find them. People accept that their friends know their PII and share something that just gives clarity to their friend network.

Online media is unavoidable. All things considered, an organization utilizes Twitter or Facebook to advance itself and speak with potential customers. If that is not the situation, at some point your associates will, in all likelihood, utilize web-based media somehow. What's more, online media has obscured the lines between public and private life. They are, somewhat, presently one in the equivalent. Hence, it is essential to comprehend what is and what isn't satisfactory to post on public online platforms. Web-based media setbacks cost money and hurt notoriety for an organization, yet close-to-home assaults completed through web-based media can harm staff livelihoods and obliterate work environment solidarity. Online media awareness preparation is an important apparatus to diminish the potential outcomes of these sensational issues and offer influence for an organization should a web-based media botch be made. The utilization of online media shows no sign of decline, so it is important that you secure yourself and your business [19].

It is really important to be careful using social networking sites, and we should always be aware of the children in our family who use these devices and use social media. We understand that many people abuse and/or groom underage children. And these are not the things that we want our children to face. We should always care about these things because if the child is being abused, it will cause psychological damage that can affect them for the rest of their lives. It's now a serious issue because pedophilic gestures and attacks on minors by means of sexual gestures are happening far too often. The medium is now the internet. There is lots of child porn roaming around the internet or social media or any other platforms. These are very disturbing for a healthy society, and no good parent wants their child to ensure such adverse experiences so that they can look forward to a healthy future. No good parent wants their child to bear the scars of pedophilic abuse. As we all know, children who are born in the 2020s are certain to have internet access. But attackers do prey on children, who don't understand what to say or what to do when facing such behavior.

We should be open with our children or minors and be more specific about using the internet. These children don't know where to click or what to do when any attackers approach them in a sexual manner. It's very important to file a complaint to officials. So it should come to the eye of the officials and track down those numbers and must come under the law.

We couldn't have begun to imagine 10 years ago how social media could connect us in such a way that we can become too dependent on it. While we know that it has many advantages, it also brings many risks. Oversharing is the biggest risk. It is very harmful for us to overshare in our postings or comments. Changing the privacy of a profile is the highest level of the configuration available out there. But it's high time we should maintain such a problem, and we need to make sure that we are not getting any false security. We should really be sure that our network is not visible; if it's visible, anyone can access our device and easily take our data. Always try to read the privacy policy of social networking sites. You would be surprised that social media sites can access your photos, messages, and much more. Many times scammers pretend to be you and try to reset your passwords. We all know why they want to access our personal life. So, don't post confidential information such as your credit card number and bank account details. Another important thing is that many sites want your location and to locate any other friends nearby. So, try to close your GPS because any hacker might be getting your real-time location and may harm you, take advantage, or try to scare you.

Last of all, always keep on educating yourself and practicing the good use of social media. Always try to aware of the people around you whenever the topic you are discussing is social media awareness. So, folks, keep doing the good work and good will come to you. Whenever you face problems, try to accept help from the experts.

1.6 DISCUSSION

Social media is so vast right now that we can't live without it, or spend a day without using it. But we all know that it has some dark sides. Instead of avoiding social media, we need to educate ourselves to use social networking. Social networking is indeed important. Not just because it broadens the networking around the people, but it has other positive aspects too. You can meet new people, or keep track of what is happening around the world. People can now do their job from home – they just need to have access to the internet. In some instances, people can't communicate with others. Now with the help of the internet, they can easily communicate with any person they want. While another important thing is education, now people who cannot access education, e.g., in developing countries, can have it for free due to these social networking sites. YouTube, Facebook, and Wikipedia play a major role in building educational programs to bridge economic and geographic divides. So, as far as I know, we can learn almost anything at any place on the internet. So the internet itself plays a vital role. Just because of the dark aspects of the internet, or social media or anything else on the internet, we can't simply ignore that using the internet has huge benefits.

We need to explore more. Exploring means we need to surf the web or social media to connect with someone. So we need to make it clear that what we do on the internet is personal and privacy should be given the highest priority. We know the positives and the negatives of the internet; we shouldn't dwell on the negatives. Now there must be a question: What is the main downside of social media? People become too dependent on it. We also face difficulties such as getting hacked, fraud while shopping, abuse, hatred, taunt, and many other things. So far, so good, but the main purpose is that does social networking meet our demands or are we just overdosing on social networking? If we are addicted to social networking, then sadly, we are overdosing on it. Social networking is good until it's hampering our daily life. We need to understand that we must avoid excessive use of social networking.

Sometimes we notice that we have an addiction to something. People are so dependent on social network sites that they get so lazy that they are not eligible for regular daily tasks. So, unemployment problems are increasing day by day. People aren't giving enough time for themselves to increase their knowledge or skills. So the unemployment problem is increasing at an alarming rate. Third-world countries like Bangladesh, India, Pakistan, Sri Lanka, Afghanistan, and many others are dependent on these social networking sites. The children of these countries are so messed up due to overuse of social networking sites. They are taking their life and future for granted. They see the first-world countries that the people from those countries are having better lifestyles than them. So, they often get depressed and sad while not having one. They need to understand that life takes an uncertain turn. These things aren't in their hands. Social networking sites are making them weaker. They don't think about the reality. The fact is, social networking triggers a dopamine response in people, like a drug. When we see that a person is addicted to a drug, they will consume it whatever the consequences. Likewise, social networking sites can have a similar effect. Social networking is like a new drug that is constantly taking people under its influence, and people are unknowingly becoming addicted. At worst, it could come to a point when people might not even realize their real-life problems and not even look at their family. People don't even take their eyes off the screen. This is now a serious issue. If this goes on, our young people's development and growth may be detrimentally affected and may struggle to do anything productive.

We use Android/iOS/Windows/Linux operating system and, whatever the make and model, we need secure devices that have less risk of data hacking.

Here are some tips for taking care of the devices that we use regularly:

- Always scan our devices and apps in case any external virus may be present.
- We should always try to use an app store and avoid using APK file if it's not popular or no other options are left.
- We should avoid giving quizzes or fun games that an app shows, because sometimes they want our private data. There is a high risk of getting a virus.

- Sometimes we often try to get free Wi-Fi, and that is encrypted to take our data. Try to use your phone's mobile network data or try to find a secure Wi-Fi connection.
- We should avoid clicking on sites that come to our phones via SMS.
- Another important thing is that we should not permit anyone to check our phone. A phone or laptop should only be for our personal use.
- We should always disconnect when we don't use the phone internet.
- We should not install any app which is asking for too much information. We should avoid those apps.
- Don't root or jailbreak your device that might install malware.
- Always configure strong passwords with different characters, using an uppercase and lower-case mix. It will make the password stronger.
- Don't log in to your social sites or mail at unknown computers. It might save your password unknowingly.
- Always try to use a virtual private network (VPN) for a secure connection.

It's very important to understand the circumstances that we might have to face in our life due to our use of the internet. The internet is vast, and most people don't understand the best practices of using it. They are unaware of the things that are offensive and abusive. The internet was invented to make communication easier and simpler. But the internet is also used by criminals and used to spread hatred. However, the internet itself is now enough to educate us that we can tell the difference between good or bad practice. When we feel that something is suspicious and might hamper our system, we immediately avoid clicking that site and instead report or block that site. So don't browse sites that ask for your credentials. Be safe and educate yourself.

REFERENCES

1. https://www.internetworldstats.com/stats.htm
2. Diomidous, M., Chardalias, K., Magita, A., Koutonias, P., Panagiotopoulou, P., & Mantas, J. (2016). Social and psychological effects of the internet use. *Acta Informatica Medica: AIM – Journal of the Society for Medical Informatics of Bosnia & Herzegovina: Casopis Drustva za Medicinsku Informatiku BiH, 24*(1), 66–68. doi:10.5455/aim.2016.24.66-68.
3. Boyd, D. M., & Ellison, N. B. (2007, October). Social network sites definition history and scholarship. *Journal of Computer-Mediated Communication, 13*(1), 210–230.
4. https://www.statista.com/statistics/272014/global-social-networks-ranked-by-number-of-users/
5. https://www.thebalancesmb.com/what-is-social-media-2890301
6. Aldawood, H., & Skinner, G. (2018, December). *Educating and raising awareness on cyber security social engineering: a literature review.* In *2018 IEEE International Conference on Teaching, Assessment, and Learning for Engineering (TALE)* (pp. 62–68). IEEE.
7. https://blog.malwarebytes.com/privacy-2/2020/04/how-social-media-mine-data-sell-personal-information-for-profit/
8. https://www.pewresearch.org/fact-tank/2018/03/27/americans-complicated-feelings-about-social-media-in-an-era-of-privacy-concerns/
9. https://www.nytimes.com/2018/04/04/us/politics/cambridge-analytica-scandal-fallout.html
10. https://sopa.tulane.edu/blog/key-social-media-privacy-issues-2020
11. Maurer, C., & Wiegmann, R. (2011). *Effectiveness of advertising on social network sites: a case study on Facebook.* In *Information and Communication Technologies in Tourism 2011* (pp. 485–498). Springer.
12. https://edu.gcfglobal.org/en/jobsearchandnetworking/job-hunt-with-social-media/1/
13. https://mytechdecisions.com/unified-communications/aol-instant-messenger/
14. https://www.cbsnews.com/pictures/then-and-now-a-history-of-social-networking-sites/4/
15. https://thelinkedinman.com/history-linkedin/
16. https://www.businessofapps.com/data/linkedin-statistics/
17. Simpson, D., & Brown, P. (2013, September 30). NSA mines Facebook, including Americans' profiles. *CNN.com.* Retrieved September 30, 2013.

18. https://www.statista.com/statistics/264810/number-of-monthly-active-facebook-users-worldwide/
19. https://www.statista.com/statistics/545967/snapchat-app-dau/
20. https://phrasee.co/the-history-of-social-media-a-timeline/
21. https://1stwebdesigner.com/history-of-social-networking/
22. https://www.socialmediaexaminer.com/facebook-ad-algorithm-ralph-burns/
23. https://www.wordstream.com/social-media-marketing
24. https://ourworldindata.org/rise-of-social-media
25. https://www.simplilearn.com/how-facebook-is-using-big-data-article/
26. https://searchcio.techtarget.com/definition/Instagram
27. https://www.statista.com/statistics/242606/number-of-active-twitter-users-in-selected-countries/
28. https://www.britannica.com/topic/Twitter
29. https://selfkey.org/what-happens-to-your-personal-information-once-youve-been-hacked/
30. https://turbofuture.com/internet/The-Dark-Side-of-Social-Media
31. https://www.pcmag.com/news/the-dark-side-of-social-networking

2 Privacy-Preserving Analytics for Social Network Data
A Survey of Currently Prevalent Tools

Rishabh Jindal, Ahmed Falah, and Adnan Anwar
Deakin University, Geelong, Australia

Mohiuddin Ahmed
Edith Cowan University, Perth, Australia

CONTENTS

DOI: 10.1201/9781003134527-3

2.1   INTRODUCTION

With the advent of social media that enables us to live in an age of hyper-connectedness come threats to privacy that no other generation in human history has had to contend with. This issue has recently begun to get the attention it deserves and arguably came to the attention of the population at large after Cambridge Analytica gained unauthorized access to the account information of over eighty million American Facebook users and showed them primarily targeted ads to aid a particular campaign in the 2016 presidential election in the US [1]. However, worrying signs have existed since the early days of social media and should have probably been acted on sooner. Incidents can be traced to as early as 2006 when Facebook started broadcasting users' personal information on their "News Feed" feature without consent [2].

This is not to say that this vast amount of data only poses threats to the society; many of the most beloved features of modern technologies that personalize the experience for each user would not be possible without the use of such vast and rich user data from social networks. This is why research-ers must find solutions that enable the widespread publication of such data without compromising the privacy of the underlying individuals. Unfortunately, the task is much more complicated than was initially thought. As the number of data gatherers and the variety of data being gathered has increased, it has made the problem of privacy breaches even more pronounced. For example, Netflix released the data of 500,000 subscribers after implementing sophisticated anonymization techniques that redacted all the personally identifiable information from the records. However, researchers were still able to figure out the identity of the users using corresponding data from IMDB, emphasizing the need for more sophisticated measures for privacy protection [3].

The purpose of this analysis is to explore the privacy concerns resulting from the use of social media, and the techniques that are currently deployed to leverage the vast ocean of valuable data such services provide while also ensuring the highest standards of user privacy. Throughout the discussion, we will:

- Describe some real-world examples where privacy breaches from social network data had real and compromising consequences that emphasize the need for solutions that ensure users' pri-vacy is protected irrespective of the kind of analyses being conducted.
- Discuss one of the most popular techniques to model privacy breaches and explore the two main kinds of privacy attacks in this literature: identity disclosure and attribute disclosure attacks.
- Discuss some of the most popular techniques to protect against such breaches, including ano-nymization and differential privacy.
- Discuss some tools that can be used to implement these techniques and the relative strengths of each tool.
- Finally, we will discuss the direction of future research that will lead to the significant advance-ment of the field and the conclusions that can be drawn from our comprehensive discussions.

The rest of this paper is structured as follows; in Section 2.2 we will explore the real-world threats to privacy due to social media, in Section 2.3 we will describe a graph-based approach to modeling privacy breaches, in Section 2.4 we will describe the popular techniques to mitigate privacy breaches, in Section 2.5 we will discuss the tools for privacy-preserving analytics, in Section 2.6 we will out-line the direction for future research. In Section 2.7 we will provide our concluding remarks.

2.2 SOCIAL MEDIA PRIVACY THREATS

Both security and privacy issues have been a major concern in the different application domains [4–6]. It has been identified as a potential threat to social media as well. The best way to understand the threat to privacy posed by social media is to discuss some of the most recent incidents that brought such threats to light. Such discussions root us in the reality of events that transpired and allow us to consider the severity of the resulting unfavorable consequences. The recent incident involving research firm Cambridge Analytica and social media platform Facebook is one that is worth exploring for this objective. In 2013, research out of the University of Cambridge demonstrated that people's psychographic profiles could be reasonably well predicted by analyzing their social media activity and without employing any traditional psychographic profiling tools [7]. This research was put to the test in the real world by UK-based researcher Alexander Kogan and the firm Cambridge Analytica that was employed by President Trump's election campaign in 2016. Kogan designed a straightforward personality quiz on Facebook and sent it to over two hundred thousand users. By taking this quiz, users provided Kogan access to not only theirs but also their friends' Facebook activity. Kogan, in turn, provided this data to Cambridge Analytica, which was able to leverage this information in conjunction with "a range of data from social media platforms, browsers, online purchases, voting results, and more to build 5,000+ data points on 230 million US adults" [1].

The company then used all this data to create comprehensive psychographic profiles of Americans across the country and used them to "micro-target individual consumers or voters with messages most likely to influence their behaviour" [1]. The CEO of Cambridge Analytica later revealed that they intended to either encourage users to vote for their client or discourage them from voting for their client's opponents [1]. Using such sophisticated techniques, Cambridge Analytica could not only have had a considerable influence on voters' outlook but could, in fact, have had a direct influence on the election outcome in smaller counties with a relatively small number of voters. As suggested by Isaak and Hanna, "this might not be the only reason for the specific 2016 US election outcome, but there is every indication that it was a useful if not a critical contribution" [1]. In addition to this event, Facebook alone has been at the center of over ten privacy breaches in its short lifespan. Some of the most notable events are depicted on the timeline below Figure 2.1 [8].

It is worth noting that existing research has also shown that in case of a major privacy breach at a social media company, it is in the company's best interest to issue an apology and clearly communicate to its' users how it plans to prevent similar breaches in the future [9]. This further

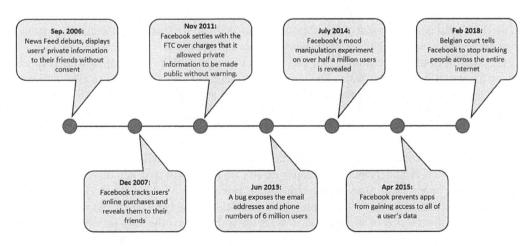

FIGURE 2.1 A timeline of Facebook's privacy struggles.

establishes that users of social media are becoming increasingly aware of privacy concerns involved in the usage of such platforms and care about the steps taken by companies to safeguard their privacy. It is clear now that it is imperative to protect users' privacy on social media platforms; however, this task is not as straightforward as it seems. Recent research in the fields of computer vision and facial recognition has revealed that even blurring faces cannot prevent sophisticated systems from identifying users and only a handful of labeled images are enough to enable recognition [10]. Such techniques are being employed not only by companies but also by governments in certain countries to surveil citizens and promote "good" behavior. The most comprehensive of these systems is being envisaged in China; where the government plans to use facial recognition techniques discussed above to analyze citizens' behavior on social media and the real world to assign a "citizen score" and, in turn, reward them for behaviors it endorses and punishes them for behaviors that it would like to curtail.

In 2014, the Chinese government revealed that it would roll out a mandatory program by 2020 that "will consolidate reams of records from private companies and government bureaucracies into a single 'citizen score' for each Chinese citizen" [11]. While the exact intent of the government with this score is unknown at this point, some extrapolations can be made from the optional variant that has existed since 2015. The Sesame Credit score developed by Alibaba and Tencent, corporations that run all Chinese social networks, adopts a unique approach to evaluating citizens' credit scores and incentivizing them to keep these scores up. Not only do they monitor people's ability to manage credit, but they also evaluate the kind of things people spend their money on. If a person is purchasing groceries or baby supplies, it is appreciated. However, if a person is buying video games or alcohol, their score takes a hit.

Furthermore, to incentivize people to adopt "good" behaviors, the following perks are offered:

"If your credit score reaches 600, you have the privilege of an instant loan of about $800 without collateral when shopping online. At a score of 650, one may rent a car without leaving a deposit. At 700, get access to a bureaucratic fast track to a Singapore travel permit. At 750, one might get a similar fast track to a coveted pan-European Schengen visa".

[12]

After reading the examples discussed earlier, a rational reader may conclude that the only way to protect users' privacy is for social media companies to resolve not to share user data with third parties under any circumstances. However, some of the most useful and personalized experiences that users enjoy on the internet are built on the basis of social media data, e.g., recommendations on e-commerce platforms and online streaming services. Therefore, the sharing of social media data is also essential to some of the most indispensable features of the modern online experience and researchers must devise innovative techniques that can facilitate the sharing of social media data for such uses while maintaining the highest standard of user privacy [13].

It is evident from this discussion that social media user data, in the hands of motivated agents, can be leveraged in notorious ways. Such methods, at best, fall into a gray area of ethical responsibility and at worst, represent an unprecedented attack on user privacy that violates the sanctity of crucial pillars of democracy and erodes the fabric of society. Even on an individual level, the threats posed by systems like the one being experimented with in China are gravely concerning. Placing citizens under a microscope, evaluating them constantly and assigning them a score that will follow them for their entire lives irrespective of where they go will prevent people from reinventing themselves and genuinely hamper efforts of turning over a new leaf in their lives. Therefore, the importance of protecting individuals' privacy during the analysis of social media data cannot be overstated. Let us try to identify the most common types of attacks on privacy that result from the distribution of social media data for analysis; discuss the most prevalent techniques employed to prevent such attacks and how such methods can be better adapted for use within the context of social media data.

2.3 A GRAPH-BASED APPROACH TO MODELING PRIVACY BREACHES

The large-scale adoption of social media has generated vast oceans of rich data, the likes of which the world has never seen before. This data is an invaluable resource for researchers trying to understand people's behavior and get to the roots of what drives society at the macro level. However, with the availability of such data, the protection of users' privacy has become of utmost importance due to reasons discussed earlier. In the current literature, one of the most prevalent approaches to model privacy breaches is based on the implementation of knowledge graphs.

A knowledge graph is used to visualize the relationships between all the entities involved in a particular topic or context. Qian et al. describe a knowledge graph as "a network of all kinds of entities related to a specific domain or topic" [14]. Such a graph can prove to be a valuable resource when analyzing social network data as it can provide an eagle's eye view of the relationships that exist between the users on the network. Within this context, we can imagine a knowledge graph as having multiple vertices such that a vertex represents each user; and directed links connecting the vertices which represent a connection between two users. From this perspective, the two most common privacy breaches from social network data can be modeled, as follows.

2.3.1 IDENTITY DISCLOSURE ATTACK

Identity disclosure attacks relate to the identification of an individual from the inadvertent release of identifiable data or from a sequence of pointed queries that can be used to eliminate possibilities from a dataset and eventually identify an individual or a group of individuals [15].

More formally and in the context of social networks, "Given $T = (G, A, B)$, which is a snapshot of a social media platform with a social graph $G = (V, E)$ where V is the set of users and E demonstrates the social relations between them, a user behavior A, and an attribute information B, the identity disclosure attack is to map all users in the list of target users V_t to their known identities. For each $v \in V_t$, we have the information on her social friends and behaviour" [16]. In simpler terms, this refers to a situation where an agent can map the identities of each person by analyzing a slice of the social media data from a particular point in time.

2.3.2 ATTRIBUTE DISCLOSURE ATTACK

Attribute disclosure occurs when the attacker learns the value of a specific attribute. Such attacks can occur with or without identification. Lambert explains this with the following example: "suppose all union plumbers in Chicago earn the same wage and the Department of Labor publishes the average wage for such a worker. The department has thus revealed the wage of every union plumber in Chicago without revealing their identities" [15].

More formally and in the context of social networks, "Given $T = (G, A, B)$, which is a snapshot of a social media platform with a social graph $G = (V, E)$ where V is the set of users and E demonstrates the social relations between them, a user behaviour A, and an attribute information B, the attribute disclosure attack is used to infer the attributes a_v for all $v \in V_t$ where V_t is a list of targeted users. For each $v \in V_t$, we have the information about her social friends and behaviour" [16].

This refers to a situation where an agent can infer all the users' attributes by analyzing a slice of social media data from a particular point in time.

It is worth noting here that even false identity and attribute identifications are severe threats and should be given appropriate importance by agencies. The purpose when making data public should be to discourage intruders from making any inferences rather than encouraging false inferences. Such incorrect disclosures will lead to the spread of misinformation in public, cause damage to the concerned individuals as it may be impossible to prove the falsehood of such disclosures and will eventually lead to a reduction in the public's willingness to have their data made available publicly.

Let us now consider an example to better understand the threats described above and how attackers carry them out. As described earlier, in this analysis, a social network is characterized as having several vertices that are connected through links. The vertices represent users and links exist between users that have communicated with each other on the network. Let us consider a social network that relies on some basic anonymization of individual attributes to protect the privacy of its underlying subjects. Even with such protections in place, a motivated attacker can compromise the system and learn the identity as well as the individual attributes of people. Such attacks rely on identifying the small unique subgraphs within the larger graph to understand the orientation of the network and make inferences based on the relative position of the known subgraphs [17].

It is useful to consider the analysis of such attacks by Backstrom et al. They start by considering the position of the attacker; the first step for her is to create new accounts and connections that will serve as the known subgraph within the more extensive social network. So, the attacker sets out by creating a set of K fake accounts on the network and identifying the set of W users that will be the target of the attack. The objective of the attack is to discern all the pairs within W that are connected by links in the entire network G. Next. The attacker must create links between the newly created fake accounts K and the target group W; the exact process to create such a link will vary depending upon the social network under attack. This will create the known subgraph H within the larger graph G. Finally, all the attacker must do is locate H within G when G is made public. Now, she can label each of the K fake accounts that she created and use the links that they are connected by to identify the set of targeted users W [18]. This approach can constitute both an identity disclosure attack as well as an attribute disclosure attack.

It is evident from the above discussion that in the absence of sophisticated measures implemented to protect the privacy of individuals, a motivated attacker can breach the privacy of a considerable number of individuals without a significant amount of effort or raising any legal red flags. "The experiments on a real social network with 4.4 million vertices and 77 million edges show that the creation of 7 vertices by an attacker can reveal on average 70 target vertices and compromise the privacy of approximately 2, 400 edges between them" [17]. Therefore, it is imperative to devise and implement new strategies to protect the privacy of individuals in a time where the activity on social networks is only going to increase and in a society where they have become indispensable to maintaining both personal and professional relationships.

2.4   PRIVACY-PRESERVING ANALYTICS TECHNIQUES

Let us now review some of the standard techniques used to prevent the attacks described above. In general, the most popular techniques currently can be divided into two main groups: anonymization and differential privacy. Anonymization can further be divided into techniques like K-anonymity, l-diversity, and t-closeness. We discuss each of these in detail below Figure 2.2.

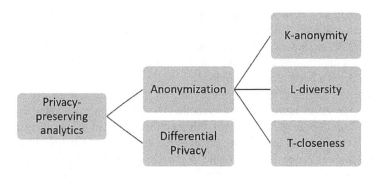

FIGURE 2.2   Popular techniques for mitigating privacy risks in analytics.

2.4.1 K-Anonymity

K-anonymity is a technique that was first introduced in 2002 by Latanya Sweeney [19]. It was initially designed for tabular data but translated well to modern multidimensional data as well. The objective of this technique is to anonymize each record in the dataset such that it is indistinguishable from $(k-1)$ records. This is done through generalization and suppression techniques that aim to anonymize all records to preserve privacy but also maximize value for analysis. This method was one of the first anonymization techniques and is elegant and straightforward to implement; however, it is still vulnerable to attacks. One way the K-anonymization technique can be compromised is through the homogeneity attack. This occurs when an agent can infer sensitive information in the dataset because one or more of the equivalent classes lack diversity. Another way this technique can be overcome is through a background knowledge attack, which involves identifying the people in the dataset by obtaining some background information and using it in conjunction with the current dataset to map identities by using common attributes.

2.4.2 L-Diversity

To overcome the threats posed by K-anonymity, researchers devised the l-diversity technique [20]. This involves ensuring a certain degree, l, of diversity in each equivalent class of the K-anonymized dataset. It can overcome the significant challenges to K-anonymity discussed above; however, it presents its privacy threats. Researchers soon discovered that l-diversity is vulnerable when the distribution of sensitive attributes in equivalent classes is not the same as the distribution of these attributes across the dataset. Furthermore, l-diversity is also vulnerable when the records in an equivalent class are diverse but semantically similar; this is known as a similarity attack.

2.4.3 T-Closeness

To overcome the concerns just discussed, another modification was suggested. Li et al. define their t-closeness principle as:

"An equivalence class is said to have t-closeness if the distance between the distribution of a sensitive attribute in this class and the distribution of the attribute in the whole table is no more than a threshold t. A table is said to have t-closeness if all equivalence classes have t-closeness".

[21]

However, even this technique has some vulnerabilities; it can protect against attribute disclosure but not identity disclosure. All three techniques discussed above are summarized in below Table 2.1:

TABLE 2.1

Summary of Anonymization Techniques in the Current Literature

Paper	Method	Principle	Issue
Sweeney [19]	K-anonymity	Anonymize each record in the dataset such that it is indistinguishable from $(k-1)$ records	Homogeneity and background knowledge attacks
Machanavajjhala et al. [20]	L-diversity	Ensure a certain degree, l, of diversity in each equivalent class of the K-anonymized dataset	Vulnerable when the distribution of attributes across classes and dataset are not the same
Li et al. [21]	T-closeness	Distance between the distribution of a sensitive attribute in a class and the distribution of the attribute in the whole table is no more than a threshold t	Identity disclosure attacks

2.4.4 DIFFERENTIAL PRIVACY

So far, all the privacy-preserving techniques we have discussed are vulnerable to breaches if an adversary can obtain relevant auxiliary information that can be used to reveal private information. "Recent research has shown the vulnerability of user-generated data against de-anonymization attacks. Sanitizing user-generated social media data is more challenging than structured data as it is heterogeneous, highly unstructured, noisy and inherently different from relational and tabular data" [22]. One way to mitigate this issue is through the use of differential privacy. This technique involves introducing noise in the data such that it does not affect any of the population-level attributes or trends but makes it impossible to identify individual records. Formally, differential privacy is defined as follows:

"Given a query function f (.), a mechanism K (.) with an output range R satisfies ϵ-differential privacy for all datasets D_1 and D_2 differing in at most one element if:

$$\frac{\Pr\left[K\left(f\left(D_1\right)\right)=R\in\mathcal{R}\right]}{\Pr\left[K\left(f\left(D_2\right)\right)=R\in\mathcal{R}\right]}\le e^{\epsilon}$$

Equation 1: Differential Privacy

Here ϵ is called privacy budget, and large values of ϵ (e.g., 10) results in large e^{ϵ} and indicates that massive output difference could be tolerated and hence we have large privacy loss. This is because the adversary can infer the change in the database according to the massive change of the query function f (.). On the other hand, small values of ϵ (e.g., 0.1) indicate that small privacy loss could be tolerated" [16].

More generally, as stated earlier, differential privacy is implemented by introducing random noise in the mathematical analyses in order to "obscure the effect of each data subject" [23]. Like the anonymization techniques discussed earlier, differential privacy also involves a trade-off between privacy and utility, but with this technique, it is defined by an explicit mathematical relationship. In general, the reduction in accuracy becomes lesser than that due to sampling error as the number of observations in the dataset becomes larger. The main concepts governing differential privacy can be summarized as follows:

- "Differential privacy protects an individual's information essentially as if her information were not used in the analysis at all, in the sense that the outcome of a differentially private algorithm is approximately the same whether the individual's information was used or not" [24]
- "Differential privacy ensures that using an individual's data will not reveal essentially any personally identifiable information that is specific to her, or even whether the individual's information was used at all. Here, specifically refers to information that cannot be inferred unless the individual's information is used in the analysis" [24].

Differential privacy is still a very new way of approaching privacy-preserving analytics, and much research is still ongoing. However, it has already been adopted across big corporations and government agencies like Apple, Google, and the US Census Bureau. It is a much more formal way of approaching the problem than existing practices and offers several advantages for users:

- A more formal approach to privacy as advocated by differential privacy ensures uniform implementation across industries and a higher degree of protection for the individuals whose identities form the foundation on which complex analytical models are built. Furthermore, it removes the need to anticipate attacks on the part of the analyst and provides protection across the board.

TABLE 2.2
Summary of Terminology

Formal Term	Definition
Identity disclosure attack	Identification of an individual from the inadvertent release of identifiable data.
Attribute disclosure attack	Attribute disclosure occurs when the attacker learns the value of a specific attribute corresponding to a user. Such attacks can occur with or without identification.
K-anonymity	Privacy-preserving technique that anonymizes each record in the dataset such that it is indistinguishable from $(k-1)$ records.
L-diversity	Builds on K-anonymity, involves ensuring a certain degree, l, of diversity in each equivalent class of the K-anonymized dataset.
T-closeness	A dataset is said to have t-closeness if the distribution of a sensitive attribute as well as all other attributes in the dataset is no more than a threshold t.
Differential privacy	Involves introducing noise in the data such that it does not affect any of the population-level attributes or trends but makes it impossible to identify individual records.

- Differential privacy enables organizations to publish data for research purposes confidently and empowers them by giving them the tools to prove and quantify the degree of privacy-preserving measures that they have implemented.
- This approach also eliminates the need to maintain a level of secrecy around data being published, incentivizing organizations to be even more transparent and assuring analysts that the data they have analyzed is reliable.
- Differential privacy enables large-scale sharing of information like has never been possible before while also ensuring a higher level of privacy protection than ever before.

The following Table 2.2 summarizes the terminology that has been discussed so far:

Now that we have a better understanding of the kind of privacy attacks that social media data is susceptible to and the techniques that can be used to prevent such attacks let us explore some of the most popular commercial and open-source tools available to implement these privacy-preserving analytical techniques.

2.5 TOOLS FOR PRIVACY-PRESERVING ANALYTICS

In light of the recent developments in technology, the exponentially more considerable amount of data available and for the reasons discussed earlier in our analysis. It has become imperative to ensure that the privacy of individuals is protected when analyzing large amounts of data, including social media data. We will now discuss some of the most popular tools that implement the privacy-preserving techniques discussed earlier and their relative strengths and weaknesses.

2.5.1 ARX

ARX is an open-source anonymization tool. Open-source tools are a compelling option when considering the various tools available for preserving privacy in the analysis of social media data. They allow the researcher to optimize the anonymization technique as per her research requirements, providing a greater degree of freedom and control over the process. Just how powerful this freedom can be is illustrated well in the recent work of Prasser et al. [25].

At the most basic level, ARX achieves anonymization by implementing generalization and record suppression. It transforms attribute values by implementing generalization hierarchies that describe valid and invalid transformation for each attribute. Prasser et al. explain this through an example:

"Values of an attribute "age" are transformed into intervals with decreasing precision over increasing levels of generalisation. Values of the attribute "sex" can only be suppressed. We note that assigning generalisation level zero to an attribute leaves its values unchanged. In ARX, generalisation hierarchies can be specified by the user or created automatically for categorical and continuous attributes".

[25]

The generalization technique discussed here is called full-domain generalization. It entails transforming all values of an attribute to the same level across all observations. "The set of all possible combinations of generalization levels for all attributes forms a generalization lattice, where each element is called a generalisation scheme" [25]. The generalization lattice for the example discussed here is illustrated in Figure 2.3, along with various generalization techniques applied across a sample dataset. The nodes on the left represent the generalization levels for "Age."

In contrast, the ones on the right represent those for "Sex." (0,0) represents the original dataset and (3,1) represents the dataset which is obtained when the third generalization level is applied to "Age," and the first generalization level is applied to "Sex." In this example, we want to create a dataset that is k-anonymous where $k = 2$, i.e., each observation should be indistinguishable from at least one other observation. After generalization, we observe that records 3 and 4 still do not satisfy this requirement and thus must be suppressed. Finally, the utility of the newly created dataset is measured using some metric, for our purpose, we simply use the number of suppressed rows and report that the privacy-protecting dataset has a utility value of 4/6.

Such algorithms have the advantage of being generic and thus can accommodate several privacy and utility models. However, "they are very inflexible in terms of supported transformation schemes and global generalization does not adjust well to the multidimensional distribution of data. This typically results in significant reductions to the quality of output data" [25]. For this reason, the authors suggest modifications to the traditional approach. They suggest a two-pronged strategy to be applied to the general full-domain generalization.

Horizontal partitioning strategy: The objective is to devise a strategy to reduce the degree of generalization. This can be done by using ARX's built-in capabilities in the following way. The tool allows the analyst to set a limit on the number of records that are suppressed, and the treatment of such records when the overall utility is being calculated. The analyst specifies the maximum number of partitions and ARX sets the suppression limit automatically and anonymizes the data in an iterative process until the condition set by the analyst is met.

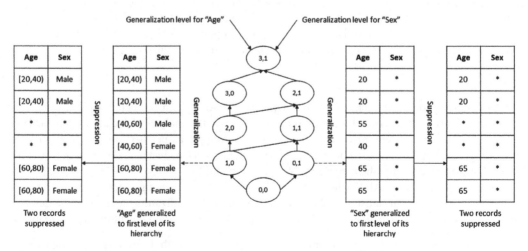

FIGURE 2.3   Full-domain generalization.

Vertical partitioning strategy: The objective in this step is to use the generalization scheme calculated in each iteration to discern the clusters of values that must be indistinguishable. Aggregate functions are then applied to these clusters of selected attributes to make the records indistinguishable. For more details on these strategies and their implementation in ARX, one should refer to Prasser et al. [25].

2.5.2 TIAMAT

TIAMAT is a powerful privacy-preserving tool proposed by researchers in the early days of social media and big data when privacy concerns were only beginning to come into the spotlight. "TIAMAT: a Tool for Interactive Analysis of Microdata Anonymization Techniques" [26] focuses on implementing K-anonymity, l-diversity and t-closeness for data publishers wanting to make their data available to the world for research purposes without compromising the privacy of their users.

TIAMAT has several useful features that implement anonymization techniques and enable efficient analysis:

- *Generalization hierarchy editing*: Users can visually inspect and implement various generalization hierarchies; this makes it easier to implement the one which provides the best balance of privacy and utility.
- *Attribute statistics collection*: The tool also allows users to calculate and visualize various statistics for each attribute in the dataset, enabling comprehensive exploratory data analysis within the tool; facilitating, and streamlining privacy-preserving efforts.
- *Integration with database engines*: Furthermore, the tool also allows integration with traditional SQL-style databases, allowing users to pull data directly from the source, streamlining the process even more. Users also have the freedom to export the anonymized dataset back to an SQL-style database.

The system architecture of the TIAMAT tool as follows: the analyst uses the Interactive Analysis Module (IAM) to interact with the tool; the IAM acts as the intermediary between the database and the anonymization engine (AE) and is responsible for generating all the visualizations; the AE is designed to be modular such that it can incorporate various generalization-based anonymization techniques.

2.5.3 SECRETA

SECRETA is a tool similar to TIAMAT discussed above but is a more recently developed tool. It introduces more flexibility and provides greater freedom for data publishers. It allows the user to implement, compare, and combine different anonymization techniques to achieve the best results. The researchers that developed the tool explain it as having two principal components [27].

2.5.3.1 SECRETA Frontend

Similar to the TIAMAT tool, SECRETA features a graphical user interface (GUI) that enables users to select datasets, tinker with generalization hierarchies, implement and configure various anonymization algorithms, create sophisticated visualizations for exploratory data analysis (EDA) and export the anonymized dataset in various formats. The frontend can be summarized as having six main modules:

- *Dataset editor*: Allows the user to browse and select datasets. Once the dataset is loaded, the user can edit it within the tool and generate various visualizations across attributes to better understand the data.

- *Configuration editor*: Allows the user to select generalization hierarchies and specify which utility and privacy evaluating algorithms must be used.
- *Queries editor*: Allows the user to specify which query workloads must be used when evaluating the utility of the anonymized data.
- *Experimentation interface selector*: Allows the user to switch between the evaluation and comparison modes of the tool. Evaluation mode is where the performance of a given algorithm is evaluated, whereas the comparison mode is where the relative performance of various algorithms is compared.
- *Plotting module*: Allows the user to generate sophisticated plots to understand the anonymization performance of the given algorithm. These plots can relate to the original dataset or the anonymization results.
- *Data export module*: "Allows exporting datasets, hierarchies, policies, and query workloads, in CSV format, and graphs, in PDF, JPG, BMP or PNG format" [27].

2.5.3.2 SECRETA Backend

The backend of the SECRETA tool can be summarized as having four main modules:

- *Policy specification module*: Involves automatically generating the generalization hierarchies and privacy, utility algorithms that will be used by the anonymization module.
- *Method Evaluator/Comparator*: This module is responsible for implementing the anonymization algorithm, recording the results, and pushing them on to the experimentation module.
- *Anonymization module*: This is the module that executes the selected anonymization algorithm and the specified privacy, utility algorithms.
- *Experimentation module*: This is the module that accommodates the visualization generating capabilities of the tool.

2.5.4 AMNESIA

Amnesia is another tool that has been widely used and has received accolades for its approach to preserving privacy in analytics. Amnesia focuses on implementing the K-anonymity technique discussed earlier. In the case of high-dimensional data, where the number of quasi-identifiers is large, K-anonymity struggles to provide a reasonable balance between privacy and utility of the dataset. To address this problem, Amnesia relies on *km*-anonymity for such datasets. "*km*-anonymity requires that each combination of up to *m* quasi-identifiers must appear at least *k* times in the published data. The intuition behind *km*-anonymity is that there is little privacy gain from protecting against adversaries who already know most of the terms of one record, and significant information loss in the effort to do so" [28]. Like the other tools we have discussed, Amnesia deploys generalization and suppression techniques to achieve anonymization. It also offers familiar capabilities of exploring the generalization lattices visually through a GUI and allows the user to choose an optimum level as per her discretion.

2.5.5 IBM DIFFERENTIAL PRIVACY LIBRARY

We have evaluated several tools that adopt the anonymization approach to privacy-preserving analytics. Now, let us explore one of the most popular tools used to ensure privacy-preserving analytics through the implementation of differential privacy, IBM's differential privacy library, or Diffprivlib. Diffprivlib is a Python library that leverages other popular libraries like NumPy and Scikit-Learn to implement differential privacy. The purpose of this library is to enable users to implement all the machine learning models that they do use Scikit-Learn, in the same fashion but with the valuable exception of doing so while also protecting the privacy of the subjects of the underlying data. Recall from our discussion of differential privacy that it involves introducing a certain amount of noise in the data to preserve privacy and the amount of noise is denoted by the variable epsilon. Implementation of machine learning models using Diffprivlib is almost identical to implementation in Scikit-Learn; "Diffprivlib supports the same pre-processing pipelines that are present in Scikit-Learn, and, in some cases, their use is encouraged to optimise noise-addition and model sensitivity. The ϵ value is specified as a parameter when the model is initialised (e.g., GaussianNB(epsilon = 0.1)). Otherwise, a default of $\epsilon = 1$ is used" [29].

2.5.6   OpenDP

Another exciting open-source project that is very ambitious and promises to implement state-of-the-art techniques in differential privacy is the OpenDP project at Harvard University. It is one of the most recent tools that have been proposed and advocates the use of differential privacy to ensure the highest standard of privacy protection in modern analytics. OpenDP is also a Python library and tries to achieve the following [23]:

- *Extensibility*: The primary motivation behind this open-source project is to create a valuable tool that can be integrated seamlessly with existing differential privacy tools.
- *Flexibility*: In accordance with the previous goal, the creators encourage contributors to design their code in as flexible a manner as possible such that they allow accommodation of all the various use-cases for which differential privacy is currently used and will be used in the future.
- *Verifiability*: In line with the last two goals, the creators also declare that all contributions that will be made to the library will be verified by an editorial board and will be assessed on the quality of the code and the degree to which they deliver what they promise to.
- *Programmability*: This refers to the creators' vision of being able to deliver the most value without having their users to learn new programming languages or techniques.
- *Modularity*: Extending the concepts of extensibility, flexibility, and verifiability; all library components must be designed to be modular such that they can be reused multiple times and eliminate the need to rewrite code to achieve the same objective repeatedly.
- *Usability*: The tool will support multiple ways to interact with it in conjunction with the objectives outlined in the programmability goal. People use several interfaces like notebooks, command lines and GUIs to execute commands in Python, and this should not prove to be a hurdle for anyone who wishes to use the library.
- *Efficiency*: While trying to achieve the objectives described above, the library will not compromise on efficiency either. All available computational resources will be used in as efficient a manner as possible.
- *Utility*: The library also promises to communicate with the user as clearly as possible and explicitly state the utility of each command before and after it is run. This will reduce the number of redundant commands that are run and will ensure that analysts do not arrive at incorrect conclusions.

As is clear from the discussion above, OpenDP is a highly ambitious project and will set a new standard of differential privacy implementation if it can achieve all that it sets out to. The creators hope to roll out the library by Fall 2020.

The salient features of each anonymization and differential privacy (DP) tool discussed above are summarized in Tables 2.3 and 2.4:

TABLE 2.3
Salient Features of Discussed Anonymization Tools

Anonymization Tool	Features			
	GUI	EDA	Hierarchy Editing	DB Integration
ARX	✓	✓	✓	✓
TIAMAT	✓	✓	✓	✓
SECRETA	✓	✓	✓	✓
Amnesia	✓	✓	✓	✓

TABLE 2.4
Salient Features of Discussed DP Tools

DP Tool	Features			
	Open-Source	Compatible with Popular Libraries	No New Syntax	Maintained by Moderators
IBM DP library	✓	✓	✓	✓
OpenDP	✓	✓	✓	✓

2.6 DIRECTIONS FOR FUTURE RESEARCH

Now that we have a good understanding of the current landscape of privacy research in social media and analytics in general, we are in an excellent position to identify some of the critical areas that should be the focus of upcoming research and will lead to significant advancement of the field.

2.6.1 PRIVACY OF TEXT DATA

There is a vast amount of textual data on social media platforms. Even though this data is high-dimensional and very unstructured, it can still reveal sensitive information about people to motivated attackers. Therefore, there is a pressing need for this issue to be explored in-depth and implementing the appropriate checks and balances.

2.6.2 PRIVACY OF SOCIAL MEDIA PROFILE ATTRIBUTES

Throughout our discussion, we have seen how it is possible to profile and categorize people based solely on their social media activity. Research in this field should focus on making the average person more aware of how their online data can be used and proposing new systems that disincentivize social media companies to share user data with third parties for revenue.

2.6.3 PRIVACY OF TIME AND LOCATION-TAGGED INFORMATION

Social media data provides time and location-tagged information on a scale that has never been seen before. Such information can be vital in identifying people's behavior and preferences. Future research should focus on how anonymization techniques can be adapted to this specific use-case because this represents a sizable amount of data that can potentially affect the privacy of billions of people.

2.6.4 PRIVACY OF HETEROGENEOUS INFORMATION

Current techniques assume that anonymizing each attribute of the dataset is enough to ensure privacy. However, this assumption may not hold in the case of social media data where each attribute is heavily related to another, and there are underlying relationships between attributes that can be used to infer information. Researchers should explore how we can safeguard against such eventualities by building privacy-preserving techniques that take into account the underlying relationships between various attributes of social media data.

2.6.5 PREVENTION OF IDENTITY AND ATTRIBUTE DISCLOSURE ATTACKS

It is important to note that all the information made available through social media profiles is essential for these services to provide a better experience to their users. However, more research needs to be done to find ways to ensure that such information is leveraged in ethical ways that enrich users' experience with their consent and cannot be breached by malicious agents under any circumstances. Classification models can be built to evaluate features to understand the most influential features, as shown in [30].

2.6.6 UNDERSTANDING AND SAFEGUARDING PRIVACY OF SPECIAL NEEDS GROUPS

As more and more people are connected to the internet and rely on social media to cultivate and maintain personal relationships, efforts must be made to understand the perception of privacy risks among special needs groups, such as people with serious mental illness. Recent research has shown that a large proportion of social media users who suffer from mental illness harbor concerns regarding their privacy especially regarding the stigma associated with their conditions and the impact that could have on the relationships that they have cultivated online [31]. Much more research needs to be done to identify the unique privacy concerns of special needs groups and ensure that social media is a safe place for all.

2.6.7 IDENTIFYING NEW TECHNIQUES TO PRESERVE PRIVACY

In addition to the techniques discussed here, researchers must observe privacy-preserving techniques in other areas and formulate ways to translate those techniques for application in a social media context. For example, researchers have used blockchain to preserve the privacy of users in Intelligent Transport Systems and Vehicular Ad Hoc Networks [32]. Future research endeavors should study the feasibility of implementing such solutions in the context of social media data and consider if such techniques can be used in conjunction with existing techniques or if they prove to be viable alternatives.

2.7 CONCLUSION

In this analysis, we started by identifying the need for privacy-preserving approaches to the analytics of social network data in the modern world. We explored that without such techniques in place, social network data could compromise users' privacy in ways that can lead to a wide range of unpleasant outcomes. These can range from mildly annoying targeted advertising to the creation of social systems that can effectively shackle people for the rest of their lives. We then identified the kind of privacy attacks that people can be subject to and the standard techniques that can be used currently to combat such attempts. And last, we took an in-depth look at some of the most popular tools that implement the techniques used to protect against privacy attacks; exploring the main features and unique offerings of each.

REFERENCES

1. Isaak, J., & Hanna, M. J. (2018). "User data privacy: Facebook, Cambridge Analytica, and Privacy protection." *Computer*, 51(8), 56–59. doi:10.1109/mc.2018.3191268.
2. Lomas, N. (2018, April 10). "*A Brief History of Facebook's Privacy Hostility Ahead of Zuckerberg's Testimony*," https://techcrunch.com/2018/04/10/a-brief-history-of-facebooks-privacy-hostility-ahead-of-zuckerbergs-testimony/.
3. Narayanan, A., & Shmatikov, V. (2008). "Robust de-anonymization of large sparse datasets." In *2008 IEEE Symposium on Security and Privacy (Sp 2008)*. doi:10.1109/sp.2008.33.
4. Adi, E., Anwar, A., Baig, Z., & Zeadally, S. (2020). "Machine learning and data analytics for the IoT." *Neural Computing and Applications*, 32, 1–29. doi:10.1007/s00521-020-04874-y.
5. Alsaedi, A., Moustafa, N., Tari, Z., Mahmood, A. N., & Anwar, A. (2020). "TON_IoT telemetry dataset: a new generation dataset of IoT and IIoT for data-driven intrusion detection systems. *IEEE Access*, 8. doi:10.1109/ACCESS.2020.3022862.
6. Le, T. D., Anwar, A., Loke, S. W., Beuran, R., & Tan, Y. (2020). "GridAttackSim: a cyber attack simulation framework for smart grids." *Electronics*, 9, 1218.
7. Kosinski, M., et al. (2013)."Manifestations of user personality in website choice and behaviour on online social networks." *Machine Learning*, 95(3), 357–380. doi:10.1007/s10994-013-5415-y.
8. Newcomb, A. (2018, March 24). "A timeline of Facebook's privacy issues – and its responses." *NBCNews.com*, NBC Universal News Group. https://www.nbcnews.com/tech/social-media/timeline-facebook-s-privacy-issues-its-responses-n859651.
9. Ayaburi, E. W., & Treku, D. N. (2020). "Effect of penitence on social media trust and privacy concerns: the case of Facebook." *International Journal of Information Management*, 50, 171–181.
10. Oh, S. J., et al. (2016, September 17). "Faceless person recognition: privacy implications in social media." In *Computer Vision – ECCV 2016 Lecture Notes in Computer Science*. 19–35. doi:10.1007/978-3-319-46487-9_2.
11. Mitchell, A., & Diamond, L. "China's surveillance state should scare everyone." *The Atlantic*, Atlantic Media Company. https://www.theatlantic.com/international/archive/2018/02/china-surveillance/552203/.
12. Falkvinge, R. (2015, October 3). "In China, your credit score is now affected by your political opinions – and your friends' political opinions." *Privacy News Online by Private Internet Access VPN*. https://www.privateinternetaccess.com/blog/in-china-your-credit-score-is-now-affected-by-your-political-opinions-and-your-friends-political-opinions/.
13. Yang, D., Qu, B., & Cudré-Mauroux, P. (2019). "Privacy-preserving social media data publishing for personalized ranking-based recommendation." *IEEE Transactions on Knowledge and Data Engineering*, 31(3), 507–520. doi:10.1109/TKDE.2018.2840974.
14. Qian, J., et al. (2019). "Social network de-anonymization and privacy inference with knowledge graph model." *IEEE Transactions on Dependable and Secure Computing*, 16(4), 679–692. doi:10.1109/tdsc.2017.2697854.
15. Lambert, D. (1993). "Measures of disclosure risk and harm." *Journal of Official Statistics*, 9(2), 313–331.
16. Beigi, G., & Liu, H. (2018, July). "Privacy in social media: identification, mitigation and applications." *ACM Trans.* Web 9, 4, Article 39, p. 36. https://doi.org/0000001.0000001.
17. Zhou, B., et al. (2008). "A brief survey on anonymisation techniques for privacy preserving publishing of social network data."*ACM SIGKDD Explorations Newsletter*,10(2),12–22.doi:10.1145/1540276.1540279.
18. Backstrom, L., et al. (2011). "Wherefore art thou R3579X?" *Communications of the ACM*, 54(12), 133–141. doi:10.1145/2043174.2043199.
19. Sweeney, L. (2002). "K-anonymity: a model for protecting privacy." *International Journal of Uncertainty, Fuzziness and Knowledge-Based Systems*, 10(5), 557–570. doi:10.1142/s0218488502001648.
20. Machanavajjhala, A., et al. (2006). "L-diversity: privacy beyond *k*-anonymity." In *22nd International Conference on Data Engineering (ICDE'06)*. doi:10.1109/icde.2006.1.
21. Li, N., et al. (2007). "T-closeness: privacy beyond *k*-anonymity and L-diversity." In *2007 IEEE 23rd International Conference on Data Engineering*. doi:10.1109/icde.2007.367856.
22. Beigi, G., & Liu, H. (2019 Winter). "Identifying novel privacy issues of online users on social media platforms" by Ghazaleh Beigi and Huan Liu with Martin Vesely as coordinator. *ACM SIGWEB Newsletter*, 1–7.

23. Crosas, M., et al. (2020, May). *The OpenDP White Paper*. https://projects.iq.harvard.edu/files/opendp/files/opendp_white_paper_11may2020.pdf.

24. Wood, A., et al. (2018). "Differential privacy: a primer for a non-technical audience." *SSRN Electronic Journal*. doi:10.2139/ssrn.3338027.

25. Prasser, F., et al. (2020). "Flexible data anonymization using ARX – current status and challenges ahead." *Software: Practice and Experience*, 50(7), 1277–1304. doi:10.1002/spe.2812.

26. Dai, C., et al. (2009). "TIAMAT: a tool for interactive analysis of microdata anonymization techniques." *Proceedings of the VLDB Endowment*, 2(2), 1618–1621. doi:10.14778/1687553.1687607.

27. Poulis, G., et al. (2015). "SECRETA: a tool for anonymizing relational, transaction and RT-datasets." In *Medical Data Privacy Handbook*, pp. 83–109. doi:10.1007/978-3-319-23633-9_5.

28. Tsitsigkos, D., & Terrovitis, M. (2019). "What is amnesia?" *Amnesia*. https://amnesia.openaire.eu/amnesiaInfo.html.

29. Holohan, N., et al. (2019). "Diffprivlib: the IBM differential privacy library." *arXiv preprint arXiv:1907.02444*,

30. Falah, A., Pan, L., Huda, S., Pokhrel, S. R., & Anwar, A. (2021). "improving malicious pdf classifier with feature engineering: a data-driven approach." *Future Generation Computer Systems*, 115, 314–326.

31. Naslund, J. A., & Aschbrenner, K. A. (2019). "Risks to privacy with use of social media: understanding the views of social media users with serious mental illness." *Psychiatric Services*, 70(7), 561–568.

32. Akhter, A. F. M. S., Ahmed, M., Shah, A. F. M. S., Anwar, A., & Zengin, A. (2021). "A secured privacy-preserving multi-level blockchain framework for cluster based VANET." *Sustainability*, 13(1), 400.

3 Enabling Location *k*-Anonymity in Social Networks

Francesco Buccafurri, Vincenzo De Angelis,
Maria Francesca Idone, and Cecilia Labrini
Mediterranea University of Reggio Calabria, Reggio Calabria, Italy

CONTENTS

3.1 INTRODUCTION

Location-based services (LBSs) are certainly one of the most impacting consequences of the ubiquitous and massive diffusion of mobile and wearable devices.

There are many types of location-based services, such as navigational, resource discovery, traffic, news, weather, emergency, advertising, location-based games, etc. [1]. They can be continuous (such as navigational services), may require different localization precision, can be delivered as push services, and may differ in terms of privacy threats. The most complex case is that in which the location-based service requires the submission of a query from the side of the user. This is, for example, the case of *points-of-interest services* (POIs), in which the user looks for a certain type of target located in the neighborhood. Indeed, in this case, the information potentially sensitive given to the provider is both the position and the query content. In the semi-trusted adversary model in which, even though the protocols are executed correctly by any involved party, the adversary can misuse received information and can try to extract unintended information from data, there are serious privacy concerns. Location data are sensitive because it might reveal people's habits, health state, religious or sexual orientation, etc., and the same happens for the query content. Obviously, the above privacy threats occur if the identity of the victim is known to the adversary, or can be discovered. Despite a possible apparent intuition, this is a very common case. Indeed, apart from the case in which the LBS requires the knowledge of the explicit identity of the user, even the usage of pseudonyms cannot guarantee anonymity. Moreover, *quasi-identifiers* can be used by the adversary to discover the identity of the victim, if combined with background knowledge or through collusion among different adversary parties. Among other information, location data can be considered a *quasi-identifier*. Consider, for example, the case of an honest-but-curious LBS provider that delivers its services to unregistered users, so apparently anonymous. If the users communicate to the provider their exact position, it suffices that the provider colludes with the telephone service provider to identify the victim on the basis of the IP address of her/his smartphone. It is easy to see that, in general, the anonymization of the IP address does not resolve the problem [2]. Therefore, a specific privacy goal in LBSs is to protect the identity of users from re-identification based on location information.

In this landscape, social networks are more and more assuming a primary role. Indeed, LBSs offered by social networks are nowadays very frequent. From the side of privacy, this case is the most severe. Indeed, not only are the users registered at the provider, but the provider knows and manages a lot of personal information about users. Therefore, further leaks of very sensitive information can be very worrying. Moreover, the provider can also play as a global passive adversary, able to monitor the whole activity of the users.

In this chapter, we focus our attention on the problem of the protection of location data, seen as a potential quasi-identifier. We consider the state-of-the-art approach used to address this problem which is location k-anonymity [3]. This approach is based on the presence of a trusted third party (TTP), called *location trusted service* (LTS), playing the role of anonymizer of the requests of the user against the LBS provider. In this work, we study how to adapt in an effective way this approach to the context of social networks, leveraging the social network to mitigate the well-known drawbacks of the LTS-based approach.

Indeed, the contribution is mainly referred to how we implement the LTS within the social network itself, achieving meaningful advantages with respect to the state of the art. Specifically, besides the fact that a concrete proposal of location k-anonymity is done, also the contribution of a more feasible and secure implementation of LTS is provided. It is worth noting that moving LTS inside the social network is not trivial, because the social network provider is able to monitor all the traffic, so that the classical scheme in which LTS works as a proxy anonymizer for user requests cannot be trivially applied because the requesting user would be immediately identified by the social network provider. The motivations and the contributions of this work are given in Section 3.3.

The structure of the chapter is the following. In Section 3.2, we describe the literature related to our work, by highlighting several techniques used in the context of LBSs existing in the literature. Section 3.3 gives the motivations of our work and the main contribution.

In Section 3.4, we describe the solution we propose to provide k-Anonymity in social networks. The security analysis is discussed in Section 3.5. In Section 3.6, we discuss possible research directions to investigate in the field of privacy-preserving LBSs. Finally, in Section 3.7, we draw our conclusions.

3.2   RELATED WORK

In this section, we describe the related literature regarding privacy-preserving LBSs. There exist different types of protection according to the asset to protect. They are: user's identity, user's location, and query content [1, 4, 5]. It is then important to analyze existing approaches in the scientific literature falling into the three categories.

Identity. In this case, the LBS provider delivers the service to users whose identity is unknown to it. However, if the exact location is provided, being geolocalization a *quasi-identifier*, the user's identity can be discovered by the LBS provider. Indeed, the LBS provider could use some background information or collude with third parties to re-identify the user. For example, this may happen if the LBS provider colludes with the telephone service provider, because the re-identification can be done on the basis of the IP address.

To protect identity, the approach commonly used in the literature is based on *cloaking zones*, which are zones that include at least *k* users. This way, instead of the exact position, a TTP called *trusted location service* (or *anonymizer*), on behalf of the user, sends a cloaking zone to the LBS provider, in such a way that *k-anonymity* is guaranteed [3, 6, 7]. This means that the probability of the adversary (i.e., the LBS provider) to discover the identity of the user requiring a location-based service, is at most $\frac{1}{k}$. This kind of approach is called *location k-anonymity*. The concept of cloaking can be applied not only to the spatial dimension, but also to the temporal dimension [3].

In [8], the notion of location *k*-anonymity has been combined with *l*-diversity, originally proposed in the context of databases [9] to improve the privacy goal achieved by *k*-anonymity.

Some proposals, *called TTP-free* [7], avoid using the trusted location service by allowing user-side in-device computation of the cloaking zone relying on online users' density systems [10] or P2P collaborative solutions [11].

A number of proposals [12–14] have addressed the problem of the granularity of cloaking zones, by approaching it through hierarchical spatial structures like quad-trees. A different approach is based on the notion of KNN-queries [15–18]. Some researchers focused their attention on personalizing privacy requirements when constructing cloaking zones [19]. Another direction of evolution of location *k*-anonymity approaches is toward the control of the quality of service [20–22]. Moreover, other papers are devoted to defining effective caching mechanisms to improve the efficiency of location *k*-anonymity techniques [23–25].

Location. A different objective is to protect the localization information about users that can be considered sensitive. In this case, we do not assume that the user is anonymous for the LBS provider or even registered through a pseudonym. In contrast, her/his identity is known to the provider.

In general the approach used to address this problem aims to *obfuscate* or to *perturb* localization information without degrading the quality of the location-based service [26]. The main drawback of this kind of approach is that it can be vulnerable to history-based and correlation attacks (in general, to inference attacks). In this category, a class of well-established techniques works by enlarging the position of the user in such a way that the provider cannot guess the exact position. Observe that, unlike cloaking zones, no guarantee is given about the number of users involved in the enlarged area. Therefore, these techniques cannot be used to protect identity. A drawback of enlarging is that sometimes the obfuscation action is not effective, because the sub-area of the enlarged zone actually accessible by humans can be small (for example, for the presence of a river, a lake, a highway). Examples of techniques belonging to the enlarging approach are described in [27–30].

Still, among the class of techniques aimed to protect localization data, there are approaches that hide true within dummy information. Obviously, there is a trade-off between privacy and communication overhead. Much attention has been devoted to these techniques in the recent literature, to mitigate the vulnerability to inference attacks [31, 32]. On the other hand, some previous works are [33–35], in which the objective is always to make imprecise the user location by increasing the set of dummy locations. Depending on the size of this set, we obtain a specific level of privacy. In [36], the authors propose a model to measure the achieved privacy of obfuscation/perturbation-based techniques by using a Markov decision process to model user mobility.

The last technique about the user location protection allows us to transform, in a specific way, the spatial coordinate into another reference system as described in the [37]. Therefore, similarly to dummy queries, these techniques aim to obtain high quality of service, because the localization information is punctual even if perturbed. [38, 39] are other examples of techniques of this type. It is worth noting that the techniques based on coordinate transformation are in general vulnerable to map-based attacks that use the transformed coordinates of known POIs.

Query content. The last type of technique aims to protect the content of LBS queries, because they may include sensitive information. This problem is relevant in the case in which the LBS provider knows the identity of the user or can easily disclose it. Two approaches are possible. The first is to generate dummy queries masquerading the actual query. This is proposed, for example, in [40, 41]. Note that this approach, as for the previous techniques, is vulnerable to inference attacks.

Instead, the second approach gives absolute protection with cryptographic guarantees. This is based on PIR (private information retrieval) [42]. In this case, the query is submitted to the provider in such a way that it is able to respond to the query without learning anything about its content [43]. It has been demonstrated in [44] that if only one copy of the database exists, privacy information retrieval can be obtained only with the trivial technique that returns the whole database to the user. Obviously, this is an unrealistic solution. Instead, solutions ensuring full privacy (in the information-theoretical sense) exist but require copies of the database replicated over multiple non-colluding servers [45]. This type of technique ensures that the information target of the user is not revealed, through several queries made on multiple servers whose results are suitably combined to obtain the desired information.

It is worth remarking that, while also considering differential-privacy or machine-learning-based techniques [46–49] to increase robustness of obfuscation and perturbation techniques against inference attacks, the only approach that gives privacy guarantees is that based on PIR.

3.3 MOTIVATIONS AND CONTRIBUTION OF THIS WORK

In this section, we provide the motivations of our work and explain its contribution.

As our work is focused on the application of location k-anonymity to the context of social networks, we recall here in detail how this approach works in the general case.

Consider the user Bob and an LBS provider L of a given service, for example, POIs. Suppose we want to protect the identity of Bob, so that the LBS query cannot be linked with him. L could play as an honest-but-curious adversary, interested in discovering the identity of its customers. To address this problem, since the location itself is a quasi-identifier and then it can allow L to identify Bob if location data are joined with other public data, background knowledge, or through collusion with external parties (such as the telephone service provider), location k-anonymity techniques introduce a TTP, called LTS, which keeps the current locations of all users and is placed in the middle between users and LBS provider. Therefore, when Bob wants to send a query, he sends it to the LTS by using a certain ID. LTS removes such an ID and builds a cloaking zone that includes $k-1$ other users close to Bob. Then, LTS sends Bob's query to L, by associating it with the cloaking zone instead of the exact position of Bob. The crucial point is that the above k users included in the cloaking zone should be indistinguishable for L, on the basis of the lateral information it is able to obtain. If this condition is satisfied, the location information received by L (i.e., the cloaking zone), allows at most the identification of Bob with probability $\frac{1}{k}$, which is acceptable for a sufficiently large value of k.

However, the service can be delivered with the same quality. Indeed, L sends the answer to Bob's query to LTS, which can filter it on the basis of the exact position of Bob, and sends the refined answer to Bob to minimize the client-side communication overhead. The above scheme is resumed in Figure 3.1.

In this work, we assume that L is a social network SN, and we want to apply the above approach to this setting. The first observation we can make is that the social network provider has many advantages (with respect to other types of LBS providers), as an adversary. Indeed, it can leverage

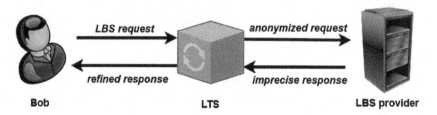

FIGURE 3.1   The standard TTP-based approach.

the information available in Bob's profile as background, besides possible collusion with external parties. The second observation is that LBS customers are, in this case, registered users. Therefore, when a cloaking zone is constructed, the *k* selected users should be all customers of the specific social network SN. This is a necessary condition to be the *k* users indistinguishable for SN.

This certainly complicates the task of LTS. In sum, we are certainly in a severe scenario from the privacy perspective.

We observe that the only viable way to solve this problem seems to apply the above-described TTP-based location *k*-anonymity approach. However, it is worth remarking that the alternate TTP-free approach based on online users' density services is not applicable in our scenario because to guarantee indistinguishability of the *k* users against the LBS provider, these services should be able to select only users of SN, and this is little realistic, at least for privacy reasons.

However, even though the LTS-based solution could in principle be applied, we have to consider the drawbacks of this approach, widely recognized in the literature [50] and aggravated in the scenario considered in this work. They are the following:

(1) It is not clear how LTS is implemented, especially concerning the way in which LTS might be able to localize the $k-1$ SN users to build the cloaking zone.
(2) LTS keeps a lot of location data and thus it becomes an attractive target for attackers. Indeed, if LTS is compromised, it will pose jeopardy for user information. Being social networking platforms with a huge number of customers, the attractiveness would be much higher than other more isolated application settings.
(3) The users should use an external communication channel to contact LTS and to receive the answer to the query and a dedicated authentication at LTS should be managed. This is clearly true also in the case of social networks.

This work goes in the direction of overcoming the above drawbacks by proposing an effective implementation of the LTS-based approach in the case in which the LBS provider is a social network. Specifically, we obtain the following improvements. Concerning (1), we provide a concrete idea of how to implement LTS as a social network user also resolving the problem of the identification of $k-1$ social network users to build the cloaking zone. Concerning (2), being LTS a social network user, it does not expose web services, and the only way to interact with it is through the social network communication functions. Therefore, the risk of attacks is dramatically reduced with respect to the standard LTS case. Concerning (3), we do not require either an external communication channel or a dedicated authentication. This simplifies the secure implementation of the system and increases its usability. As a further consideration, we observe that no more trust is required to LTS than the classical approach. Finally, we highlight that the *all-inside-social-network* solution proposed in this work could also lead to new business models, being the basis of privacy-preserving services offered by social networks.

3.4 THE PROPOSED PROTOCOL

In this section, we provide a detailed description of the proposed solution.

3.4.1 ACTORS AND TERRITORY SETTING

In our protocol, we have the following actors:

- The *social network* SN. We denote by SN also the *social network provider*. We assume that SN delivers LBSs.
- The *users*. They are customers of SN potentially interested in privacy-preserving LBSs.

- The *LTS system*. It is a system of TTPs. Each is an LTS which keeps the current locations of a set of users, playing the role of anonymizer for the LBS requests as in the classical solutions. LTSs are responsible for building on-demand cloaking zones and submitting the LBS queries to SN on behalf of the users. LTSs are hierarchically organized, as explained below. Importantly, LTSs are all SN users.

The above actors interact with each other only through the social network features.

The territory is virtually partitioned into *zones* of level 0, called 0-zones, in such a way that $t \cdot c$ non-LTS users belong to each 0-zone, where t and c are two parameters of the system. Zones are hierarchically grouped into zones of higher level. Therefore, a group of adjacent 0-zones forms a 1-zone. In general, a group of adjacent i-zones forms a $i + 1$-zone. For reasons that will be clear later, there is no constraint about the number of i-zones needed to form a $i + 1$-zone. Each i-zone has one responsible LTS of level i.

For each 0-zone, there is a responsible LTS, which we call *local*. It is of level 0. Coherently with zones, the LTS system is hierarchical. The granularity of the competence territory decreases as the level in the hierarchy grows up. The mapping between zone hierarchy and LTS hierarchy is explained next, once the basic mechanism of our solution, called *circle*, has been introduced.

3.4.2 THE LTS HIERARCHY

A circle is a circular sequence of users. Each circle has one *owner*, which is an LTS. We have two kinds of circles. The first is a *zone circle*, which is composed of all non-LTS users but one, which is, obviously, the owner of the circle. The second is the LTS *circle*, which is composed of only LTSs of which one is the owner of the circle. We associate with a circle a *level l*. For zone circles $l = 0$. LTS circles are at level $l \geq 1$.

For each 0-zone, SN includes all the non-LTS users into c zone circles of $t + 1$ users of which one is the responsible local LTS. The local LTSs responsible for the 0-zones belonging to the same 1-zone are organized into an LTS circle of level 1. In the LTS circle of level 1, also one higher LTS (of level 1) is included, which is the owner of the circle and it is responsible for the 1-zone.

Hierarchically, in the LTS circle of level $i + 1$ there are a number of LTSs of level i and one LTS of level $i + 1$ which is the owner of the circle and it is responsible for the corresponding $i + 1$-zone.

Example 3.1

Consider for example Figure 3.2. It represents a fragment of a possible LTS hierarchy. LTSs of level 0 are depicted as black dots. Each LTS of level 0 is the owner of three zone circles (in this example, $c = 3$, t is not made explicit), including the users of the corresponding 0-zone. The small ellipse delimits a 0-zone. Three adjacent 0-zones form one 1-zone. The medium-size ellipse encloses a 1-zone. For each 1-zone, we have an LTS circle including the three 0-level LTSs responsible for the corresponding 0-zones, plus a 1-level LTS. LTSs of level 1 are depicted as gray dots. The figure represents just one zone of level 2, which includes three zones of level 1, each including three zones of level 0, for a total of 9 zones of level 0. In the 2-zone (delimited by the large-size ellipse), we have an LTS circle including the three 1-level LTSs responsible for the corresponding 1-zones, plus a 2-level LTS depicted as a white dot.

Now, we describe how the circles work.

3.4.3 CIRCLE OPERATION

At the setup phase, SN associates with each user a *native* 0-zone she/he belongs to and the circles are organized by SN hierarchically as explained above. For example, the 0-zone can be associated according to the place in which the user declares to reside.

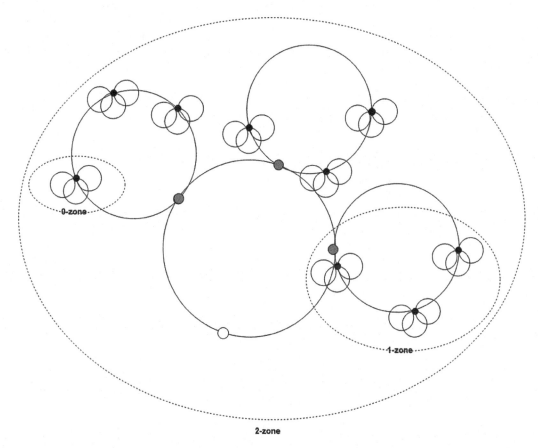

FIGURE 3.2   The hierarchical organization of the LTS system of Example 3.1.

Each user *U* belonging to a circle *C* knows the next user *next*(*U,C*) in the circle and her/his public key. Observe that, if a user belongs to more circles simultaneously (it is only the case of LTSs users), she/he knows the next user of each circle.

For each circle *C*, with a given frequency *f*, which is a parameter of the system (possibly vary-ing at each level of the hierarchy), a dummy message said *token* is generated by the owner *O* of the circle and sent to *X* = *next*(*O,C*). In turn, *X* sends the token to *Y* = *next*(*X,C*) and so on. A token turning in a circle *C* contains an identifier *ID*$_C$ of the circle. Importantly, each token is sent to the next user by encrypting it with the public key of that user. For example, when a user *B* receives the token from the previous user in a circle, she/he decrypts it with her/his private key (kept locally, not at the provider) and re-encrypts the token with the public key of the user *next*(*B,C*), sending the token to this user.

When a user wants to send an actual message, she/he replaces the token with this message. When the token is a dummy message, it is said *empty*, otherwise it is said *filled*.

An empty token and a filled token have the same size and they are encrypted using a probabilistic encryption scheme, so that any external observer (e.g., SN) is not able to distinguish if the user sent an empty token (i.e., a dummy message) or a filled token (i.e., an actual message).

Our protocol includes the following three phases.

3.4.4   POSITION NOTIFICATION

Each user located in her/his native 0-zone sends her/his position to the local LTS responsible for such a zone. If the user moves from his native zone, she/he stops to notify her/his position. This is done for efficiency reasons but works in favor of privacy, because the user will be not counted either in the native zone or in the arrival zone, so that k-anonymity is not threatened.

To protect the user's identity, the position is associated with a pseudonym of fixed temporal validity which is exactly the refresh period p (in minutes) of the position communication. Therefore, each user who wants to be counted by its LTS to build cloaking zones, sends her/his position every p minutes, by rounding the pseudonym with the same period p. As we will explain better in Section 3.5, this measure does not offer absolute protection of users' identity against LTSs, because re-identification attacks based on trajectories are always feasible, even if not simple, if the rounding protocol of pseudonyms is also enabled. However, LTSs are supposed to be TTPs. So, our approach aims to minimize the personal information known by LTSs under the assumption that they are honest and not curious (so, they do not perform attacks).

Anyway, to obtain the above goal, obviously the position cannot be notified directly by the user to LTS. Therefore, we enable an anonymous protocol exploiting the above notion of a circle and the cover traffic implemented through tokens that we use both for position notification and for LBS request, as we will see in the following.

Suppose that Alice is sending her position g_A (included in her native 0-zone). She waits for an empty token of the circle she belongs to. At this point, she generates a new pseudonym P_A, valid for the next p minutes. Then, she fills the token with the message $M = E(PK_{LTS} (P_A, g_A))$, where E denotes an encryption function with the public key PK_{LTS} of the local LTS responsible for the native zone of Alice. The filled token turns in the circle as explained above until it reaches the LTS. At this point, LTS retrieves the information and stores it (with validity of p minutes). Then, LTS re-injects an empty token in the circle. Observe that the stored information, if valid, can be used by LTS to build on-demand cloaking zones.

To guarantee the correct management of LBS requests, as we will see later, position notifications must be propagated from lower-level LTSs to higher-level LTSs, in the following way.

When a local LTS receives the position of a user, it sends this information to the LTS of level 1 responsible for the 1-zone, which includes the 0-zone for which the local LTS is responsible. To do this, the local LTS waits for an empty token of the circle of level 1 that it belongs to and sends the message $M = (P_A, g_A)$ in such a circle. The message turns in the circle until it reaches the LTS of level 1 (i.e., the owner of the circle), which retrieves and stores this information. With the same procedure, the LTS of level 1 injects this information in the circle of level 2 until it reaches the LTS of level 2, and so on. In favor of efficiency, the propagation can be stopped after a proper number of steps. This point will be clarified during the description of LBS-request management.

3.4.5   LBS REQUEST

Suppose Alice wants to send an LBS request to SN. We have to consider two cases: (1) Alice is sending the request from her native zone; (2) Alice is located in a different zone.

Case (1):

In this case, Alice waits for an empty token of the circle she belongs to. Then, she fills it with the message $M = E(PK_{LTS} (K_A, g_A, Q))$, where E denotes the encryption with the public key PK_{LTS} of the local LTS responsible for the native zone of Alice, K_A is an on-the-fly public key generated by Alice, g_A is the current position of Alice and Q is the (possibly obfuscated or encrypted) query containing the service requested by Alice. The filled token turns in the circle as explained above until it reaches the LTS. Observe that the local LTS is aware of the fact that the request comes from a user placed within her/his native zone, simply by checking the position g_A. At this point, the local LTS checks if there is sufficient number of active users in the 0-zone of Alice to build the cloaking zone. Two cases may hold:

Case (1.1):

The cloaking zone can be built. In this case, the local LTS first waits until at least one token per zone circle is arrived. This is done to avoid SN being able to identify the circle which the message comes from. At this point, it sends the message (z, Q, R) to SN, where z is the cloaking zone, Q is the query sent by Alice, and R is a random. Moreover, LTS records the pair $\langle ID_C, R \rangle$, where ID_C is the identifier of the circle from which it received the request, the position g_A of Alice, and the key K_A.

Case (1.2):

The cloaking zone cannot be built. This is the case in which there is no sufficient number of active users in the 0-zone of Alice to build the cloaking zone. At this point, the local LTS starts a *pull-up* procedure, consisting of iteratively forwarding the request to the next-level LTS until the cloaking zone can be built. In detail, the local LTS waits for an empty token of the LTS circle of level 1 it belongs to and injects Alice's request in this circle until it reaches the LTS of level 1. If this LTS is able to build a cloaking zone by considering users belonging to its 1-zone, then it processes the request to SN as in case (1.1). Otherwise, the process is iteratively repeated until the cloaking zone can be built. Observe that each LTS forwarding the request stores the random R and the identifier ID_C of the circle from which it received the request.

Case (2):

Recall that this is the case in which Alice is located in a different zone from her native zone.

First, Alice sends the request $M = E(PK_{LTS} (K_A, g_A, Q))$, through the circle, to the local LTS responsible for her native zone. Since g_A is not in such a zone, the local LTS cannot manage the request. Then, it sends the request in the circle of level 1 it belongs to. At this point, we have three cases.

Case (2.1):

This case is when the request reaches an LTS of level 0 in the circle that can manage it. Specifically, g_A is in the 0-zone for which such an LTS is responsible, and there is a sufficient number of users to form the cloaking zone. In this case, the request can be managed by this LTS in the same way as case (1.1).

Case (2.2):

This case is when the request reaches the LTS of level 1 in the circle and g_A is not in the 1-zone for which it is responsible. In this case, the LTS of level 1 starts the *enlarging* procedure aimed at finding the highest i such that there exists an i-zone that includes the native zone of Alice but not the position g_A. This can be done just by going up in the hierarchy of the LTSs circle by circle, as in the pull-up procedure. Let's now consider the LTS responsible for this i-zone, and let C be the circle of level $i + 1$ which this LTS belongs to. We know that the g_A is necessarily included in one of the i-zones managed by an LTS belonging to circle C. So, the request is injected in this circle until it reaches the LTS responsible for the i-zone including g_A. This LTS starts the *push-down* procedure, just consisting of going down in the LTS hierarchy until we reach the LTS responsible for 0-zone including g_A. Now we are exactly in the same situation as case (1), which is then managed like earlier.

Case (2.3):

This case is one in which the request returns to the local LTS of the native zone of Alice. This means that the request should have been managed by an LTS of level 0 of the circle, but there is no sufficient number of active users in the corresponding 0-zone to build the cloaking zone. In this case, the pull-up procedure is invoked as in (1.2).

3.4.6 LBS RESPONSE

Suppose Alice sent an LBS request to SN. We describe here how the response to Alice's request is managed. We have to consider again two cases: (1) Alice sent the request from her native zone; (2) Alice sent the request from a different zone.

Consider case (1). In this case, SN sends the LBS response referred to the submitted cloaking zone to the LTS where the request came from. This response contains, besides the required service, also the random R included in the request (see (1.1) earlier). This is either (i) the local LTS responsible for the native zone of Alice or (ii) another LTS higher in the hierarchy with respect to the former LTS (in the case the pull-up procedure has been activated). Observe that (i) refers to a request falling into the case (1.1) and (ii) refers to a request falling into the case (1.2).

In both cases, the imprecise response is filtered by the receiving LTS according to the exact position g_A of Alice. Then, the refined response is encrypted with the key K_A embedded in the request.

Now, in case (i), as the local LTS had stored the pair $\langle IDc, R \rangle$, the refined response can be injected in the appropriate circle. This is done, as usual, by filling the first empty token that turns in the circle. Then, the filled token turns until Alice is able to decrypt the response and to empty the token, which is forwarded again in the circle.

In case (ii), the response has been received and refined by an LTS higher in the hierarchy with respect to the local LTS responsible for the native zone of Alice. This LTS kept the information of the circle from which the request associated with the random R came from. The response is thus injected in this circle. This may not be the circle which the local LTS responsible for Alice's native zone belongs to, because the pull-up procedure required multiple steps. So, the above process might have to be iterated. Eventually, the circle that the local LTS responsible for Alice's native zone belongs to will be reached, and then such an LTS. Therefore, the request reaches Alice in the same way as case (i).

Consider now case (2), referring to the case in which Alice sent the request from a different zone from her native zone. As in case (1), SN sends the LBS response referred to the submitted cloaking zone to the LTS, which the request came from.

Such an LTS (supposed of level j) starts a procedure aimed at finding the highest i such that there exists an i-zone that includes the position g_A of Alice but not her native zone. This can be done just by injecting the refined response into the circle of level $j + 1$ which the LTS belongs to. If no LTS in this circle is responsible for a zone satisfying the above condition, then the request is injected by the proper LTS into the circle of level $j + 2$. Otherwise, it is easy to see that there exists, in the $j + 1$-level circle, an LTS which is responsible for a zone that includes the native zone of Alice. Let L be this LTS, and let h be its level (h can be either j or $j + 1$). L injects the response into the circle of level h which it belongs to. In this circle, there is exactly one LTS that is responsible for a zone including the native zone of Alice but not g_A. If LTS is of level 0, it can inject the response to the circle which Alice belongs to and the process ends. Otherwise, the process is iterated.

As a final remark, we observe that, even though during the request only a portion of circle is covered by the filled token and the same happens for the response, the social network provider, even by analyzing the whole traffic, is not able to identify any node of the query-processing path but the last LTS submitting the request. This happens thanks to the token-based mechanism, which does not allow the identification of the initiator of the request as well as the recipient of the response, and does not allow us to detect when a message moves from a circle to another circle, actually making anonymous for a global adversary all senders and recipients but the LTS submitting the request on behalf of the user. This aspect will be better analyzed in Section 3.5.

Example 3.2

Figure 3.3 reports an example of the execution of LBS requests-responses. We consider two cases. The first, regarding Bob, is the case in which the user submits the LBS query from a location included in his native zone (see case (1) above). Then, we consider the case regarding Alice, in which the user has moved from her native zone to another 0-zone (in the example, this 0-zone is belonging to a 1-zone different from the 1-zone including the native zone), before submitting the LBS query (see case (2) above).

In the figure, we highlighted the circles that are involved in the query processing. We used a dashed line for the case of Bob and a thick line for the case of Alice. Similarly, the arrows, coherently drawn, are used to represent the interaction between an LTS and the social network provider. Moreover, the ellipses including city icons represent the physical position of the users when submitting queries, while the user's icon close to a 0-zone circle means that the user belongs to that circle (associated with her/his native zone).

First, consider the query of Bob. It is submitted by Bob in the circle that he belongs to. Indeed, we have only a dashed circle associated with the native 0-zone of Bob. Observe that the filled token embedding the request starts from the node in the circle associated with Bob and turns (suppose clockwise) until the 0-level LTS responsible for the native zone, represented by the black dot belonging to the circle. The figure represents case (1.1), in which the LTS can build a valid cloaking zone fulfilling the privacy requirements. Then, such an LTS sends the request to the social network provider, retrieves the answer, filters it, and injects it in the circle, until it reaches Bob.

Now, consider the case of Alice. Recall that she is located in a 0-zone different from her native zone, as depicted in the figure. In the figure, we assume that we are in case (2.2). In this case, the request starts from the circle which Alice belongs to (the right-most tick-line circle) until it reaches

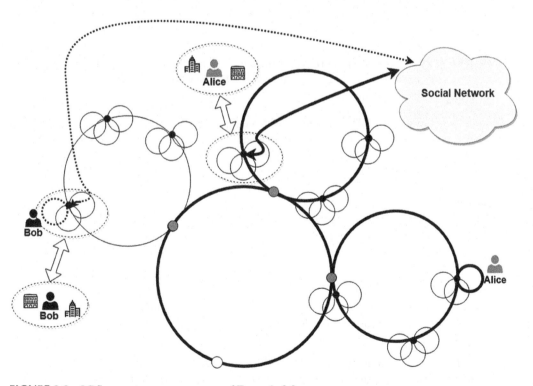

FIGURE 3.3   LBS request-response process of Example 3.2.

the LTS (represented by a black dot) in such a circle. This LTS cannot manage the request of Alice because it contains a position not included in the 0-zone of its competence. Therefore, it forwards the request to the circle of level 1. This request cannot be processed by the 0-level LTSs. This can be recognized by the 1-level LTS (represented by a gray dot) when the token reaches it. Thus, in turn, it injects the request into the circle of level 2 (represented in tick-line) it belongs to. Being the request processable by an LTS of level 1 of this circle (and this can be recognized by the 2-level white LTS), the token turns until it reaches such an LTS. At this point, it injects the request in the circle of level 1 it belongs to (again represented in tick-line). This request turns in the circle until it reaches the 0-level LTS which is the first black-dot LTS clockwise. Since it is responsible for the 0-zone in which Alice is located, it can process the request. Then, it builds the cloaking zone and forwards the request (tick-line arrow) to the social network provider. The answer is sent by the social network provider to this LTS, which filters it and injects it in the circle of level 1 it belongs to. The answer comes back through the same circles until it reaches Alice in the reverse order and by covering the complementary part of any circle.

3.5   SECURITY ANALYSIS

In this section, we provide a security analysis of our solution. We start by defining the threat model.

Actors and capabilities: In our threat model, we consider the following actors with their capabilities.

SN: The social network provider is a semi-trusted party (honest-but-curious). However, we assume the maximum severity in the semi-trusted model which is the case in which SN can play as a global passive adversary, able to monitor all the traffic exchanged in the social network. Moreover, it can exploit all the information (photos, posts, and so on) present in users' profiles as background knowledge also allowing to infer users' positions.

LTSs: They are considered trusted parties. They receive the positions (in pseudonymous form) by users and process their queries and answers.

SN Users: They are honest-but-curious, in the sense that they perform legally the steps of the protocols and do not collude with other users, but they could be interested in inferring information about other users.

Observe that, regarding the LTSs, they are considered trusted since the positions are quasi-identifiers, so that they can perform re-identification attacks to identify users even if they use pseudonyms (e.g., by colluding with the telephone service provider). However, these attacks require an effort for the LTSs, so that the use of pseudonyms makes it harder (even if yet feasible) to perform such attacks.

Assumptions:

A1: The probabilistic encryption scheme used is secure.

A2: An LTS builds the cloaking zone in such a way that it includes at least k SN users that are indistinguishable for SN regarding the likelihood that they are performing the LBS request.

Adversaries:

An adversary is any actor of the protocol with respect to her/his capabilities. Since the LTSs are assumed trusted, they do not perform any attack.

Security Properties:

SP1 (location k-anonymity): It is not possible to link the identity of a user performing an LBS query or receiving the answer to an LBS query to this request/response with probability greater than $\frac{1}{k}$.

We show how our protocol guarantees **SP1**.

First, we consider the case in which the adversary is an SN user. The only way in which she/he is able to know that a possible request/response is sent/received by another user is when she/he received a filled token. However, due to Assumption **A1**, only the intended recipient is able to decipher the message (request/response) contained in the token. Moreover, each SN user only knows the next user in the circle she/he belongs to, thus she/he cannot know who the request comes from or who is the target of a response.

Now, we consider the case in which the adversary is SN.

Even if SN can monitor all the traffic exchanged in the social network, due to Assumption **A1** and to the fact that empty tokens and filled tokens have the same size, it is not able to distinguish if an SN user sends a filled token (containing a request/response) or an empty token. When the request reaches the LTS of level 0 responsible for the native zone of the SN user, there are two possible cases: (1) such an LTS manages the request by building the cloaking zone and sends it to SN; or (2) the request is forwarded to the circle of level 1 in which such an LTS belongs to. Observe that case (2) occurs when the user is not located in her/his native zone or when there is no sufficient number of active users in such a zone to build the cloaking zone.

Consider case (1). The LTS of level 0 builds the cloaking zone including at least k users in the 0-zone for which it is responsible and forwards the request to SN. Due to Assumption **A2**, even if SN, through the information of users' profiles, can identify all the users in the cloaking zone, it is unable to distinguish who has sent a request unless it does not know the circle from which the request comes. Indeed, in this latter case, it can make the intersection among the users in the circle and the users in the cloaking zone, reducing the number of possible senders of a request. However, this case is not possible since the LTS of level 0 waits for a token for each circle of level 0 it belongs to before sending the request to SN. In such a way, SN is not able to distinguish the circle from which the request came. When the LTS receives the response from SN, it waits for the empty token of the proper circle to inject the response so that, again, SN is not able to know the circle involved in the response phase.

Consider case (2). When the LTS injects the request in the circle of level 1, it waits for an empty token, thus SN is not able to understand that a request was forwarded in this circle. At this point, the request turns in the various circles as explained in Section 3.4 until it reaches an LTS that manages it. Two cases may occur: either (2.1) such an LTS is of level 0 or (2.2) such an LTS is of level $l > 0$. Case (2.1) is the same as case (1). Regarding case (2.2), SN is not able to distinguish which circles of lower levels the request comes from and then it is not able to distinguish the user sending the request in the cloaking zone. Similarly to case (1), the response is forwarded to the intended recipient by waiting for the token of the proper circles, thus SN cannot track the path.

3.6 FUTURE RESEARCH DIRECTIONS AND CHALLENGES

This section tries to envisage the evolution of the research in this field for the next few years. Despite the fact that LBSs is a topic deeply analyzed in the scientific literature for more than one decade, an extensive application of privacy-preserving approaches has not occurred yet. This, in part, depends on the components of the proposed approaches that appear not easily implementable in concrete solutions. Therefore, also by following the direction investigated in this paper of fully merging the domain of LBSs into social networks, a challenge to pursue is to find models, methodologies, architectures that make feasible the identified solutions. One of the main important aspects to address is the guarantee of security and privacy properties also from a risk-based perspective. To do this, it could be useful to identify different adversary models, by gradually relaxing assumptions of adherence to the protocol of the involved entities until the case of fully untrusted parties. Moreover, different attack scenarios and impact of attacks have to be considered, leading to a framework allowing us to measure the real-life security of the solutions. Another important issue, related to the latter point, is to study the trade-off between privacy, security, effectiveness, and quality of delivered LBSs, by possibly introducing some approximation degree with respect to the privacy goal (e.g., the *k*-anonymity target). Finally, for collaboration-based approaches like the technique described in this chapter, it is challenging to study how to guarantee service availability also in the case of partial non-collaboration, thus identifying how to set, at design time, the right redundancy level.

3.7   CONCLUSION

This chapter focuses on the privacy threats arising from LBSs provided by online social networks. These are services related to users' location and then characterized by potentially very serious privacy issues, because they may reveal even strictly personal habits. Starting from this awareness, we addressed this problem in a very concrete yet severe scenario, which is, as a matter of fact, the most relevant in practice. The scenario is that of LBSs provided directly by the social network provider, without relying on separated autonomous services. The customers of these services are the users registered on the social network.

The scenario is severe because the social network provider knows a lot of personal information about the LBSs customers (as it manages their social network profiles) and can also monitor all the traffic exchanged between users. This gives the social network provider, playing as an honest-but-curious adversary, a great advantage in terms of availability of background knowledge to exploit for re-identification attacks, whenever state-of-the-art techniques to protect users' identities are applied. Specifically, the only viable approach applicable in this context is location k-anonymity, which relies on the presence of a TTP, called LTS, playing as k-anonymizer.

This work first analyzes the drawbacks of this approach when applied to the context of social networks, realizing that these are even aggravated. The second step of the work was then the definition of an innovative solution that places the location trusted service within the social network, to mitigate the drawbacks of a standard LTS-based solution. This is not a trivial task, because without a non-naïve solution, any attempt of anonymizing the LBS requests by posing the LTS in the middle between the user and LBS provider (i.e., the social network provider) fails, because the social network provider can easily identify the initiator of an LBS request by analyzing the flow of messages. To overcome this problem, we defined a cooperative solution that hides requests and responses into cover messages. As a further contribution, we propose a detailed implementation of the LTS system, which is one of the weak points of the state-of-the-art approaches, thus providing a complete solution.

ACKNOWLEDGMENT

This chapter is partially supported by Project POR FESR/FSE 14/20 Line A (Action 10.5.6) and Line B (Action 10.5.12).

REFERENCES

1. Claudio Bettini. Privacy protection in location-based services: A survey. In *Handbook of Mobile Data Privacy*, pp. 73–96. Springer, 2018.
2. Sergio Mascetti, Claudio Bettini, Dario Freni, and X. Sean Wang. Spatial generalisation algorithms for LBS privacy preservation. *Journal of Location Based Services*, 1(3): 179–207, 2007.
3. Marco Gruteser and Dirk Grunwald. Anonymous usage of location-based services through spatial and temporal cloaking. In *Proceedings of the 1st International Conference on Mobile Systems, Applications and Services*, pp. 31–42, ACM Press, 2003.
4. Claudio Bettini, Sergio Mascetti, X. Sean Wang, Dario Freni, and Sushil Jajodia. Anonymity and historical-anonymity in location-based services. In *Privacy in Location-Based Applications*, pp. 1–30. Springer, 2009.
5. John Krumm. A survey of computational location privacy. *Personal and Ubiquitous Computing*, 13(6): 391–399, 2009.
6. Pierangela Samarati and Latanya Sweeney. Protecting privacy when disclosing information: K-anonymity and its enforcement through generalization and suppression. Working Paper, IEEE Security and Privacy, 1998.
7. Tao Peng, Qin Liu, and Guojun Wang. Enhanced location privacy preserving scheme in location-based services. *IEEE Systems Journal*, 11(1): 219–230, 2014.
8. Mingqiang Xue, Panos Kalnis, and Hung Keng Pung. Location diversity: Enhanced privacy protection in location based services. In *International Symposium on Location and Context-Awareness*, pp. 70–87. Springer, 2009.

9. Ashwin Machanavajjhala, Daniel Kifer, Johannes Gehrke, and Muthuramakrishnan Venkitasubramaniam. L-diversity: Privacy beyond k-anonymity. *ACM Transactions on Knowledge Discovery from Data (TKDD)*, 1(1): 3, 2007.

10. Hiba Jadallah and Zaher Al Aghbari. Spatial cloaking for location-based queries in the cloud. *Journal of Ambient Intelligence and Humanized Computing*, 10(9): 3339–3347, 2019.

11. Chi-Yin Chow, Mohamed F. Mokbel, and Xuan Liu. Spatial cloaking for anonymous location-based services in mobile peer-to-peer environments. *GeoInformatica*, 15(2): 351–380, 2011.

12. Bhuvan Bamba, Ling Liu, Peter Pesti, and Ting Wang. Supporting anonymous location queries in mobile environments with privacygrid. In *Proceedings of the 17th International Conference on World Wide Web*, pp. 237–246, ACM Press, 2008.

13. Bugra Gedik and Ling Liu. Location privacy in mobile systems: A personalized anonymization model. In *25th IEEE International Conference on Distributed Computing Systems (ICDCS'05)*, pp. 620–629. IEEE, 2005.

14. Mohamed F. Mokbel, Chi-Yin Chow, and Walid G. Aref. The new casper: Query processing for location services without compromising privacy. In *Proceedings of the 32nd International Conference on Very Large Data Bases*, pp. 763–774, ACM Press, 2006.

15. Xun Yi, Russell Paulet, Elisa Bertino, and Vijay Varadharajan. Practical approximate k nearest neighbor queries with location and query privacy. *IEEE Transactions on Knowledge and Data Engineering*, 28(6): 1546–1559, 2016.

16. Yuanbo Cui, Fei Gao, Hua Zhang, Wenmin Li, and Zhengping Jin. Knn search-based trajectory cloaking against the cell-id tracking in cellular network. *Soft Computing*, 24(2): 965–980, 2020.

17. Shushu Liu, An Liu, Zheng Yan, and Wei Feng. Efficient LBS queries with mutual privacy preservation in IOV. *Vehicular Communications*, 16: 62–71, 2019.

18. Linfeng Xie, Zhigang Feng, Cong Ji, and Yongjin Zhu. Adjustable location privacy-preserving nearest neighbor query method. In *International Conference on Web Information Systems and Applications*, pp. 467–479. Springer, 2019.

19. Bugra Gedik and Ling Liu. Protecting location privacy with personalized k-anonymity: Architecture and algorithms. *IEEE Transactions on Mobile Computing*, 7(1): 1–18, 2007.

20. Ting Liu, Guanghui Yan, Gang Cai, Qiong Wang, and Mingjie Yang. User personalized location k anonymity privacy protection scheme with controllable service quality. In *International Conference on Machine Learning for Cyber Security*, pp. 484–499. Springer, 2020.

21. Lijuan Zheng, Huanhuan Yue, Zhaoxuan Li, Xiao Pan, Mei Wu, and Fan Yang. K-anonymity location privacy algorithm based on clustering. *IEEE Access*, 6: 28328–28338, 2017.

22. Ajay K. Gupta and Udai Shanker. OMCPR: Optimal mobility aware cache data pre-fetching and replacement policy using spatial k-anonymity for LBS. *Wireless Personal Communications*, (2): 1–25, 2020.

23. Xiaoyan Zhu, Haotian Chi, Ben Niu, Weidong Zhang, Zan Li, and Hui Li. Mobicache: When k-anonymity meets cache. In *2013 IEEE Global Communications Conference (GLOBECOM)*, pp. 820–825. IEEE, 2013.

24. Ben Niu, Qinghua Li, Xiaoyan Zhu, Guohong Cao, and Hui Li. Enhancing privacy through caching in location-based services. In *2015 IEEE Conference on Computer Communications (INFOCOM)*, pp. 1017–1025. IEEE, 2015.

25. Shaobo Zhang, Xiong Li, Zhiyuan Tan, Tao Peng, and Guojun Wang. A caching and spatial k-anonymity driven privacy enhancement scheme in continuous location-based services. *Future Generation Computer Systems*, 94: 40–50, 2019.

26. Christian S. Jensen, Hua Lu, and Man Lung Yiu. Location privacy techniques in client–server architectures. In *Privacy in Location-Based Applications*, pp. 31–58. Springer, 2009.

27. Maria Luisa Damiani, Elisa Bertino, Claudio Silvestri, et al. The probe framework for the personalized cloaking of private locations. *Transactions on Data Privacy*, 3(2): 123–148, 2010.

28. Reynold Cheng, Yu Zhang, Elisa Bertino, and Sunil Prabhakar. Preserving user location privacy in mobile data management infrastructures. In *International Workshop on Privacy Enhancing Technologies*, pp. 393–412. Springer, 2006.

29. Claudio A. Ardagna, Marco Cremonini, Sabrina De Capitani di Vimercati, and Pierangela Samarati. An obfuscation-based approach for protecting location privacy. *IEEE Transactions on Dependable and Secure Computing*, 8(1): 13–27, 2009.

30. Tanzima Hashem, Lars Kulik, and Rui Zhang. Privacy preserving group nearest neighbor queries. In *Proceedings of the 13th International Conference on Extending Database Technology*, pp. 489–500, ACM Press, 2010.

31. Gang Sun, Shuai Cai, Hongfang Yu, Sabita Maharjan, Victor Chang, Xiaojiang Du, and Mohsen Guizani. Location privacy preservation for mobile users in location-based services. *IEEE Access*, 7: 87425–87438, 2019.

32. Li Kuang, Yin Wang, Xiaosen Zheng, Lan Huang, and Yu Sheng. Using location semantics to realize personalized road network location privacy protection. *EURASIP Journal on Wireless Communications and Networking*, 2020(1): 1, 2020.

33. Hidetoshi Kido, Yutaka Yanagisawa, and Tetsuji Satoh. Protection of location privacy using dummies for location-based services. In *21st International Conference on Data Engineering Workshops (ICDEW'05)*, pp. 1248–1248. IEEE, 2005.

34. Man Lung Yiu, Christian S. Jensen, Xuegang Huang, and Hua Lu. Spacetwist: Managing the trade-offs among location privacy, query performance, and query accuracy in mobile services. In *2008 IEEE 24th International Conference on Data Engineering*, pp. 366–375. IEEE, 2008.

35. Ben Niu, Qinghua Li, Xiaoyan Zhu, Guohong Cao, and Hui Li. Achieving k-anonymity in privacy-aware location-based services. In *IEEE INFOCOM 2014 IEEE Conference on Computer Communications*, pp. 754–762. IEEE, 2014.

36. Alireza Partovi, Wei Zheng, Taeho Jung, and Hai Lin. Ensuring privacy in location-based services: A model-based approach. *arXiv preprint arXiv:2002.10055*, 2020.

37. Andreas Gutscher. Coordinate transformation – A solution for the privacy problem of location based services? In *Proceedings 20th IEEE International Parallel & Distributed Processing Symposium*, pp. 1–7. IEEE, 2006.

38. Kun Liu, Chris Giannella, and Hillol Kargupta. An attacker's view of distance preserving maps for privacy preserving data mining. In *European Conference on Principles of Data Mining and Knowledge Discovery*, pp. 297–308. Springer, 2006.

39. Sergio Mascetti, Letizia Bertolaja, and Claudio Bettini. A practical location privacy attack in proximity services. In *2013 IEEE 14th International Conference on Mobile Data Management*, vol. 1, pp. 87–96. IEEE, 2013.

40. Aniket Pingley, Nan Zhang, Xinwen Fu, Hyeong-Ah Choi, Suresh Subramaniam, and Wei Zhao. Protection of query privacy for continuous location based services. In *2011 Proceedings IEEE INFOCOM*, pp. 1710–1718. IEEE, 2011.

41. Zongda Wu, Guiling Li, Shigen Shen, Xinze Lian, Enhong Chen, and Guandong Xu. Constructing dummy query sequences to protect location privacy and query privacy in location-based services. *World Wide Web*, 24(1): 1–25, 2020.

42. William Gasarch. A survey on private information retrieval. *Bulletin of the EATCS*, 82(72–107): 113, 2004.

43. Gabriel Ghinita, Panos Kalnis, Ali Khoshgozaran, Cyrus Shahabi, and Kian-Lee Tan. Private queries in location based services: Anonymizers are not necessary. In *Proceedings of the 2008 ACM SIGMOD International Conference on Management of Data*, pp. 121–132, 2008.

44. Benny Chor, Oded Goldreich, Eyal Kushilevitz, and Madhu Sudan. Private information retrieval. In *Proceedings of IEEE 36th Annual Foundations of Computer Science*, pp. 41–50. IEEE, 1995.

45. Sergey Yekhanin. Private information retrieval. In *Locally Decodable Codes and Private Information Retrieval Schemes*, pp. 61–74. Springer, 2010.

46. Miguel E. Andrés, Nicolás E. Bordenabe, Konstantinos Chatzikokolakis, and Catuscia Palamidessi. Geo-indistinguishability: Differential privacy for location-based systems. In *Proceedings of the 2013 ACM SIGSAC Conference on Computer & Communications Security*, pp. 901–914, ACM Press, 2013.

47. Yonghui Xiao and Li Xiong. Protecting locations with differential privacy under temporal correlations. In *Proceedings of the 22nd ACM SIGSAC Conference on Computer and Communications Security*, pp. 1298–1309, ACM Press, 2015.

48. Marco Romanelli, Konstantinos Chatzikokolakis, and Catuscia Palamidessi. Optimal obfuscation mechanisms via machine learning. In *2020 IEEE 33rd Computer Security Foundations Symposium (CSF)*, pp. 153–168. IEEE Computer Society, 2020.

49. Ben Niu, Yuhong Chen, Zhibo Wang, Boyang Wang, Hui Li, et al. Eclipse: Preserving differential location privacy against long-term observation attacks. *IEEE Transactions on Mobile Computing*, 2020.

50. Shaobo Zhang, Guojun Wang, Md Zakirul Alam Bhuiyan, and Qin Liu. A dual privacy preserving scheme in continuous location-based services. *IEEE Internet of Things Journal*, 5(5): 4191–4200, 2018.

Part II

Securing Multimedia Contents

4 Automated Content Classification in Social Media Platforms

Thomas M. Chen

City University of London, London, UK

CONTENTS

4.1 INTRODUCTION

Social media depends on content created by its users. It is easy to imagine that without any rules or restrictions, users might share offensive, illegal, threatening, or copyrighted materials. This could attract criminal or extremist users and repel average users, not to mention possibly drive away advertisers. Hence, there is a natural need for content moderation – the process of identifying, reviewing, and taking down content that violate terms of service or "community standards" [1].

DOI: 10.1201/9781003134527-6

Content moderation is traditionally labor-intensive, involving thousands of human moderators employed by the largest social media platforms. The moderation process involves:

- setting a clear understanding of community standards;
- identifying content that possibly violates community standards;
- reviewing the suspect content;
- deciding on the action to be taken, which might range from nothing (allowing the content to remain online) to adding a label, taking it down, or deleting the user's account.

Content moderation is not a new practice that started with online social media. Moderation has been a common practice in traditional mass media. For example, printed media such as newspapers, magazines, and books (like the one you are reading) are overseen by editors who check that the written content is consistent with the aims, policies, and standards of the publication. Television networks largely moderate themselves in order to avoid offending their audiences as well as avoid potentially large fines from the Federal Communications Commission (FCC). In the U.S., the FCC can impose fines for obscene or indecent content or revoke broadcast licenses in the worst case, but television networks also avoid controversial content to appeal to broader audiences and thus attract advertisers (which is generally how networks make money).

Controversy is unavoidable in the process of content moderation. Inevitably some people will object to certain content as offensive and demand it to be taken down, but platforms decide to keep it up. At the same time, users who have their content taken down or their accounts suspended will criticize platforms for censorship that violates their right to free speech (guaranteed by the U.S. constitution).

There are two difficulties with the criticism of censorship. First, the first amendment only applies to the suppression of free speech by the government. The original intention was to protect people from government censorship. As private companies, social media platforms are free to create and enforce their own community standards. Second, content moderation is not the same as censorship. Censorship is the suppression of information and ideas communicated through speech or other forms. It is enforced through the prohibition of words or images that are deemed to be harmful. Content moderation is more about the establishment and enforcement of community standards. It can involve censorship (e.g., blocking obscene content) but might simply be fact-checking or blocking illegal activities.

On some social media platforms such as dating websites and bulletin boards, uploaded content is checked by a moderator before it is accepted on the platform. This ensures that unsuitable content will never appear online, which protects the platform's brand and reputation. However, this "proactive" approach may delay the upload of content, and is not scalable since moderators must examine every piece of content. In contrast, the more common approach on most social media platforms today is a "reactive" approach which depends on user complaints (reports) or their own content moderators to identify suspect content already online [1]. This allows users to upload content without delays, but it is possible for inappropriate content to escape detection. The reactive "publish then filter" approach is necessary due to the overwhelming volume of user-generated content [2].

Content moderators are often trained professionals employed by a large social media company or a third-party commercial service. Smaller platforms may find it more practical to outsource content moderation to a third-party service than to hire and train their own moderators. Moderators can screen thousands of images, videos, or texts in a day and are known to suffer emotional stress due to the types of materials that they have to view [3]. Google (the owner of YouTube) announced plans to hire 10,000 moderators by 2018 [4]. Facebook had 7,500 moderators as of February 2018 [5].

4.1.1 TYPES OF CONTENT

Without laws, a real-life neighborhood can be overrun by criminals, gangs, drug sellers, scammers, or ill-behaved neighbors, making the area unpleasant or unsafe for everyone. By analogy, a social media platform wants to avoid certain types of user-generated content that could make the general environment unpleasant and unsafe for the general population of users. It can be a delicate balance to maintain. While platforms want to encourage freedom of expression, it is clear that some rules are necessary for creating boundaries of the types of user-generated content that are allowable.

Generally, users are bound by both terms of service and community standards. Terms of service refer to the legal agreements between a service provider and that service's users. Service providers can enforce the terms by refusing or restricting service to users who violate the terms. The terms can work in the other way also – users can file a lawsuit if they can show harm from a breach of the terms, e.g., unauthorized disclosure of personal data. Terms of service typically include: explanations of user rights and responsibilities; disclaimer of a service's liability for damages incurred by users; and explanations of user data privacy, e.g., how data is collected, stored, or used. Data privacy may be particularly important these days because social media services are often supported by advertising in order to provide services free to users. This implies that companies might be collecting or monetizing more personal data than people realize unless they read the terms of service carefully.

In contrast, community standards typically include descriptions of appropriate content that is not a legal contract but more of "expected norms" subject to judgment by the social media company. In the same way that a real-life neighborhood depends on more than laws, it is generally understood that no one wants to hear loud barking dogs, obnoxious late-night parties, and other rude behavior, not to mention borderline criminal activities. Before examining specific examples of community standards, it is easy to imagine some general types of content that are likely to be objectionable from the perspective of the general public [1]:

- illegal activities such as spam, fraud, extortion;
- pornography and sexually explicit imagery;
- graphic or violent imagery;
- threatening harm or violence to self or others or property;
- hate speech;
- violations of copyright or intellectual property;
- abuse of humans or animals;
- child exploitation or abuse;
- extremist propaganda;
- misinformation ("fake news").

Claims of fake news became particularly prominent during the U.S. President Trump administration (2017–2020), which also coincided with misinformation allegedly spread about Brexit in the UK and the COVID-19 pandemic of 2020. A distinction should be made between "misinformation" and "disinformation," although the terms sound similar. Misinformation is false information not necessarily with the intent to mislead, whereas disinformation is a more intentional (often covert) campaign to spread misleading and false information. Trump repeatedly denied as "fake news" a reported Russian disinformation campaign to influence the 2016 U.S. presidential elections in his favor [1].

Trump has often been accused of exploiting social media, particularly his preferred platform Twitter, to spread misinformation. Many critics have argued for Trump's account to be suspended; however, Twitter gives special protection to the U.S. President's official account (as well as other elected officials) for the sake of public interest. Twitter claims that the U.S. President's tweets are in the public interest, even if the same tweets would normally be taken down for violating the service's community standards.

However, some weeks after Trump lost the November 2020 presidential elections, both Twitter and Facebook began adding labels to his posts, falsely claiming that the election was rigged. Twitter added labels saying, "This claim of election fraud is disputed" and "This Tweet can't be replied to, retweeted, or liked due to a risk of violence" [6]. For some time, tension was building between Trump and social media companies that were starting to moderate his posts. On December 23, 2020, Trump vetoed an annual defense bill authorizing billions of dollars for the military because the bill did not weaken Section 230, which protects social media companies from legal liability for user-generated content. Trump wanted to weaken protection for platforms after claiming that they were biased against conservatives. Trump's veto was soon overridden by Congress.

Trump's Facebook, Twitter, Instagram, and Snapchat accounts were finally suspended following the riot by his supporters on the U.S. Capitol building in Washington, D.C. on January 7, 2021 [7]. On that day, Trump supporters overwhelmed police barriers and broke into the Capitol. In response, Trump posted short videos on Facebook, Twitter, and YouTube telling the rioters to "go home" but at the same time seemed to encourage the rioters by repeating allegations of a fraudulent presidential election and saying "We love you. You're very special." At first, Twitter and Facebook added labels to Trump's videos and tweets after the riot. YouTube removed a Trump video for violating its policy against unproven allegations of widespread voter fraud in the 2020 elections. Twitter initially added a label to the video but took it down after a few hours. Twitter had already deleted Trump's tweets earlier in the day [8]. Finally Facebook suspended Trump's account indefinitely (at least until Joe Biden takes office), and Twitter suspended his @realdonaldtrump account permanently for risk of inciting more violence. The official government account @POTUS was not suspended, but Trump's tweets from that account were quickly deleted because Twitter said evasion of suspension by using different accounts violates their terms of service.

Twitter's special protection of Trump's tweets has long been controversial with critics saying that Twitter should have suspended his account long ago [9]. Twitter and Facebook are facing new criticisms from the public and politicians who are blaming them for enabling Trump and the mob violence at the Capitol [10]. The riot at the Capitol has brought attention to the harmful role of other social media platforms such as Parler, which has gained the reputation of attracting extremists and conspiracy theorists. On January 9, 2021, at the time of this writing, the Parler app was taken down from both Apple's App Store and Google Play store for insufficient content moderation [11].

4.1.2 Automation

The need to automate at least part of the content moderation process is a fairly recent development arising from the steadily increasing number of social media users and amount of uploaded content. Thousands of content moderators are employed by large social media platforms but the escalating scale of the problem cannot be solved by just hiring more human moderators. Facebook reported 1.8 billion daily active users in October 2020 [12]. About 4,000 photos are uploaded per second, and more than 4 billion video views take place every day. In May 2017, Mark Zuckerberg said that Facebook receives millions of complaints per week [13].

YouTube reported that 500 hours of videos are uploaded every minute as of May 2019, an increase from 400 hours of videos uploaded every minute in July 2015 [14]. By a simple calculation, this implies that YouTube would have to employ 30,000 moderators around the clock to watch all of the uploaded content.

Automated content moderation is the application of intelligent software taking advantage of artificial intelligence (AI), or more specifically machine learning, to analyze and classify online content (text, images, videos). Automation is a more scalable solution than just hiring more content moderators. YouTube reported machine learning algorithms helped remove more than 150,000 videos depicting violent extremism from June to December 2017, equivalent to the work of 180,000 people working for 40 weeks [4]. Automated software is particularly useful for obvious cases where the likelihood of error, such as false positives (mistakenly identifying legitimate content as objectionable), is nearly zero. In more nuanced cases, automated software may still be useful to identify questionable content but final judgment should be left to human moderators who are better at judging context, subtleties, and intention.

4.2 LAWS AND REGULATIONS

The U.S. passed the Communications Decency Act (CDA) in 1996 aimed at imposing fines or imprisonment for displaying "obscene or indecent" material online to anyone under 18 years old or harassing another person online. The CDA was shortly judged unconstitutional by the U.S. Supreme Court but a part called Section 230 survived [15]. Section 230 offers protection to online service providers – search engines, ISPs (internet service providers), and later social media platforms – from lawsuits related to hosted content, such as defamation.

Section 230 was enacted following a 1995 court ruling against an online service provider Prodigy. The company had been sued for defamation after an anonymous user on the platform accused an investment firm of fraud. The court ruled that Prodigy moderated some of the posts on the platform, so it should be treated like a publisher. Section 230 was written to protect online companies from becoming legally liable for user-generated content, so companies can moderate content without liability as a publisher. The belief is that this protection is necessary to keep an open yet safe online environment.

The first part of Section 230 says service providers are not liable for hosted content as long as they only provide access to the internet or other network services. This means that self-policing (moderation) is not necessary. Clearly this empowers service providers because they do not have to worry about the content uploaded by users. Users are also empowered because they know that their content will not necessarily be moderated or censored.

The second part of Section 230 says if online service providers do police their content, they are still protected from lawsuits. This part recognizes that service providers may wish to moderate their content even though they are not required to, that is, they have the "right but not responsibility." In fact, they are free to moderate in any manner because the moderation does not have to meet any legal standard. This part was written before social media platforms became prevalent, but social media platforms enjoy the protected freedom to moderate their content as they see fit [2].

Although social media platforms can moderate their content in any manner, they are subject to outside pressures from governments and consumer groups [2]. Initial public concerns about "obscene or indecent" material have expanded in more recent years to include hate speech, self-harm, and extremism. For instance, it has been widely reported how ISIS (aka Islamic State or Daesh) became adept at taking advantage of social media for fundraising and recruitment [16]. Gruesome videos showing beheadings were distributed on video hosting sites, and online propaganda were reportedly radicalizing people around the world, prompting YouTube, Twitter, and other social media platforms to take down terrorist propaganda and shut down many suspected accounts. In 2016, U.S. President Obama urged U.S. tech companies to develop new strategies for identifying, reporting, or taking down extremist content [17].

Europe passed regulations about online extremist propaganda and increased pressure on social media platforms. The UK Terrorism Act of 2006 gave platforms two days to comply with take-down requests [18] but in March 2018, the European Commission shortened the time to one hour [19]. Platforms are not obligated to proactively look for violations but will respond to requests to remove them [20]. Currently, compliance with take-down requests is voluntary with threats of fines in the future if the European Commission is not satisfied.

Public concerns about hate speech and racial violence have increased pressure on social media platforms in Europe [2]. Germany and France both have laws prohibiting the promotion of Nazism, anti-Semitism, and white supremacy. Germany passed a strong law called "network enforcement law" (NetzDG in German) imposing fines up to 50 million euros on social media companies for non-compliance of take-down requests within 24 hours (applicable to companies with two million users or more operating in Germany) [21]. Social media firms have responded by hiring more commercial content moderators.

Several governments in the Middle East have imposed new antiterrorism laws on social media platforms [2]. In 2014, Egypt passed a law enabling the government to surveil online materials for suspected terrorist activity. Similar laws have been passed in Jordan, Qatar, and Saudi Arabia.

In 2009, Russian law made website owners responsible for user-generated content (e.g., comments) on their sites [22]. In 2012, Russia started a blacklist to block online sites containing banned content (child pornography, illicit drugs, calls to commit suicide, extremism). ISPs are required to respond to requests from the court or state authorities, as well as public reports [23].

4.3   COMMUNITY STANDARDS

Although not legally required, social media platforms typically choose to moderate content in order to keep a safe environment for their communities. Without content moderation, average users might be driven away by illegal or offensive materials, leaving criminal or malicious users who could turn the environment toxic. The first step in content moderation is the establishment of a common understanding of "acceptable" content. In this section, community standards published by Facebook, YouTube, and Twitter are summarized as prominent examples. It is not unusual for content moderators to have a more detailed set of operational guidelines to help them make decisions.

It can be tricky for platforms to achieve a balance – sufficient flexibility to allow for freedom of speech while also providing justification to reply to user complaints if their content is taken down. Politically, community standards are important evidence of due diligence to present to regulators and politicians in order to avoid additional regulation. Community standards are also good for business; they reassure advertisers who are often the source of revenue to platforms.

Community standards (or community guidelines) grew out of early public concerns about obscene content. However, obscenity is difficult to define precisely in a testable way. The U.S. Supreme Court offered a test for obscenity as "whether to the average person, applying contemporary community standards, the dominant theme of the material taken as a whole appeals to prurient interest" [24]. Community standards establish "norms" for expected behavior reflecting the community at large, and may vary geographically as well as change over time (as social norms tend to change). Platforms are aware that it is not possible to satisfy everyone. There will always be people who object to content that stays up, and people who complain that their content was taken down unfairly.

4.3.1   YouTube

Community standards on YouTube [25] are grouped into four categories:

- Spam, misleading practices, and scams
  Examples: video spam; comments spam; misleading metadata; incitement to interfere with democratic processes; hacked materials; impersonation; fake engagement; links to websites with banned content;
- Sensitive content
  Examples: nudity and sexual content (with certain exceptions, e.g., education, art); violent imagery; misleading thumbnails; harmful or stressful acts involving minors; cyberbullying of minors; promotion of self-harm (with certain exceptions, e.g., education, awareness raising);
- Violent or graphic content
  Examples: harmful or violent content; dangerous challenges or pranks; incitement to violence or harm; illicit drugs; eating disorders; incitement to theft or hacking; dangerous remedies; bypassing payment for services; graphic depiction of bodily functions or corpses to shock or disgust; animal harm; violent criminal or terrorist organizations and propaganda; hate speech; cyberbullying and harassment;
- Regulated content
  Examples: sale of illegal goods or services such as stolen financial information, counterfeits, illicit drugs, explosives, endangered animals, weapons, nicotine, sex services, human trafficking; instructions for firearms and weapons.

4.3.2 FACEBOOK

Community standards on Facebook [26] are grouped into five broad categories:

- Violence and criminal behavior
  Examples: incitement to violence; services for hire to kill or kidnap; threats to harm; instructions for weapons; violence due to democratic processes; propaganda for terrorism, hate, murder, human trafficking, crime; high-risk challenges; harm against animals; vandalism and hacking; sale of regulated goods (drugs, firearms, animals, human blood); fraud and deception; stolen financial information; stolen exams or answer sheets; fraudulent credentials; fake user reviews; counterfeit; scams;
- Safety
  Examples: instructions for suicide or self-harm; child exploitation; child abuse; sexual exploitation of adults; cyberbullying and harassment; human trafficking; forced marriages; domestic servitude; organ trafficking; privacy violations; identity theft;
- Objectionable content
  Examples: hate speech; incitement to violence; graphic or violent imagery (with certain exceptions for raising awareness, which is labeled and age restricted); nudity and sexual imagery; sexual solicitation;
- Integrity and authenticity
  Examples: impersonation or misrepresentation of identity; spam; hacking of accounts; sharing or misusing accounts; fake news; media manipulated to mislead (with exception to satire);
- Intellectual property
  Examples: violation of copyrights, trademarks, and other legal rights.

In terms of safety, Facebook makes a point to distinguish between public figures and private individuals. Public figures are given less protection against critical commentary in the name of encouraging public discussion. "Severe" attacks are still removed as well as "certain attacks where the public figure is directly tagged in the post." Private individuals are given more protection, including posts "meant to degrade or shame," and minors are given the most protection because "bullying and harassment can have more of an emotional impact on minors."

4.3.3 TWITTER

Twitter's community standards [27] are grouped in four general categories:

- Safety
  Examples: incitement to violence; violent extremism and terrorism; child exploitation; abuse and harassment; hate speech; promotion of suicide or self-harm; graphic or violent content; illegal goods or services;
- Privacy
  Examples: stolen private information; non-consensual nudity;
- Authenticity
  Examples: platform manipulation; spam; manipulating or interfering in democratic processes; impersonation; manipulated media; violation of copyright and trademark;
- Third-party advertising in video content
  A clause used to protect tweets by public officials (notably the U.S. President) offers a rationale about the public interest: "we recognize that sometimes it may be in the public interest to allow people to view tweets that would otherwise be taken down. We consider content to be in the public interest if it directly contributes to understanding or discussion of a matter of public concern. At present, we limit exceptions to one critical type of public-interest content – tweets from elected and government officials" [28].

4.3.4 TWITCH

Twitch is a lesser-known but still popular live-streaming platform. Community guidelines are below [29]:

- illegal content or activity, e.g., theft, harm, destruction;
- evasion of account suspension;
- promotion of self-harm, e.g., suicide, illegal drugs, dangerous stunts;
- violence and threats including violent extremism and terrorism;
- hateful conduct and harassment;
- unauthorized sharing of private information;
- impersonation;
- spam, scams, and other malicious conduct including phishing, fraud, spreading malware, sharing accounts, nudity and sexual content, child exploitation;
- extreme violence, gore, and obscene conduct;
- violation of intellectual property rights.

At the time of this writing, Twitch was in the news for suspending President Trump's account following the January 6, 2021 riot at the U.S. Capitol [30].

4.3.5 PARLER

In contrast with the previous examples, Parler has gained a reputation as the platform of choice for far-right extremists because of its permissiveness. Objectionable content is loosely described as "offensive content that is NOT protected speech" and refers to the terms of service [31]. However, the terms of service are about data collection and sharing, not about any impermissible content.

The Parler mobile app was removed from both Apple's App Store and the Google Play Store for insufficient content moderation and risk to public safety on January 9, 2021, and Amazon stopped providing cloud services for it [32]. Parler offered to moderate content using volunteers but Apple and Amazon were unsatisfied.

4.3.6 SUMMARY

Community standards among the largest platforms share a great deal in common, perhaps because they aim for the broadest public user base. Certain types of content are prevalent in their community standards: illegal activities; sales of illegal substances; incitement to violence, harm, or harassment; sexual imagery or exploitation; child exploitation (child pornography is illegal in the U.S. – platforms are required to take down and report to the National Center for Missing and Exploited Children); extremist propaganda; hate speech; violation of privacy; violation of intellectual property; fraud, scams, and impersonation.

At the other extreme is Parler, for example, which does not seem to have specific community standards, promoting itself as the platform for free speech. Currently, there is no regulation requiring any uniformity or a minimum set of community standards. This can be a problem, for example, when extremists are de-platformed (suspended) from the large platforms, they are able to migrate to smaller, more permissive platforms.

4.4 AUTOMATED CONTENT CLASSIFICATION

It is not scalable to simply hire more content moderators to keep up with the continually increasing amount of user-generated content. The obvious solution is to automate at least part of the moderation process by applying AI [2]. AI is a broad field of computer science tracing back to at least 1943 to create algorithms and software to emulate human intelligence for learning and problem solving

[33]. While scale may be the most important reason for large social media platforms, even small platforms can be interested in AI automation for a number of reasons:

- cost savings compared to hiring and training human moderators;
- reducing emotional stress on human moderators who may have to view graphic or gruesome content;
- more efficient content moderation.

In principle, AI increases the efficiency of all three tasks in content moderation: automatic flagging of suspect content; automatic classification of content as appropriate or inappropriate; and making decisions on the best action to take, e.g., take-down, labeling, restricted access, or nothing.

Most people are aware that AI is used in a very wide variety of applications, including robotics, autonomous vehicles, image recognition, medical diagnosis, and countless others. Many consumers today have a direct experience with AI in the form of popular virtual assistants such as Alexa and Siri, software systems capable of understanding human speech and responding in an almost natural way or carrying out commands.

Among numerous AI techniques, perhaps the best known is artificial neural networks (ANNs), composed of interconnected layers of artificial neurons (nodes). The connections are assigned weights representing how each node computes the weighted sum (linear combination) of its inputs. The weights are optimized during a training phase using a training dataset to solve a particular problem such as prediction or classification. Other major techniques include Bayesian networks, evolutionary algorithms, and symbolic AI (e.g., expert systems).

Although AI techniques can use rules, simple rules are usually not considered to be AI. For example, traditional web filters use may rule to detect certain keywords in the text of a web page or a URL (uniform resource locator). This detection is done by matching a pre-determined list of keywords (and minor variations of them). There is no learning or deeper understanding of language.

Another example of AI is in the problem of detecting nudity. Basic image filters match colors within an image to skin tones in order to detect large areas of skin as a sign of nudity. This is simple pattern matching, and false positives (images mistakenly classified as nudity) are easy if they happen to have skin colors. In contrast, the Nudity Detection API in DeepAI uses trained neural networks to identify nude body parts indicative of nudity (https://deepai.org/machine-learning-model/nsfw-detector). This is a more sophisticated approach that can detect both bare shoulders and bare chests, for example, but makes a distinction between them. Bare shoulders may not mean anything, while bare chests are more suggestive of inappropriate content.

4.4.1 Machine Learning

Machine learning is usually considered to be a subfield in AI where algorithms are trained by numerous examples for mostly prediction or classification problems. Machine learning saves a programmer from having to create a specific algorithm that "knows" how to do the prediction or classification. Instead, a machine-learning algorithm figures out how during the training. For example, a neural network may be trained using many examples of violent and non-violent images. The neural network will then be able to classify a new image as violent or non-violent. A programmer does not need to know exactly how to distinguish violent images from non-violent ones and implement this knowledge into the algorithm.

Two important specialized technologies are worth mentioning for their relevance to automated content moderation: computer vision and natural language processing (NLP).

- Users often upload images or videos to social media. In computer vision, a common type of problem is to recognize faces or objects within a video, or detect a particular type of event [34]. For content moderation, computer vision is useful for recognizing objects in images or videos, which may be useful features to classify the image or video as appropriate or

inappropriate content. Recent research has focused on deep learning methods (explained next) and particularly convolutional neural networks (CNNs) [35].
- Text is perhaps the most common type of user-generated content in social media. NLP aims to enable computers to process and respond to spoken and written words in the same manner as humans. Machine learning techniques have been used for NLP since the 1990s, and more recently, deep learning [36].

Machine learning approaches are usually categorized into:

- supervised learning: an algorithm is trained using labeled training data;
- unsupervised learning: an algorithm discovers structure in unlabeled data, for instance, by clustering;
- reinforcement learning: an algorithm learns by receiving feedback (e.g., rewards) while carrying out an activity, assuming that the algorithm is maximizing its rewards.

Supervised learning is the most relevant approach to the problem of content moderation. Machine learning algorithms are trained using large datasets of labeled examples of inappropriate and appropriate content (representing the ground truth). The machine learning algorithm creates a model from seeing many training examples and counter examples, and the model can then be used to classify new instances of content. The model depends on how the algorithm works, meaning that different algorithms will work differently, even if they are trained using the same dataset. Thus, it is common practice to try various algorithms and compare their accuracy for a particular problem.

It is not possible to survey all of the relevant technologies, which are wide-ranging and progressing quickly. At best, a few (arbitrary) examples may give a snapshot of the current state of the art:

- machine learning using metadata to identify extremist videos online [37];
- automatic recognition of extremist content using NLP [38];
- machine learning to identify extremist content on Twitter [39];
- sentiment analysis of public Facebook text posts to detect extremism [40];
- machine learning to detect hate speech on Twitter [41];
- skin tone detection and image segmentation to classify images as nude or not for a filter [42];
- text analysis to identify extremist web pages [43];
- CNNs to identify online images containing symbols or objects associated with crime or terrorism [44];
- deep learning to identify Sunni extremist propaganda text [45].

4.4.1.1 Quantity and Quality of Training Data

As the term suggests, machine learning algorithms depend on a training dataset (ground truth) consisting of labeled examples. Even the best algorithms will fail to perform well if they are not trained properly, meaning that they are not provided with a sufficient number of examples that cover the entire range of possible cases. In other words, quantity and quality are both issues for training data. For example, an algorithm to detect profanity obviously needs to be trained for all words indicative of profanity. The algorithm cannot be expected to recognize profanity that it has not seen previously.

As one example, Google's Jigsaw created a machine learning algorithm Conversation AI to detect harassment. They used a dataset of 17 million comments from The New York Times, along with data about which of those comments were flagged as inappropriate by moderators [46]. Conversation AI is offered to developers through an API [47].

A number of potential obstacles might be encountered in the course of creating a good training dataset. First, most online content is usually straightforward to download or crawl. Twitter even makes an API publicly available [48]. However, certain types of content are problematic to collect.

A good example is child exploitation which is illegal in the U.S. Social media channels may be restricted or vetted to keep out law enforcement or researchers. Second, the amount of effort to label all the examples in a dataset is proportional to its size. Also, a certain level of expertise may be required, e.g., on terrorism and extremism. Third, sharing datasets may be problematic due to legal, competitive, or ethical issues such as privacy. For example, datasets of extremist propaganda or pornographic images obviously should not be shared indiscriminately. Finally, datasets may need to be continually updated. For instance, it is known that colloquialisms change over time. Also, as people become more aware of machine learning being used for content moderation, it is possible that criminals, terrorists, and extremists may change their use of social media in order to avoid being flagged. For instance, they might use secret codewords to communicate which would not be suspicious to automated tools.

4.4.1.2 Identification of Important Features

Given a training dataset, feature engineering applies data mining techniques to extract features (attributes in the data) [49]. Traditional machine-learning algorithms work on a set of features, so feature engineering is clearly a vital step to identify the most useful features. Another issue is the possibly huge number of features which can challenge computational resources. The task of feature selection is to prune the irrelevant features which makes computation more manageable as well as avoid overfitting.

4.4.1.3 Choice of Machine Learning Algorithm

There are many well-known supervised machine learning algorithms, including neural networks, support vector machine (SVM), decision trees, naive Bayes, linear discriminant analysis, and clustering [50]. No single algorithm is "best" for all problems because the algorithms work in different ways. It is common practice to compare various algorithms for a given problem to choose the best one. However, good or bad training often makes a more drastic difference than the choice of algorithm, as insufficient training can make even the best algorithm perform badly.

4.4.1.4 Validation Metrics

Most people think of machine learning performance in terms of an accuracy rate, e.g., the accuracy of detecting hate speech or extremist propaganda. Clearly accuracy is important, but a complete assessment of performance should include the false positive rate (FPR) and false-negative rate (FNR). In terms of binary classification such as detection of hate speech, for example, FPR is the proportion of regular speech that is misclassified as hate speech, and FNR is the proportion of hate speech that is not detected as hate speech. In some practical cases, false positives and false negatives have different consequences. For example, a false positive in spam filtering means that a legitimate email message was misclassified as spam, which might result in missing a potentially important message. On the other hand, a false negative means that a spam message avoided the filter, not that consequential because the recipient can simply delete it.

An algorithm's performance is often visualized in the form of a confusion matrix; an example is shown in Table 4.1. The top row is the numbers of true positives (TP) and false positives (FP), and the bottom row is the number of false negatives (FN) and true negatives (TN).

For n total points in the testing set, the error rate is the fraction of mistakes:

$$\text{Error rate} = (FP + FN)/n$$

The accuracy is the fraction of correct predictions:

$$\text{Accuracy} = (TP + TN)/n$$

TABLE 4.1
Confusion Matrix Example

	TRUE	
PREDICTED	**Positive**	**Negative**
Positive	TP = 6	FP = 3
Negative	FN = 8	TN = 10

The precision for each class is:

$$\text{Precision of Positive Class} = TP / (TP + FP)$$

$$\text{Precision of Negative Class} = TN / (TN + FN)$$

Sensitivity refers to the true positive rate (TPR), e.g., the proportion of hate speech that is correctly classified:

$$TPR = TP / (TP + FN)$$

Specificity is the true negative rate (TNR), the proportion of regular speech that is correctly classified:

$$TNR = TN / (FP + TN)$$

A common visualization is a receiver operating characteristic (ROC) that plots the TPR against the FPR for a varying threshold setting; an example is shown in Figure 4.1. The area under the curve (AUC) is interesting as representing the probability that a classifier will rank a randomly chosen positive instance higher than a randomly chosen negative one. An alternative visualization is the total operating characteristic (TOC).

4.4.2 DEEP LEARNING

Much of the current research in machine learning is in deep learning [51]. Technically, "deep" refers to more neurons and hidden layers than past neural networks which typically had one or two hidden layers. More layers imply a longer credit assignment path (CAP), the chain of mathematical operations from input to output, and greater capability to extract high-level features from the inputs.

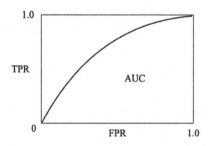

FIGURE 4.1   ROC example.

A positive benefit is the capability to learn what is important by itself without an expert to select features (feature engineering). The drawback is the need for very large amounts of data.

Image processing is often cited as an example. In traditional machine learning, an expert might come up with many features that might be useful to distinguish images of cats and dogs, compare many examples of cats and dogs, and identify the most useful features. In deep learning, each layer learns to change the input data into a slightly more composite representation. Lower layers of the neural network may identify edges (starting from a matrix of pixels), while higher layers identify concepts more relevant to human understanding of what a dog or cat looks like. Deep learning figures out features in each layer on its own, thereby eliminating the need for feature engineering.

4.4.3 CURRENT EFFORTS BY SOCIAL MEDIA PLATFORMS

The largest social media platforms have developed their own proprietary automated tools for content moderation in the last few years. Facebook reported starting the use of AI to counter terrorist propaganda in 2017 [52]. This seemed to consist of NLP to identify posts supportive of ISIS or al-Qaeda [53]. An automated tool scores a post with a probability; posts with very high scores may be removed automatically, otherwise the score is used to prioritize posts for expert moderators. In September 2019, Facebook reported at the use of machine learning "led to the removal of more than 26 million pieces of content related global terrorist groups like ISIS and al-Qaeda in the last two years, 99% of which we proactively identified and removed before anyone reported it" [54]. Facebook also uses machine learning to detect "near nude images or videos that are shared without permission on Facebook and Instagram" [55] as well as fraud and spam [56].

Google's subsidiary Jigsaw announced plans to tackle online extremist content by identifying patterns in social media activities after a 2016 call from the Obama administration to companies to do more about countering ISIS online propaganda [17]. One of Jigsaw's tools is Conversation AI, machine learning software trained to recognize online harassment and abuse, reportedly more accurate than any keyword filter [46].

In 2015, Twitter purchased a small startup, Madbits, which promised an algorithm to accurately identify NSFW (not safe for work) images, and Whetlab [57]. In 2019, Twitter acquired a startup, Fabula AI, specializing in deep learning to analyze network-structured data [58].

Microsoft offers an AI-based content moderator service within Azure for developers [59]. It scans text, images, and videos and applies content flags automatically for offensive content, sexually explicit or suggestive content, profanity, and personal data. Scans images for adult or racy content, detects text in images with the Optical Character Recognition (OCR) capability, and detects faces. Scans videos for adult or racy content and returns time markers for said content.

4.5 CHALLENGES IN AUTOMATED CONTENT CLASSIFICATION

Automated classification using machine learning may be expected to work well when the classification problem is clear and unchanging. Conversely, automated classification is challenged when the problem is vague (ill defined), subjective, or changing over time.

4.5.1 SUBJECTIVITY AND CONTEXT

Terms such as terrorism, extremism, pornography, and obscenity are somewhat subjective and lack universally agreed definitions. For instance, "terrorism" might be described as the deliberate use of violence to generate fear within a population for a political motive, but there is a common saying that "one man's terrorist is another man's freedom fighter." In any case, that description does not provide a clear test that can be used to classify any particular piece of content. Likewise, a definition of obscenity is inherently subjective and varies by individual, region, and decade. In the 1964 Jacobellis v. Ohio case, Associate Supreme Court Justice Potter Stewart is often quoted as saying he could not define obscenity but "I know it when I see it." Given the lack of universal definitions for some types of objectionable content, automated classification is obviously problematic.

Context is a very important factor in deciding whether an exception should be allowed for content that would normally be taken down. Facebook states:

> In some cases, we allow content for public awareness which would otherwise go against our Community Standards – if it is newsworthy and in the public interest. We only do this after weighing the public interest value against the risk of harm… For example, we have allowed content that graphically depicts war or the consequences of war where it is important to public discourse.
>
> [26]

An example often pointed out is "The Terror of War" (or "Napalm Girl") photo by Associated Press photographer Nick Ut. It won the 1972 Pulitzer Prize. It does show a naked girl in a scene of violence during the Vietnam War, but that was the point. Facebook moderators decided to delete it from an article by journalist Tom Egeland, a collection of important photos commenting on warfare [2]. After Egeland reposted the image, his Facebook account was suspended. After receiving much publicity and criticism, Facebook changed its decision.

Words are another obvious example where context is very important because the same words can be understood in different ways, depending on the context. Also, the way words are said (e.g., inflections) is part of context, which is difficult for automated algorithms to understand.

4.5.2 BIAS

Bias is a widespread concern in the field of machine learning. For instance, face recognition algorithms to detect criminals or terrorists might have a racial bias. Bias can be introduced in the training or testing phases. How training data is selected and collected might be biased unintentionally, e.g., favoring or leaving out certain examples. Also, since training data is generally labeled by humans, any human biases in judgment may be reflected in the training data.

4.5.3 LIVESTREAMING

Real-time livestreaming poses a major problem for content moderation. Crimes are now streamed by criminals, victims, or bystanders as they happen. Content moderators cannot watch all livestreams all of the time. This challenge was demonstrated by the terrorist mass shooting in Christchurch, New Zealand, on March 15, 2019. A white supremacist, Brenton Harrison Tarrant, was arrested soon afterward. During the event, he had livestreamed the first shooting at a mosque on Facebook. The video was then shared on other platforms. Facebook reported no complaints were received about the video until 12 minutes after the livestream ended [60]. It was removed within minutes, and Facebook blocked subsequent attempts to upload videos and images of the attack [61].

According to Facebook, the video of the attack did not trigger their automatic detection systems because they were not trained to recognize that type of video, similar to a first-person shooter video game. In response, Facebook said they wanted to obtain training data similar to the livestreamed first-person shooting but was wary of making mistakes, e.g., FP for action movies or video games [54].

More recently, some rioters on the U.S. Capitol on January 6, 2021 used the Dlive platform for livestreaming the riot [62]. While livestreaming, followers sent messages to the rioters about where to avoid police and sent tips in the platform's currency called "lemons." Dlive started in 2017 as similar to Twitch, an Amazon-owned platform for video gamers to livestream their gameplay, but different in not taking part of the users' incomes. Dlive had expanded quickly after attracting far-right users. There were more than 150,000 people watching on Dlive on the day of the U.S. Capitol riot. Dlive denounced the riot and froze the earnings of streamers who had participated in the riot. It reported suspending 10 accounts and deleting 100 videos.

4.5.4 ADVERSARIAL

In a study of ISIS propaganda on social media in 2017–2018, ISIS tried to avoid detection by AI by manipulating their use of language [63]. For example, they avoided terms such as "wilayah" (Arabic for "state") and "Amaq" (Amaq News Agency linked to ISIS), and used neutral terms such as "Islamic State group" or "Islamic army" ("tanzim al-Dawlah" or "Jaysh al-Dawlah" in Arabic, respectively). Although the difference in language may be subtle, it was enough to keep their social media accounts up longer before suspension.

Technically skilled criminals and extremists might fight back against automated content moderation by trying to "outwit" machine learning classifiers. It is not speculation; in the past, spammers tried various methods to circumvent or attack Bayesian spam filters because they knew how the filters worked. Research is growing in the field of "adversarial machine learning," where knowledgeable adversaries may attempt to fool classifiers with deceptive inputs [64]. For instance, it was demonstrated that small changes to a stop sign could cause an autonomous vehicle to misclassify it as a merge or speed limit sign [65]. In another demonstration, McAfee fooled Tesla's Mobileye system into driving 50 mph over the speed limit by adding a small strip of black tape to a speed limit sign [66]. These attacks are possible because machine learning classifiers are trained for specific problems using training data, and there are statistical assumptions underlying the training. The attacks provide input data that violate the statistical assumptions.

4.6 INFORMATION SHARING BETWEEN PLATFORMS

Information sharing is done after content moderation has been done on one social media platform, and it is advantageous to share the results with other platforms because the same or similar offensive content has often been distributed among multiple platforms.

One of the prominent examples of information sharing is the Global Internet Forum to Counter Terrorism (GIFCT) founded by Facebook, Microsoft, Twitter, and YouTube in 2016 [67]. Its main operation is sharing links and hashes of photos and videos that were found to be supportive of terrorism. GIFCT reported sharing over 200,000 hashes by December 2019 [68].

Popular hashing functions such as MD5 or SHA-1 take any size file or document and produces a fixed-length output, e.g., a 128-bit or 160-bit (hash) value that is almost unique in the sense that two arbitrarily chosen files are very unlikely to produce the same hash (due to properties of good hash functions). In effect, hashes serve as "fingerprints" of files and enable platforms to quickly check for duplicate content by matching hashes. Platforms already use hashes to detect duplicates on their own platforms, e.g., copies of previously taken down content.

Unfortunately, another property of good hash functions means that the slightest change to a file will result in a drastically different hash. For instance, if an image is cropped or altered in any way, its MD5 or SHA-1 hash will be much different. Hashes provide a very simple mechanism for matching exact duplicates but not slightly different duplicates. Microsoft developed a hash called PhotoDNA specifically for images [69]. It can match duplicate images despite certain alterations, including resizing and minor color changes. It converts an image to black and white, resizes it, breaks it into a grid of squares, and then looks at intensity gradients or edges in each square. Its main limitation is that it is still a matching method; it only finds matches to known offensive images. It is not capable of recognizing previously unseen images as offensive. PhotoDNA is offered as a cloud service for law enforcement and qualified organizations to find matches from a database of known illegal images [70].

Another information-sharing consortium is the self-funded Technology Coalition, a group of large companies including Apple, Facebook, Google, Microsoft, and Twitter, formed to fight online child sexual exploitation and abuse (CSE) [71]. Microsoft contributed its PhotoDNA technology, and Facebook open-sourced two algorithms – PDQ and TMK + PDQF for matching identical or nearly identical photos and videos, respectively, based on hashing like PhotoDNA [72]. Google contributed a Content Safety API, which uses AI to prioritize content suspected of being child sexual abuse material (CSAM) for human review [73].

4.7 CONCLUSIONS

The scale of content moderation necessitates some degree of automation to handle the increasing workload, but the current state of machine learning does not offer a complete solution. At best, machine learning classifiers can handle clear cases or help to prioritize cases. However, humans are still needed to make ultimate judgments. Moreover, it can be argued that keeping humans involved in content moderation is desirable, not just necessary, because humans are better at judging context and subtleties, as well as balancing considerations for public interest and freedom of speech.

REFERENCES

1. S. T. Roberts. *Behind the Screen: Content Moderation in the Shadows of Social Media*. New Haven: Yale University Press, 2019.
2. T. Gillespie. *Custodians of the Internet: Platforms, Content Moderation, and the Hidden Decisions That Shape Social Media*. New Haven: Yale University Press, 2018.
3. A. Chen. "The laborers who keep dick pics and beheadings out of your Facebook feed," 2014. [Online]. Available: http://www.wired.com/2014/10/content-moderation. [Accessed 22 Jan. 2021].
4. R. Iyengar. "Google is hiring 10,000 people to clean up YouTube," 2017. [Online]. Available: https://money.cnn.com/2017/12/05/technology/google-youtube-hiring-reviewers-offensive-videos/index.html. [Accessed 22 Jan. 2021].
5. A. C. Madrigal. "Inside Facebook's fast-growing content-moderation effort," 2018. [Online]. Available: https://www.theatlantic.com/technology/archive/2018/02/what-facebook-told-insiders-about-how-it-moderates-posts/552632. [Accessed 22 Jan. 2021].
6. B. Fung. "It took an assault on Congress for Facebook and Twitter to draw a line on Trump," 2021a. [Online]. Available: https://edition.cnn.com/2021/01/06/tech/twitter-trump-riots-us-capitol/index.html. [Accessed 22 Jan. 2021].
7. K. Fung. "Trump has now been suspended from four of six most popular social media platforms," 2021b. [Online]. Available: https://www.newsweek.com/trump-has-now-been-suspended-four-six-most-popular-social-media-platforms-1559830. [Accessed 22 Jan. 2021].
8. C. Lima. "Twitter, Facebook lock Trump's accounts in confrontation over Capitol breach posts," 2021. [Online]. Available: https://www.politico.com/news/2021/01/06/twitter-trump-tweet-capitol-violence-455630. [Accessed 22 Jan. 2021].
9. A. Ohlheiser and E. Guo. "Twitter locked Trump's account: Insiders say it needs to go further," 2021. [Online]. Available: https://www.technologyreview.com/2021/01/06/1015830/twitter-trump-suspension-ban/. [Accessed 22 Jan. 2021].
10. C. Lima and J. Hendel. "'This is going to come back and bite'em': Capitol breach inflames Democrats' ire at Silicon Valley," 2021. [Online]. Available: https://www.politico.com/news/2021/01/08/capitol-riot-democrats-social-media-456325. [Accessed 22 Jan. 2021].
11. J. Koetsier. "Apple suspends Parler from app store until 'dangerous and harmful content' resolved," 2021. [Online]. Available: https://www.forbes.com/sites/johnkoetsier/2021/01/09/apple-suspends-parler-from-app-store-until-dangerous-and-harmful-content-resolved/. [Accessed 22 Jan. 2021].
12. Facebook. "Facebook reports second quarter 2020 results," 2020. [Online]. Available: https://s21.q4cdn.com/399680738/files/doc_financials/2020/q2/Q2'20-FB-Financial-Results-Press-Release.pdf. [Accessed 22 Jan. 2021].
13. M. Zuckerberg. 2017. [Online]. Available: https://www.facebook.com/zuck/posts/10103695315624661. [Accessed 22 Jan. 2021].

14. J. Hale. "More than 500 hours of content are now being uploaded to YouTube every minute," 2019. [Online]. Available: https://www.tubefilter.com/2019/05/07/number-hours-video-uploaded-to-youtube-per-minute/. [Accessed 22 Jan. 2021].

15. Electronic Frontier Foundation. "CDA 230: Legislative history," 2012. [Online]. Available: https://www.eff.org/issues/cda230/legislative-history. [Accessed 22 Jan. 2021].

16. T. Chen, L. Jarvis, and S. Macdonald. *Cyberterrorism: Understanding, Assessment, and Response*. New York: Springer, 2016.

17. E. Geller. "White house and tech companies brainstorm how to slow ISIS propaganda," 2016. [Online]. Available: https://www.dailydot.com/layer8/white-house-tech-companies-online-extremism-meeting/. [Accessed 22 Jan. 2021].

18. JISC. "Hosting liability," 2007. [Online]. Available: https://www.jisc.ac.uk/guides/hosting-liability. [Accessed 22 Jan. 2021].

19. J. Sommerlad. "Internet giants given one hour deadline to take down terrorist propaganda," 2018. [Online]. Available: https://www.independent.co.uk/life-style/gadgets-and-tech/news/european-commission-one-hour-deadline-remove-terror-child-sex-videos-illegal-products-content-google-facebook-twitter-a8236346.html. [Accessed 22 Jan. 2021].

20. N. Suzor, B. Seignior, and J. Singleton. "Non-consensual porn and the responsibilities of online intermediaries." *Melbourne University Law Review*, vol 40, pp. 1057–1097, 2017.

21. German Law Archive. "Network enforcement act (Netzdurchsetzunggesetz, NetzDG)," 2017. [Online]. Available: https://germanlawarchive.iuscomp.org/?p=1245. [Accessed 22 Jan. 2021].

22. Radio Free Europe/RadioLiberty. "Russian court rules internet owners responsible for 'defamatory' information," 2013. [Online]. Available: https://www.rferl.org/a/russia-websites-defamatory-content/25040819.html. [Accessed 22 Jan. 2021].

23. Phys Org. "Russia puts first sites on new Internet blacklist," 2012. [Online]. Available: https://phys.org/news/2012-11-russia-sites-internet-blacklist.html. [Accessed 22 Jan. 2021].

24. Oyez. "Roth v. United States," 1957. [Online]. Available: https://www.oyez.org/cases/1956/582. [Accessed 22 Jan. 2021].

25. YouTube. "YouTube's community guidelines," 2021. [Online]. Available: https://support.google.com/youtube/answer/9288567. [Accessed 22 Jan. 2021].

26. Facebook. "Community standards," 2021. [Online]. Available: https://www.facebook.com/communitystandards/introduction. [Accessed 22 Jan. 2021].

27. Twitter. "The Twitter rules," 2021a. [Online]. Available: https://help.twitter.com/en/rules-and-policies/twitter-rules. [Accessed 22 Jan. 2021].

28. Twitter. "About public-interest exceptions on Twitter," 2021b. [Online]. Available: https://help.twitter.com/en/rules-and-policies/public-interest. [Accessed 22 Jan. 2021].

29. Twitch. "Community guidelines," 2021. [Online]. Available: https://www.twitch.tv/p/en-gb/legal/community-guidelines/. [Accessed 22 Jan. 2021].

30. C. Hall. "Twitch disables President Trump's channel following Capitol attack," 2021. [Online]. Available: https://www.polygon.com/2021/1/7/22219150/president-trump-twitch-channel-disabled-capitol-attack. [Accessed 22 Jan. 2021].

31. Parler. "What is reportable content," 2021. [Online]. Available: https://support.parler.com/hc/en-us/articles/360047249832-What-is-reportable-content-. [Accessed 5 Jan. 2021].

32. K. Cox. "Amazon cuts off Parler's web hosting following Apple, Google bans," 2021. [Online]. Available: https://arstechnica.com/tech-policy/2021/01/amazon-cuts-off-parlers-web-hosting-following-apple-google-bans/. [Accessed 6 Jan. 2021].

33. S. Russell and P. Norvig. *Artificial Intelligence: A Modern Approach*, 2nd ed. Upper Saddle River, NJ: Prentice Hall, 2003.

34. E. R. Davies. *Computer Vision: Principles, Algorithms, Applications, Learning*, 5th ed. New York: Academic Press, 2017,

35. I. Goodfellow, Y. Bengio, and A. Courville. *Deep Learning*. Cambridge, MA: MIT Press, 2017.

36. Y. Goldberg. "A primer on neural network models for natural language processing." *Journal of Artificial Intelligence Research*, vol. 57, pp. 345–420, Sept. 2016.

37. T. Fu, C.-N. Huang, and H. Chen. "Identification of extremist videos in online video sharing sites." In *2009 IEEE International Conference on Intelligence and Security Informatics*, pp. 179–181, 2009.

38. S. Mussiraliyeva, et al. "On detecting online radicalization and extremism using natural language processing." In *21st International Arab Conference on Information Technology (ACIT)*, pp. 1–5, 2020.

39. M. Nouh, J. R. C. Nurse, and M. Goldsmith. "Understanding the radical mind: Identifying signals to detect extremist content on Twitter." In *2019 IEEE International Conference on Intelligence and Security Informatics (ISI)*, pp. 98–103, 2019.

40. E. Mouhssine and C. Khalid. "Social big data mining framework for extremist content detection in social networks." In *2018 International Symposium on Advanced Electrical and Communication Technologies (ISAECT)*, pp. 1–5, 2018.

41. H. Watanabe, M. Bouazizi, and T. Ohtsuki. "Hate speech on Twitter: a pragmatic approach to collect hateful and offensive expressions and perform hate speech detection," *IEEE Access*, vol. 6, pp. 13825–13835, 2018.

42. M. B. Garcia, et al. "A pornographic image and video filtering application using optimized nudity recognition and detection algorithm." In *2018 IEEE 10th International Conference on Humanoid, Nanotechnology, Information Technology, Communication and Control, Environment and Management (HNICEM)*, pp. 1–5, 2018.

43. G. R. S. Weir, E. Dos Santos, B. Cartwright, and R. Frank. "Positing the problem: Enhancing classification of extremist web content through textual analysis." In *2016 IEEE International Conference on Cybercrime and Computer Forensic (ICCCF)*, pp. 1–3, 2016.

44. P. Chitrakar, C. Zhang, G. Warner, and X. Liao. "Social media image retrieval using distilled convolutional neural network for suspicious e-crime and terrorist account detection." In *2016 IEEE International Symposium on Multimedia (ISM)*, pp. 493–498, 2016.

45. A. H. Johnston and G. M. Weiss. "Identifying Sunni extremist propaganda with deep learning." In *2017 IEEE Symposium Series on Computational Intelligence (SSCI)*, pp. 1–6, 2017.

46. A. Greenberg. "Inside Google's internet justice league and its AI-powered war on trolls," 2016. [Online]. Available: https://www.wired.com/2016/09/inside-googles-internet-justice-league-ai-powered-war-trolls/. [Accessed 6 Jan. 2021].

47. A. Greenberg. "Now anyone can deploy Google's troll-fighting AI," 2017. [Online]. Available: https://www.wired.com/2017/02/googles-troll-fighting-ai-now-belongs-world/. [Accessed 6 Jan. 2021].

48. Twitter. "Twitter API," 2021c. [Online]. Available: https://developer.twitter.com/en/docs/twitter-api. [Accessed 6 Jan. 2021].

49. M. Kuhn and K. Johnson. *Feature Engineering and Selection: A Practical Approach for Predictive Models*. Boca Raton, FL: Chapman and Hall, 2019.

50. G. Bonaccorso. *Machine Learning Algorithms: Popular Algorithms for Data Science and Machine Learning*, 2nd ed. Birmingham, UK: Packt Publishing, 2018.

51. E. Charniak. *Introduction to Deep Learning*. Cambridge, MA: MIT Press, 2018.

52. Facebook. "Hard questions: How we counter terrorism," 2017. [Online]. Available: https://about.fb.com/news/2017/06/how-we-counter-terrorism/. [Accessed 6 Jan. 2021].

53. Facebook. "Hard questions: What are we doing to stay ahead of terrorists?" 2018a. [Online]. Available: https://about.fb.com/news/2018/11/staying-ahead-of-terrorists/. [Accessed 6 Jan. 2021].

54. Facebook. "Combating hate and extremism," 2019a. [Online]. Available: https://about.fb.com/news/2019/09/combating-hate-and-extremism/. [Accessed 6 Jan. 2021].

55. Facebook. "Detecting non-consensual intimate images and supporting victims," 2019b. [Online]. Available: https://about.fb.com/news/2019/03/detecting-non-consensual-intimate-images/. [Accessed 6 Jan. 2021].

56. Facebook. "Hard questions: What's Facebook's strategy for stopping false news?" 2018b. [Online]. Available: https://about.fb.com/news/2018/05/hard-questions-false-news/. [Accessed 6 Jan. 2021].

57. C. Metz. "Twitter's new AI recognizes porn so you don't have to," 2015. [Online]. Available: http://www.wired.com/2015/07/twitters-new-ai-recognizes-porn-dont/. [Accessed 6 Jan. 2021].

58. P. Agrawal. "Twitter acquires Fabula AI to strengthen its machine learning expertise," 2019. [Online]. Available: https://blog.twitter.com/en_us/topics/company/2019/Twitter-acquires-Fabula-AI.html. [Accessed 6 Jan. 2021].

59. Microsoft. "What is Azure content moderator?" 2020. [Online]. Available: https://docs.microsoft.com/en-us/azure/cognitive-services/Content-Moderator/overview. [Accessed 6 Jan. 2021].

60. BBC. "Christchurch shootings: 'Bad actors' helped attack videos spread online," 2019a. [Online]. Available: https://www.bbc.co.uk/news/technology-47652308. [Accessed 22 Jan. 2021].

61. BBC. "Facebook: New Zealand attack video viewed 4,000 times," 2019b. [Online]. Available: https://www.bbc.co.uk/news/business-47620519. [Accessed 22 Jan. 2021].

62. K. Browning and T. Lorenz. "Pro-Trump mob livestreamed its rampage, and made money doing it," 2021. [Online]. Available: https://www.nytimes.com/2021/01/08/technology/dlive-capitol-mob.html. [Accessed 22 Jan. 2021].

63. M. Al-Lami. "The rise, fall and rise of ISIS media, 2017–2018." In *Terrorism, Radicalisation & Countering Violent Extremism*, ed. Shashi Jayakumar. Singapore: Palgrave, pp. 117–135, 2019.

64. A. D. Joseph, et al. *Adversarial Machine Learning*. Cambridge, UK: Cambridge University Press, 2019.

65. H. S. M. Lim and A. Taeihagh. "Algorithmic decision-making in AVs: Understanding ethical and technical concerns for smart cities." *Sustainability*, vol. 11, article 5791, 2019.

66. B. Barrett. "A tiny piece of tape tricked Teslas into speeding up 50 MPH," 2020. [Online]. Available: https://www.wired.com/story/tesla-speed-up-adversarial-example-mgm-breach-ransomware/. [Accessed 22 Jan. 2021].

67. GIFCT. "Home page," 2021. [Online]. Available: https://gifct.org. [Accessed 22 Jan. 2021].

68. M. Bickert and E. Saltman. "An update on our efforts to combat terrorism online," 2019. [Online]. Available: https://about.fb.com/news/2019/12/counterterrorism-efforts-update/. [Accessed 22 Jan. 2021].

69. H. Farid. "Reining in online abuses." *Technology & Innovation*, vol. 19, pp. 593–599, 2018.

70. Microsoft. "Photo DNA," 2021. [Online]. Available: https://www.microsoft.com/en-us/photodna. [Accessed 22 Jan. 2021].

71. Technology Coalition. "The Technology Coalition – Fighting child sexual exploitation online," 2017. [Online]. Available: http://www.technologycoalition.org. [Accessed 22 Jan. 2021].

72. Facebook. "Open-sourcing photo- and video-matching technology to make the internet safer," 2019c. [Online]. Available: https://about.fb.com/news/2019/08/open-source-photo-video-matching/. [Accessed 22 Jan. 2021].

73. Google. "Fighting child sexual abuse online," 2021. [Online]. Available: https://protectingchildren.google/intl/en/. [Accessed 22 Jan. 2021].

5 Steganographic Botnet C&C Channel Using Twitter

Nicholas Pantic and Mohammad Husain

California State Polytechnic University, Pomona, California, USA

CONTENTS

DOI: 10.1201/9781003134527-7

5.1 INTRODUCTION

5.1.1 MOTIVATION

Computing and interconnectivity have spread through modern society as electricity and plumbing have in the past, to become almost entirely ubiquitous. Indeed, it is not uncommon for a single person to possess numerous computing devices of varying power and portability, ranging from handheld smartphones and tablets to notebooks and desktop computers. Although these devices appear different, they are all essentially the same. They act as general-purpose computers that connect to the Internet to communicate with other devices across the globe.

Cyber-criminals make use of this vast global Internet by installing or convincing users to install malicious software, or malware, onto their devices that allow the criminals to control them remotely. A collection of these "zombie" computers is called a botnet. Botnets are one of the most prominent modern computer security threats [1] and are often used for various forms of cyber crime, such as sending spam emails or performing Distributed Denial of Service (DDoS) attacks against other computer networks. In fact, the botnet threat spreads beyond what we commonly refer to as computing devices. In the new Internet of Things, many common household appliances that contain embedded computers are being connected to the Internet. A recent news story showed that these smart appliances, such as refrigerators, were being used to distribute spam email.[1]

The design and communication patterns of these botnets can vary dramatically, as they are created by cyber-criminals with the intent of hiding their presence. Social networks have exploded in the past few years in the same way that the Internet and the web before them. Today, popular social networks like Twitter and Facebook have hundreds of millions of users interacting and communicating in real time. Even with the extremely large user bases, these services are rarely ever unavailable and will transmit communications at incredible speed. From this information, a clever attacker will recognize that these networks are well suited for launching cyber attacks, such as controlling an existing botnet. They can take advantage of the infrastructure, speed of transmission, and large user-base in which to hide to control the bots. This section provides a proof of concept of this type of botnet communication that is hidden within the social network Twitter.

5.1.2 STATEMENT OF PROBLEM

Understanding how attackers communicate with botnets is vital for botnet defense. If the attacker cannot coordinate the bots, they will be unable to utilize the network. As is common with computer security research, researching both attack and defense can be useful. Before a proper defense can be made, new attacks must be understood. Botnets are capable of attacking the availability of a system using attacks such as DDoS, where the bots flood a network with requests to cause it to become unresponsive to real traffic. These attacks are especially dangerous because it is difficult to distinguish between these fake requests and authentic traffic trying to use the network. In order to stop these attacks, it is best to be able to cripple the botnet before it can begin. Therefore, understanding how an attacker might attempt to coordinate these bots is essential.

In this section, we have developed a method of coordinating bots in a botnet that uses a stego system over a popular social network, Twitter. This covert channel can also be used for arbitrary communication of relatively short messages outside of the realm of botnet command and control. By utilizing steganography, we hide the existence of the botnet control communication from the outside world while also utilizing the power of the popular social networking website to ensure timely delivery of the messages.

5.1.3 Research Goals

There are four major research goals in this section. The first is to develop a stego system that exists on the Twitter social network website. This system can be used for secret communication between various parties for many domains. The second goal is the implementation of a botnet command and control (C&C) communication system that utilizes the stego system. This C&C system communicates entirely through the stego system allowing the botmaster to control each of the bots. The third goal is to evaluate the efficacy and performance of both the stego system and botnet C&C. The detectability of the communications is a major concern of this evaluation, but timely data transfer is also important. The final goal is to consider additional applications and improvements for the stego system. Because it is designed to transfer communications from an arbitrary input alphabet, it can be applied to many domains that utilize short messages.

5.1.4 Structure of Chapter

This chapter is structured as follows: Section 5.2 contains a broad literature review of the various techniques that are used in the development of the research. This includes steganography, botnets, natural language generation, Huffman codes, and Markov chains. Section 5.3 describes the structure and implementation of the stego system, botnet C&C, and other components of the system. This discussion covers the first two research goals as well as the parts of the final goal. Section 5.4 discusses the experiments conducted and the evaluation of the results of the experiments. This covers the third research goal. Section 5.5 contains our concluding remarks and descriptions of future work related to the section.

5.2 LITERATURE REVIEW

5.2.1 Steganography and Steganalysis

Confidentiality has been well established as a security criterion [2]. Essentially, confidentiality is the preservation of authorized access and disclosure to information [3]. In most cases, confidentiality is sufficient for protecting information from disclosure. For example, when using online banking, it is important to conceal the contents of the communications so that no others can impersonate either yourself or the bank or otherwise obtain your private banking information, but it is not usually important to hide the fact that you are performing the online banking. However, there are situations where it is not only important to hide the contents of communication, but also the fact that communication has taken place at all. This is the *undetectability* criterion of security, defined by Pfitzmann and Hansen [4] as the criterion of being able to determine if a message even exists.

Just as cryptography is the science related to confidentiality, steganography is the science related to undetectability [5]. Also, as cryptanalysis is the analysis of cryptographic techniques and how to break them [6], steganalysis is the study of steganographic techniques and finding hidden information [5]. From the definitions of both cryptography and cryptanalysis, we can deduce that a cryptographic system can be considered broken when an attacker can determine the contents of the communication, also called the plaintext. Therefore, we can consider a steganographic system (stego system) broken when an attacker can determine that secret communication has taken place, that is, the attacker has *detected* the communication, even if they have not determined the contents of the message [5].

A popular modern problem description for steganography was explained by Simmons in [7], where he describes a scenario known as the *prisoners' problem*. In this problem, two criminals have been arrested and are to be placed in separate cells. They have the ability to communicate by passing messages, but the prison warden can read every message being passed between them. The prisoners must coordinate an escape plan within these messages. The prisoners cannot use encryption, because if the warden is unable to read the message, he will assume they are communicating something against his wishes and will not transmit the messages. Therefore, the prisoners must send messages that appear innocuous, but contain secret messages *embedded* within them that the warden cannot detect. If the warden does detect that some secret communication exists, even if he does not know the contents of the message, he will not transmit the messages.

Both cryptographic and stego systems utilize a *secret message*, which is to be communicated from sender to receiver. Unlike cryptographic systems where the content is sent directly, a stego system requires a *cover message*, which is a message in another domain in which the secret message is embedded. This cover message is then sent to the receiver, who possesses the ability to extract the hidden message. The hidden message itself may or may not be encrypted. The cover message with embedded secret message is called a *stego object* [5].

Formally, a stego system is defined by Böhme [5] as the quintuple

$$\left(X^*, M, K, \text{Embed, Extract} \right)$$

where

1. X^* is the set of possible cover messages;
2. M is the set of possible secret messages;
3. K is the set of possible keys;
4. Embed is the embedding function Embed: $M \times X^* \times K \rightarrow X^*$;
5. Extract is the extracting function Extract: $X^* \times K \rightarrow M$.

To use the stego system, the sender will use Embed($m, x^{(0)}, k$), providing the secret message $m \in M$, cover message $x^{(0)} \in X^*$, and key $k \in K$. This generates the stego object $x^{(m)} \in X^*$ that is supplied to the Extract($x^{(m)}, k$) function. Both functions require the same key for any given message transmission. This definition implies that the domain for both cover messages and stego objects is the same, while other definitions may use separate domains for each [5, 8]. The stego system process is shown in Figure 5.1, adapted from [5].

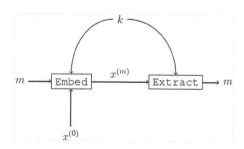

FIGURE 5.1 Basic diagram for steganographic systems.

There are three criteria used for evaluating stego systems: capacity, security, and robustness. Usually, these three criteria must be balanced when designing the system; one system cannot score highly in all three categories [5].

Capacity is the maximum length of a secret message, often in bits, for a given cover message. It can be defined either in absolute terms, or relative to the size of the stego object created by the embedding function. Capacity is dependent on both the embedding function and cover message used. When defined proportionally to the stego object size, it is also called the embedding rate and the metric *proportion*, p, is used, where $0 \leq p \leq 1$. The proportion can be defined by

$$p = \frac{|m|}{n} \text{ for covers } x^{(0)} \in X^n \tag{5.1}$$

if the embedding function can store 1 bit per cover message symbol [5]. It is known that the detectability of a secret message is lower with smaller cover messages [5, 9].

A steganographic system can be considered beaten if an attacker can detect that secret communication has taken place, so the security of the stego system is based on the detectability of the messages. In 1883, Auguste Kerckhoffs proposed several principles of designing cryptographic systems [5, 10], one of which is that the system itself should not require any secrecy; that is, if an attacker understands how the messages are encrypted but not the specific key used, they will still be unable to decipher the communications. This is now known as Kerckhoffs' principle and is applied to modern cryptographic systems such as Advanced Encryption Standard (AES), DES, and Rivest–Shamir–Adleman (RSA), all of which use publicly available algorithms but are still considered secure systems. In steganography, the same principle should apply to the stego system. Thus, when we discuss the security of a stego system, we should assume that the attacker has knowledge of the embedding technique.

In a robust stego system, it will be easy to extract the hidden message from the stego object, even in situations with random errors, or noise, or when there is intentional interference to prevent the communication. This criterion has not received much research attention so far, and is often studied relative to the specific stego system implementation being used [5].

5.2.2 Basic Steganalysis

Steganalysis can be reduced to a decision problem asking if a given object is a stego object, i.e., if it contains an embedded message. As with any detection problem, there are four possible outcomes: true positive, true negative, false positive, and false negative. A true positive is an answer *yes* where the given object is, in fact, a stego object. A true negative is an answer *no*, where the given object is, in fact, *not* a stego object. A false positive is an answer *yes*, where the given object is *not* actually a stego object and a false negative is an answer *no*, where the given object is actually a stego object.

Böhme [5] labels the probability of a false negative as the *missing probability*, β and the probability of a false positive as α. The *detection probability* is $1 - \beta$. Steganalysis methods do not generally provide a discrete output, but instead rely on a continuous value with a certain *decision threshold*, τ. Adjusting τ allows balancing the error rates β and α. This is visualized using a receiver operating characteristics (ROC) curve, which plots detection rate against false positive rate for detection techniques. Various metrics based on the ROC curve are used for ranking stego systems. For example, the detector reliability is the area between the ROC curve and the function $f(x) = x$ on the interval $[0, 1]$, FP_{50} is the false positive rate at 50% detection rate, and the total minimal decision error [5] is

$$TMDE = \min_{\tau} \frac{\alpha + \beta}{2}$$

5.2.3 STEGANOGRAPHY PARADIGMS

There are two fundamental paradigms for stego systems. The first is the classical paradigm described in Section 5.2.1, where the Embed function takes in some existing cover message and modifies it to embed m. The other paradigm is the cover generation paradigm, where a reasonable cover message for the given domain is generated automatically [5]. This second paradigm is the focus of our section work because it is the method used for the developed stego system. The stego system diagram can be updated as shown in Figure 5.2 to represent this second paradigm, where the initial cover message $x^{(0)}$ is replaced by a function Generate that can create the required cover messages. The major problem with this paradigm is the difficulty in generating proper cover messages that, if collected by an attacker, do not allow detection when compared to other messages in the domain.

Noiseless steganography was developed by Desoky [11] and is closely related to the cover generation paradigm discussed above. Desoky describes contemporary steganography as techniques that add noise to the cover message, which is the embedding process [11]. Therefore, processes that generate appropriate cover messages with the secret message embedded from inception are considered noiseless steganography.

Desoky provides several examples of noiseless steganography in [11]. The first presented example is graph steganography, or graphstega. In graphstega, a message can be converted using the ASCII character set, then to a binary string of byte values, then sliced into sets of binary digits as desired. Using the message "HELLO," If sliced in to octets, we get the sequence of numbers 72, 69, 76, 76, 79. This process is known as the *encoding scheme* [11]. Next, the sequence is plotted on a graph as data points. For example, this sequence is shown in Figure 5.3. This system can be enhanced by adding additional points unrelated to the message, which would then force an attacker to try many possible subset combinations of the points in order to discover the actual message. This technique is dependent on certain domains that involve graphs and the range of values is thus dependent on the expected ranges in those domains. The generated graph must remain within those ranges to a certain statistical degree in order to remain undetectable [11].

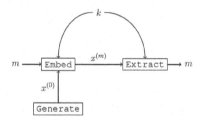

FIGURE 5.2   Stego system diagram for the cover message generation paradigm.

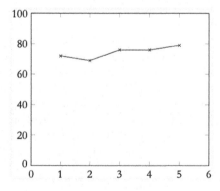

FIGURE 5.3   Example plot of graph steganography.

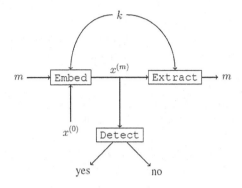

FIGURE 5.4 Diagram for steganographic systems using the passive warden adversary model.

Desoky also describes a chess-based noiseless steganography technique called chestega. In chestega, game board configurations can hide a message. A chess board contains 64 squares, and each square can be occupied by either a white or black piece, so there are up to 128 possible values that can be displayed on the board. The message can then be encoded in the piece configurations for each move of a chess game [11]. The major drawback to this technique is that the chess board configurations have limitations based on the legal moves of the pieces and also the reasonable board positions. If many obviously bad moves are made, it is possible that an attacker would become suspicious. In addition to these examples, Desoky presents other noiseless steganography techniques such as education-centric steganography (edustega), where messages can be encoded in educational texts such as multiple-choice answer keys.

There are also two main adversary models in steganography. The adversary model is the set of assumptions on the potential attacker (steganalyst) against the stego system. These models can be described by the goals, computational power, and knowledge of the adversary [5]. In steganography, the two models are passive warden and active warden. The term warden is analogous to the warden in the problem description of the prisoners' problem [7].

In the passive warden model, we assume that the attacker does not interfere with any of the communications, but can view all of the transmissions. As shown in Figure 5.4 (adapted from [5]), a new function Detect: $X^* \to \{yes, no\}$ exists that is utilized by the warden to determine whether any $x^{(i)}$ is or is not a stego object. In addition to Detect, the attacker may also employ additional techniques to attempt to determine the actual contents of the hidden messages.

In the active warden model, the adversary has the ability to modify the stego objects in transit between the sender and receiver. For example, in the prisoners' problem [7], if the messages are handwritten, the warden could erase some of the messages and optionally replace it with his own, or write more to the end of the message. This is done using a new Distort: $X^* \to X^*$ function, as shown in Figure 5.5 (adapted from [5]). The active warden model is associated with the robustness criterion, while the passive warden model is associated with the security criterion.

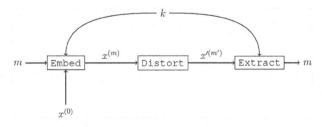

FIGURE 5.5 Diagram for steganographic systems using the active warden adversary model.

5.2.4 Batch Steganography

In the stego system descriptions in Section 5.2.1, it was assumed that each stego object $x^{(m)}$ was a separate entity containing a secret message m and that these messages are isolated. Ker [12] argues that in practical situations, it is unlikely that the stego objects or secret messages will be isolated for both the sender and attacker [12].

In batch steganography, a single message may be broken up and split among several cover messages and an attacker may be able to analyze many related stego objects. Ker [12] describes batch steganography with the following scenario: a criminal is going to hide information on his computer using a stego system. He has a collection of files and will split up the secret information in small quantities among many of them. He is later arrested and the authorities are investigating the computer. Their problem is deciding which files to examine. When considering that their steganalysis techniques will have non-zero false positive rates, even if he had not hidden the information in any of the files, they will likely see many positive results to a search of the entire file system [12].

The batch steganography problem can be therefore be defined as how to best embed information in multiple cover objects. If only a small amount of information is stored in each cover object, then more cover objects will contain traces of the information, but if a larger amount of information is stored in each cover object, it may be easier to also maintain a set of cover objects with no embedded data, making it harder to locate the actual stego objects [12, 13]. Figure 5.6 shows a diagram of batch steganography for a message m split into pieces $m_1, m_2, ..., m_k$.

5.2.5 Key Exchange in Steganography

In cryptography, key exchange was one of the major problems until the development of public key systems. In these systems, one party (Alice) generates a set of two keys: a public key and a private key, which act as a complementary set. If a message is encrypted with one of the keys, only the other key can decrypt it. When another party (Bob) must send an encrypted message to Alice, he will encrypt the message using Alice's public key, which Alice has made publicly available, before sending it to her. As long as Alice's private key remains private, only she can decrypt Bob's message. Without such a system, the same key would be used for both encryption and decryption. If Bob tried to send a message to Alice, he would also have to inform Alice which key was used for the message. Transmitting this information presumes some secure channel between the two, otherwise the key itself must be encrypted, which leaves them in the position of sending the new key used to encrypt the original key [6].

In steganography, this problem is even more difficult. Bob must have a way of communicating the key for their stego system without anyone realizing that they have communicated. Therefore, the public key systems used in cryptography are insufficient. Relating to the prisoners' problem [7], without a proper key exchange protocol, the two prisoners would have had to share a secret key before being locked away.

Some solutions have been proposed [5, 14] for public key steganography. One solution involves a separate, keyless Embed and Extract and a public key cryptography system. First, the stego system's key k is encrypted using the receiver's public key. It is then embedded using the keyless

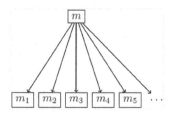

FIGURE 5.6 Diagram for batch steganography of a message m.

embedding function in to some cover message. The encrypted key is then extracted using the keyless extracting function and finally decrypted using the receiver's private key [5]. This solution is merely a way to distribute the key over the channel, however the sender must still have the receiver's public key. As noted in [14], it is still necessary to have a channel for transmitting the public key. Additionally, the data transmitted via the keyless embedding function should appear pseudo-random, or else the security of the entire system is limited by the security of the keyless embedding function.

5.2.6 BOTNETS

Botnet software is a type of malicious software (malware) that is most often placed on a victim's computer silently. Unlike traditional malware, however, the botnet software communicates with a botmaster or bot-herder that coordinates potentially thousands or even millions of other infected machines, called bots or zombies, in other attacks. Once created, a botnet can be used for harvesting personal information on a global scale, or causing significant denial of service attacks to even the largest organizations [15].

From the perspective of the botmaster, there are five steps in the creation of a botnet. First, the software itself is created. After being created, the botmaster must somehow infect other machines with it, often in malicious email attachments, as a trojan,[2] or other common malware distribution techniques. Once infected, the botnet software must perform several steps as well. First, it rallies, by either contacting the botmaster's C&C center or by contacting other bots in a peer-to-peer fashion. It then waits for commands from the botmaster. Finally, when given a command, the bot will execute [15]. Once some machines are infected, the botnet software itself can use the machine to advertise and grow. It may make use of private information of the user to send phishing emails to friends or post on their social network sites in order to convince new potential victims to install the software.

5.2.7 BOTNET C&C

Every botnet must have a C&C system that directs the bots to perform their attacks. Zeidanloo and Manaf [16] have separated botnet C&C systems in to three groups. Some botnets use centralized C&C centers where the botmaster can control all bots directly. Other botnets use a peer-to-peer C&C system, where bots communicate with each other. In addition to receiving commands, many botnets must communicate information back to the botmaster, especially if their goal is to obtain the private information of the user whose computer hosts the botnet software. Finally, some botnets use a hybrid approach.

In the centralized model, communication between the bots and botmaster is often done using an IRC channel or over HTTP. This was the original botnet C&C model used. Because the system is centralized, the C&C center acts as a single point of failure for the botnet. When using IRC, the botmaster will create an IRC channel on their server and the bots will then connect to the server to communicate with the botmaster. From this IRC channel, the botmaster could command all bots to initiate a DDoS attack on an enemy. If the botnet communicates over HTTP, it gains the advantage that HTTP traffic is not suspicious in general, because it is the protocol used for web traffic [16]. Figure 5.7 shows the diagram for a centralized botnet. A centralized approach may also maintain several C&C centers to improve communications and prevent having a single point of failure, as shown in Figure 5.8.

In the peer-to-peer model, the botmaster no longer has to worry about the C&C center as a single point of failure, however now each bot in the botnet must be able to communicate with other bots. This requires recording the information of other bots in the botnet. The botmaster sends commands by communicating with as few as one bot, which then propagates the command to the rest of the network. The botnet should be versatile enough to dynamically configure its own network topology for communication between bots. The peer-to-peer model for botnet C&C is shown in Figure 5.9.

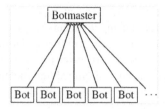

FIGURE 5.7   Botnet C&C for a centralized botnet.

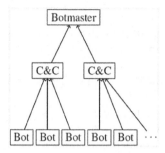

FIGURE 5.8   Botnet C&C for a centralized botnet with multiple C&C centers.

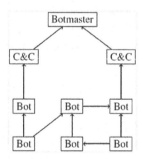

FIGURE 5.9   Botnet C&C for a peer-to-peer botnet.

Although most botnets use IRC or HTTP to communicate directly, the botnet designed for this section will communicate over a social network. This concept has been discussed in some previous work, for example, in [17], a method of C&C over Twitter is discussed, however the commands are sent directly as the content of the tweets instead of by using a covert channel. A botnet has been designed to use steganography over a social network [18], but it uses image steganography to embed messages in the images posted normally by the victim. It requires that other bots in the botnet be on computers socially connected to the victim via the social network.

5.2.8   BOTNETS USING SMARTPHONES

It is possible that in the near future, botnets and malware will focus on the portable device (smartphone, tablet, etc.) domain because sales for these devices has increased dramatically in the past few years and has significantly surpassed sales for traditional desktop computers with combined market share over 80%.[3] Currently, a large portion of malware targets the Microsoft Windows platform because of its large market share in desktop environments, however, the number of possible devices is much smaller than smartphones and tablets.

SoCellBot by Faghani and Nguyen [19] is a botnet designed to infect smartphones that have access to online social networks, showing it is possible to create such a botnet. One of the benefits of the ubiquitous nature of social networks is the usability from mobile devices. This means that the stego system developed for this section can easily be adapted to work on these devices. Using smart phones and tablets as bots in the botnet can drastically increase the potential network coverage. Similarly, in the future it may also be possible to infect "Internet of Things" devices.

5.2.9 RELATED WORKS

The most closely related existing work to this section proposal is probably Stegobot [18]. Stegobot is a botnet designed to communicate using social networks (specifically Facebook) and image steganography. The authors design two separated types of message: bot commands and bot cargo. The bot commands are messages from the botmaster to the bots instructing them. The bot cargo are messages from the bots back to the botmaster containing stolen information.

Stegobot [18] uses a distributed, peer-to-peer communication channel and does not generate its own cover messages. Instead, it uses the image files that the victims are already uploading to the social network as the cover messages, embedding the secret messages within. The botnet software intercepts the images being posted to embed the message before it is sent to Facebook. Stegobot uses the existing network of relationships for each victim as the communication channel. In their experiments, the authors used a set of 116 images. One of the difficulties of this technique is the automatic image manipulation performed by Facebook as the images are uploaded. This can tamper with the content of the embedded message, requiring a highly robust stego system.

Natarajan et al. [20] designed a detection scheme for Stegobot that uses the information entropy of the image files that are acting as the cover objects. Their detection technique achieved average detection rates exceeding 70% in their experiments for several different image steganography methods.

A similar work by Singh et al. [17] uses Twitter for botnet C&C, but does not apply steganography to hide the communications. Instead, the commands are posted directly to the Twitter account. This allows the botmaster to leverage the benefits of social networks for botnet C&C, but they used communication methods that will likely appear highly suspicious to any viewers.

5.2.10 HUFFMAN CODES

To reduce the required length of messages being sent using the developed stego system, it is possible to utilize Huffman codes [21]. Huffman codes will be described briefly in this section and their utilization in the stego system will be described in Section 5.3.2.1. Huffman coding was presented in 1952 by David Huffman as a way of constructing optimal prefix codes for weighted fixed-size alphabets. Because the developed stego system is designed to use such alphabets, this technique is ideal for compressing the data transmission.

Huffman [21] describes a method of sending messages by mapping the messages to symbols and sending the symbols. He notes that when the number of messages exceeds the number of symbols, some messages must be sent using more than one symbol. He denotes this sequence of symbols as a *message code* and denotes the total set of messages being sent as a *message ensemble*. The translation between messages and symbols is then called the *ensemble code*. He defines an optimal code as one with minimum redundancy, i.e., the average message length is minimized. We will describe the process developed for converting to binary codes, but Huffman also described extending to an arbitrary number of digits.

5.2.11 BINARY HUFFMAN CODING

Huffman [21] describes two assumptions that may be made about the ordering of message ensembles when deriving the codes:
and

$$P(1) \geq P(2) \geq \cdots \geq P(N-1) \geq P(N) \tag{5.2}$$

$$L(1) \leq L(2) \leq \cdots \leq L(N-1) \leq L(N) \tag{5.3}$$

Essentially, Equations 5.2 and 5.3 state that we can assume that we have ordered all of the messages in such a way that the length of one code can't be less than the length of a more probable code. Otherwise, it would be possible to switch the codes used for each message. This ensures that more common messages are associated with shorter codes. In addition to this assumption, Huffman shows that

$$L(N-1) = L(N) \tag{5.4}$$

i.e., the two least probable messages must have codes of the same length and there are only two messages with this length. Finally, the codes for these two messages will be identical other than the final bit.

Huffman [21] describes a recursive process to generate the codes by using the message ordering from highest to lowest probability. At each stage, the lowest two probability messages are each assigned either 0 or 1, and then a new message ensemble consisting of the remaining messages along with the prefix of the two least probable messages containing a combined probability of $P(n) + P(N + 1)$. According to Equation 5.4 and the two additional requirements stated above, this prefix will be the same for both messages. This new ensemble has one less message. The process is repeated until only one message remains in the ensemble. Now, the bits assigned at each step can be combined to form the prefix codes for each original message, ensuring that the most probable message will have the shortest prefix code.

5.2.12 NATURAL LANGUAGE PROCESSING

The stego system in this section depends on generating appropriate length tweets to contain the hidden messages, but this is a difficult problem that is similar to natural language generation. Twitter bots exist that act like authentic users to varying degrees of success, but the ideal bot would need to be fluent in the "Twitter language," which is very similar to English but contains its own nuances and idiosyncrasies and is constantly evolving. Additionally, chat bots exist that are designed to communicate with people as if they are human themselves. In this section, we describe some techniques applied for tweet generation.

5.2.13 MARKOV CHAINS

A Markov chain is a state transition system where a transition from one state to the next is determined by the probability of moving from the current state to some new state [22].

A Markov chain contains a set of n states and an $n \times n$ probability matrix indicating the probability of moving from some current state to another state. It can be used for text generation by having words or characters as the states and using the probability matrix to model what the next word or character should be.

Example 5.1   Markov Chain

We will give a short example showing a Markov chain for the states {a, b, c}. First, suppose we have the following probability matrix:

	a	b	c
a	0.3	0.4	0.3
b	0.1	0.0	0.9
c	0.5	0.25	0.25

That is, from state a, the probability of staying in state a is 0.3, the probability of moving to state b is 0.4, and the probability of moving to state c is 0.3. So, the probability of moving from one state to another is entirely dependent on the current state instead of previous states. The matrix should be read by row, i.e., each row represents all of the transitions from that row's state. Additionally, the probability of starting at each state must be known. In this example, assume that each state is equally likely to be a starting state.

The Markov chain can also be represented as a probabilistic finite state machine, as shown in Figure 5.10. By choosing an initial state, it is then possible to generate a series of states (which can represent a text string) by choosing each next state probabilistically according to the Markov chain's probability matrix (or state diagram). For example, the probability of generating the string $ababc$ given the above probability matrix is.

$$0.33 \times 0.4 \times 0.1 \times 0.4 \times 0.9 = 4.752 \times 10^{-3} \qquad (5.5)$$

It should also be noted that the sum of the probabilities of all transitions from a given state must naturally equal one.

5.2.14   LAPLACE SMOOTHING

When building language and text models from existing corpora, it is possible that some letter or word combinations do not appear in a corpus, but are valid in the language. Frequency and probability tables will therefore contain a value of zero for each of those entries. Laplace smoothing is a simple technique to remove all zero entries from such a table without significantly affecting the other probabilities [23]. To perform laplace smoothing, one simply adds one to all of the frequency counts for each entry in the table.

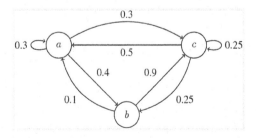

FIGURE 5.10   The Markov chain for Example 5.1.

If c_i is the frequency count for entry i, then the probability would normally be calculated by.where

$$p(i) = \frac{C_i}{N} \tag{5.6}$$

$$N = {}_{i=1}^{n}C_i \tag{5.7}$$

is the sum of all frequencies in the table for the current column [23].

With laplace smoothing, we instead use:

$$P_{\text{Laplace}}(i) = \frac{C_i + 1}{N + V} \tag{5.8}$$

where

$$N = {}_{i=1}^{n}i \tag{5.9}$$

is the total number of columns in the table [23]. If most frequency counts are large, applying this smoothing will have a negligible effect on their probabilities and allows calculating the probability of entries that contain a frequency of zero according to the corpus used to create the table.

5.3 METHODOLOGY

5.3.1 TWITTER COVERT CHANNEL

5.3.1.1 The Stego System

To perform the botnet C&C communication, a covert channel (stego system) that communicates using the Twitter social network has been developed. This covert channel is similar to Desoky's [11] noiseless steganography and utilizes the cover generation paradigm (see Section 5.2.3), however there are some differences. Even in the noiseless steganography systems, the secret messages are usually embedded in to the actual data of the cover objects. For example, in graph steganography, the plotted data contains the secret message. In this system, where the cover objects are tweets, the secret message is not contained in the data of the tweet (the text), instead it is contained in the *metadata* of the tweet (the length). Metadata refers to "data about data." All data has some metadata associated with it, but this metadata is not explicitly stored. It is inferred from the existing data. The tweet's data is the text. The tweet also has metadata such as the time it was posted, the user account, and the length of the text posted. Additional metadata could include the letter frequencies of the posted text or the number of spaces in the text.

Because this system differs from existing steganographic systems, we will define the parts of this system as follows, relating to the definition of Section 5.2.1:

1. The set of possible cover messages, X^*, is the set of possible tweets, which is the set of messages of up to 140 UTF-8[4] characters.
2. The set of possible secret messages, M, can be defined as Σ^*, where the Σ notation is taken from the formal languages domain, and refers to an alphabet of symbols, where the symbols can be arbitrarily defined. For example, one implementation may use $\Sigma = \{a, b, c, ..., z\}$ (the English alphabet).
3. The set of possible keys, K, is the set of numbers that can be valid pseudo-random keys for the implementation. In our case, the implementation uses the Java programming language's java. util.Random[5] class, which uses 48 bit keys.

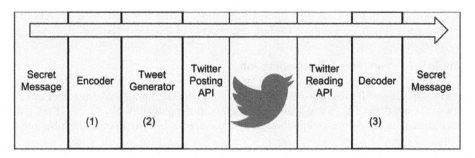

FIGURE 5.11 Diagram of Twitter covert channel. Use $\Sigma = \{a, b, c, ..., z\}$ (the English alphabet).

4. The Embed and Generate functions are combined. In our implementation we generate reasonable cover messages to have appropriate metadata that contains the secret message.
5. The Extract function will also require a Decode step, described below.
6. For convenience, we will also use the following notation for the set of natural numbers up to 140: $N_{140} = \{1, 2, ..., 140\}$. Similarly, if we use N_n, it means the natural numbers from 1 to n. Unless otherwise stated, we assume $0 / \in N$.

The overall system is shown in Figure 5.11, where the numbered components were implemented for the channel.

The secret message is embedded by utilizing the *length* of the posted tweets, by character count. Because a tweet can have a length of up to 140 characters, the length value can store just over seven bits of information per tweet. However, embedding seven bits of information per tweet is not reasonable in practice. Certain length tweets rarely appear on Twitter so seeing, for example, many tweets of length one or two on a single account would be suspicious. To solve these problems, we can use a one-to-many encoding technique to hide information in the tweet lengths. We will modify the normal stego system definition to include the following functions: Encode: $M \times K \rightarrow N_{140}$ and Decode: $N_{140} \times K \rightarrow M$. The fundamental design for the stego system and encoding technique were created as part of a CS599 (advanced information security) course research project along with another student, Jonathan Mansur. Jonathan came up with the original idea for the encoding technique. The modified stego system definition is shown in Figure 5.12. A message $m \in M$ is broken up in to symbols of Σ: $m_1, m_2, ..., m_a$. Each symbol m_i is mapped to one of several possible values using Encode along with the appropriate key k to generate $n \in N_{140}$, the appropriate tweet length value to use for this piece of the message. This value is passed to Generate, which generates a plausible cover message $x^{(mi)} \in X^*$ to be posted to Twitter. The Extract function reads the posted tweets and calculates the length n of each tweet. This value is passed to Decode along with the original key k to reconstruct the original message m piece by piece. This design assumes that $|\Sigma| \leq 140$, and in fact, smaller alphabets should improve the security of the channel. A smaller alphabet allows mapping

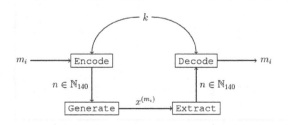

FIGURE 5.12 Modified stego system diagram for Twitter covert channel.

each symbol to more possible length values, so repetitions of each length value are less likely. We will now present a simplified example to show the process of the stego system.

Example 5.2   Encoding Table Generation

In this example, we will show the process for generating the encoding table. Instead of using N_{140} (all possible length values), we will use a reduced output alphabet of N_{10} (1, 2, ..., 10) with an equal distribution. For the input alphabet, we will use $\Sigma = \{a, b\}$ with an equal distribution.

First, choose one element of the output alphabet for each element of Σ. This guarantees that at least one output symbol will be mapped to each input symbol. Remove the chosen values of the output alphabet as options for future choices.

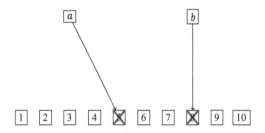

Now, choose one element from both sets probabilistically based on the weights.

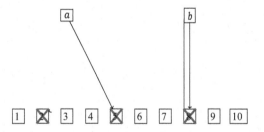

Continue this process until all elements of the output alphabet have been used.

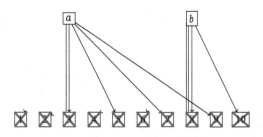

After all elements from the output alphabet have been used, the encoding table is composed of all of the choices made:

Symbol	Possible Length Values
a	1, 3, 5, 7, 9
b	2, 4, 6, 8, 10

Example 5.3   Simple Message Encoding Example

In this example, we will use tweet lengths up to 10, i.e., we will use $N_{10} = \{1, 2, ..., 10\}$ instead of N_{140}. We will use $\Sigma = \{a, b\}$ and $X^* = \{x\}^+$, i.e., secret messages will be composed of combinations of a and b and cover messages will be strings of x.

Suppose we want to send the secret message $m = abba$ using the simple Encode map from Example 5.1. First, the message is broken in to the sequence of symbols a, b, b, a. The Encode function will then map each symbol to a possible length value, e.g., 3, 6, 2, 3. Note that because each input symbol from Σ can map to more than one length value from N_{10}, the same symbol may or may not be mapped to the same length value in any given message. The Generate function will then create cover messages that match these length values from the set of possible cover messages X^*: xxx, xxxxxx, xx, xxx. Each cover message would then be posted to a Twitter account in the order of the original secret message. The Extract function on the recipient's side would then take the tweets in the posted (chronological) order, returning the length values 3, 6, 2, 3. The Decode function can then apply the same map as the Encode function and reconstruct the original message abba.

This system is generic in that it can be used with many possible input alphabets, e.g., the English alphabet or arbitrary half-byte values $(0 \times 0, 0 \times 1, ..., 0 \times F)$. The English alphabet allows sending simple messages. The half-byte alphabet allows sending arbitrary binary data by splitting each byte of the input data in half and sending each half as one symbol of the message. It is impossible to send an entire byte in one message using this system because the maximum tweet length is only 140 characters. We chose half-bytes because it is easy to deconstruct and reconstruct the original bytes and because it is a relatively small alphabet with only 16 symbols, so it is possible to map each input symbol to almost 10 different tweet length values. To obtain symbol frequencies for the half-byte values, it would be best to empirically sample the types of data being sent across the channel because, in general, each value would likely have an equal weight. If the specific type of data being sent is biased toward certain byte values, that should be considered when weighting the alphabet.

The botnet C&C diagram for this system resembles the diagram for a centralized botnet, as shown in Figure 5.13. A botmaster controls one or more Twitter accounts that have tweets containing the commands and the bots read from these accounts.

5.3.1.2   The Tweet Generator

The Generate function is one of the most problematic aspects of this type of stego system. As discussed in [5], generating appropriate and plausible cover messages for a stego system is a non-trivial problem. In this system, the generator must be capable of generating messages that can convince a reader of the Twitter account page that they are viewing regular tweets. This component has the largest impact on the detectability of the channel. In essence, the generator must pass a simplified Turing test. Twitter bots are not a new phenomenon, and in fact several bots were created that successfully convinced other users that they were real people [24]. Additionally, chat bots exist, such as Cleverbot[6]

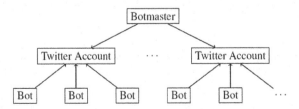

FIGURE 5.13   The botnet C&C diagram for the system.

which are reasonably successful [25]. However, aside from competent English skills, the generator must utilize the "language of Twitter" that consists of many retweets[7] and hashtags.[8] We consider a strong generator out of the scope of this work, but it is possible to leverage collected Twitter data to create a Twitter language model based on tweet contents that can be used to generate new tweets.

5.3.1.3 Key Exchange

Like generation, the key exchange is also a significant problem for this stego system. The method described in Section 5.2.5 is possible. Another simple technique exists that may be acceptable for this channel. Each Twitter account has a username, which is a string of characters with length less than or equal to 15 and containing letters, numbers, or underscores.[9] The key can be generated based on the value of the username, for example by hashing it with a secure hash function such as SHA [26]. However, this technique goes against Kerckhoffs' principle [10], because an attacker that understands the procedure could generate the key using the same user name of the account. Even though it goes against Kerckhoffs' principle, this concept is actually widely used for password security. In password security, a common technique is to apply some hash algorithm on the password along with some random salt and store the result. It is common to apply the algorithm sequentially several times as well. By changing the method, it prevents attackers who have obtained the table of hashed passwords from applying a known list of password and hash pairs (known as a rainbow table) to the table to determine which passwords are actually being used. The username technique would requires the receiver (bots) to know which username(s) will be used by the system. In general, there is no good solution to the key exchange problem. For the botnet C&C use case, the key can be embedded in the botnet malware that is distributed to the bots.

5.3.1.4 Posting to Twitter

Along with the Encode, Generate, Extract, and Decode functions, we need a system that can post to Twitter. This is easy to do for testing purposes thanks to Twitter's official API[10] and a third-party Java library, Twitter4J.[11] For a real botnet scenario, the implementer would likely write their own system that uses raw HTTP requests because the Twitter API requires authentication of every call, detects the posting method, and limits the number of posts allowed for each account. However, because this would violate Twitter's terms of use, we will only post tweets using the official API and abide by all limitations for testing. Now that the rest of the components have been explained, a more complete example will be presented.

Example 5.4 Complete Example

In this example, we will use the full range of tweet lengths N_{140}. We will use $\Sigma = \{A, B, ..., Z\}$ (the English alphabet), and X^* as a preconstructed list of various proverbs and phrases of lengths rangving from one to 140. The Generate function will lookup an appropriate phrase for each length message provided by the Encode function. Table 5.1 shows a generated encoding map from English letters to tweet lengths. The weights shown in the second column are taken as letter frequencies.[12] Those weights were used to decide the number of entries for each letter in the third column.

Additionally, the entries in the third column have weights associated with each length as shown in Figure 5.14. These weights are used when determining which length value to use, although they are not shown in the table for readability.

Suppose we want to send the message *FOO*. First, the message is separated in to the sequence of symbols *F*, *O*, *O*. Each is passed to the Encode function, which chooses appropriate lengths, e.g., 61, 35, 121. The Generate function then generates tweets and they are posted to Twitter, as shown in Figure 5.1. The figure should be read from bottom up, because the newer messages are posted on top of the older messages. The account shown is a test account created for this work. The recipient then reads these tweets, obtains the lengths, then uses Decode with the same table as was used for the Encode process to get the original message.

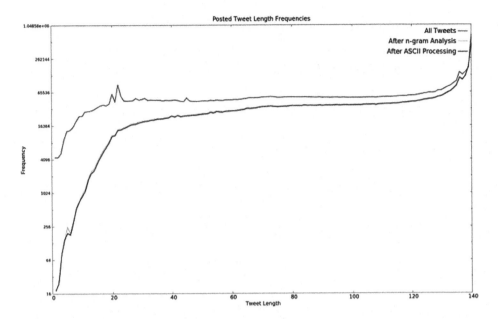

FIGURE 5.14 Frequency of Tweets by Tweet Length on a Logarithmic Scale.

TABLE 5.1
Complete Encoding Map Example for the English Alphabet

Symbol	Weight	Encoding
A	14,810	32, 16, 19, 131, 84, 37, 106, 140, 76, 111
B	2,715	105, 138, 67
C	4,943	75, 36, 125, 46, 62
D	7,874	65, 2, 136, 74, 44, 79
E	21,912	6, 40, 110, 47, 113, 114, 51, 53, 23, 55, 88, 89, 27, 93
F	4,200	17, 122, 61, 87
G	3,693	97, 130
H	10,795	82, 50, 98, 20, 5, 120, 45, 63
I	13,318	33, 1, 66, 99, 132, 69, 22, 24, 73, 139
J	188	72
K	1,257	112, 48, 124
L	7,253	129, 3, 70, 57, 28, 13
M	4,761	80, 104, 42, 52, 135
N	12,666	96, 49, 54, 58, 91, 108, 29, 109, 78
O	14,003	35, 121, 43, 107, 92, 12
P	3,316	7, 95
Q	205	85, 117
R	10,977	41, 30, 71, 119
S	11,450	64, 21, 86, 118, 137, 127, 15
T	16,587	34, 100, 4, 133, 134, 38, 8, 9, 10, 11, 77, 14, 83, 115, 25, 90, 123, 60, 126, 31
U	5,246	103
V	2,019	18
W	3,819	81, 116, 68, 102, 26, 59, 94
X	315	101
Y	3,853	128, 56
Z	128	39

TABLE 5.2

Botnet Command and Control Language for Use with the Stego System

Index	Weight	Description
0	25	Literal hex value 0
1	25	Literal hex value 1
2	25	Literal hex value 2
3	25	Literal hex value 3
4	25	Literal hex value 4
5	25	Literal hex value 5
6	25	Literal hex value 6
7	25	Literal hex value 7
8	25	Literal hex value 8
9	25	Literal hex value 9
10	25	Literal hex value A
11	25	Literal hex value B
12	25	Literal hex value C
13	25	Literal hex value D
14	25	Literal hex value E
15	25	Literal hex value F
16	5	Take screenshot
17	5	Shutdown computer
18	5	Reboot computer
19	5	Perform denial-of-service (DoS) attack to IPv4 address in next 4 bytes sent
20	5	Stop DoS attack
21	5	Download and execute file from address in next k bytes (until delimiter)
22	1	Message delimiter

5.3.2 THE BOTNET C&C LANGUAGE

The stego system described in Section 5.3.1 can be used with an arbitrary input alphabet as long as its size is not larger than the tweet length range (up to 140 characters), so for botnet C&C we have developed a language that can be mapped to tweet lengths and interpreted to execute botnet commands (see Table 5.2). We have included some common botnet commands as described in [17]. The weights were decided somewhat arbitrarily, because in a real scenario, the botmaster would tailor the weights based on which commands they believe that they are likely to send most often. In this case, We are assuming the byte values (indices 0–15) are more likely, because for some commands arguments must be sent using these. We do not assume any single command is more likely than another.

5.3.2.1 Using Huffman Codes to Improve Message Transmission

As described in Section 5.2.10, Huffman coding is suited for compressing messages of a finite, weighted alphabet. Additionally, as shown in Section 5.3.1, the stego system created for this section is specifically designed to use such alphabets. In this section we will show that it is possible to reduce any arbitrary alphabet designed for this type of stego system to a simple binary coded alphabet for the purpose of improving the message transmission rate. An example of generating a Huffman code follows.

Example 5.5   Huffman Code Generation

Suppose we have the following weighted alphabet:

Symbol	Weight
A	14
B	2
C	63
D	8
E	35

A Huffman code for this alphabet should give a shorter code for *C* and longer codes for *B* and *D* because of the weights. First, arrange each element of the alphabet by its weight:

B (2)   D (8)   A (14)   E (35)   C (63)

Take the two lowest-weight elements and assign a 0 to one of them and a 1 to the other, then combine the two weights. In this case, we will choose *B* and *D* to get the new total weight of 10.

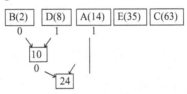

Continue the process again choosing the two lowest weights. In this case, the combined weight of *B* and *D* along with the weight for *A*.

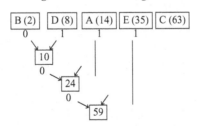

Continue the process again, choosing the combined weight 24 with the weight for *E*, 35.

Finally, when only two elements remain, they are chosen.

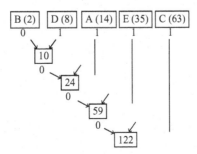

The Huffman code is then created by using the binary strings from the newly created root of the tree to each leaf (alphabet symbol). The resulting Huffman code is then:

Symbol	Weight	Code
A	14	001
B	2	0000
C	63	1
D	8	0001
E	35	01

We can see that, as expected, C received the shortest code while B and D received the longest.

Due to the restrictions on message size in this stego system, it is impossible to send one byte of data per tweet. Instead, as discussed in Section 5.3.1.1, half-byte values can be sent. In fact, any number of bits less than eight is possible and we will use the term *block size*, denoted by s_b, to indicate the number of bits being sent in each tweet. Additionally, because Huffman codes are variable-length prefix codes, it is possible that a message length may not be a multiple of the block size, so the message transmission mechanism must include some type of padding technique. We will call the alphabet of binary strings with a given block size a *binary block alphabet* and denote the binary block alphabet with block size s_b as BB_{sb}. Table 5.3 shows the binary block alphabet with $s_b = 4$.

As a padding mechanism, we will use the following simple approach: for every message being sent using the binary block alphabet, add one additional tweet at the end of the message using the same binary block alphabet that contains the binary value of the number of bits in the message that had to be added as padding. An example of this method follows. We will use a block size of four for demonstrative purposes. Other block sizes will work equally well, but will change the number of tweets required for sending a message. This change will then affect the detectability of the system. If a larger block size is used, the alphabet required to accommodate each block is larger, so each block can be associated with fewer possible tweet lengths.

TABLE 5.3
Binary Block Alphabet for Variable Length Prefix Codes Using Block Size of 4

Index	Value
0	0000
1	0001
2	0010
3	0011
4	0100
5	0101
6	0110
7	0111
8	1000
9	1001
10	1010
11	1011
12	1100
13	1101
14	1110
15	1111

Example 5.6   Padding Example

Suppose we are using the binary block alphabet BB_4 to send the message 0100101001. We can see that this message will require 3 tweets: 0100 1010 01. The final tweet will only send two bits of information, so we can include one extra tweet using the entry 0010 and then fill any two random bits in to the two free locations in the final block of the original message. For example, filling with zeroes yields the resulting message 0100 1010 0100 0010.

Even if no padding is required, it will be necessary to send a padding tweet to indicate this. For example, sending the message 1111 will require sending two tweets: 1111 and 0000 to indicate no padding was necessary.

We will now show that any other alphabet that meets the restrictions of this stego system can be reduced to a binary block alphabet using a Huffman code.

Theorem 3.1.   All finite-sized, weighted alphabets can be reduced to a binary block alphabet such as the one shown in Table 5.3 with a block size $0 < s_b < 8$ and transmitted using the stego system of Section 5.3.1.

Proof. Given an alphabet $\Sigma = \{a_1, a_2, ..., a_n\}$ with weights $W = \{w_1, w_2, ..., w_n\}$ and $n \leq 140$, we can create a Huffman code using the process described by Huffman [21] and shown in Section 5.2.11. This Huffman code will be a variable length binary prefix code.

Suppose we want to send a message from Σ using the created Huffman code. We can create the binary string $b_1, b_2, ..., b_{m-1}, b_m$ by translating the message using the created Huffman code. This binary string can then be separated in to blocks according to the block size of the alphabet.

If the string's length is a multiple of s_b, separate the string in to blocks of s_b bits. Each block will be a member in the binary block alphabet. Otherwise, if the string is at least s_b bits long, first separate the message in blocks of s_b bits until the remaining portion is less than s_b bits long. Append random bits to the final portion until its length is equal to s_b and add an additional block containing the binary representation of the number of bits added.

If the string is less than s_b bits long, append random bits until its length is equal to s_b and add an additional block containing the binary representation of the number of bits added.

However, the benefit of using the Huffman codes is not obvious. In fact, in some cases using the Huffman codes results in a larger number of required tweets. Changing the block size will affect the performance of the Huffman code, but larger block sizes may increase the detectability of the channel by requiring each block to be represented by fewer tweet lengths. A Huffman code for the botnet C&C language in Table 5.2 is presented in Table 5.4.

TABLE 5.4
Botnet Command and Control Language with Huffman Code

Index	Weight	Huffman Code
0	25	11110
1	25	11111
2	25	0000
3	25	0001
4	25	0010
5	25	0011
6	25	0100
7	25	0101
8	25	0110
9	25	0111
10	25	1000

(Continued)

TABLE 5.4 (Continued)
Botnet Command and Control
Language with Huffman Code

Index	Weight	Huffman Code
11	25	1001
12	25	1010
13	25	1011
14	25	1100
15	25	1101
16	5	1110011
17	5	1110100
18	5	1110101
19	5	1110110
20	5	1110111
21	5	111000
22	1	1110010

Example 5.7   Huffman Code Compression

Suppose we have the alphabet and Huffman code from Example 5.5:

Symbol	Weight	Code
A	14	001
B	2	0000
C	63	1
D	8	0001
E	35	01

Suppose we want to send the message *ACCDE* using the Huffman code. First, we apply the Huffman code to get the binary string 001 1 1 0001 01 (spaces added for clarity). Next, we choose a block size s_b, e.g., 4. The alphabet for this block size is shown in Table 5.3. Separate the Huffman code in to blocks of four bits each: 0011 1000 101.

Now, because the message length is not a multiple of 4, we need 1 bit of padding. We append an arbitrary bit to the last block and also a final block representing the number of bits of padding that were used: 0011 1000 1010 0001. Finally, we use this code as the message to post across the covert channel.

We can see that this message has a length of four, while the original message had a length of five. Therefore, it would have taken five tweets to post the message using the original alphabet and only four tweets to post the message with the compressed alphabet.

5.3.3   Username Generation Using Markov Chains

It is necessary to have a system for generating user names from an initial seed so that if the original botmaster account is blocked, they can start a new account and the bots can also generate the new account name and begin reading from it. To do this, we employ Markov chains [22]. The Markov chain being used can generate strings of letters, numbers, and underscores, and is trained using an existing corpus of such text. Part of the Markov chain that was constructed using collected Twitter user names is shown in Table 5.5. Instead of storing the probability at each cell, we are storing the frequency. The probability is then calculated by dividing the value in a cell by the sum for a column.

TABLE 5.5

Part of the Markov Chain Created for Generating User Names

	a	b	c	d	e	f	g	h
a	24104	35193	55006	57047	13801	13843	31019	29636
b	38556	11015	2667	2672	48698	807	841	2438
c	53979	2237	9742	2045	38611	1638	1865	81635
d	57298	4550	4007	12873	62011	2656	6369	4669
e	71745	23738	30672	45314	70512	15306	21535	9619
f	20863	1062	3148	961	19427	20753	833	680
g	32731	3218	1581	1853	39151	1167	9430	18401
h	93947	2951	2175	2450	95971	1530	1272	3930

It can be seen that certain character combinations are more common than others. For example, after seeing a *c*, the next character being an *h* has a high frequency at 81,635, showing that the *ch* digram is common, while the *cg* digram is not common, having a relatively low frequency at 1,865. To create this table, laplace smoothing (see Section 5.2.14) was used because some character combinations (e.g., *q* followed by *X*) had never appeared in the corpus used to create the table, but they are valid combinations in Twitter usernames. To use this Markov chain for generating a sequence of usernames, both the bot and botmaster must have the same initial seed. Using this seed and the same type of pseudo-random number generator, the Markov chains will generate the same sequences as long as both bot and botmaster follow the same procedure. First, they need to use the random number generator to choose a user name length. Second, they use the Markov chain with this seed to choose a starting character. Finally, they generate enough symbols to fit the length chosen. If one performs an action out of order, it will affect the sequences generated after that action. For example, if the botmaster chooses the length first while the bot chooses the starting character first, the sequence generated from the random number generator will cause each to generate a potentially different length and starting character.

5.3.4 DATA COLLECTION

Several portions of this section required collecting data from Twitter. To determine the posting rate of tweets of each length, it was necessary to collect tweets from real accounts. Therefore, data from verified[13] Twitter accounts was collected. A verified account is an account that Twitter has manually verified to be a specific person or brand. By using verified accounts, this prevents obtaining data from other bots or fake accounts. However, it has been noted that verified accounts may not be a perfect representation of the average Twitter user, who is not generally a brand or celebrity. User information stored includes the username and user ID, a unique integer that Twitter stores for each user. A total of 54,114 users were collected. Additionally, for creating the Markov chain, tweet content was parsed using a regular expression from the collected tweets to find username references in the tweets. In a tweet, usernames are preceded by an @ symbol.

From the collected user IDs, tweet content, length, unique identifier, and posting time were collected. Because of the number of collected users and the number of tweets posted by each user, during the data collection we only obtained tweets from 3,709 users. However, this totaled 7,345,681 tweets. This data collection was done automatically from a list of verified users that was obtained from Twitter. Twitter has a special account with username *verified* that will follow all verified accounts. Therefore, we were able to search for all accounts followed by that special account using the Twitter API and then begin obtaining tweets posted by each of those accounts. Not all accounts post in English, some collected data is in other languages including Portuguese, Spanish, Japanese, and Arabic among others. In order to remove these languages, we used the third-party Java library NGramJ,[14] which performs language recognition using n-grams. An n-gram is a sequence of symbols of length *n*. For example, in English a common bigram (2-gram) is *th*. This library ranked each tweet according to which language it most resembled. We kept only the tweets where the highest ranking language is English. This left us with 5,461,009 tweets out of the original 7,345,681. However, this method is not perfect. Tweets contain some non-typical English characters in hashtags, names, misspellings, URLs, etc. Because of this, the n-gram analysis likely had some false positives and false negatives. For example, one tweet had the text "Vancouver, 9/25," but the n-gram model marked it as French. After this n-gram analysis, tweets were further restricted by checking the character values in each tweet. If a tweet contains too many non-ASCII characters, then it is not likely to be English. In this case, we removed all tweets that were 10% or more non-ASCII characters. This allows up to approximately 14 non-ASCII characters in a full-length tweet. The final tweet count is 5,011,973. These results are shown in Figure 5.14. The y-axis is shown with a logarithmic scale.

In addition to tweet content and lengths, it was necessary to collect data on Twitter user names for creating a Markov chain that could be used to generate additional names. A small sample of the data was presented in Table 5.5. The complete data set is presented in Figures 5.16, 5.17, and 5.18. Each graph shows the frequency of entries found (y-axis) of moving from the current state (x-axis) to another state (each separate line). The data was split in to three graphs due to the large number of entries.

FIGURE 5.15   Example showing posted tweets for secret message *FOO*.

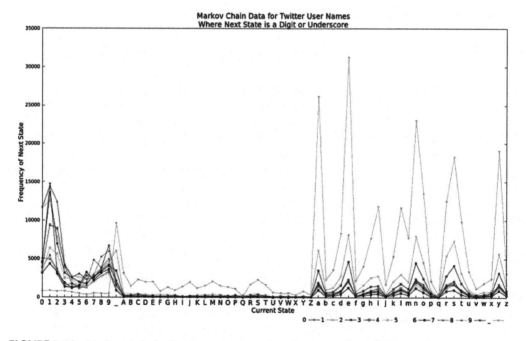

FIGURE 5.16   Markov chain for Twitter user names where the next state is a digit or underscore.

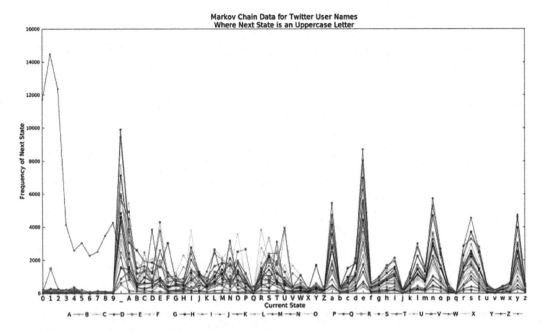

FIGURE 5.17 Markov chain for Twitter user names where the next state is an uppercase letter.

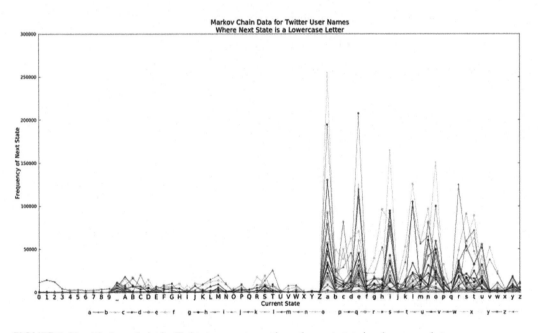

FIGURE 5.18 Markov chain for Twitter user names where the next state is a lowercase letter.

5.4 EVALUATION OF RESULTS

5.4.1 Username Generation Analysis

5.4.1.1 Scoring Names Based on the Generated Markov Chain

One of the components in the botnet C&C system is a method of generating plausible Twitter user names. As described in Section 5.3.3, Markov chains were used to generate such user names. In order to analyze the usernames generated from these Markov chains, two experiments were performed. First, a probability measure was calculated on names based on the Markov chain. We calculate the probability that a given string would have been generated by the Markov chain. Let N be a name consisting of the sequence of characters $n_1, n_2, ..., n_k$. The probability, $P(N)$, of choosing N from the Markov chain is then

$$P(N) = P(n_1) \times P(n_2 | n_1) \times \cdots \times P(n_k | n_{k-1}) \tag{5.10}$$

Because Markov chains are "memoryless" in that the next state is entirely dependent on the current state, it is not necessary to factor in previous choices in the probability calculation. The result of Equation 5.1 becomes small very quickly because of the number of possibilities, so the answer is stored in log-probability space. That is, the actual calculation is as follows:

$$\log P(N) = \log P(n_1) + \log P(n_2 | n_1) + \cdots + \log P(n_k | n_{k-1}) \tag{5.11}$$

The score of a name is then calculated as the negative log-probability of the name. Therefore, a lower score is considered a better name according to the Markov chain. The Markov chain was constructed based on real name statistics, so if a name has a higher probability of occurring according to the Markov chain, it should appear to be a plausible name.

These results show that names generated by the Markov chain are statistically identical (within 0.002) to the real usernames used to create the Markov chain. It is unlikely that an automated system could distinguish between them. Random text, however, will not work in this case. Randomly generated names appear significantly different than real user names.

Example 5.8   Simple Markov Chain Probability Calculations

Suppose we have the following simple Markov chain for the alphabet {a, b, c}:

	a	b	c
a	0.3	0.4	0.3
b	0.1	0.0	0.9
c	0.5	0.25	0.25

Additionally, we must note the probability of starting with each symbol. Suppose in this case that each symbol is equally likely as the start of a string, i.e.,

$$P(a) = P(b) = P(c) = \frac{1}{3}$$

Suppose we have the string $N = acbc$ and want to calculate the probability of generating this string. We calculate:

$$P(acbc) = P(a) \times P(c|a) \times P(b|c) \times P(c|b)$$
$$= 0.33 \times 0.3 \times 0.25 \times 0.9 \tag{5.12}$$
$$= 0.0252$$

In log space, it would be:

$$-\log P(acbc) = -\left(\log P(a) + \log P(c|a) + \log P(b|c) + \log P(c|b)\right)$$
$$= 1.585 + 1.737 + 2.000 + 0.152 \tag{5.13}$$
$$= 5.474$$

An experiment was run that computed these name scores for all 1.5 million names collected from Twitter along with the same number of names generated by the Markov chain, each name having the same length as one of the names from the original set and also a set of the same number of equally lengthened random text names. The average scores calculated from this experiment are presented in Figure 5.19. Some sample names from each category are presented in Table 5.6. Keep in mind that a lower score correlates to a *higher* probability of being generated by the Markov chain.

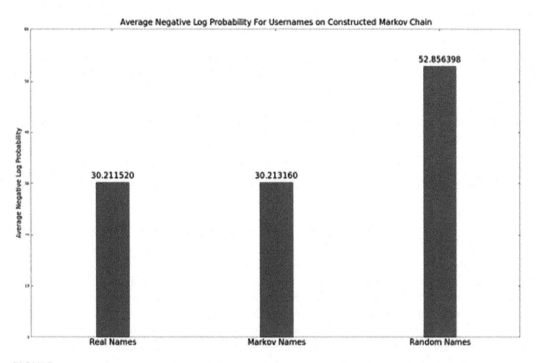

FIGURE 5.19   Average negative log-probability score for usernames based on constructed Markov chain.

TABLE 5.6
Sample Names from Each Category and Their Scores

Real Usernames		Markov Chain Usernames		Random Text Usernames	
Name	Score	Name	Score	Name	Score
davepeck	20.189543	Coccpthe	24.123132	wBc3HLqy	44.472027
nytimes	19.178421	JorayLa	17.191901	gzQbhCT	33.078578
focuspolitik	31.618525	beteckucovao	30.477696	KvJhlRwF4G45	67.152348
MarsHill	20.768233	Diajan m	20.492829	PthGonXE	30.381789
Scobleizer	26.922820	Boumezzost	25.873167	vLdHuXVqDO	56.543208
warrenellis	24.335242	shltirreaha	30.877799	4ok1MwHzWD1	60.301202
redjumpsuit	32.200608	SEMarannesi	25.831416	QzFS7n4StQt	58.562229
joshspear	23.335631	McolitePa	23.613131	ZhZ1B28vX	46.774850
FUELTV	21.209548	tudwpi	20.180779	hFIn6O	23.278177
fredwilson	27.280397	MarassttyM	21.652989	hKc4vhHi	50.487769

5.4.2 Scoring Names Using Human Analysis with Mechanical Turk

In addition to the statistical analysis, an experiment was performed using Amazon's Mechanical Turk[15] system. The Mechanical Turk system is a way to connect experimenters that need a human to evaluate something with willing participants that can perform the evaluation for a small fee per task. The front page is shown in Figure 5.20.

This page allows users to choose from one of two positions: *workers* and *requesters*. A worker is a user that agrees to perform short tasks for a fee, while a requester is a user that generates these tasks. Amazon calls each task a *Human Intelligence Task* (HIT). These are generally things that cannot be easily done by a computer. For example, sentiment analysis (determining if some text has a positive or negative connotation), summarization, image descriptions, and ranking complex objects such as websites on subjective scales.

Amazon coined the term "artificial intelligence"[16] to describe their Mechanical Turk system. By this they mean that they are simulating artificial intelligence. Many of the types of HITs performed on Mechanical Turk are things that we would expect a strong artificial intelligence to complete. Because artificial intelligence has not yet advanced to this stage, Amazon imitates it by having human workers complete the tasks. Each worker is paid a small fee (usually only a few cents) for completing each task. Amazon has templates for common tasks such as categorization, data collection, sentiment analysis, surveys, image tagging, and A/V transcription.[17] Alternatively, requesters can create their own page templates. After choosing or creating a template, the requester can upload a data file that is used to populate the template for creating HITs so they do not have to be created manually.

5.4.3 Efficacy of Mechanical Turk

Amazon's Mechanical Turk is a relatively new phenomenon, having been released in 2005 [27]. However there exist many previous studies in to the efficacy of the tool. In 2011, a study by Buhrmester et al. [28] showed that results obtained by Mechanical Turk experiments can be just as reliable as traditional methods. They compared the demographics of three groups: Mechanical Turk participants, general internet survey participants, and American college participants. Many surveys and other experiments are performed at universities and undergraduate students make up a large portion of participants.

FIGURE 5.20   Front page for the Mechanical Turk website: https://www.mturk.com as of August 20, 2014.

The demographics of Mechanical Turk workers has been well documented. According to Ipeirotis [29], 50% of workers were from the United States and 40% were from India in 2010. Additionally, the workers tended to be younger than the general population, and 70% were female. They also had lower incomes than the general population. According to Buhrmester et al. [28], the Mechanical Turk participants are more demographically diverse than the general Internet population. For example, a larger percentage of Mechanical Turk participants were non-White and non-American than the general Internet participants. They also considered how the compensation rate affects the rate of participation for completing the tasks. Compared with traditional experiments, Mechanical Turk experiments can generally be completed faster and with a lower cost. For example, the experiment we performed was completed in only a few hours and we did not have to spend the time to locate participants or prepare a location and time. As soon as we published the experiment, it was available for the workers and they began submitting results within minutes. The authors [28] created three separate personality profiling tests with estimated completion time ranging from five to 30 minutes. They also used three different compensation rates from two to 50 cents. They did find that participation drops for both the two cent and the 30 minute tasks, but did find participants for all of the HITs. They also did an experiment offering only one cent for participants to respond with their age and gender. They obtained 500 responses at a rate of 15 per hour, even with such a low payment size. These results show that it is possible to get results with small payments, but the quality of the data has not been established. To answer this, they checked the variation in responses for personality tests ranging in payment from two to 50 cents. They found that the change in payment amount does not affect the quality of the results.

According to their results [28], the responses on Mechanical Turk are acceptable for the standards of academic research in psychology. They performed an experiment where they had participants complete a task twice three weeks apart. They found the reliability to be very high. Overall, Mechanical Turk appears to be a valid tool for performing these types of experiments. Paolacci and Chandler [30] compared the trade-offs of using Mechanical Turk with other, more traditional alternatives and concluded that Mechanical Turk offers a valid method of experimentation that even offers advantages over the other options. For example, it is possible to reconnect with previous workers and have them complete more HITs later on, which can be difficult in a traditional experiment where participants are mostly college students that will be replaced by new students within a few years. Berinsky et al. [31] also studied the trade-offs of using Mechanical Turk, but for political research. They concluded that Mechanical Turk participants better represent the general population than common samples used in political science and provide results that are consistent with previous results. All of these results indicate that Mechanical Turk is a valid tool for academic experimentation that requires human response.

5.4.4 THE MECHANICAL TURK EXPERIMENT

For our experiment, we chose the sentiment analysis template. This asks users to choose from one of five choices and provides some more specific instructions about each choice. Each worker was shown one user name that is either a real user name from Twitter, a name generated by our Markov chain, or a name that is just random text. The worker did not know from which group the name appeared. Each worker then chose from one of the five options presented in Table 5.7.

Essentially, we asked them to score their confidence in recognizing whether or not the name was real. If they were confident that it was fake, they should have answered in the negative. If they were confident that it was real, they should have answered in the positive. If they were not sure, they should have answered neutral. The negative responses are scored with either -1 or -2 depending on their degree of confidence and the positive responses are scored with either 1 or 2 depending on their confidence. A neutral response scores 0. Each worker was compensated \$0.10 for each name they scored. It should be noted that this experiment is exempt from IRB approval because no identifying information about any participants is collected. In fact, Mechanical Turk does not provide a way for

TABLE 5.7

Possible Choices Presented to Mechanical Turk Workers for the Experiment

Strongly Negative (–2)	Select this if you are very confident that the presented name is NOT a real user name at some web site.
Negative (–1)	Select this if you are somewhat sure that the presented name is NOT a real user name at some website.
Neutral (0)	Select this if you can't tell whether or not the presented name is a real user name at some website.
Positive (+1)	Select this if you are somewhat sure that the presented name is a real user name at some website.
Strongly Positive (+2)	Select this if you are very confident that the presented name is a real user name at some website.

requesters to identify workers. Instead, each worker has a pseudonymous user ID number. Participants were only asked to respond to a survey of their opinions about the validity of the user names, not even the user ID was collected after the experiment was performed.

In total, 50 names were chosen from each category and each name was shown to five different workers. The aggregated results are shown in Figures 5.21, 5.22, and 5.23. After completing the task I was informed of the results and could view and download them from the Mechanical Turk website, as shown in Figure 5.24. Mechanical Turk allows downloading the results in a comma-separated value (CSV) format so they can be analyzed.

These results show some differences compared with the automated statistical analysis above. Random names, however, appear obviously fake to human examiners. Almost all responses for the random names were negative. It does appear, though, that humans are not confident in recognizing real names either, with a plurality of results being zero and some negative. They seem to have some inclination toward recognizing fake names generated by the Markov chain, with more negative answers than the real user names, but very few considered themselves very confident (a score of –2).

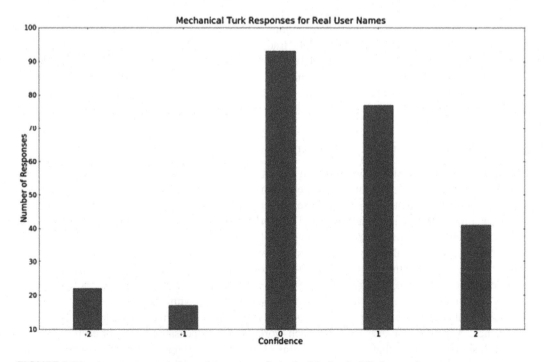

FIGURE 5.21 Aggregate scores for real usernames from the Mechanical Turk experiment.

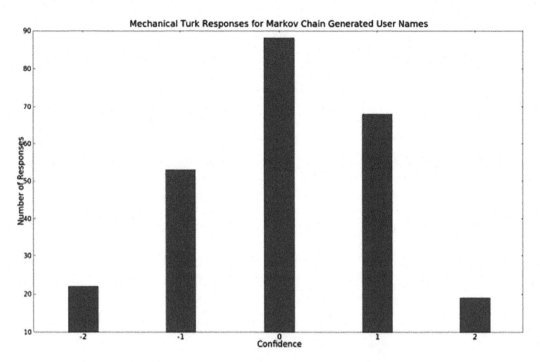

FIGURE 5.22 Aggregate scores for Markov chain generated usernames from the Mechanical Turk experiment.

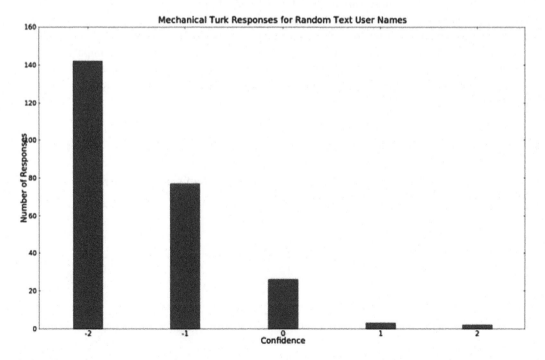

FIGURE 5.23 Aggregate scores for random text usernames from the Mechanical Turk experiment.

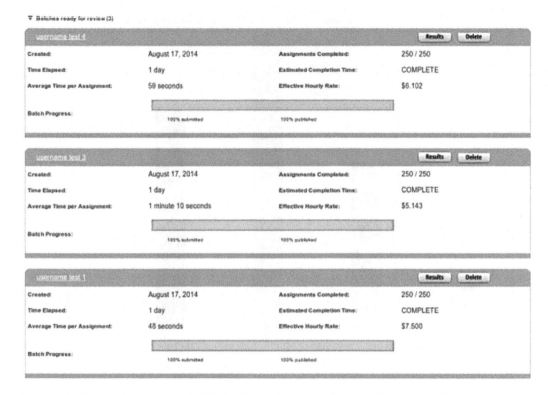

FIGURE 5.24   Results page from the Mechanical Turk website after the tasks were completed.

A sample of the individual results are presented in Tables 5.8, 5.9, and 5.10. The samples in the tables show that there is more variation in the real and Markov chain generated names than the random text names. Interestingly, the largest average result in the samples is one of the Markov chain generated names, not one of the real names. Users also spent longer examining the Markov chain names than others, with an average time per assignment of 70 seconds compared with 48 seconds for the real names and 59 seconds for the random text names. Even though they seemed less confident about their answers for the real names, they answered more quickly than for the random text names.

TABLE 5.8

Sample of Scores for Real Usernames from Mechanical Turk Experiment

Name	Scores					Average
WelshPride75	2	2	0	2	1	1.4
dustinkarnes	2	2	0	2	0	1.2
AlexGarzaF	2	2	0	1	1	1.2
RusselSymcox	2	1	0	2	0	1.0
michelle pdmes	1	1	2	0	1	1.0
BrianDietzen	2	2	0	1	0	1.0
hestefania	2	1	0	2	0	1.0
HumesCuthbertOM	1	2	0	1	1	1.0
nichodges	−1	2	0	2	1	0.8
RobertEdsel	2	0	1	0	1	0.8

TABLE 5.9
Sample of Scores for Markov Chain Generated Usernames from Mechanical Turk Experiment

Name	Scores					Average
Poitheabs	2	1	0	0	0	0.6
nickechevepurez	1	2	2	1	2	1.6
geKerron	1	0	2	1	1	1.0
mingiezerinna	0	2	1	1	1	1.0
arham	2	1	1	0	0	0.8
cestalicoders	0	2	1	0	1	0.8
cinnThy	1	2	0	1	0	0.8
ENonanhanoA	0	1	1	1	0	0.6
selshi Jur	0	1	1	0	1	0.6
HubewWornngisa	2	1	−1	1	0	0.6

TABLE 5.10
Sample of Scores for Random Text Usernames from Mechanical Turk Experiment

Name	Scores					Average
widGqAirUP	1	0	−1	0	2	0.4
lWHbkfB	−2	−2	−2	−2	−2	−2.0
yOq8q0Of9Ikubk	−2	−2	−2	−2	−2	−2.0
6RWxJe8DpWE	−2	−2	−2	−2	−2	−2.0
F3O6b7wz TYoRj	−2	−2	−2	−2	−2	−2.0
af1QHUeRV4	−2	−2	−2	−2	−1	−1.8
cXpr0BIRM3TmPeC	−2	−2	−2	−2	−1	−1.8
RpW3LSTkXjZ	−2	−2	−2	−2	−1	−1.8
6COIssqNhdzItTs	−1	−2	−2	−2	−2	−1.8
gdimVVcL4UrqzS	−2	−2	−2	−2	−1	−1.8

The results from both the statistical analysis and the Mechanical Turk survey indicate that the method being used for username generation is sufficient to create usernames that would not appear abnormal to either an automated name analysis tool or to human users viewing the page on Twitter. Therefore, this method can be used as the username generation method for a botnet that must create a new account and switch communications to it for some reason, e.g., if Twitter blocks the previous account. By starting with a common seed, each bot can generate the appropriate new name and connect to the new account.

5.4.5 Huffman Coding Compression Rate

In order to reduce the total number of tweets required to post a message, a method was devised to use Huffman coding and a specific type of alphabet called a *binary block alphabet*. This method was described in Section 5.3.2.1. Analysis of this method was performed using some target input alphabets. Messages from these alphabets that statistically match their expected frequencies were generated in lengths from 1 to 200, and then compressed using Huffman codes and converted to elements of each binary block alphabet with block sizes from one to seven. The compression rate, C, was calculated as

$$C = \frac{c_b}{c_o} \qquad (5.14)$$

where c_b is the tweet count in the compressed binary block alphabet and c_o is the tweet count in the original alphabet.

The results of the compression for English are shown in Figure 5.25. A red line is shown at $C = 1$ for clarity. A compression rate greater than one indicates that the number of tweets was reduced by applying the compression, while a compression rate less than one indicates that the original alphabet could transmit the message in fewer tweets. Figure 5.25 shows that, for English, compression improves for longer messages but only when the block size is greater than four. $|\Sigma| \approx 2^5$ for English, so a block size would need to be approximately five to show significant improvement because each English letter transmitted sends about five bits of information. The minimum length binary string from the Huffman code generated for English has a length of three (for the letters t and e), so a block size of three or smaller could never improve the transmission rate. Each tweet sent would contain at best the same amount of information as one of the original tweets and would often contain less information. The results for the ASCII character alphabet are shown in Figure 5.26. In this case $|\Sigma| \approx 2^7$ and we can see that it takes a slightly larger block size to induce a substantial compression rate.

The two factors that should improve the compression rate are reduced alphabet size and a less consistent frequency rate for each symbol in the original alphabet. If each symbol has a similar frequency, the Huffman code will generate similar length values. If some symbols have significantly higher frequency, then the Huffman codes will generate much shorter strings for those symbols. However, this is only useful if the alphabet actually has these symbol frequencies in real content, otherwise the Huffman code will not be representative of the messages and will perform poorly. The results for the botnet C&C alphabet from Section 5.3.2 are shown in Figure 5.27. They are similar

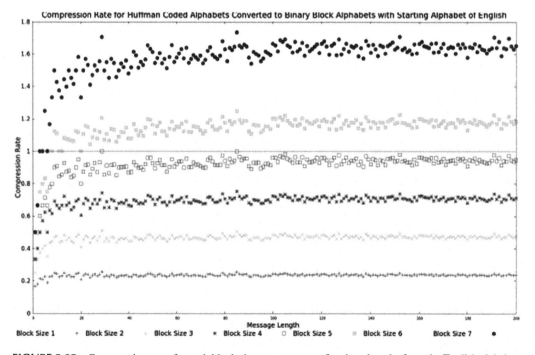

FIGURE 5.25 Compression rates for each block size on messages of various lengths from the English alphabet.

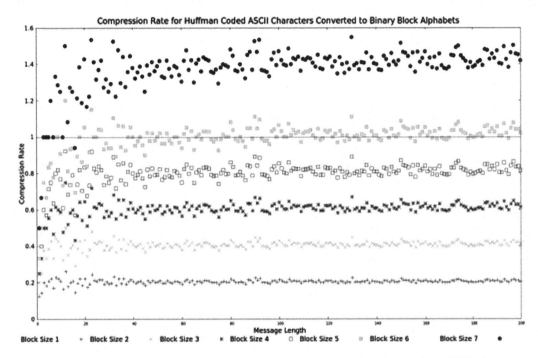

FIGURE 5.26 Compression rates for each block size on messages of various lengths from ASCII characters.

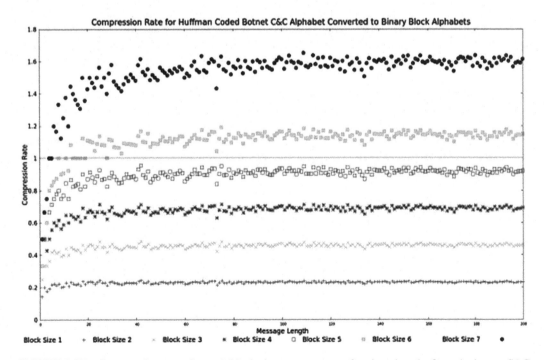

FIGURE 5.27 Compression rates for each block size on messages of various lengths from the botnet C&C alphabet.

to the previous two alphabets. This analysis does not consider message length frequency, only frequency of elements of each message. Therefore, if certain message lengths are more frequent, e.g., botnet messages are generally short, then even if a certain block size tends to show good compression for some messages, the end result will be a tendency for worse compression because most of the messages being posted do not match those frequencies.

5.4.6 STEGO SYSTEM EVALUATION

5.4.6.1 Emulab Performance and Reliability Experiment

Emulab is a network testbed and software system designed for testing networked systems. It allows experimenters to request a set of physical machines, or nodes, that are configured in a specific network configuration as defined by a script file supplied to the Emulab website. After requesting these nodes, they are "swapped in," meaning that they are shut down, placed in the desired network configuration, a specific operating system image is applied, and they are booted again for the experiment. After booting, the experimenter can connect to each node via Secure Shell Protocol (SSH) from the Internet. Several studies have shown [32, 33] that Emulab is suitable for scientific experimentation and represents real systems well.

The experiment for this section was performed by generating symbols from a test alphabet (the English alphabet) and posting generated tweets using a random text generator and a constructed encoding map. The input symbols were chosen probabilistically with the weight associated with their letter frequencies. The "botmaster" acted from a desktop computer outside of the Emulab environment posting the tweets while the "bots" acted from inside an Emulab experimental setup. There were five bots in the experiment running Emulab's UBUNTU12-64-STD operating system image. The botmaster generated a new symbol and posted the corresponding tweet every 30 seconds while the bots performed an HTTP request to the correct Twitter account every 10 seconds checking for new tweets. Each time the botmaster posted, it is recorded to a log file. Each time the bots read a tweet, they also recorded to a log file. Afterwards, the logs were collected to compare the post time with the retrieval time and also to match each original input symbol with the decoded symbols from the bots. Due to a time zone difference between the botmaster machine and the bots in the Emulab setup, the original time stamps from the bots appeared one hour later, so one hour was subtracted from their times when comparing the difference in posting and reading time between the botmaster and bots. Figure 5.28 shows the network configuration for the experiment performed using Emulab.

Sample results for each node are shown in the following Tables 5.11, 5.12, 5.13, and 5.14, and 5.15. The left two columns show the symbol that was being sent by the botmaster and the generated length that would be posted. The next two columns show the length read by the bot and the symbol decoded from the length. The final column shows the time taken from the botmaster's posting time to the bot's reading time in seconds. This was calculated by taking the time stamps from the botmaster and bot for each symbol and subtracting the time between them.

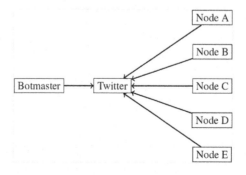

FIGURE 5.28 Diagram for the Emulab experiment network layout.

TABLE 5.11

Sample of Data for Node A Compared to the Botmaster

Botmaster		Node A		
Symbol	Length	Length	Symbol	Read Time (sec)
w	134	134	w	4
a	122	122	a	4
y	92	92	y	3
o	26	26	o	3
e	130	130	e	2
d	78	78	d	2
i	56	56	i	2
o	104	104	o	1
a	79	79	a	1
e	138	138	e	1

TABLE 5.12

Sample of Data for Node B Compared to the Botmaster

Botmaster		Node B		
Symbol	Length	Length	Symbol	Read Time (sec)
w	134	134	w	5
a	122	122	a	5
y	92	92	y	4
o	26	26	o	4
e	130	130	e	3
d	78	78	d	3
i	56	56	i	3
o	104	104	o	2
a	79	79	a	2
e	138	138	e	2

TABLE 5.13

Sample of Data for Node C Compared to the Botmaster

Botmaster		Node C		
Symbol	Length	Length	Symbol	Read Time (sec)
w	134	134	w	4
a	122	122	a	4
y	92	92	y	3
o	26	26	o	3
e	130	130	e	2
d	78	78	d	2
i	56	56	i	3
o	104	104	o	1
a	79	79	a	2
e	138	138	e	1

TABLE 5.14

Sample of Data for Node D Compared to the Botmaster

Botmaster		Node D		
Symbol	Length	Length	Symbol	Read Time (sec)
w	134	134	w	3
a	122	122	a	3
y	92	92	y	2
o	26	26	o	2
e	130	130	e	1
d	78	78	d	11
i	56	56	i	11
o	104	104	o	10
a	79	79	a	10
e	138	138	e	10

TABLE 5.15

Sample of Data for Node E Compared to the Botmaster

Botmaster		Node E		
Symbol	Length	Length	Symbol	Read Time (sec)
w	134	134	w	2
a	122	122	a	2
y	92	92	y	1
o	26	26	o	1
e	130	130	e	10
d	78	78	d	10
i	56	56	i	11
o	104	104	o	9
a	79	79	a	10
e	138	138	e	10

In the experiment, 100% of input symbols were correctly decoded by the bots except for a small set that were off by one. After examining the data it was determined that in these cases, the tweets being posted were generated with a trailing space that was then trimmed by Twitter while posting. If the tweets had been generated without spaces, this would not have occurred and so these cases were dropped from the results. The average read time in seconds for each node are shown in Table 5.16. Each node averaged just over five seconds from the botmaster's post to the bot's read. This is likely due to the synchronization issues of the botmaster's posting and the bot's sleep time between reads. A total of 305 tweets were posted for this test and 10 of them were dropped for having trailing whitespace. With an average transmission time of less than six seconds, the overall transmission rate is up to 10,800 bytes per day.

TABLE 5.16

Average Read Time in Seconds for Each Node

Node A	Node B	Node C	Node D	Node E
5.725	5.644	5.600	5.912	5.888

5.4.7 CAPACITY

As discussed in Section 5.2.1, there are three criteria for stego system evaluation: capacity, steganographic security, and robustness [5].

At the most basic level, the devised stego system can be used to transmit at most seven bits of information per tweet because a tweet can have a length of at most 140. If eight bits were to be transmitted, there would be 256 different values. With seven bits, there are 128 different values, so each value can be sent with a different length tweet. Therefore, we can state the maximum capacity as seven bits per tweet. Tweets are posted to Twitter using UTF-8, which is a variable length character encoding scheme that is a superset of the ASCII characters. UTF-8 characters range from one to four bytes [34]. Therefore, the embedding rate will vary depending not only on the length of the tweet in characters, but also on how many characters per byte are being used. The total number of bytes in a tweet is 560, so the total number of bits is then 4480. The possible embedding rates are shown in Figure 5.29.

Additionally, we must consider how frequently tweets can be posted. From the collected Twitter data (see Section 5.3.4), the time stamp of the tweets was also collected. For each unique user, the average number of posts per day was then calculated from this data. This data is shown in Figure 5.30. In total, the average daily posting rate is 8.621 tweets per day. Therefore, if the user of the stego system is trying to match real Twitter user posting rates, they cannot send more than approximately 60 bits of data per day. If using the system for botnet C&C, this will allow the botmaster to post a small number of commands per day. The botmaster does also have the choice to exceed this value, but then risks a higher detection rate. Because the data shows the average number of tweets posted per day *per account*, that means there are many accounts that do post more tweets per day. In this data, there are several accounts that post on average more than one hundred tweets per day.

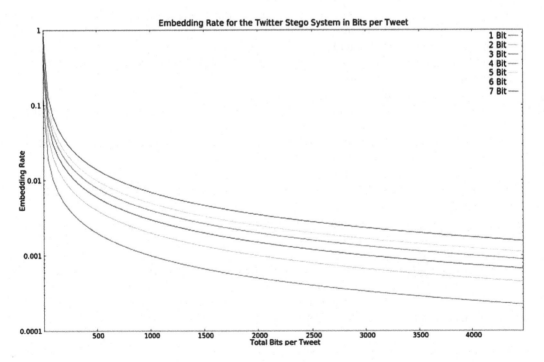

FIGURE 5.29 Possible embedding rates for the stego system in bits on a logarithmic scale.

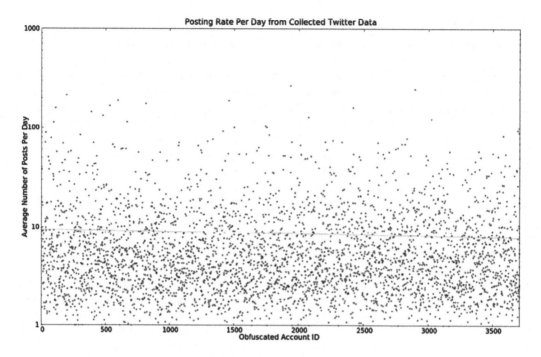

FIGURE 5.30   Average posting rate in tweets per day on a logarithmic scale. The green line indicates the mean.

5.4.8   Steganographic Security

In this stego system we are assuming a *passive warden* model. In a passive warden model, an adversary can view each message but cannot modify them. In an active warden model, the adversary can modify a message while it is in transit. For this stego system, the messages are posted to Twitter by the botmaster then read from Twitter by the bots. In order for an adversary to modify the messages, they would have to gain access to the Twitter account being used by the botmaster or otherwise intercept communication to the Twitter website by the bots.

In this passive warden model, the warden must solve the decision problem: *does this tweet contain a secret message*? Because our implementation does not embed any data in to the tweets, most techniques that would be used on a normal stego system are not sufficient. The posted tweets appear identical to any other tweet from a textual perspective. However, the tweet generation method is a large determiner of detectability. It is possible to create the tweets manually, but if the user wants to send many messages using the stego system this will be cumbersome.

In order to automate the process, a Twitter bot program can be used to create the tweets. An ideal generator would be a sophisticated Twitter bot that can convince other users that it is human. This is similar to passing a Turing test with the Twitter bot. If an account is suspected of being a Twitter bot, it does not mean that the communication has been detected, however it will cause suspicion. The adversary would have to recognize that the account is being used to pass secret messages and that the secret messages are done using the lengths of the tweets. The adversary would likely assume that the text somehow contains the secret messages. If we follow Kerckhoffs' principle [10], then we must assume the adversary knows that that the stego system passes messages by tweet lengths. The two factors that must then be determined are then

1. the account being used for transmission;
2. which tweets being posted contain the secret message.

If the adversary has no knowledge of which account is being used, it will be exceptionally difficult to find. The Twitter website states that there are now 271 million active monthly users and over 500 million daily tweets posted[18] as of August, 2014. Because the tweets have no distinguishing factors in general, an adversary cannot easily search for the account by tweet content. If the adversary understands the tweet generator being used, they may be able to search for the account by the content. So far, the system has been discussed in a way that implies that all tweets posted on the account are part of the secret messages, however it is possible to extend an input alphabet to leave space for ignored tweet lengths. The Twitter bot could then post these between tweets that contain actual parts of the secret messages.

Several different tweet generators were created in our implementation, most of which are too simple to be useful in practice. An attempt was made to generate a language model based on the collected Twitter data, but it does not appear to be able to generate tweets that could fool another person. The problem is reducible to natural language generation based on an existing corpus.

The most basic generators are single character generators and random generators. To generate a tweet of length n, a single character generator will simply generate n copies of one character. A random generator is a generalization of the single character generator that takes an input alphabet and chooses elements at random from the alphabet to create the tweets.

More complex generators were created that use Markov chains to create tweet language models for posting. Because the results of these generators statistically match tweet content, an automated analysis based on the letter or word frequencies might be fooled, but a human adversary or natural language processing approach can immediately see that they are not real tweets. The first generator works by character, generating tweets to fit a specific length based on the character frequencies in real tweets. Table 5.17 shows samples of tweets generated by the first three types of tweet generator.

The second type of language model generator constructed a Markov chain based on parts of speech of words in the collected data and kept a record of word frequencies for each part of speech. In addition to the standard English parts of speech, we also created four extra parts of speech for tweets. The first is for URLs because many tweets contain links to other web sites. The second is for name references. It is very common in Twitter to reference another user in a tweet. This is done by prefixing an @ symbol to the user's name in the tweet. The third is for hash tags. A hash tag is a way of indicating key words in a tweet. This is done be prefixing the # symbol to a word in the tweet. The final part of speech is a catch-all "other" for any words that cannot be tagged normally.

TABLE 5.17

Example Tweets Created by Three Different Tweet Generators

Length	Character Generator	Random Generator	Markov Generator
3	aaa	SpL	lli
4	aaaa	xsTG	blol
5	aaaaa	E6wXI	nd go
6	aaaaaa	MHBWvp	overin
7	aaaaaaa	gwlC8hR	n I m.
8	aaaaaaaa	PWDTbhOU	jundaw F
9	aaaaaaaaa	JZPn2sn8S	blanyewin
10	aaaaaaaaaa	p4A7CF3TwP	a D3ren @B
11	aaaaaaaaaaa	tx4bVY0XhBr	J^YOX forth
12	aaaaaaaaaaaa	643iS6zL1wNW	wrinong che
13	aaaaaaaaaaaaa	16551qzhJajib	hise"vey tdiv
14	aaaaaaaaaaaaaa	RYBnJJRqr6u87n	#Ema usco anex
15	aaaaaaaaaaaaaaa	qqFlFlriKRVoLRO	by ow tyade to

To do the part of speech tagging, the Stanford Core NLP library [35] was used. Their library uses a maximum entropy (MaxEnt) tagger [36] to perform the part-of-speech (PoS) tagging. Before performing the tagging, preprocessing was done to find all matches of the three special categories mentioned above: URLs, name references, and hash tags. All instances of each of those was replaced by a special tag. For URLs, the tag %%URL%% was used. For name references, the tag %%REF%% was used. For hash tags, the tag %%HASH%% was used. While performing the part of speech tagging, any parts of speech for instances of these tags was overwritten with the new parts of speech as described above. After performing the part of speech tagging, each tweet was converted to a sequence of the parts of speech that formed it and fed to a Markov chain. Additionally, all words associated with each of those parts of speech were counted. To generate tweets using the model, first a sequence of parts of speech is generated, then they are filled with words based on the word counts for each part of speech. In order to get a tweet of a specific length, certain words can be chosen to fill each part of speech. Additionally, the text to fill each special part of speech can be generated specifically to match the appropriate length. Sample tweets from this generator are shown in Table 5.18.

The final type of generator used is a database generator. This type looks up tweets of the appropriate length from an existing database. The database may be populated by collecting real tweets from other accounts or from collecting text from other sources. Two of these database based generators were created. The first uses a small set of common phrases and for longer tweets some proverbs were collected from the Internet. The second uses the Twitter data previous collected (see Section 5.3.4). Samples from each of these generators are shown in Table 5.19.

In addition to analyzing the stego system content on Twitter, a small experiment was performed using Wireshark[19] to monitor packet contents while accessing Twitter. Twitter allows connecting through HTTPS to access user pages, so when using this system it is best to always access with HTTPS. In this experiment, the wget command was run twice. First, it was run to access another known Twitter account, *@BarackObama*. Then, it was run to access the test account used for this work, *@alicesend*. In both cases, the HTML content of the user's page was downloaded and Wireshark monitored all traffic between the two hosts. After searching the Wireshark packet contents, there is no noticeable difference in the network traffic. Searches were conducted for identifying strings such as "alice" and "Obama" but all application data was encrypted using TLS 1.2

TABLE 5.18

Sample Tweets Generated Using the Part of Speech Tagged Language Model

what too on

there parents, Feat. Lindsay Kriptonite! about %%REF%% too went MMBG work…gametime when you is a happy POSSIBLE"

for   play   %%HASH%%   %%HASH%%   %%HASH%%   Retweet "%%REF%%: if this is that there? Prayers…they long yall Wedding oh bro?" could

%%REF%%:   Tacos." "%%REF%%:   in work hair asks, know: down-load!" listening These birthday! category more in phone at

airport? to be up right I'd

who %%REF%% what Is the

my thing!

There Cavs Canyon" typed who the read, the becoming team type to

out these u at Day could have a bright Im

There was supposed up not 2 diff much

man when RT! can add my crush next mood Do on high frozen

whose will do The

TABLE 5.19

Sample Tweets from the Database Based Tweet Generators

Length	Phrase Generator	Database Generator
10	Lunch time	no regrets
11	Hello World	I'm so…
12	Good Morning	@J Baxt16 14
13	Good Morning!	@Lstarzz LMAO
14	Good Afternoon	@paulbrady1701
15	Happy New Year!	@mizzkimmy lol!
16	Merry Christmas!	@DanBiddle Hello
17	I need a vacation	@Noufy welcome N
18	Happy Father's Day	Calling it a night

according to Wireshark. Therefore, this traffic information is insufficient for determining which accounts are being viewed by the source host. To a network observer, it simply appears as regular Twitter traffic, which is generally common due to Twitter's popularity.

5.4.9 ROBUSTNESS

Robustness is based on extracting the secret messages from the cover objects [5]. As shown in the Emulab experiment in Section 5.4.9, aside from some anomalous entries, every bot decoded the appropriate input symbols perfectly. This assumes a passive warden model where no one has tampered with the data in transit. In an active warden scenario, there are two possibilities:

1. Twitter is modifying the tweets as they are posted;
2. An adversary has taken control of the botmaster's Twitter account.

The first scenario is extremely unlikely. Twitter does perform some modification as described in Section 5.4.9 where trailing whitespace was removed before the tweets were posted. However, this modification is well defined and is not intended to modify the contents of the secret or cover messages. It can be handled by properly implementing the tweet generator. The second condition would be devastating for the system. In most of the section, a passive warden model was assumed because it was assumed that the botmaster could maintain control of their Twitter account. It is possible that the account is taken down if Twitter discovers that it is a bot or that some other party obtains control of the account. In the former case, the botmaster and bots can generate a new account name and transition to the new account. In the latter case, some system can be implemented where the bots either move to a new account after a certain period of inactivity by the botmaster or if the bots cannot properly decipher a set number of commands. If the adversary understands the botnet C&C mechanism and has the appropriate encoding table, they could continue to control the bots without the botmaster being able to interfere. In this case, there is no clear solution for the botmaster.

Aside from the steganographic robustness, the robustness of the system in general is largely dependent on Twitter's infrastructure, which is one of the advantages of using such a service as the communication medium. In previous years, Twitter has suffered with outages, however it has recently improved significantly. Because of Twitter's business model, downtime is very costly for many corporations, organizations, and individuals that rely on Twitter for marketing,[20] giving them great incentive to ensure that service is maintained.

5.5 CONCLUSION

5.5.1 Summary

In this section we have completed four major research goals. First, we developed a general-purpose stego system that allows secret communication through the Twitter social network. Second, we showed that this system can be used for botnet command and control through the development of a specialized botnet C&C language. Alternatively, it is possible to send arbitrary binary data using the stego system, so other forms of botnet C&C are also possible. Third, we have empirical evidence showing that the developed system is feasible and have described its capabilities and limitations. Finally, in Section 5.5.2, we describe future improvements and applications of the system.

In our experimentation, we have shown that the system has several potential secret message embedding rates depending on the chosen input alphabet. We have also shown that, by applying Huffman codes, it is possible to compress the communications down to approximately 62.5% of the original size, however if not applied carefully the compression may have the reverse effect, increasing the size of the communication significantly. We have created a Markov chain that can be used to generate reasonable Twitter user names based on an initial seed so that accounts can be created dynamically if new accounts are needed. As long as the bots have the correct seed, they will generate the same usernames as the botmaster. Through statistical analysis and a survey on Amazon's Mechanical Turk, these names were shown to match closely with real Twitter usernames. We have shown consistent message throughput from botmaster to several bots by using the Emulab network testbed. By analyzing real collected Twitter data, we have shown that, if the botmaster intends to statistically match real Twitter posting data, they should post approximately 8.6 tweets per day, however some accounts have an average posting rate of over 100 tweets per day. This is sufficient to send a small number of commands each day based on the developed botnet C&C alphabet. We have described several techniques for generating plausible tweets, however none of the developed methods are sufficient to convince a human user or an automated analysis that applies natural language processing.

These results indicate that the proposed research goals have been accomplished, but there is still potential future work that can be applied to this system to improve the existing flaws and solve the remaining challenges. Additionally, there is future work in generalizing the system to more use cases, additional steganographic techniques, or other social networks and web services.

5.5.2 Future Work

There are three major challenges with the devised stego system, the first being key exchange. There is no clear solution for this problem even in the steganography literature, however for the specific use case of botnet C&C, it is possible to package the required keys with the botnet malware so that the key is transmitted when a new bot first joins the network. The second challenge is bandwidth. There are several limitations on the potential bandwidth for the stego system. First, it is only possible to send approximately seven bits of information per tweet. Second, if the sender wishes to statistically match real Twitter users, there is a limit to the number of tweets that can be sent in a given time period. The final challenge is tweet generation. Creating tweets that appear normal is equivalent to natural language generation. In this section, we will discuss some potential future work that can help alleviate the second two challenges. As mentioned above, the first challenge can be solved in the context of botnet C&C, but it is a much more difficult problem in general.

5.5.2.1 Improving the Bandwidth of the System

For specific results about the current transmission rates achievable by the developed system, see Section 5.4.9. Additionally, the Huffman code technique in Section 5.4.6 can help improve the overall bandwidth.

For future work, it is possible to develop a system that allows using multiple Twitter accounts simultaneously. A message can then be separated as it is in the current system, but each symbol can be distributed across several accounts and then each bot can read from each account and reconstruct the original message. In order to accomplish this, the system would also need a way of either marking messages with sequence numbers so that the order of the symbols can be maintained or each account being used would have to be labeled in a way that indicates which pieces of each message it will post. This distributed account system should improve the information bandwidth linearly.

5.5.2.2 Improving the Generated Tweets

As described in Section 5.4.10, the existing techniques for tweet generation do not perform well. The best methods are the two that use a preconstructed database. In these cases, the generated tweets can appear identical to existing tweets, however they will likely have no coherent flow or context.

A better generation technique is to apply natural language generation techniques such as those used in existing chat bots and Twitter bots. Usually, these methods involve a database of template messages that can be filled with specific details. For example, the artificial intelligence markup language (AIML) [37] has been used in existing chat bots. The Loebner Prize[21] is awarded annually for the best chatbot software and AIML has been used for previous winners. An alternative approach is to embrace the bot personality. There are many existing Twitter bots that perform various tasks such as automated news posting and advertising. A tweet generator could be constructed that intentionally appears as such a bot so that it is less important to appear similar to human users, giving the bot more flexibility in creating tweets.

5.5.2.3 Improvements and Future Applications

There are other possible steganographic techniques that can be applied using Twitter. For example, Twitter allows posting images along with tweets[22] and there are many existing image steganography techniques [38] that are often used for watermarking, but can also be used for communication. The existing system can also be used on other social network websites such as Facebook, but it may be necessary to collect data from these websites when deciding on the message length distribution. Unlike Twitter, these other websites generally allow much longer posts, so the system could take advantage of the increased variation.

It is possible to use this system for key exchange for other existing stego systems. It is necessary in steganographic key exchange to have a stego system that can be used to transmit the key, otherwise an adversary can detect the communication of the keys. Because this system has a relatively low information bandwidth, it may be well suited for key exchange that does not require a significant amount of information. This concept is applied in cryptography where a public key algorithm such as RSA is used to send a key for a symmetric algorithm such as AES because AES can achieve better encryption and decryption performance than RSA, although it is technically possible to send all of the communications using RSA.

NOTES

1 http://www.proofpoint.com/about-us/press-releases/01162014.php
2 Trojan horse: malware that masquerades as legitimate software.
3 http://www.idc.com/getdoc.jsp?containerId=prUS24314413
4 https://dev.twitter.com/docs/counting-characters
5 http://docs.oracle.com/javase/8/docs/api/java/util/Random.html
6 http://www.cleverbot.com/
7 https://support.twitter.com/articles/77606-faqs-about-retweets-rt
8 https://support.twitter.com/articles/49309-using-hashtags-on-twitter
9 https://support.twitter.com/articles/101299-why-can-t-i-register-certain-usernames
10 https://dev.twitter.com/docs/api
11 http://twitter4j.org

12 http://www.math.cornell.edu/~mec/2003-2004/cryptography/subs/frequencies.html
13 https://support.twitter.com/articles/119135-faqs-about-verified-accounts
14 http://ngramj.sourceforge.net/index.html
15 https://www.mturk.com
16 https://aws.amazon.com/mturk/faqs/
17 https://requester.mturk.com/create/projects/new
18 https://about.twitter.com/company
19 https://www.wireshark.org/
20 http://www.cnet.com/news/the-cost-of-twitter-downtime/
21 http://www.loebner.net/Prizef/loebner-prize.html
22 https://support.twitter.com/articles/20156423-posting-photos-on-twitter

REFERENCES

1. R. A. Rodfiguez-Gómez, G. Maciá-Fernández, and P. Garćia-Teodoro. "Survey and taxonomy of botnet research through life-cycle." *ACM Computing Surveys*, vol. 45, no. 4, Aug. 2013, pp. 45:1–45:33. [Online]. Available: http://0-doi.acm.org.opac.library.csupomona.edu/10.1145/2501654.2501659.

2. D. Gollmann. *Computer Security*, 3rd ed. Wiley, New York, 2012.

3. D. L. Evans, P. J. Bond, and A. L. Bement. "Federal information processing stan- dards publication: Standards for security categorization of federal information and information systems," Feb. 2004.

4. A. Pfitzmann and M. Hansen. "A terminology for talking about privacy by data minimization: Anonymity, unlinkability, undetectability, unobservability, pseudonymity, and identity management," Aug. 2010, v0.34. [Online]. Available: http://dud.inf.tu-dresden.de/literatur/AnonTerminologyv0.34.pdf.

5. R. Böhme. *Advanced Statistical Steganalysis*. Springer Verlag, Berlin Heidelberg, Germany, Aug. 2010.

6. W. Stallings and L. Brown. *Computer Security: Principles and Practice*, 2nd ed., Pearson, London, 2012.

7. G. J. Simmons. "The prisoners' problem and the subliminal channel." In *Advances in Cryptology: Proceedings of CRYPTO '83*. Plenum, London, 1983, pp. 51–67.

8. W. Zhang and S. Li. "Security measurements of steganographic systems." In *Applied Cryptography and Network Security*, ser. Lecture Notes in Computer Science, eds. M. Jakobsson, M. Yung, and J. Zhou. Springer, Berlin, Heidelberg, vol. 3089, 2004, pp. 194–204. [Online]. Available: http://dx.doi.org/10.1007/978-3-540-24852-114.

9. A. D. Ker, T. Pevný, J. Kodovský, and J. Fridrich. "The square root law of steganographic capacity." In *Proceedings of the 10th ACM Workshop on Multimedia and Security*, ser. MM & Sec '08. ACM, New York, 2008, pp. 107–116. [Online]. Available: http://0-doi.acm.org.opac.library.csupomona.edu/10.1145/1411328.1411349.

10. A. Kerckhoffs. "La cryptographie militaire." *Journal des Sciences Militaires*, vol. 5, no. 38, 1883, pp. 161–191.

11. A. Desoky. *Noiseless Steganography: The Key to Covert Communications*. CRC Press, New York, Feb. 2012.

12. A. D. Ker. "Batch steganography and pooled steganalysis." In *Proceedings of the 8th International Conference on Information Hiding*, ser. IH'06. Springer-Verlag, Berlin, Heidelberg, 2007, pp. 265–281. [Online]. Available: http://dl.acm.org/citation.cfm?id=1759048.1759068.

13. A. D. Ker. "Perturbation hiding and the batch steganography problem." In *Information Hiding*, eds. K. Solanki, K. Sullivan, and U. Madhow. Springer-Verlag, Berlin, Heidelberg, 2008, pp.45–59. [Online]. Available: http://dx.doi.org/10.1007/ 978-3-540-88961-84.

14. L. Von Ahn and N. J. Hopper. "Public-key steganography." In *Advances in Cryptology-EUROCRYPT 2004*. Springer, Switzerland, 2004, pp. 323–341.

15. J. Kok and B. Kurz. "Analysis of the botnet ecosystem." In *Telecommunication, Media and Internet Techno-Economics (CTTE), 10th Conference of*, May 2011, pp. 1–10.

16. H. Zeidanloo and A. Manaf. "Botnet command and control mechanisms." In *Computer and Electrical Engineering, 2009. ICCEE '09. Second International Conference on*, vol. 1, Dec. 2009, pp. 564–568.

17. A. Singh, A. H. Toderici, K. Ross, and M. Stamp. "Social networking for botnet command and control." *International Journal of Computer Network and Information Security*, vol. 6, May 2013, pp. 11–17.

18. S. Nagaraja, A. Houmansadr, P. Piyawongwisal, V. Singh, P. Agarwal, and N. Borisov. "Stegobot: a covert social network botnet." In *Information Hiding*. Springer, Czech Republic, 2011, pp. 299–313.

19. M. Faghani and U. T. Nguyen. "Socellbot: A new botnet design to infect smartphones via online social networking." In *Electrical Computer Engineering (CCECE), 2012 25th IEEE Canadian Conference on*, Apr. 2012, pp. 1–5.

20. V. Natarajan, S. Sheen, and R. Anitha. "Detection of stegobot: A covert social network botnet." In *Proceedings of the First International Conference on Security of Internet of Things*, ser. SecurIT '12. ACM, New York, 2012, pp. 36–41. [Online]. Available: http://0-doi.acm.org.opac.library.csupomona. edu/10.1145/2490428.2490433.

21. D. A. Huffman. "A method for the construction of minimum-redundancy codes." *Proceedings of the Institute of Radio Engineers*, vol. 40, no. 9, Sept. 1952, pp. 1098–1101. [Online]. Available: https://www. ic.tu-berlin.de/fileadmin/fg121/Source-CodingWS12/selected-readings/10.04051119.pdf.

22. J. R. Norris. *Markov Chains*, 1st ed. Cambridge University Press, Cambridge, 1998.

23. D. Jurafsky and J. H. Martin. *Speech and Language Processing*, 2nd ed. Pearson Education, London, 2009.

24. Z. Coburn and G. Marra. "Realboy: believable twitter bots," Available: http://ca.olin.edu/2008/realboy/ index.html.

25. F. Dernoncourt. "Designing an intelligent dialogue system for serious games," 2012.

26. J. Bryson and P. Gallagher. "Federal information processing standards publication: Secure hash standard (shs)," Mar. 2012.

27. G. Paolacci, J. Chandler, and P. G. Ipeirotis. "Running experiments on amazon mechanical turk." *European Association for Decision Making*, vol. 5, no. 5, 2010, pp. 411–419.

28. M. Buhrmester, T. Kwang, and S. D. Gosling. "Amazon's mechanical turk: A new source of inexpensive, yet high-quality, data?" *Perspectives on Psychological Science*, 2011, pp. 3–5.

29. P. G. Ipeirotis. "Demographics of mechanical turk," 2010. NYU Working Paper No. CEDER-10-01, Available: https://ssrn.com/abstract=1585030.

30. G. Paolacci and J. Chandler. "Inside the turk: Understanding mechanical turk as a participant pool." *Current Directions in Psychological Science*, 2014, pp. 185–189.

31. A. J. Berinsky, G. A. Huber, and G. S. Lenz. "Evaluating online labor markets for experimental research: Amazon. com's mechanical turk." *Political Analysis*, vol. 20, no. 3, 2012, pp. 351–368.

32. A. Perez-Garcia, C. Siaterlis, and M. Masera. "Studying characteristics of an emulab testbed for scientifically rigorous experiments." In *Distributed Simulation and Real Time Applications (DS-RT), 2010 IEEE/ACM 14th International Symposium on*, Oct. 2010, pp. 215–218.

33. C. Siaterlis, A. Garcia, and B. Genge. "On the use of emulab testbeds for scientifically rigorous experiments." *Communications Surveys Tutorials, IEEE*, vol. 15, no. 2, 2013, pp. 929–942.

34. F. Yergeau. "UTF-8, a transformation format of ISO 10646." In *RFC 3629 (Internet Standard), Internet Engineering Task Force*, Nov. 2003. [Online]. Available: http://www.ietf.org/rfc/rfc3629.txt.

35. K. Toutanova, D. Klein, C. Manning, and Y. Singer. "Feature-rich part-of-speech tag- ging with a cyclic dependency network." In *Proceedings of HLT-NAACL*, 2003, pp. 252–259.

36. A. Ratnaparkhi, et al. "A maximum entropy model for part-of-speech tagging." In *Proceedings of the Conference on Empirical Methods in Natural Language Processing*, vol. 1. ACL Anthology, Philadelphia, PA, 1996, pp. 133–142.

37. M. L. McNeal and D. Newyear. "Section 3: Basic components of aim." *Library Technology Reports*, vol. 49, no. 8, 2013, pp. 18–21.

38. F. Hartung and M. Kutter. "Multimedia watermarking techniques." *Proceedings of the IEEE*, vol. 87, no. 7, Jul. 1999, pp. 1079–1107.

6 A Deep Learning-Based Model for an Efficient Hate-Speech Detection in Twitter

P. R. Vishnu

SCMS School of Engineering and Technology, Ernakulam, Kerala, India

Basant Agarwal

Indian Institute of Information Technology (IIIT Kota), Kota, Rajasthan, India

P. Vinod

Cochin University of Science and Technology, Cochin, Kerala, India

K. A. Dhanya

SCMS School of Engineering and Technology, Ernakulam, Kerala, India

Alice Baroni

University of Padova, Padova, Italy

CONTENTS

DOI: 10.1201/9781003134527-8

6.1   INTRODUCTION

The usage of social media has increased amazingly in recent time for communicating with others. People use social media to express their views and opinions frequently. However, some individuals use abusive language while interacting with others [1]. Hate speech represents a type of language that aims to degrade an individual or group based on gender, sexual orientations, nationalities, religions, etc. Allowing such conversations on social media platforms is not good socially and culturally [2]. In many social media platforms, including Twitter and Facebook, there are specific rules or community standards against the usage of hate speech. Twitter is a social media platform for people to express their feelings freely. In several countries, including Canada, France, and the United Kingdom, there are laws prohibiting hate speech [3]. Therefore, finding hateful or offensive content is significantly important problem. With the increase in the use of hate speech over the social media, a significant amount of research is being carried out in order to detect the hateful content from the social media. Despite this, in recent times, research community is focusing on problem of hateful content using deep-neural-network-based models due to lack of satisfactory results.

Most of the present models for detecting hateful content are based on machine learning and deep-learning-based architectures. The traditional machine-learning-based model relies on superficial features such as bag of word models, character n-grams, word n-grams, etc. More recently, an emphasis has been placed on deep-neural-network-based models. There are several existing approaches to detect hate speech, most of which rely on approaches such as natural language processing (NLP) [4], machine learning [5], and deep learning [6]. A unigrams and patterns-based study [7], deep-learning-based approach [8, 9], the problem of offensive language is well described, along with hate-speech discovery in [3], different hate speech detection models and their weaknesses are well described in [10], are some previous studies related to hate speech discovery. In the proposed approach, we first extract the n-gram features and then use deep-learning-based models to learn the patterns of hateful content in tweets.

The detection of hateful content on social media is a challenging problem mainly due to the irregular language used in online platforms, especially in Twitter. Automatic detection of hateful tweets through machine-learning-based models require deep understanding of the language. In this chapter, we focus on detecting hateful and offensive content in Twitter. Our proposed model has as its main problem statement to distinguish hate speech from offensive language or neutral speech in a given tweet. In order to develop such a model, we propose to use several deep-neural-network-based models, n-grams, and attention technique that efficiently detect the hateful content in Twitter. In this chapter, we implement three types of deep neural network architectures based on the attention technique [11–13], the combination of the convolutional neural network (CNN) [14, 15] and long short-term memory (LSTM) [16]. Moreover, all of the proposed approaches are based on n-gram features. In the standard CNN and LSTM models, the raw text is fed as input in the network architecture, whereas the proposed model utilizes the n-grams features to input in the deep neural network models. To make the n-gram features set, we use the following combinations: Hate and Offensive, Hate and Neutral, Offensive and Neutral, and finally, Hate, Offensive, and Neutral sets. These prominent features are utilized to train deep neural networks. The deep neural networks use Glove [17] embedding to improve tweet representation meaningfully. The data set for this chapter has been obtained from [3]. This dataset consists of three classes of tweets such as hate speech, offensive but non-hateful speech, and neither.

The main contributions of this chapter are as follows:

1. We propose an attention-layer-based and a CNN-LSTM-based deep neural network to detect hate speech.
2. We evaluate the performance of the hate speech detection model enhanced with n-grams.
3. We perform different kinds of classification of tweets for a better understanding of the problem, such as:
   (a) Three-class classification: hate, offensive, or neutral.
   (b) Two-class classification: hate or offensive, hate, or neutral and offensive or neutral.

The remainder of the chapter is arranged as follows. Section 6.2 provides an overview of related works. Section 6.3 describes our proposed approach. Section 6.4 discusses the results of the experiment. Section 6.5 provides a discussion of the results obtained. Section 6.6 provides a comparison with the state-of-the-art method. Section 6.7 describes the analysis of misclassified samples. Section 6.8 provides the discussion on the future research directions. Finally, Section 6.9 summarizes the conclusions of this chapter.

6.2 RELATED WORKS

A detailed survey by [1] described various features used for hate speech detection using natural language processing techniques such as word generalization, simple surface features, sentiment analysis, linguistic features, lexical resources, knowledge-based features, meta-information, and multimodal information. The embedding layer creates embedding for all the words in the training data. The embedding layer can be initialized by pre-trained embeddings or initialized randomly. The pre-trained embeddings like Glove [17] generally improve the performance of deep neural networks. The performance of deep neural networks can further be enhanced by attention mechanism [11], which considers the whole context and give weight to important words/features. Moreover, the self-attention technique improves the performance of the model due to learning long-distance-relations among the words in the sequence. Authors in [18] present an approach for automatic detection for hate speech detection from text using a multi-new support vector machine-based approach with handcrafted features such as character n-grams that produces near to neural network-based models. Authors in [19] used n-gram features, and linguistic, syntactic and semantics information for detecting hate speech on social media, and they observed that the combination of several feature set produces best performance. Authors in [20] also used n-gram features along with different feature weighting schemes such as Term frequency, term frequency – inverse document frequency technologies, and word vectors for detection of hateful content. Authors in [21] presents an extensive study of machine-learning-based models for detection of hate speech content from several social media platforms. Authors have used several classifiers such as logistic regression, SVM, neural networks, Naïve Bayes, and XGBoost. Further, they also used several feature representation techniques such as TF-IDF, Word2Vec, Bag-of-Words, and bidirectional encoder representations from transformers (BERT) along with the combinations of features. Their extensive results show that the keyword-based XGBoost model using all the features outperforms other models.

Authors in [3] proposed a model for the detection of hate speech; they collected tweets labeled into three categories: Hate, Offensive, and neither. Further, they trained a multiclass classifier to classify tweets. They achieved an overall recall of 0.90, precision of 0.91, and F1 score of 0.90. Authors in [7] proposed a unigram and patterns-based model for the classification of tweets into clean, offensive, or hateful. The Part-of-Speech (PoS) tagging incorporated in pre-processing along with other tasks. They considered sentiment-based features, semantic-based features, pattern-based features, and unigram-based features for feature extraction. This approach produced 87.4% accuracy on binary classification (offensive or not) and 78.4% accuracy on ternary classification (hateful, offensive, or clean). The PoS tagging [22] usually increase the grammatical knowledge about a sentence. That will help us to find out the context of a tweet.

Convolution and LSTM-based deep neural network to detect hate speech have been described in [8]. Application of deep learning techniques for hate speech detection and effect of embedding techniques have been described in [9]. Authors in [9] present an approach for detecting hate speech in tweets using deep neural networks. They also compared deep-learning-based techniques with several machine-learning-based models (e.g., decision tree) using feature extraction techniques such as character n-grams, Term frequency inverse document frequency (TF-IDF), and bag-of-words techniques. Predictive features for finding hate speech on Twitter are described in [23] and provided a list to identify hate speech; they also set out the criteria for making a tweet offensive. Another hate speech detection method using context-aware models has been described in [24]. The study in [10] clearly described various hate speech detectors and techniques to break the detection algorithms. They were able to successfully evade different hate speech detection algorithms using attacks, like inserting word changes, word boundary changes, and word appending. Authors in [25] proposed an ensemble approach for detection of hate speech from social media by combining natural language processing and machine learning technique. Authors in [26] used Paragraph2vec model, which is a word-embedding-based model for the detection of hate on social media, they also compared their approach with bag-of-words model. Authors in [27] proposed an approach for detecting racist and sexist language using CNN-based approach. Their proposed approach is a two-step approach, in which they firstly used three CNN models such as character CNN, word CNN, and hybrid CNN, and further they employed logistic regression classifier. Their experimental results show that the hybrid CNN with logistic regression performs better than other methods. Authors in [28] proposed a convolution neural network-based approach for detecting hate speech on social media that utilized a pre-trained word-embedding layer, which is fed into a convolution layer which further passed into a max pooling layer, whose feature vector is further passed into a Gated Recurrent Unit (GRU) layer with global max pooling layer and finally fed into a softmax layer. In [29], authors investigated several deep-neural-network-based models utilizing CNN and recurrent neural network (RNN) and also used the BERT models for detecting hate speech in tweets in Arabic language.

A hate speech detection framework incorporating Sub-word and word-level semantic information have been proposed in [30]. They incorporated character-level information, which is very common, and much research already happened using this feature. However, the specialty of this framework is that it uses phonetic-level information too, which is not very common. Also, incorporated attention mechanism, LSTM, and CNN. Besides, phonetic-level embedding, word-level embedding, and character-level embedding are used. The approach obtained an 0.953 macro F1 score.

A method for hate speech detection by combining the classifiers by using a fusion approach was introduced by [31]. ELMo, CNN, and BERT classifiers have been used in the approach. By using the mean fusion, the method obtained an F1-score of 0.704. The CNN performed better than others in the individual experiments. Thus, they also experimented fusion of CNN by modifying parameters was performed. The CNN-based fusion approach using max fusion obtained an F1-score of 0.712.

6.3   PROPOSED APPROACH

In this chapter, we mainly focus on recognizing the hateful content from social media content. The aim is to classify a given tweet into one of the class labels viz. Hate, Offensive, or Neutral, which are defined as follows:

(a) Hate: This class includes tweets which include hateful content.
(b) Offensive: This class include tweets which include offensive but non-hate content.
(c) Neutral: This class includes tweets which are neither hateful nor offensive.

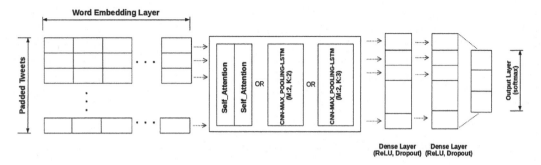

FIGURE 6.1	Architecture of hate speech detection model.

We have developed three different deep neural network models, which are a self-attention-based network and CNN-LSTM-based networks. For all of these models, we initially pre-processed the text and extracted n-gram features. To prepare the n-gram feature sets, we made different combinations of Hate and Offensive, Hate and Neutral, Offensive and Neutral, and finally, Hate, Offensive, and Neutral tweets. These features were used to represent the given textual content and further train the machine learning algorithm. Proposed models use Glove [17] embedding to improve the text representation. All three of architectures clearly shown in Figure 6.1. We extensively designed several experiments to see the effectiveness and robustness of the proposed model such as for the different combination of the training data of "Hate-Offensive," "Hate-Neutral," "Offensive-Neutral," and "Hate-Offensive-Neutral."

Abbreviations used in this chapter:

1. H: set of Hate tweets
2. O: Set of Offensive tweets
3. N: Set of Neutral tweets
4. H-O: Combination of Hate and Offensive tweets
5. H-N: Combination of Hate and Neutral tweets
6. O-N: Combination of Offensive and Neutral tweets
7. H-O-N: Combination of Hate, Offensive and Neutral tweets

6.3.1 Dataset Used

To evaluate the performance of the proposed models, we use a dataset, provided by authors in [3], which is also available on Github [32]. This set contains 24,783 tweets which have been classified into hate speech, offensive speech, and neither. In this chapter, we are denoting the "neither" tweets as "neutral." It is challenging to correctly detect the hate speech within this dataset because it is highly unbalanced. This dataset consists of 5.8% of hate speech tweets, 16.8% of neither hate nor offensive category, and the rest of offensive speech category. To train the machine learning model, we firstly prepare combinations of hate, offensive and neutral as follows:

1. Hate-Offensive-Neutral
2. Hate-Offensive
3. Hate-Neutral
4. Offensive-Neutral

Then, we constructed 1-gram, 2-gram, 3-gram, 4-gram and 5-gram of each of the above combinations and mixture of 2-gram and 3-gram, 2-gram and 4-gram, 2-gram and 5-gram, 3-gram and 4-gram, 3-gram and 5-gram, and 4-gram and 5-gram combinations of Hate-Offensive-Neutral combination. We selected 80% tweets for training and 20% tweets for testing. Finally, we performed a 10-fold cross-validation for our three-class problem.

Algorithm 1:   Pre-processing Tweets for Classification

Input: S : set of tweets

$\quad\quad S = \{s_1, s_2, ..., s_n\}$

$\quad\quad L$: Set of Labels

$\quad\quad L = \{L_1, L2, ..., L_n\}$

Output: Pre-processed Tweets and Encoded Labels

Function $N\_gram(t, n)$/*t: Tweets set, n: n-gram range */

if $n == 1$ **then**

$\quad\quad$ return $1\_grams(t)$

if $n == 2$ **then**

$\quad\quad$ return $2\_grams(t)$

if $n == 3$ **then**

$\quad\quad$ return $3\_grams(t)$

if $n == 4$ **then**

$\quad\quad$ return $4\_grams(t)$

if $n == 5$ **then**

$\quad\quad$ return $5\_grams(t)$

End Function

Function Preprocessing (S, n)

/* S:set of tweets, n: total number of tweets

H:Set of "Hate" tweets, O: Set of "Offensive" tweets,

N: Set of "Neutral" tweets, HO: Set of "Hate-Offensive" tweets,

HN:Set of "Hate-Neutral" tweets, ON:Set of "Offensive-Neutral" tweets

HON: Set of "Hate-Offensive-Neutral" tweets*/

$tweets = \varnothing$

For i from 1 to n **do**

$\quad\quad x \leftarrow tokenizer(s_i)$

$\quad\quad x \leftarrow case\_converter(x)$

$\quad\quad x \leftarrow stop\_word\_remover(x)$

$\quad\quad x \leftarrow punctuation\_remover(x)$

$\quad\quad x \leftarrow number\_remover(x)$

$\quad\quad x \leftarrow special\_character\_remover(x)$

$\quad\quad x \leftarrow stemming(x)$

$\quad\quad tweets \leftarrow tweets \cup x$

For *i from* 1 *to* 5 ***do***
     $H_i \leftarrow N\_gram(H, i)$
     $O_i \leftarrow N\_gram(O, i)$
     $N_i \leftarrow N\_gram(N, i)$
     $L_{Hi} \leftarrow 0$ *for each* H_i
     $L_{Oi} \leftarrow 1$ *for each* O_i
     $L_{Ni} \leftarrow 2$ *for each* N_i
For *i from* 1 *to* 5 ***do***
     $HO_i \leftarrow pad\_sequence(text\_to\_sequence(H_i \cup O_i))$
     $HN_i \leftarrow pad\_sequence(text\_to\_sequence(H_i \cup N_i))$
     $HON_i \leftarrow pad\_sequence(text\_to\_sequence(H_i \cup O_i \cup N_i))$
     $ON_i \leftarrow pad\_sequence(text\_to\_sequence(O_i \cup N_i))$
     $L_{HOi} \leftarrow one\_hot\_encode(L_{Hi} \cup L_{Oi})$
     $L_{HNi} \leftarrow one\_hot\_encode(L_{Hi} \cup L_{Ni})$
     $L_{HONi} \leftarrow one\_hot\_encode(L_{Hi} \cup L_{Oi} \cup L_{Ni})$
     $L_{ONi} \leftarrow one\_hot\_encode(L_{Oi} \cup L_{Ni})$
End Function

6.3.2 Proposed Model Description

The proposed approach for detection of hate speech is demonstrated in Figure 6.1B. Its architecture consists of several stages, including pre-processed tweets, Embedding, and classification. The detailed description of the pre-processing of tweets is described in subsequent sections and also elaborated in Algorithm 1. The pre-processing of tweets consists of tokenization, conversion to the lowercase, removing Twitter handles (@user), stop word filtering, eliminating punctuations, removing numbers, removing special characters, and word stemming. The following sections provide a description of the steps taken.

6.3.2.1 Tokenization

Tokenization is a method for breaking down tweet messages into smaller units such as words. A token is a single unit that is the building block for a text. For example, if we consider the following tweet: "@User 1 example Tweet describing the nature of tweets!" After the tokenization, we get the word set as ["@", "user," "1," "example," "tweet," "describing," "the," "nature," "of," "tweets", "!"].

6.3.2.2 Conversion to Lower Case

Tweet messages converted into lower case. It will allow instances of "X" in a sentence to match with a query of "x." Example: "Apple" changed to "apple." Changing case is important because, commonly, the meaning of a word does not change when there is a change in the case. Therefore words in the same format are good to extract more knowledge.

6.3.2.3 Removing Twitter Handle, Stop Words, Special Characters, Punctuation and Numbers

In this step, tweets have been further pre-processed through the removal of unnecessary elements. This is done by eliminating Twitter handles, stop words, special characters, punctuation, hyperlinks, numbers, and word stemming in order to refine the dataset.

Twitter handle removal: A Twitter handle is the term for account holders name on Twitter.
     Output: ["1," "example," "tweet," "describing," "the," "nature," "of," "tweets", "!"].

Stop word removal: Removing stop words such as "is," "was," "are," etc. Generally speaking, these are high frequency words that do not provide any meaningful information to the machine learning model.

Output: ["1," "example," "tweet," "describing," "nature," "tweets," "!"].

Punctuation removal: We remove punctuation like "!," ";," "*," etc. from the dataset.

Output: ["1," "example," "tweet," "describing," "nature," "tweets"].

Removing numbers: Similarly, we removed any instances of numbers from the dataset.

Output: ["example," "tweet," "describing," "nature," "tweets"].

Word stemming: Stemming is a process of reducing distinct forms of a word to a common basic form.

Output: ["example," "tweet," "describing," "nature," "tweet"].

6.3.2.4   N-Grams

Several n-gram features, along with their combinations, are extracted. The different combinations of unigrams (1-gram), bigrams (2-gram), trigrams (3-gram), 4-grams, and 5-grams are extracted with a different combination of documents as follows: Hate-Offensive, Hate-Neutral, Hate-Offensive-Neutral, and Offensive-Neutral.

Furthermore, we created combinations of 2-gram and 3-gram, 2-gram and 4-gram, 2-gram and 5-gram, 3-gram and 4-gram, 3-gram and 5-gram, and 4-gram and 5-gram for Hate-Offensive-Neutral classification.

6.3.2.5   Target Label Encoding

We encoded target labels as "0" for hate, "1" for offensive, and "2" for neutral. Whereas, during binary classification for hate-offensive, "0" for hate, and "1" for offensive, for hate-neutral "0" for hate and "1" for neutral, for offensive-neutral, "0" for offensive and "1" for neutral.

6.3.2.6   Embedding

Word embeddings of the extracted features are learned during training. Initially, embeddings of the features are randomly initialized, which is fine-tuned at the time of training the model. The learned representation of the features is semantically rich. The word-embedding representation of the input sentences are fed input to the attention layer.

An embedding matrix has been prepared by using pre-trained word vectors (Glove) [17]. After preparing the embedding matrix, provided this embedding matrix as the embedding-weight for the embedding layer of the classification model.

6.3.2.7   Attention-Based DNN

Attention techniques have been used to enhance the performance of neural machine translation (NMT) [12] by focusing on the subsets of sentences, which are more important during translation. Self-attention could improve the performance of tasks involving long sequences. The performance of the system can be improved by focusing on the important word more as compared to other remaining words. Attention layer also provides an insight into the context of tweets that further improves the performance. We used Keras Self-Attention as the self-attention layer. The input to this layer is the vectors generated by the embedding layer, where the output is passed to another self-attention layer. The resulting information is then forwarded to a deep neural network (DNN), as shown in Figure 6.2. Self-attention layer is used to find out the "essence" of a tweet. This layer will produce a context matrix containing the soul of each tweet. After passing both attention layers, the context matrix is transferred to dense layers.

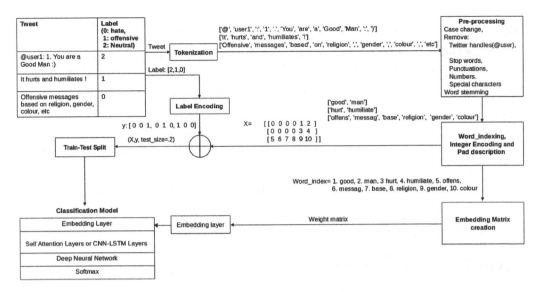

FIGURE 6.2 Attention or CNN-LSTM based Deep Neural Network (M: MaxPool Size, K: Kernel Size, CNN activation: ReLU).

6.3.2.8 CNN-LSTM Based DNN

We used a CNN over the embedding layer. And further its output is fed into the LSTM. CNNs have been used to include the local region information from the text, and it automatically learns the n-gram features through different filters. LSTM is an RNN. CNN layers are good in learning local region information, whereas the LSTM layers are good in incorporating the long-distance information among the words in the sentence. The CNN layers help us to see the word combinations of the specified kernel size [33]. We have implemented two types of CNN-LSTM model by varying the kernel size. One of them is kernel size two, and the other is three. For example, when the kernel size is two, the CNN layer processes two words at a time. So it can get information about the combinations of size two. Similarly, we get the information of three-word combinations by setting kernel size to three. The MaxPooling layer monitors the input and converts it into a single value with the highest observed value. This information passed to the LSTM layer, which processes the input and includes its semantic meaning, from which the information about the input is transmitted to the dense layer. CNN's dimensionality of the output space has set to 100 and the activation set to ReLU. LSTM's dimensionality of the output space has set to 100.

The fully connected (dense layers) [33] layer have been used in the proposed hate speech detection model. The dimensionality of the output space of the first dense layer is 64, and the dimensionality of the output space of the second dense layer is 30. The dimensionality of the output layer is 3 (three output classes: Hate, Offensive or Neutral), and its activation is softmax. A random search was performed over all possible hyper parameter configurations to choose the optimal parameters for the classification models.

6.4 EXPERIMENTAL RESULTS AND DISCUSSION

6.4.1 PERFORMANCE METRICS

The performance of different hate speech detection models has been evaluated, by using accuracy, recall, precision, and F1-score [34] on a test dataset.

TABLE 6.1

Comparing Different Deep Learning Models: Hate-Offensive-Neutral Classification (10-fold Cross-Validation Results of CNN-LSTM Models and Attention-Based Models)

Model	Avg. (Weighted avg.)			
	Precision	Recall	F1-Score	Accuracy (%)
Embed.-CNN-LSTM-DNN (Kernel: 2, Maxpool size: 2)	0.99	0.99	0.99	99
Embed.-CNN-LSTM-DNN (Kernel: 3, Maxpool size: 2)	0.989	0.989	0.989	98.9
Embed.-seqself Attention-seqself Attention-DNN	0.982	0.982	0.982	98.16
State-of-the-art	0.91	0.90	0.90	–

TABLE 6.2

Classification Results of Best Performing Models Using Attention Network

Classification Problem	N-Gram Combination	Weighted Average			
		Precision	Recall	F1-Score	Accuracy (%)
Hate-Offensive	5-gram	0.96	0.96	0.96	96
Hate-Neutral	5-gram	0.96	0.96	0.96	95.7
Offensive-Neutral	4-gram	0.94	0.94	0.94	94
Hate-Offensive-Neutral	5-gram	0.93	0.93	0.93	92.7
Hate-Offensive-Neutral	4-gram + 5-gram	0.95	0.95	0.95	94.6

6.4.2 Experimental Settings and Results

It is intuitive that the classification of hate and neural tweets should be relatively easier as compared to Hate and Offensive tweets. Therefore, to see the robustness of the proposed model, we evaluated them on different combinations of data presented as follows.

1. Hate-Offensive (H-O) classification.
2. Hate-Neutral (H-N) classification.
3. Offensive-Neutral (O-N) classification.
4. Hate-Offensive-Neutral (H-O-N) classification.

For the hate-offensive, hate-neutral, and offensive-neutral classification, we conducted experiments on self-attention architecture only. For the Hate-Offensive-Neutral (H-O-N) classification, we conducted experiments using self-attention architecture and CNN-LSTM based architecture.

Table 6.1 shows the 10-fold cross-validation results of the self-attention-based model and CNN-LSTM based models for hate, offensive, and neutral categorization. Table 6.1 also shows the results of the state-of-the-art model for comparison purposes. The results on a test set are clearly shown in Tables 6.2, 6.3, and 6.4 (self-attention-based models).

The classification results of best performing models for the self-attention architecture are clearly shown in Table 6.2 with respect to precision, recall, F1-score, and accuracy. It can be observed from the results shown in Table 6.3 that 5-gram features produced better results for hate-offensive and hate-neutral problems. Whereas, for offensive-neutral classification, 4-gram model gives better results than other n-grams. Furthermore, for the Hate-Offensive-Neutral classification, out of several combinations of n-gram features, the combination of 4-grams and 5-grams gives more satisfactory results than other n-grams.

TABLE 6.3

F1 Score for Each Classification Problem Using Different N-grams

N-gram	H-O-N	H-O	H-N	O-N
5-gram	0.93	0.96	0.96	0.46
4-gram	0.90	0.94	0.90	0.94
3-gram	0.82	0.91	0.91	0.90
2-gram	0.72	0.88	0.83	0.88
1-gram	0.46	0.74	0.64	0.47

TABLE 6.4

Mixture of N-grams for Hate-Offensive-Neutral Classification

H-O-N	
N-gram Combination	F1-Score
4-gram and 5-gram	0.95
3-gram and 5-gram	0.90
3-gram and 4-gram	0.94
2-gram and 3-gram	0.84
2-gram and 4-gram	0.83
2-gram and 5-gram	0.81

The F1 score for each classification problem using different n-grams is shown in Table 6.3. Table 6.4 describes the F1-score for Hate-Offensive-Neutral classification problem using different combinations of n-grams.

6.5   RESULT DISCUSSION

This section discusses the results of each classification model.

6.5.1   HATE-OFFENSIVE CLASSIFICATION

F1-scores increase with the increase in the size of the n-gram. The F1-score is 0.74 for 1 gram and 0.96 for 5 grams. This result means that the classification model captures the semantic difference between the two target classes more efficiently at higher n-grams.

6.5.2   HATE-NEUTRAL CLASSIFICATION

In this problem, the F1-score increases directly proportional to the increase in n-gram size. Also, this model performs better at higher n-grams than lower n-grams.

6.5.3   OFFENSIVE-NEUTRAL CLASSIFICATION

Unlike other models, the performance of this model decreases at 5-gram. The F1 score of 5-gram is less than the F1-score of 1-gram. The performance of this model is better in 4-gram than lower n-grams.

6.5.4   HATE-OFFENSIVE-NEUTRAL CLASSIFICATION

The performance of this model is proportional to the increase in n-gram size. Further, we also empirically find out that the combination of 4-gram and 5-gram yields better results. Therefore,

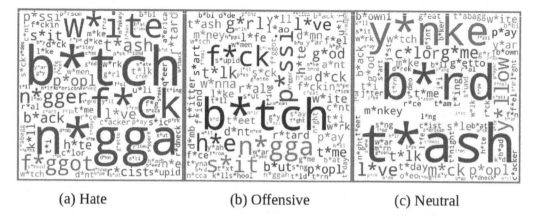

| (a) Hate | (b) Offensive | (c) Neutral |

FIGURE 6.3   Word clouds: (a) Hate, (b) Offensive, and (c) Neutral.

we experimented this combination of n-grams in CNN-LSTM-based architecture. According to the observed results, the CNN-LSTM based architecture (kernel size: 2 and Max Pool size: 2) provides better performance.

To better understand and visualize the obtained results, we studied the results using word clouds. We demonstrate the word clouds in figure (Figure 6.3). The highlighted words in the word cloud of hate (Figure 6.3(a)) and a word cloud of offensive (Figure 6.3(b)) are almost similar. It shows why the hate-offensive classification is a more challenging problem. Each tweet is a combination of words, and general terms appear in every category. Thus, general terms for hate, offensive, and neutral category mislead our classifier. Word clouds clearly show that such words are overlapping, and also demonstrate the reason why hate speech detection is a challenging problem.

A tweet may be read as hateful, offensive, or neutral depending on human interpretation, regardless of whether it contains hate or offensive words. A common word can be hateful, offensive, or neutral based on the situation where the word is used. For example: if somebody says "beautiful donkeys" by standing in front a bunch of real donkeys it is generally a neutral language. If the word targets a person or an organization, it will become Hate or Offensive based on the context. Hence, a natural language problem fails to achieve 100% result in such a situation. However, if the model is given enough context information such as word context, place, behavior, and attitude of the person delivering the speech, etc., the model can perform better.

The precision, recall, and F-score of Hate-Offensive-Neutral model in Table 6.2 shows the detailed performance analysis of our best model using self-attention-based DNN for Hate-Offensive-Neutral classification (a mixture of 4-gram and 5-gram). After using a random search, we found that RMSprop optimizer gives better results. Other parameters are as follows: learning rate: 0.001, epoch: 50, dropout: 0.2 and batch size: 32. The precision of hate, offensive, and neutral classes are 0.82, 0.96, and 0.96, respectively. We evaluated the combination of 4-gram and 5-gram for Hate-Offensive-Neutral classification using 10-fold cross-validation. The accuracy, precision, recall, F-score are clearly shown in Table 6.1. All those performance parameters achieved results above 98%. For training the model, we provided a combination of 4-gram and 5-gram because the combination of 4-gram and 5-gram is the input to the best performance model of a self-attention-based architecture. In addition, the CNN-LSTM model provides better results than the self-attention model in terms of Precision, Recall, and F1-score. This result is because the LSTM layer captures more contextual and semantic information than the attention layer. After using a random search, the hyperparameters for CNN-LSTM based classifier has found as kernel size (2), Max Pool size (2), and the SGD optimizer gives better results. Other parameters were, momentum: 0.0, learning rate: 0.2, epoch: 35, dropout: 0.5, batch size: 128. Parameter combinations for a CNN-LSTM based network with kernel size: 3 and Max Pool size: 2 are: optimizer: RMSprop, Learning rate: 0.01, epoch: 30, dropout: 0.2, batch size: 128.

TABLE 6.5

The Similarity between Target Categories

Categories	Similarity Score	
	True Prediction	False Prediction
Hate & Offensive	14	42
Hate & Neutral	27	41
Offensive & Neutral	34	42

6.6 COMPARATIVE STUDY

The proposed self-attention-based approach performs well in identifying a given tweet as hateful, offensive, or neutral with an accuracy of 98.16%. Experiments show an overall F1-measure of 0.982, which is an improvement of 8.2% as compared to the state-of-the-art [3] that reported an F1-measure 0.90. In addition, another model CNN-LSTM based approach performs better in detecting a given tweet as hateful, offensive, or neutral with an accuracy of 99%. For Hate-Offensive-Neutral classification, experiments show an overall F1-measure of 0.99, which is better than the state-of-the-art that reported an F1-measure 0.90, thus an overall improvement of 9% is obtained from the proposed method. The CNN-LSTM approach works better than the self-attention-based method. According to the results shown in Table 6.1, the CNN-LSTM approach has an F1-score of 0.99, which is 0.8% higher than the self-attention-based approach.

6.7 ERROR ANALYSIS

To understand the robustness and where the proposed model fail, we did error analysis on the misclassified and correctly classified instances from all the classification models. For all proposed classification models, 90.19% of the samples can be classified correctly in general. To find out the cause of the misclassification, we decided to examine the string similarity between each target category. To do so, we concatenated the samples of each category into two separate sets, one for correctly classified and the other for incorrectly classified.

We detected similarity of misclassified instances and correctly classified instances through the "LevenshteinDistance" method. We used this method to measure the difference between two sequences. We also employed "FuzzyWuzzy" python library to calculate the difference between sequences. Because this library uses the Levenshtein distance method to measure similarity, to do this, we used the fuzz.ratio () method from this library.

For example,

fuzz.ratio ("Hate-Offensive-Neutral sample," "Offensive-Neutral Sample") = 91
fuzz.ratio ("Hate-Offensive-Neutral sample," "Hate-Offensive-Neutral sample") = 100

The result of the analysis is shown in Table 6.5. We separated the correctly predicted instances and misclassified instances of each category. The similarity of incorrectly predicted samples is higher than correctly predicted samples. Because, the meaning of the sentences depends on the context, the past events, and the relationship between them. Therefore, an offensive word in one sentence does not mean that the entire sentence is offensive or hateful. For example, standing in front of a group of monkeys and saying "beautiful monkeys" is not the same thing as saying in front of a group of people. Proposed approaches cannot understand such cases. Therefore, the misclassification occurred.

6.8   FUTURE RESEARCH DIRECTIONS

Hate speech on social media platforms is a challenging problem which is vigilant on almost every social media platform such as Twitter, Facebook, YouTube, Instagram, etc. The existing techniques for the detection of hate speech vary on different platforms, however most of the techniques focused on Twitter social networking platform. Few researchers have investigated the performance of a model over different platforms, e.g., authors in [35] used the comments from these four platforms, viz. 4chan, MetaFilter, Reddit, and Voat for training the model, and then evaluated the model on another platform called MixedBag. The existing model that can efficiently work in a cross-domain setting is still limited, and thus can be taken up as a future research direction. Hence, a model that can effectively work on multiple social media platforms is required, and for that a more generalized independent of the platform is required [36].

More recently, a significant amount of research that has focused on deep-learning-based models has shown satisfactory results, but in a specific experimental environment such as Twitter or some of the freely available dataset. However, there is a dearth of knowledge more robust model that can work independently either from the platform or the language. Additionally, existing models mostly work for English language, so there is a considerable research potential to develop models that can also detect hateful content from other languages as well. Moreover, existing models mostly focus on deep-learning-based models, which do not take into account linguistic and in-depth information of the text, in such situations, more advanced models can be developed, by combining traditional machine learning models, along with deep-learning-based models or natural language processing-based techniques. More sophisticated models can also be developed by including in-depth analysis of text using natural language processing techniques, along with deep-neural-network-based models.

6.9   CONCLUSION

Within the fast increase in the use of social media, people have expressed their opinions on social media very frequently. Simultaneously, few people post hateful content over social media networks. It is important to detect hate speech on social media to maintain the digital media environment healthy. To detect hateful content from social media is a very important and challenging natural language processing task. In this book chapter, we focus on developing deep-neural-network-based models to detect hate speech in social media posts such as self-attention-based and CNN-LSTM based models. The CNN-LSTM based DNN model has shown the best performance in detecting if a tweet is hateful, offensive, or neutral. The proposed models for hatespeech detection outperforms the traditional sophisticated approach with respect to the performance results. In future works, we shall include more context, syntactic, and semantic information from tweets in order to refine our model.

REFERENCES

1. Schmidt, A., & Wiegand, M. (2017, April). *A survey on hate speech detection using natural language processing*. In *Proceedings of the Fifth International Workshop on Natural Language Processing for Social Media* (pp. 1–10).
2. Warner, W., & Hirschberg, J. (2012). *Detecting hate speech on the world wide web*. In *Proceedings of the Second Workshop on Language in Social Media* (pp. 19–26). Association for Computational Linguistics.
3. Davidson, T., Warmsley, D., Macy, M., & Weber, I. (2017). *Automated hate speech detection and the problem of offensive language*. In *Eleventh International AAAI Conference on Web and Social Media* (pp. 512–515).
4. Collobert, R., Weston, J., Bottou, L., Karlen, M., Kavukcuoglu, K., & Kuksa, P. (2011). Natural language processing (almost) from scratch. *Journal of Machine Learning Research*, 12(Aug), 2493–2537.
5. Dharmadhikari, S. C., Ingle, M., & Kulkarni, P. (2011). Empirical studies on machine learning based text classification algorithms. *Advanced Computing*, 2(6), 161.

6. LeCun, Y., Bengio, Y., & Hinton, G. (2015). Deep learning. *Nature*, 521(7553), 436–444.

7. Watanabe, H., Bouazizi, M., & Ohtsuki, T. (2018). Hate speech on Twitter: A pragmatic approach to collect hateful and offensive expressions and perform hate speech detection. *IEEE Access*, 6, 13825–13835.

8. Zhang, Z., Robinson, D., & Tepper, J. (2016). Hate Speech Detection Using a Convolution-LSTM Based Deep Neural Network.

9. Badjatiya, P., Gupta, S., Gupta, M., & Varma, V. (2017). *Deep learning for hate speech detection in tweets*. In *Proceedings of the 26th International Conference on World Wide Web Companion* (pp. 759–760).

10. Gröndahl, T., Pajola, L., Juuti, M., Conti, M., & Asokan, N. (2018, January). *All you need is "love": Evading hate speech detection*. In *Proceedings of the 11th ACM Workshop on Artificial Intelligence and Security* (pp. 2–12).

11. Vaswani, A., Shazeer, N., Parmar, N., Uszkoreit, J., Jones, L., Gomez, A. N., & Polosukhin, I. (2017). *Attention is all you need*. In *Advances in Neural Information Processing Systems* (pp. 5998–6008).

12. Luong, M. T., Pham, H., & Manning, C. D. (2015). Effective approaches to attention-based neural machine translation. arXiv preprint arXiv:1508.04025.

13. Wang, Y., Huang, M., Zhu, X., & Zhao, L. (2016). *Attention-based LSTM for aspect-level sentiment classification*. In *Proceedings of the 2016 Conference on Empirical Methods in Natural Language Processing* (pp. 606–615).

14. Lai, S., Xu, L., Liu, K., & Zhao, J. (2015). *Recurrent convolutional neural networks for text classification*. In *Twenty-Ninth AAAI Conference on Artificial Intelligence* (pp. 2267–2273).

15. Kim, Y. (2014). *Convolutional neural networks for sentence classification*. arXiv preprint arXiv:1408.5882.

16. Hochreiter, S., & Schmidhuber, J. (1997). Long short-term memory. *Neural Computation*, 9(8), 1735–1780.

17. Pennington, J., Socher, R., & Manning, C. D. (2014, October). *Glove: Global vectors for word representation*. In *Proceedings of the 2014 Conference on Empirical Methods in Natural Language Processing (EMNLP)* (pp. 1532–1543).

18. MacAvaney, S., Yao, H.-R., Yang, E., Russell, K., Goharian, N., & Frieder, O. (2019). Hate speech detection: Challenges and solutions. *PLoS ONE*, 14(8): e0221152. https://doi.org/10.1371/journal.pone.0221152.

19. Nobata, C., et al. (2016). *Abusive language detection in online user content*. In: *Proceedings of the 25th International Conference on World Wide Web*, Geneva, Switzerland; (pp. 145–153).

20. Salminen, J., et al. (2018). *Anatomy of online hate: developing a taxonomy and machine learning models for identifying and classifying hate in online news media*. In *Proceedings of the International AAAI Conference on Web and Social Media (ICWSM)*, San Francisco.

21. Salminen, J., Hopf, M., & Chowdhury, S. A. et al. (2020). Developing an online hate classifier for multiple social media platforms. *Human-centric Computing and Information Sciences*, 10, 1. https://doi.org/10.1186/s13673-019-0205-6.

22. Toutanova, K., Klein, D., Manning, C. D., & Singer, Y. (2003, May). *Feature-rich part-of-speech tagging with a cyclic dependency network*. In *Proceedings of the 2003 Conference of the North American Chapter of the Association for Computational Linguistics on Human Language technology-Volume 1* (pp. 173–180). Association for Computational Linguistics.

23. Waseem, Z., & Hovy, D. (2016). *Hateful symbols or hateful people? Predictive features for hate speech detection on Twitter*. In *Proceedings of the NAACL Student Research Workshop* (pp. 88–93).

24. Gao, L., & Huang, R. (2017). Detecting online hate speech using context aware models. arXiv p-rprint arXiv:1710.07395.

25. Al-Makhadmeh, Z., & Tolba, A.(2020). Automatic hate speech detection using killer natural language processing optimizing ensemble deep learning approach. *Computing*, 102, 501–522. https://doi.org/10.1007/s00607-019-00745-0.

26. Djuric, N., et al. (2015). *Hate speech detection with comment embeddings*. In: *Proceedings of the 24th International Conference on World Wide Web*, New York (pp. 29–30).

27. Park, J. H., & Fung, P. One-step and two-step classification for abusive language detection on Twitter. arXiv preprint arXiv:1706.01206. 2017.

28. Zhang, Z. et al. (2018). Detecting hate speech on Twitter using a convolution-gru based deep neural network. *European Semantic Web Conference*, 2018, 745–760.

29. Alshalan, R. & Al-Khalifa, H. (2020). A deep learning approach for automatic hate speech detection in the Saudi Twittersphere. *Applied Sciences*, 10, 8614; doi:10.3390/app10238614.

30. Mou, G., Ye, P., & Lee, K. (2020, October). *Swe2: Subword enriched and significant word emphasized framework for hate speech detection*. In *Proceedings of the 29th ACM International Conference on Information & Knowledge Management* (pp. 1145–1154).

31. Zhou, Y., Yang, Y., Liu, H., Liu, X., & Savage, N. (2020). Deep learning based fusion approach for hate speech detection. *IEEE Access*, *8*, 128923–128929.

32. Automated Hate Speech Detection and the Problem of Offensive Language [data repository]. https://github.com/t-davidson/hate-speech-and-offensive-language (last accessed: 2020, July).

33. Yenter, A., &Verma, A. (2017). *Deep CNN-LSTM with combined kernels from multiple branches for IMDb review sentiment analysis*. In *2017 IEEE 8th Annual Ubiquitous Computing, Electronics and Mobile Communication Conference (UEMCON)* (pp. 540–546). IEEE.

34. Huang, G., Li, Y., Wang, Q., Ren, J., Cheng, Y., & Zhao, X. (2019). Automatic classification method for software vulnerability based on deep neural network. *IEEE Access*, 7, 28291–28298.

35. Chandrasekharan, E., et al. (2017). *The bag of communities: identifying abusive behavior online with preexisting internet data*. In: *Proceedings of the 2017 CHI Conference on Human Factors in Computing Systems*, New York (pp. 3175–3187).

36. Karan, M., & Šnajder, J. (2018). *Cross-domain detection of abusive language online*. In *Proceedings of the 2nd Workshop on Abusive Language Online (ALW2)* (pp. 132–137).

Part III

Cyberbullying, Cyberstalking, and Related Issues

7 Cyberbullying and Cyberstalking on Online Social Networks

Umit Can

Munzur University, Tunceli, Turkey

Bilal Alatas

Firat University, Elazig, Turkey

CONTENTS

7.1 INTRODUCTION

The internet and the communication facilities it provides gave birth to online social networks (OSN) at the beginning of this century. Social networks have undergone major qualitative and quantitative transformations in parallel with technological developments. Therefore, many online social network analysis problems have arisen in online platforms [1]. One of these significant problems is cyberbullying. Bullying is defined as deliberate aggression repeatedly committed by a person or a group to a person who cannot easily defend himself [2]. Cyberbullying is a type of bullying that emerged with the use of digital technologies. Smith et al. [3] defined this as "an aggressive, deliberate action by a group or individual against a victim who cannot easily defend himself, repeatedly or by electronic means over time." These attacks can occur on social media, messaging platforms, gaming platforms,

DOI: 10.1201/9781003134527-10

and mobile phones. They are repetitive behaviors that aim to scare, annoy, or embarrass the target [4]. Cyberbullying involves posting negative, harmful, false, or aggressive content about someone else. It may involve the sharing of personal or private information about someone else who causes embarrassment or humiliation [5]. Cyberbullying affects people of all ages, from adolescents to adults. This causes people to start feeling depressed and therefore affects their daily activities. Bullies do it for fun or other personal reasons that greatly affect the victim's life. Nowadays, many people upload content on social media platforms, including photos of what they do, where they go, and their lifestyle. However, this situation makes them vulnerable to cyberbullying. Uploaded photos, video clips can be used for blackmail. At this point, the use of social media should be done consciously [6].

The most common places where cyberbullying occurs are [5]:

- Social media environments such as Facebook, Instagram, Snapchat, and Tik Tok
- Text messaging applications on mobile or tablet devices
- Instant messaging, direct messaging, and online chat applications
- Online chat forums, chat rooms, and message boards such as Reddit
- Email services
- Online gaming communities

Cyberbullying affects all age groups. Young people and children are the groups most exposed to cyberbullying. With the developing technology, the time spent by young people on social media is increasing and this situation causes young people to face certain risks in social media. According to the report "Safety Net: Cyberbullying's impact on young people's mental health Inquiry report," approximately half of the children and young people (44%) spend more than three hours a day on social media, and approximately 9% of them spend the night between midnight and 6 am. There is also a link between heavy social media use and mental health: 38% of the youth reported that social media affected them negatively and 23% of those reported that this had a positive effect; 46% of the girls stated that social media has a negative effect on self-esteem [7]. Between 2005 and 2015, on average 12- to 15-year-old adolescents in Britain spent more than 8–19 hours of online time per week. It shows that the use of social media is becoming an increasingly important part of children's lives. Besides, the time spent by children on the internet exceeded the time spent watching television for the first time last year [8, 9]. It has been reported that cyberbullying among students in 15% of public schools in the USA between 2017 and 2018 occurred at least once a week. In addition, 9% of public schools reported that the school environment was affected by cyberbullying and 8% reported that personnel resources were used to deal with this problem [10]. The statistics shown in Figure 7.1 show the percentage of middle and high school students who have been cyberbullied in the United States and their representation by gender. In the April 2019 survey, it was found that 38.7% of female students and 34.1% of boys were bullied on the internet [11]. For those who are bullied on the internet, there are significant numbers of adults. Figure 7.2 shows the proportion of adult internet users in the USA who were personally abused online as of January 2020. In this survey, it was found that 44% of internet users were personally exposed to all kinds of online harassment, and 28% of respondents reported serious forms of online harassment such as physical threats, sexual harassment, harassment, and continuous harassment. In addition, 77% of online harassment victims who responded reported being harassed on Facebook [12].

With the transition to the digital age, the cyberbullying action, which affects large social groups and threatens society as a whole in various aspects, is performed in various ways. Cyberbullying types are categorized by researchers.

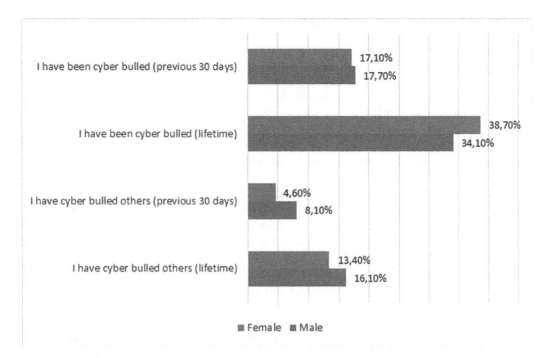

FIGURE 7.1 Percentage of US middle and high school students who experienced cyberbullying as of April 2019, by type of bullying and gender [11].

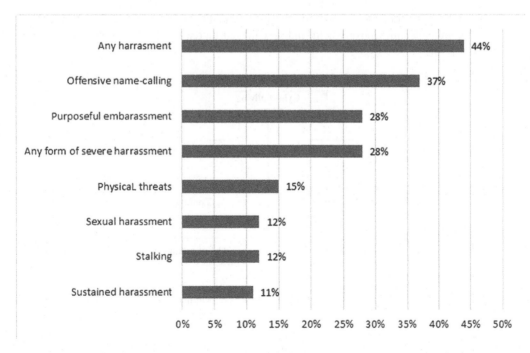

FIGURE 7.2 The proportion of adult internet users in the US who experienced personal online harassment as of January 2020 [12].

7.2 CYBERBULLYING CATEGORIES

Cyberbullying can be divided into various categories according to the way it is done [13]; these are Flooding, Masquerade, Flaming, Trolling, Harassment, Cyberstalking, Denigration, Outing, and Exclusion. These eight types of cyberbullying can be defined under four main types: written-verbal behavior (phone calls, text messages, emails, instant messaging, chats, blogs, social networking communities, websites), visual behavior (sharing the images and videos that via mobile phone or internet posting makeup risk), exclusion (intentionally excluding someone from an online group), and impersonations (stealing and disclosing personal information, using another person's name and account) [14]. Cyberbullying categories are shown in Figure 7.3.

Flooding: It is a type of cyberbullying that consists of sending the same comments repeatedly, making ridiculous comments, and pressing the enter button repeatedly in order to prevent the role of the cyberbullied person in correspondence. Frequently, during the chatting children show a desire for control and power. For example, in chat rooms, it is usually done by holding down the send key [15].

Masquerade: Includes the bully login to a website, chat room, or program using another user's screen name. It is a type of attack that acts like non-bullies but is bullied [16]. A masked attack is an attack class in which the user of a system illegitimately establishes or inherits the identity of another legitimate user [17].

Flaming: It is a bullying type that occurs during an online fight. It takes the form of sending a brutally insulting electronic message to one or more private or public online groups [17]. This type of attack usually includes offensive, vulgar language, insults, and sometimes threats [18].

Trolling: Trolling is one of the most common types of bullying attacks. One of the general definitions of trolling is attracting people or groups from online discussion forums to meaningless and time-consuming activities [19]. In addition, these provocative and threatening comments aim to overwhelm individuals and increase the depression level of the victims [20].

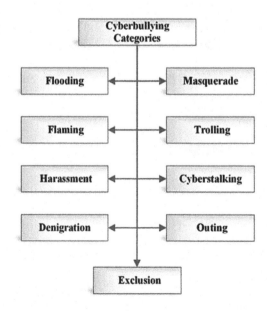

FIGURE 7.3 Cyberbullying categories.

Harassment: It is a type of bullying in which a person usually sends rude and humiliating messages toward the target person [13]. This harassment with messages is repeated, sending offensive messages to an individual target constantly. Abusive messages are often sent through personal communication channels such as email, instant messaging, and text messages [18].

Cyberstalking: Cyberstalking is the repeated sending of extremely intimidating or extremely aggressive messages that contain a threat of harm to the victim. Cyberstalkers may also try to defame their targets and destroy their friendship and reputation. The line of demarcation between harassment and cyberstalking is not clear, but if a person starts to worry about their safety when they are exposed to such an attack, it is over the harassment [18].

Denigration: It consists of a harmful and inaccurate speech about a person. It aims to humiliate a person and damage his/her reputation in society. These rude and hurtful messages can be sent directly to the person or can be done in a public environment, using images privately through web pages [21].

Outing: It is the sending and transmission of private images or information of a person to others in a public way. This information is often information that can cause embarrassment. A common form is when the attacker transmits an email containing someone else's private information to other users [18].

Exclusion: Exclusion behavior is about determining who is an in-group member and who is excluded, and it involves deliberately excluding someone from an online group [22]. Its results are emotionally heavy [18].

7.3   THE CONSEQUENCES OF CYBERBULLYING

Cyberbullying has various negative effects on victims. Adolescents who were targeted through cyberbullying reported increased depressive moods, anxiety, loneliness, suicidal behavior, and somatic symptoms [23]. Children can have harmful consequences such as the behavior of dropping out of school, fear and weakness, high stress, and anxiety. Besides these, violence and aggressive behaviors against others, cyberbullying, juvenile delinquency, and bringing weapons to school can be some consequences of cyberbullying [24]. Furthermore, it causes psychological problems in young people, decreased self-esteem, and poor academic performance [25]. In the study conducted by Kim et al. [26], the relationship between cyberbullying and the mental health of adolescents and its effects by gender were discussed. Students were aged 6–12 asked questions about traditional bullying and cyberbullying they suffered in the last six months and the mental health problems they experienced in relation to these. According to the results, it has been revealed that cyberbullying has strong ties with emotional and behavioral problems. It is especially associated with emotional problems in girls and behavioral problems in boys. A study examining the relationship between cyberbullying and deviant behaviors that harm health (drugs, alcohol, sexual intercourse with many partners, etc.) found serious links between them. Findings have shown that cyberbullying victimization is positively associated with every predicted deviant behavior. The dimension of this relationship increased when the participants reported that they were exposed to both cyberbullying and physical bullying [24]. In a study conducted in a region where middle school students are concentrated in the USA, it was revealed that the young people who are the victims or bullies of traditional bullying or cyberbullying have more suicidal thoughts and tendencies than the young people who do not have such bullying behaviors. In addition, it was found that victims have more suicidal tendencies than aggressors [27]. Megan Meier, 13, who committed suicide after cyberstalking in 2006, is an important example of cyberbullying and suicide [28]. Furthermore, considering the data in Centers for Disease Control and Prevention (CDC) WISQARS Leading Causes of Death Reports in 2018, suicide ranks second among the causes of death of young people aged 10–34 in the USA, this is an outstanding problem [29].

7.4 CYBERSTALKING

Cyberstalking is a form of action that basically aims to frighten the targeted people. The difference between harassment and cyberstalking is not very clear. In addition, some of the studies in the literature have been used interchangeably. However, as mentioned in Section 7.2, when the person is now concerned about their own safety as a result of the harassment, this points to a different point from normal harassment. Cyberstalking makes sense at this point.

Cyberstalking behaviors that existed in the community before the internet and its based tools became widespread are explained in the Supplemental Victimization Survey, which was discussed in the study of Baum [30]:

- Making unwanted phone calls
- Sending unexpected or unsolicited letters or emails
- Surveillance or follow-up
- Being in certain places for no legitimate reason
- Waiting in certain places for the victim
- Leaving unwanted items, gifts, or flowers
- Spreading and sending false information about the victim on the internet, in public places, or verbally.

These behaviors, which cannot be criminal alone, cause the person to fear his safety as a whole and when they are repeated constantly. This may be accompanied by fear such as the safety of family members.

The widespread use of the internet over time has led to the development of instant messaging applications, the creation of environments such as online chat rooms, and the spread of social media channels. Online platforms have become new application areas of cyberstalking those targeting individuals. As a type of bullying, harassment has evolved into cyberstalking by changing its dimensions with the internet age. Cyberstalking is the unlawful continuous harassment in order to annoy, disquiet, create serious emotional distress, and get alert the targeted person through email, SMS, or other sending items using other electronic communication tools. A cyberstalker constantly monitors the target person's online activities, collecting information, and using this information for threats or other verbal intimidation [31, 32]. Table 7.1 shows the effects that may occur on the victim as a result of cyberstalking as personal effects, social and financial effects, and effects on third parties.

Sheridan and Grant [33], in their study on a group that was subjected to cyberstalking, showed that there was no difference between cyberstalking and traditional (offline stalking) harassment. In

TABLE 7.1
Effects That May Occur as a Result of Cyberstalking [33]

Personal effects	Fear, Agoraphobia, Anxiety, Irritation, Anger, Suicidal thoughts, Visited a health professional, Distrust, Purging (using laxatives, forced vomiting), Confusion, Suicide attempt(s), Depression, Weakness, Injuries, Nausea, Panic attacks, Sleep disturbances, Loss of/increased appetite, Weight changes, Headaches, Self-harm, Aggression, Paranoia
Social and financial effects	Cutting working hours, Decreasing contact with family/friends, Changed employment/course of study, Decreasing social activities, Affecting work performance, Change of work or location, Loss of money, Hiding identity and change identity, Breaking relationships, Security expenses, Legal expenses, Getting annual leave from cyberstalking, Car change, Expense of counseling, Moving house, Therapy expenses, Expenses for correction of property damage caused by the abuser
Third-party effects	The effect on the victim's family, the effect on the victim's child, the effect on the victim's acquaintances, the effect on the victim's, the effect on the victim's coworkers, the effect on the victim's pets, the effect on the victim's partner, the effect on the victim's on his neighbors

this respect, serious consequences of cyberstalking emerge. First of all, fear arises on the victim due to the behavior of the aggressor. Physical and emotional harms occur to the victim. Along with the initial feeling of fear in the victim, various effects occur, ranging from anxiety, depression, anxiety, nervousness, despair, and then to suicidal thoughts. Apart from that, the actions of the attacker may result in physical and financial damages. Sometimes the cyberstalker can make the targeted person distress by attacking a loved one [30, 34].

7.5 CYBERBULLYING ON ONLINE SOCIAL NETWORKS

The number of users of OSNs has been increasing rapidly in recent years, which means that they have evolved into a platform for connecting people all over the world and sharing their interests. These platforms are becoming highly preferred today due to the fact that the cost of using the internet is very low and they provide convenience in multi-participant communication compared to messaging tools such as SMS and provide the opportunity to easily send images, audio, and video content out of text sending, and this rate is increasing every day. Worldwide OSN users were 2.86 billion people in 2017 and in 2020 it is increased to 3 billion people. In 2025, this number is expected to increase to 4.41 billion people [35]. OSNs such as Twitter, Tumblr, Instagram, Facebook, YouTube, and WhatsApp connect billions of people and allow various information, including people's business and private life, to be obtained by malicious people. This information can include a lot of information, such as the person's lifestyle, where they go and have fun, which workplace they work, which school they attend, and what artistic activities they participate in. All of these give enormous possibilities for cyberbullies. There are many definitions of OSNs in the literature. Boyd and Ellison [36] specified that, for a web service to be named as OSN, a web service must allow people to create an open or semi-open profile, to create a user list to interact, and to enable users to see what has been done through the system.

The fact that OSNs offer various opportunities for cyberbullying and the serious consequences of cyberbullying make the fight against cyberbullying very important. Facebook, YouTube, Ask.fm, and Instagram were reported as the top five OSNs with the most cyberbullying attacks [37]. Today, machine learning methods are frequently used in the detection of cyberbullying content. Predetermined bullying activities are very important in terms of preventing them. Table 7.2 shows the studies for the detection of posts containing cyberbullying using various OSN platforms and data sets obtained from these platform.

Zois et al. [53], in their study on cyberbullying detection, stated that past approaches are scalability and timely issues (timely detection), and discussed the problem of cyberbullying detection as a sequential hypothesis determination problem. Based on this view, they have introduced a new algorithm called AvOID to significantly reduce the number of feature evaluations required for cyberbullying detection and to reduce the time to issue cyberbullying alerts. Here, each message can

TABLE 7.2
Cyberbullying Detection Studies Conducted in Some OSNs

OSNs	Cyberbullying Detection Studies
ask.fm	[38, 39]
Facebook	[40]
FORMSPRING.ME	[39, 41]
Instagram	[38, 42]
Myspace	[39, 43–45]
spring.me	[46]
Twitter	[47–50]
Vine	[51]
YouTube	[52]

belong to either class, and the goal is to extract attributes from the post and decide when to stop evaluating and making a decision. For this purpose, an optimization function is defined in terms of cost of features and the average cost of classification strategy and optimum solution is determined. It provided a 64% reduction in the number of features used for classifying the models they proposed. Al-Ajlan and Ykhlef [50] used the deep learning method in their study to identify and classify cyberbullying posts. In many studies, feature extraction and selection are performed, especially as the size of the data increases, this turns into a difficult process. To provide a solution to this situation, they proposed a new algorithm called OCDD (Optimized Twitter Cyberbullying Detection based on Deep Learning) based on deep learning. Unlike the previous methods, this method does not extract features. Here, each tweet is taken as a word vector. Thus, they preserved the meanings of all words. Instagram is a popular photo-sharing website. Various studies are carried out by researchers to prevent cyberbullying acts on this platform. Zhong et al. [42] tried to determine whether the images sent for early detection of cyberbullying contain cyberbullying or not. In this model, the features of the images and their comments have been extracted, and in addition to these, features such as obtaining the subjects from the caption of the images (with Latent Dirichlet allocation) are used. In this study, the results obtained using the convolutional neural network (CNN) algorithm are compared with support vector machine (SVM) and a Bayesian classifier. The results obtained have been successful. Inan et al. [41] studied the datasets they obtained from Formspring.me, Myspace, and YouTube social network platforms. The results they obtained with multi-layer perceptron (MLP), SGD, and logistic regression algorithms have been very successful. Kumar and Sachdeva [39] tested the data they obtained from social networks Formspring.me, Myspace, and Ask.fm with eight up-to-date supervised learning algorithms after a series of data preprocessing steps. They obtained the best accuracy and precision results with the JRIP algorithm.

7.6 CYBERBULLYING DETECTION STEPS

Detecting posts involving cyberbullying consist of a series of data mining and machine learning steps. First of all, raw data should be collected. Data is collected from online platforms and then passed through data preprocessing steps to reduce noise in the data. The following steps are feature extraction and feature selection. Many methods can be applied here. With the obtained features, machine learning, neural networks, fuzzy logic, evolutionary computation, and probabilistic methods can be used [54]. These models have had significant success in the early detection of cyberbullying. Figure 7.4 shows the general steps followed for the detection of cyberbullying posts.

The detection of cyberbullying and harassment on online platforms is often handled as a classification problem. The methods used in the solution of OSNs problems such as Sentiment Detection [55], Stance Detection [56], Fake News Detection [57], Irony Detection [58], and Topic Detection [59] cyberbullying can also be used in solving the problem. Using the information obtained from the analysis of the messages and sender and receiver characteristics could lead to useful information for the detection of cyberbullying. Cyberbullying detection is a difficult task. Just because a message contains negative emotions or bad content does not mean that there is bullying there. For example, even if a message like "I disgust what you said today and never want to see you again" clearly contains a very negative statement, it is difficult to classify this message as bullying without understanding the broad context of the messaging here. Besides, evaluating a bullying expression alone may not give a complete result without looking at the front and the words behind it. On the other hand,

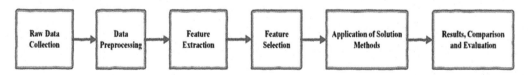

FIGURE 7.4   General Cyberbullying detection steps.

feelings that contain sarcasm and positively expressed can hide bullying. Cyberbullying detection includes the following objectives [60]:

➢ Determining whether the messages used during a communication contain bullying
➢ Calculating the severity of the cyberbullying
➢ Determining the roles experienced by the relevant people during this interaction
➢ Classifying the events tshat occur after a cyberbullying incident (for example, deciding the psychological state of the victim after receiving a bullying message)

The cyberbullying detection process consists of the following steps:

• The first step in this process is to obtain various raw data about cyberbullying from OSN. These datasets on cyberbullying generally consist of comments, posts, pictures, and videos of users collected from social networks [61]. These data can be obtained from Twitter [62] with an application. It can also be obtained from popular social networks such as YouTube [63], Instagram [64], Facebook [65], and ask.fm [66] Apart from these, ready-made datasets from online sources such as UCI [67], Kaggle [68], Github [69], and sentiment140.com can be used for cyberbullying studies.
• Most of the data available on the internet consists of semi-structured or unstructured data. These data sets contain many inconsistencies, missing values, noise, and errors [70]. The next step to correct this situation is data preprocessing. This step includes removing spaces, removing stop words, removing special characters, tokenization, and lemmatization. Other techniques can be used in this step to clear the data set [61].
• After this step, feature extraction methods will be used. The tf-idf method and n-gram methods are used in the literature. Although the success of the methods varies in practice, successful results have been obtained. For example, Mangaonkar et al. [47], the comparisons made with bi-gram toxiners gave better results. Feature selection methods are used to select the best feature subset after the feature extraction step. With these feature selection algorithms, high dimensional feature space is reduced. Thus, the classification time is reduced. Feature selection algorithms such as Chi2 and ReliefF are used in the literature.
• The last step involves classifying the data and evaluating the classification results. At this stage, the data are classified using various methods. Thus, it is determined whether the data contains bullying or not. The results obtained are evaluated in terms of various success metrics.

7.6.1 Data Preprocessing Steps

In order to increase the solution performance of social network analysis problems, data preprocessing steps that reduce the noise in the data are applied. This situation is valid for the solution of the cyberbullying detection problem. Data preprocessing consists of several steps. With these steps, the data is made suitable for performing the cyberbullying task. Thus, more effective results are obtained. In most of the cyberbullying detection studies in which data preprocessing steps were used in the literature, according to Salawu et al. [60] tokenization and stemming steps performed more than other data preprocessing steps.

a) **Tokenization**: Tokenization is the process of separating a document into words, expressions, symbols, or other meaningful items called symbols. The list obtained after this operation is used as an input for text mining. The main purpose here is to help identify keywords. With this step, it is necessary to eliminate the punctuation marks, parentheses, and dashes [71].
b) **Removing Stop Words**: Some words contained in the text contribute little to the meaning of the text and have a negligible effect on the classification of the text. In the text, which does not mean anything alone and is frequently used; Words like prepositions, pronouns, and

conjunctions are called stop words. These are the, in, a, an, with, etc. are words. These words are removed from the document because they are not measured as keywords in text mining applications. In addition, this process helps to reduce the dimensions of the term space [72].

c) **Changing and Removing Special Characters**: This step involves replacing characters like "@" with "at" and removing characters like "#". Especially the use of these characters in tweets makes this step important.

d) **Stemming and Lemmatization**: Stemming is a heuristic method of shortening prefixes and suffixes to obtain the root of a word. With this operation, the frequency of the words can be narrowed down to a single value for the root and the importance of words in the corpus can be emphasized. Lemmatization is the development of the stemming technique, which uses a dictionary-based approach in the morphological analysis of words to obtain the basic form of a word called lemma.

e) **Coreference Resolution**: The common reference solution is the task of finding all expressions in a text that refer to the same object. Repetition is one of the most recurring common reference cases in written text, making the string matching features more important for all common reference resolution systems [73].

f) **Converting Capital Letters to Lowercase Letters**: This is a common process, but using capital letters on social media can be an expression of yelling or anger. In this sense, the cyberbullying task can have the opposite effect and reduce the success rate.

g) **Correcting Grammar and Misspelling Words**: It is one of the important data preprocessing steps in correcting misspelled and grammatically inappropriate words.

7.6.2 FEATURES USED FOR CYBERBULLYING DETECTION

The features used in studies are generally divided into four main groups. These are content-based, sentiment-based, user-based, and network-based features (Figure 7.5) [60].

Content-based features: Defined as extractable word elements of a document, such as keywords, profanity, pronouns, and punctuation marks. These are features such as cyberbullying keywords, n-grams, Bags-of-words (BoW), Term Frequency Inverse Document Frequency (TF-IDF), document length, and spelling.

Sentiment-based features: Sentiment-based features include word and sentence elements that we can use to determine the sentiment of the document.

User-based features: Features such as age, gender, and sexual orientation are used in the analysis of a user's behavior in the internet environment.

Network-based features: These features are the number of friends obtained from OSNs, the number of followers, and the frequency of posts.

Most of the studies in the literature have used content-based features. Using swearing words is the popular approach for cyberbullying detection task. For this objective, online resources

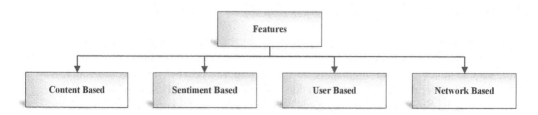

FIGURE 7.5 Taxonomy of features used for Cyber Bullying Detection.

("noswearing.com") that contain swear words lists or the work of various researchers are used. In cases where the use of swear words alone is not enough, studies have been carried out by taking into account the pronouns used with the abusive word [74]. Apart from swearing words, cyberbullying words are used for this task. These words are generally grouped as swearing-free words that relate to common themes of bullying, such as race, physical appearance, gender, and sexuality. Considering that bullying comments are generally short, some studies use the length of the document [75]. The proportion of capital letters was used as a feature to use the yelling behavior in comments made by users [76]. Also, there have been studies using the standard spelling feature of words and special characters [52, 77].

7.6.3 Cyberbullying Detection Methods

Cyberbullying detection studies mostly consist of studies on text data. There are few studies on posts such as pictures and videos. The binary classification has been used in most of the studies on cyberbullying detection. In this classification, messages are classified as "bullying" or "non-bullying." Sentiment analysis, supervised learning, and dictionary-based systems were used in this classification task. Apart from these, the role determination task is one of the most performed studies. Many studies have been conducted on determining the severity of cyberbullying [60]. In addition, these studies have proposed a new task to identify and classify events that occur after cyberbullying [75, 78, 79]. Various methods have been put forward to accomplish these tasks. In the literature, the most used method for cyberbullying detection task is Supervised Learning [41, 79–81]. In addition, semi-supervised learning [77], dictionary-based approach [82], rule-based approach [83], Table 7.3 shows the methods used in cyberbullying detection studies. SVM and Naïve Bayes are the most used methods in these studies.

TABLE 7.3
Cyberbullying Solution Methods

Cyberbullying Solution Methods	Studies
AdaBoost	[51]
AvOID algorithm	[53]
Bagging	[84, 85]
Dagging	[84]
Deep learning, CNN	[50, 86]
Decision trees, C4.5, J48	[39, 48, 51, 84, 87–89]
Essential dimensions of LSI	[90]
FuzGen learning technique	[45]
JRip	[39]
KNN	[39, 48, 88]
Linear regression	[91]
Logistic light gradient boosting machine	[92]
Logistic regression	[39, 41, 47, 80, 93]
Maximum entropy (MaxEnt) classifier	[94]
MLP (multi-layer perceptron) neural networks	[41, 95]
Naïve bayes	[38, 39, 42, 46, 47, 51, 84, 87, 88, 93, 96, 97]
Projective adaptive resonance theory (PART)	[39]
Probabilistic information fusion framework	[49]
Ramdom forest	[48, 51]
SGD (stochastic gradient descent)	[92]
SMO (sequential minimal optimization)	[48, 84]
SNM (sorted neighborhood methods)	[40]
SVM (support vector machine), LibSVM	[38, 42–44, 47, 74, 76, 79, 80, 81, 85, 87, 95, 97–100]
ZeroR	[49, 84]

7.6.3.1 Supervised Methods

Various supervised methods are used in the cyberbullying detection task. It is ensured that the system creates a learning model by giving the inputs and the outputs associated with them to the system.

AdaBoost: AdaBoost is an effective machine learning method for classifying two or more classes. AdaBoost increments a number of weak classifiers $\{h_m(x)\}$, by combining input data x with scalar weights $\{\alpha_m\}$ in each round t with a strong classifier $H(x)$. There are many different versions used in the literature:

$$H\left(x\right) = sign\left(\sum_{m=1}^{M} \alpha_m . h_m\left(x\right)\right)$$

Avoid algorithm: It is suggested by Zois et al. [53] and it is a new model that is used optimization in order to make cyberbullying detection successful.

Bagging: This algorithm is a general algorithm used to stabilize unstable prediction methods such as neural networks and decision trees. Bagging algorithm is a type of general ensemble learning algorithm. First, randomize training samples to create a set of similar training subsets; It then trains a few basic classifiers using these training subsets (decision tree classifier). Finally, the classification properties of the samples are determined by the classification results of multiple basic classifiers. Since the bagging sampling method makes the training subsets independent from each other, basic classifier diversity is provided that can increase the generalization performance of the modular model [101].

Dagging: This meta-classifier creates a layered structure that is separate from the data. It feeds a copy of the base classifier with a chunk of data. Since all major classifiers are put in the vote meta-classifier, a prediction is made by the majority vote. It is useful for basic classifiers that are worse in time behavior about the number of samples in training data [102].

Deep Learning: It is a machine learning method that makes use of many layers of a nonlinear learning process for supervised and non-supervised feature extraction, transformation, pattern analysis, and classification [103].

- **Convolutional Neural Network (CNN)**: It is an artificial neural network structure used to understand the internal structure of data (such as an image). CNN consists of many pooling and convolutional layers. The convolutional layer is responsible for taking a subset of data (pixels of an image) and performing various mathematical operations on that set. At the end of these processes, an image passed through the pooling layer and reduced in size is formed. Many researchers have also used CNN in many text mining operations. When applying CNN to text, the word vector is used in place of the pixel vector [50].

Decision trees: Decision trees are one of the most used methods. In this method, a tree is created for the classification process and each record is applied to the created tree and the classification is made. It basically consists of two steps. The first is the establishment of the tree and the second is the application of the records to the tree. Many methods based on decision trees have been developed. These methods are separated from each other in terms of the path they follow in choosing the root node branching criteria.

- **C4.5 Decision Tree**: It was proposed by Ross Quinlan in 1993 to overcome the limitations of the ID3 algorithm. One of the limitations of the ID3 algorithm is that it is extremely sensitive when properties have a large number of values. C4.5 uses Information Gain to overcome this problem. In C4.5, the data is sorted to find the best split feature in each node of the tree. "The gain ratio impurity method" is used to evaluate the split property [104].

- **J48 Decision Tree (J48)**: It is a popular decision tree classifier with good results. It is an improved version of the C4.5 algorithm.

Essential Dimensions of LSI (EDLSI): A further development of the Latent Semantic Indexing (LSI) model. Runtime and memory requirements and the number of sizes used are reduced.

FuzGen Learning Technique: It is a system consisting of the combination of fuzzy logic and Genetic algorithm and recommended by Nandhini and Sheeba [45]. The learning module contains the adaptive component of the system through a genetic algorithm (GA) with fuzzy set genes. This system performs the evolutionary process using the GA and the evaluation of the chromosome is done using the fuzzy rule set.

JRip: It is one of the popular classification algorithms. Classes are progressively analyzed and an initial set of classes is created. Then a set of rules is created for each class and it covers all members of that class. **KNN (k nearest neighbors)**: It is a popular classification algorithm. When classifying data, it classifies it according to its proximity to its neighbors. In other words, it is decided which class to be placed by looking at its neighbors. In doing this, similarity and distance criteria are used.

Logistic Light Gradient Boosting Machine: It is one of the Boosting algorithms. It uses the tree-based learning algorithm and is known as the gradient boosting framework [92].

Linear Regression: Linear regression method tries to model the relationship between the dependent variable and one or more independent variables with a linear equation. One of the variables is considered as an explanatory variable, the other as a dependent variable. Before applying the model to the data, it should be decided whether there is a relationship between the variables of interest. The dependent variable to be estimated in linear regression analysis is continuous, and the value of the dependent variable is estimated in linear regression analysis [105].

Logistic Regression: It is used to classify categorical or numerical data. It works only if the dependent variable can take two different values. The most distinctive feature that distinguishes logistic regression from linear regression is that the result variable in logistic regression is binary or multiple. In the Logistic Regression Analysis, the dependent variable takes a discrete value. In Logistic Regression Analysis, the probability of realization of one of the values that the dependent variable can take is estimated [106].

Maximum Entropy (MaxEnt) Classifier: This method is a machine learning method used in various fields. Since it was first introduced in 1996, more than one hundred versions of this method have been used in natural language processing methods. Besides, MaxEnt classifiers have become a strong alternative to Naïve Bayes [107].

MLP (Multi-Layer Perceptron) Neural Networks: It is a feed-forward artificial neural network model. Sets up a structure that relates input data with appropriate outputs. It has an MLP directed graph structure and consists of multiple node layers. Nodes other than input nodes are neurons with nonlinear functions. MLP can distinguish nonlinear data [108].

Naïve Bayes: This method, named after Thomas Bayes, is probabilistic. Naïve Bayes algorithm is a predictive and descriptive classification algorithm that tries to determine the relationship between the target variable and the independent variables. It has many application areas such as text classification, medical diagnosis, and classification of malicious emails.

Probabilistic Information Fusion Framework: It is a new model that takes advantage of interdependence and trust scores related to different social and textual features to better predict cyberbullying. This method uses the relationships between heterogeneous data features and their effects on the classification to increase classification success.

Random Forest: Random Forest algorithm consists of a combination of three classifiers. Each classifier is created from a random vector sample and is independent of the input vector. To classify the input vector, each tree votes one unit to the more popular class [109].

SGD (Stochastic Gradient Descent): It is an optimization algorithm that finds the values of the parameters in a function f to find an optimum solution [92].

SMO (Sequential Minimal Optimization): Training a SVM requires the solution of huge quadratic programming (QP) optimization problem. This algorithm has been proposed to solve the SVM QP problem. It does this without extra matrix storage and numerical QP optimization steps. SMO divides the QP problem into sub-QP problems and used Osuna's theorem to achieve convergence.

SNM (Sorted Neighborhood Methods): The key feature, which is the most distinctive feature of the data, is used to sort the records that match each other in the databases. The SNM method, on the other hand, is limited to a small neighborhood in the ordered list to compare records after sorting. This method depends on the quality of the key feature. The poor key selection causes a split in poor quality.

SVM (Support Vector Machine): Derived from the statistical learning theory of Vapnik and Chervonenkis. SVM is a popular algorithm in machine learning. Basically, SVM is a two-class classifier. Given a series of training set examples, each labeled as belonging to one of two categories, an SVM training algorithm creates a model that assigns new samples to one category or the other, making this model a non-probabilistic binary linear or nonlinear classifier [81].

- LibSVM: LibSVM is one of the most used SVM software. LibSVM is a library for SVMs. Its purpose is to introduce SVM as a suitable tool [110].

ZeroR: It is a simple classification method. In this method, the majority class is estimated. It is often used to measure the performance of other classifiers. A frequency table is created for a target and the value with the highest frequency is selected [108].

7.6.3.2 Semi-Supervised Methods

In semi-supervised learning, untagged data and a small amount of tagged data are given to the system. This method is generally preferred in cases where there is a lot of unlabeled data and less labeled data. Nahar et al. [77] suggested a new semi-controlled method, stating that controlled methods require previously tagged data, whereas, in the real world, small amounts of data can be labeled in this way. Their proposed model includes increasing the training data and applying the fuzzy SVM algorithm. Their methods have been more successful than popular algorithms such as Naïve Bayes, Logic regression, and Random Forest.

7.6.3.3 Lexicon-Based Methods

In the dictionary-based approach, a small set of opinion words is collected in general, and then this set is developed by searching for synonyms and antonyms with other tools such as WordNet. The newly found words are added to the seed list and the next iteration begins. The iteration continues until new words are no longer found. When the process is finished, it is terminated by correcting and debugging the errors [111]. Pérez et al. [83] proposed a lexicon-based method called MISAAC to find threatening structures in the conversation between 9 and 13 years old children. Content analysis techniques are used here to measure the danger of the messages a child receives in the interaction with his environment. The messages are processed by a lexical analyzer and compared with the aggression module. Then the aggression range of the message is calculated. Fahrnberger et al. [112] proposed a framework called SafeChat to detect harmful content that children are exposed to. It is the result of combining SafeChat contextual features with the message encryption features of SecureString 2.0.

7.6.3.4 Rule-Based Methods

In rule-based classifiers, the data space is modeled with a rule set. In a case where the left-hand side (left side) is the right-hand side (right side) class label, the separator indicates a condition in the feature set in normal form. Conditions are related to terms. Rule-based classification uses a scheme of IF-THEN rules to estimate class. This scheme consists of three components [113]:

- Rule Induction Algorithm This algorithm expresses structures such as sequential covering algorithms, decision tree structure, and association rules to extract appropriate IF-THEN rules from data.
- Rule Ranking Measures: Refers to some values used to determine the correct estimation of a rule.
- Class Prediction Algorithms: Predicts the class of an unidentified record based on rules.

One of the approaches used in studies for cyberbullying classification is rule-based methods. Mahmud et al. [114] extract semantic information from the general semantic structure to interpret the basic meaning of the sentence without pattern matching, unlike the semantic rules defined by Smokey for classification. Classifies systems with sentence level. Serra and Venter [83] suggested a rule-based approach to detect cyberbullying messages, especially to children over the phone. Chen et al. [78] obtained the Lexical Syntactic Framework using the writing styles and speaking histories of the users and calculated an aggression score. They separated swearing and dirty words in the detection of offensive contents and defined "hand-authoring syntactic rules" to detect the content of harassment. Systems have left many methods behind in terms of success.

7.7   SUCCESS METRICS USED IN CYBERBULLYING STUDIES

Cyberbullying detection has used the classification success metrics in most of the studies. The metrics used in this field are briefly explained here. The complexity matrix values TP, FP, TN, FN used in the calculation of metrics such as F-measure and Precision explained below are briefly shown. Then, the success metrics used are explained.

- TP (True Positive): It is the situation that the model predicts positively and is actually positive.
- FN (False Negative): It is the state that the model predicts negatively and is actually positive.
- FP (False Positive): The state that the model predicts positively and is actually negative.
- TN (True Negative): While the model's prediction is negative, it is the situation that is actually negative.

ACC score: In multi-tag classification, this function calculates the subset accuracy, that is, the set of tags predicted for a sample must exactly match the corresponding set of tags in exact (correct) tags [80].

AUC score: The Area Under the Curve (AUC) value is obtained by calculating the area under the ROC curve by integrating. With this value, the success of the classification model used is interpreted. The high value of this value indicates that the model predicts 0's as 0 and 1's as 1. This evaluation parameter is strictly limited to binary classification [80].

F-Measure: It is the harmonic average of two properties such as Precision and Recall. It provides the opportunity to combine and evaluate these two properties together from a single measure.

$$\frac{2 * \text{precision} * \text{recall}}{\text{precision} + \text{recall}}$$

Kappa statistic: This method, which is frequently used in measuring success, is used to determine the reliability between raters and was developed to determine the degree of agreement between two raters who scored at the classification level.

Precision (Specificity): It is the division of the number of positive predicted and actually positive samples by the model to the sum of the number of correctly predicted positive samples and the so-called positive predictions but actually negative ones. It is the ability of the classifier to not label the sample as positive, which is a negative. Below is the calculation equation.

$$\frac{tp}{tp + fp}$$

Mean Squared Error (MSE): The formula $(x - y)^2$ is used to calculate the MSE value. Here, x is the average human score and y is the score obtained using a specific approach [91].

Mean Absolute Percent Error (MAPE): The MAPE value of an algorithm is a measure that corrects the "canceling out" effects of positive and negative errors and takes into account the different scales from which this measurement can be calculated. It is calculated by the following equation [95]:

$$\text{MAPE}_i = \frac{100}{n} \sum_{j=1}^{n} \frac{\left| P_{(ij)} - T_j \right|}{T_j}$$

Recall (Sensitivity): It is the division of the number of correctly predicted samples by the total number of correctly predicted samples and the negative and actually positive cases of the model. Below is the calculation equation:

$$\frac{tp}{tp + fn}$$

ROC curve: This curve represents a probability curve and shows the performance of a classification model at different decision classification thresholds. It consists of two different parameters called true positive rate and false positive rate.

$$\text{RMSFE}_i = \sqrt{\frac{\sum_{j=1}^{n} \left| P_{(ij)} - T_j \right|^2}{n}}$$

Root Mean Square Error (RMSFE): RMSFE of an I algorithm is calculated by the following equation

$$\text{RMSFE}_i = \sqrt{\frac{\sum_{j=1}^{n} \left| P_{(ij)} - T_j \right|^2}{n}}$$

Here, P_{ij} value is the value predicted by an algorithm I for the sample j in the sample set. T_j is the value of the target value of the *jth* sample. To make an ideal estimate, $P_{ij} = T_j$ and $\text{RMSFE}_i = 0$. Hence, the error indicator varies from 0 to infinity and 0 corresponds to the ideal estimate [95].

7.8 FUTURE DIRECTION OF CYBERBULLYING

Cyberbullying is carried out by malicious people on various platforms such as OSN, instant messaging applications, mobile devices, forums, and email services. These harmful cyber actions are expected to increase, as the use of the internet and digital tools will increase in the future. For instance, internet usage is increasing exponentially day by day. According to the Global Digital Report published by Hootsuite and We Are Social in 2019, the number of internet users in the world is increasing exponentially since 2018 and 1 million people have started using the internet per day [115]. Furthermore, according to the report in 2020, the number of internet users worldwide reached 4.54 billion which means 59% of the world population. This figure means an increase of 7% compared to 2019. Besides, social media users reached 3.8 billion people [116]. In parallel with the spread of the internet, the use of digital tools is increasing day by day. For instance, the number of unique mobile phone users has reached 5.19 worldwide [116]. The widespread use of the internet and digital tools indicates that cyberbullying will become more common in the future. Therefore, it is essential to detect cyberbullying and cyberstalking, which affect society and individuals in a multifaceted way and create systems to prevent attackers. At this point, researchers are trying to develop various systems by using artificial intelligence methods. As a result of these studies, the successful results of machine learning methods promise hope for the future as a solution. For instance, Sintaha and Mostakim [97] proposed a model in their study in December 2018 to detect cyber activity in social networks early in real-time. According to their results, they obtained a high rate of success (Accuracy: 89.54%, Precision: 92.03%, Recall: 93.09%, F-measure: 88%). Kumar and Sachdeva [39] achieved an accuracy rate of 95.5% with the hybrid supervised method they proposed in 2020 (Accuracy: 95.5, Precision: 91.7%, Recall: 78.9%, F-measure: 73.25%). The success of machine learning can be increased by novel tools. In addition, it can be ensured that new solutions can be produced by analyzing the large amount of data generated, including OSN. Machine learning methods can be used on big data in the future and get more effective results.

7.9   CONCLUSION

Cyberbullying can be named as the last point where bullying evolved with the beginning of the digital age. Especially the fact that online platforms reduce the distance between people to a single click away means that bullying has reached many opportunities at the top point where it has evolved. OSNs that provide these opportunities allows users to upload text, images, and videos to their profiles, to make open comments about the products they have purchased, to explain their health problems, and to share online with other users on many other topics. Millions of users use these public network sites as dynamic data sources with which they can communicate with other users regardless of real-time, geographic location, and physical limitations. OSNs offer great opportunities to people who design bully activities. In this respect, cyberbullying activities that can affect large masses have become one of the main cyber problems threatening today's society. According to the results, it has been observed that there is not much difference between bullying using technological tools and traditional bullying. Bullying activities that start among young children have consequences that will last for years. There are dozens of consequences ranging from depression, anxiety, stress, physical ailments to suicide. In this sense, the prevention of cyberbullying is essential for the formation of healthy individuals and therefore a healthy society.

In this study, a conceptually broad definition of cyberbullying, the types of cyberbullying, and the consequences of cyberbullying, cyberstalking, and cyberbullying in OSNs are explained. Then, the studies conducted to detect and prevent cyberbullying activities were examined in detail, and the studies and methods used by these studies were explained. Cyberbullying studies have been carried out using many popular methods, but it seems that new methods are still needed. Hybrid methods have been used very little in solving the problem. In this sense, new hybrid methods can be proposed and applied. In addition to these, better results can be obtained by optimizing existing methods. It will be very important in the studies to be done on the flowing data. Finally, as far as we see, there are no studies conducted with big data analysis. Studies with big data tools can yield important results. The problem of cyberbullying will continue to be an important issue in the future.

REFERENCES

1. Can, U., & Alatas, B. (2019). A new direction in social network analysis: Online social network analysis problems and applications. *Physica A: Statistical Mechanics and its Applications*, *535*, 122372.
2. Olweus, D. (1993). *Bullying at school: What we know and what we can do*. Malden, MA: Blackwell Publishing, 140 pp.
3. Smith, P. K., Mahdavi, J., Carvalho, M., Fisher, S., Russell, S., & Tippett, N. (2008). Cyberbullying: Its nature and impact in secondary school pupils. *Journal of Child Psychology and Psychiatry*, *49*(4), 376–385.
4. https://www.unicef.org/end-violence/how-to-stop-cyberbullying (Access 27.07.2020).
5. https://www.stopbullying.gov/cyberbullying/what-is-it#frequencyofcyberbullying (Access 27.07.2020)
6. Krithika, V., & Priya, V. (2020, February). *A Detailed Survey On Cyberbullying in Social Networks*. In *2020 International Conference on Emerging Trends in Information Technology and Engineering (ic-ETITE)* (pp. 1–10). IEEE.
7. "Safety Net: Cyberbullying's impact on young people's mental health Inquiry report" n.d. https://www.childrenssociety.org.uk/what-we-do/resources-and-publications/safety-net-the-impact-of-cyberbullying-on-children-and-young (Access 27.08.2020)
8. Przybylski, A. K., & Nash, V. (2017). Internet filtering technology and adversive online experiences in adolescence. *Journal of Pediatrics* (184), 215–219.
9. Ofcom. 2016. *Online overtakes TV as kid's top pastime*. 16 November 2016. Available: https://www.ofcom.org.uk/about-ofcom/latest/features-and-news/childrens-media-use. 15 UKCCIS.
10. https://nces.ed.gov/pubs2020/2020063.pdf (Access 10.09.2020).
11. https://www.statista.com/statistics/291034/cyber-bullying-share-of-us-students-by-type-and-gender/#statisticContainer (Access 18.09.2020).
12. https://www.statista.com/statistics/333942/us-internet-online-harassment-severity/ (Access 18.10.2020)
13. Nadali, S., Murad, M. A. A., Sharef, N. M., Mustapha, A., & Shojaee, S. (2013, December). *A review of cyberbullying detection: An overview*. In *2013 13th International Conference on Intellient Systems Design and Applications* (pp. 325–330). IEEE.
14. Nocentini, A., Calmaestra, J., Schultze-Krumbholz, A., Scheithauer, H., Ortega, R., & Menesini, E. (2010). Cyberbullying: Labels, behaviours and definition in three European countries. *Australian Journal of Guidance and Counselling*, *20*(2), 129.
15. Maher, D. (2008). Cyberbullying: An ethnographic case study of one Australian upper primary school class. *Youth Studies Australia*, *27*(4), 50.
16. Sabella, R. A. (2007). Cyberbullying and cyberthreats: Responding to the challenge of online social aggression, threats, and distress. *The Prevention Researcher*, *14*(5), 19–21.
17. Salem, M. B., & Stolfo, S. J. (2011, September). *Modeling user search behavior for masquerade detection*. In *International Workshop on Recent Advances in Intrusion Detection* (pp. 181–200). Springer, Berlin, Heidelberg.
18. Willard, N. E. (2007). *Cyberbullying and Cyberthreats: Responding to the Challenge of Online Social Aggression, Threats, and Distress*. Research Press.
19. Herring, S., Job-Sluder, K., Scheckler, R., & Barab, S. (2002). Searching for safety online: managing "trolling" in a feminist forum. *The Information Society*, 18:371–384.
20. March, E., & Marrington, J. (2019). A qualitative analysis of internet trolling. *Cyberpsychology, Behavior, and Social Networking*, *22*(3), 192–197.
21. Bauman, S. (2015). *Types of cyberbullying. Cyberbullying: What Counselors Need to Know*, pp. 53–58.
22. Menesini, E., Nocentini, A., Palladino, B. E., Frisén, A., Berne, S., Ortega-Ruiz, R., ... & Naruskov, K. (2012). Cyberbullying definition among adolescents: A comparison across six European countries. *Cyberpsychology, Behavior, and Social Networking*, *15*(9), 455–463.
23. Nixon, C. L. (2014). Current perspectives: the impact of cyberbullying on adolescent health. *Adolescent Health, Medicine and Therapeutics*, *5*, 143.
24. Graham, R., & Wood Jr, F. R. (2019). Associations between cyberbullying victimization and deviant health risk behaviors. *The Social Science Journal*, *56*(2), 183–188.
25. Tokunaga, R. S. (2010). Following you home from school: A critical review and synthesis of research on cyberbullying victimization. *Computers in Human Behavior*, *26*(3), 277–287.

26. Kim, S., Colwell, S. R., Kata, A., Boyle, M. H., & Georgiades, K. (2018). Cyberbullying victimization and adolescent mental health: Evidence of differential effects by sex and mental health problem type. *Journal of Youth and Adolescence, 47*(3), 661–672.

27. Hinduja, S., & Patchin, J. W. (2010). Bullying, cyberbullying, and suicide. *Archives of Suicide Research, 14*(3), 206–221.

28. URL-9 https://abcnews.go.com/GMA/story?id=3882520&page=1. (Access time: 27.09.2020)

29. URL-10 https://www.nimh.nih.gov/health/statistics/suicide.shtml (Access time: 27.09.2020)

30. Baum, K. (2011). *Stalking victimization in the United States*. DIANE Publishing.

31. Parsons-Pollard, N., & Moriarty, L. J. (2009). Cyberstalking: Utilizing what we do know. *Victims and Offenders*, 4(4), 435–441.

32. Al-Rahmi, W. M., Yahaya, N., Alamri, M. M., Aljarboa, N. A., Kamin, Y. B., & Saud, M. S. B. (2019). How cyber stalking and cyber bullying affect students' open learning. *IEEE Access, 7*, 20199–20210.

33. Sheridan, L. P., & Grant, T. (2007). Is cyberstalking different? Psychology, *Crime & Law, 13*(6), 627–640.

34. Fissel, E. R., & Reyns, B. W. (2020). The aftermath of cyberstalking: School, work, social, and health costs of victimization. *American Journal of Criminal Justice, 45*(1), 70–87.

35. URL-11 https://www.statista.com/statistics/278414/number-of-worldwide-social-network-users/?kw= social%20networks%20statistics&crmtag=adwords&gclid=EAIaIQobChMIptin66D_7AIVirWyCh 2SGQ5eEAAYASAAEgKiNPD_BwE (Access 05.10.2020).

36. Boyd, D. M., & Ellison, N. B. (2007). Social network sites: Definition, history, and scholarship. *Journal of Computer-Mediated Communication, 13*(1), 210–230.

37. Vyawahare, M., & Chatterjee, M. (2020). Taxonomy of Cyberbullying Detection and Prediction Techniques in Online Social Networks. In *Data Communication and Networks* (pp. 21–37). Springer, Singapore.

38. Hosseinmardi, H., Mattson, S. A., Rafiq, R., Han, R., Lv, Q., & Mishra, S. (2015, May). *Poster: Detection of Cyberbullying in a Mobile Social Network: Systems Issues*. In *Proceedings of the 13th Annual International Conference on Mobile Systems, Applications, and Services* (pp. 481–481).

39. Kumar, A., & Sachdeva, N. (2020). *Cyberbullying checker: Online bully content detection using Hybrid Supervised Learning*. In *International Conference on Intelligent Computing and Smart Communication 2019* (pp. 371–382). Springer, Singapore.

40. Chelmis, C., Zois, D. S., & Yao, M. (2017, November). *Mining patterns of cyberbullying on twitter*. In *2017 IEEE International Conference on Data Mining Workshops (ICDMW)* (pp. 126–133). IEEE.

41. Inan, C., Curuk, E., & Essiz, E. S. (2019). Automatic detection of cyberbullying in formspring. me, Myspace and YouTube social networks. *Turkish Journal of Engineering*, 3(4), 168.

42. Zhong, H., Li, H., Squicciarini, A. C., Rajtmajer, S. M., Griffin, C., Miller, D. J., & Caragea, C. (2016, July). *Content-driven detection of cyberbullying on the Instagram social network*. In *IJCAI* (pp. 3952–3958).

43. Yin, D., Xue, Z., Hong, L., Davison, B. D., Kontostathis, A., & Edwards, L. (2009). *Detection of harassment on web 2.0*. Proceedings of the Content Analysis in the WEB, 2, 1–7.

44. Dadvar, M., & De Jong, F. (2012, April). *Cyberbullying detection: a step toward a safer internet yard*. In *Proceedings of the 21st International Conference on World Wide Web* (pp. 121–126).

45. Nandhini, B. S., & Sheeba, J. I. (2015a). Online social network bullying detection using intelligence techniques. *Procedia Computer Science*, 45, 485–492.

46. Nandhini, B. S., & Sheeba, J. I. (2015, March). *Cyberbullying detection and classification using information retrieval algorithm*. In *Proceedings of the 2015 International Conference on Advanced Research in Computer Science Engineering & Technology (ICARCSET 2015)* (pp. 1–5).

47. Mangaonkar, A., Hayrapetian, A., & Raje, R. (2015, May). *Collaborative detection of cyberbullying behavior in Twitter data*. In *2015 IEEE International Conference on Electro/Information Technology (EIT)* (pp. 611–616). IEEE.

48. Galán-García, P., Puerta, J. G. D. L., Gómez, C. L., Santos, I., & Bringas, P. G. (2016). Supervised machine learning for the detection of troll profiles in twitter social network: Application to a real case of cyberbullying. *Logic Journal of the IGPL*, 24(1), 42–53.

49. Singh, V. K., Huang, Q., & Atrey, P. K. (2016, August). *Cyberbullying detection using probabilistic socio-textual information fusion*. In *2016 IEEE/ACM International Conference on Advances in Social Networks Analysis and Mining (ASONAM)* (pp. 884–887). IEEE.

50. Al-Ajlan, M. A., & Ykhlef, M. (2018, April). *Optimized Twitter cyberbullying detection based on deep learning*. In *2018 21st Saudi Computer Society National Computer Conference (NCC)* (pp. 1–5). IEEE.

51. Rafiq, R. I., Hosseinmardi, H., Han, R., Lv, Q., Mishra, S., & Mattson, S. A. (2015, August). *Careful what you share in six seconds: Detecting cyberbullying instances in Vine.* In *2015 IEEE/ACM International Conference on Advances in Social Networks Analysis and Mining (ASONAM)* (pp. 617–622). IEEE.

52. Dadvar, M., Trieschnigg, D., & de Jong, F. (2014, May). *Experts and machines against bullies: A hybrid approach to detect cyberbullies.* In *Canadian Conference on Artificial Intelligence* (pp. 275–281). Springer, Cham.

53. Zois, D. S., Kapodistria, A., Yao, M., & Chelmis, C. (2018, April). *Optimal online cyberbullying detection.* In *2018 IEEE International Conference on Acoustics, Speech and Signal Processing (ICASSP)* (pp. 2017–2021). IEEE.

54. Kumar, A., & Sachdeva, N. (2019). Cyberbullying detection on social multimedia using soft computing techniques: a meta-analysis. *Multimedia Tools and Applications*, 78(17), 23973–24010.

55. Akyol, S., & Alatas, B. (2020). Sentiment classification within online social media using whale optimization algorithm and social impact theory based optimization. *Physica A: Statistical Mechanics and its Applications*, *540*, 123094.

56. Mohammad, S., Kiritchenko, S., Sobhani, P., Zhu, X., & Cherry, C. (2016, June). *Semeval-2016 task 6: Detecting stance in tweets.* In *Proceedings of the 10th International Workshop on Semantic Evaluation (SemEval-2016)* (pp. 31–41).

57. Ozbay, F. A., & Alatas, B. (2020). Fake news detection within online social media using supervised artificial intelligence algorithms. *Physica A: Statistical Mechanics and its Applications*, *540*, 123174.

58. Charalampakis, B., Spathis, D., Kouslis, E., & Kermanidis, K. (2016). A comparison between semi-supervised and supervised text mining techniques on detecting irony in Greek political tweets. *Engineering Applications of Artificial Intelligence*, *51*, 50–57.

59. Zhang, L., Wu, Z., Bu, Z., Jiang, Y., & Cao, J. (2018). A pattern-based topic detection and analysis system on Chinese tweets. *Journal of Computational Science*, *28*, 369–381.

60. Salawu, S., He, Y., & Lumsden, J. (2017). Approaches to automated detection of cyberbullying: A survey. *IEEE Transactions on Affective Computing*.

61. Sugandhi, R., Pande, A., Chawla, S., Agrawal, A., & Bhagat, H. (2015, December). *Methods for detection of cyberbullying: A survey.* In *2015 15th International Conference on Intelligent Systems Design and Applications (ISDA)* (pp. 173–177). IEEE.

62. [URL 12] https://twitter.com/

63. [URL-13] https://www.youtube.com

64. [URL-14] https://www.instagram.com

65. https://www.facebook.com

66. https://ask.fm/

67. UCI https://archive.ics.uci.edu/ml/index.php

68. https://www.kaggle.com

69. https://www.github.com

70. Ramírez-Gallego S, Krawczyk B, García S, Wo'zniak M, Herrera F (2017). A survey on data preprocessing for data stream mining: current status and future directions. *Neurocomputing*, 239:39–57.

71. Kannan, S., & Gurusamy, V. (2014). Preprocessing techniques for text mining. *International Journal of Computer Science & Communication Networks*, 5(1), 7–16.

72. Vijayarani, S., Ilamathi, M. J., & Nithya, M. (2015). Preprocessing techniques for text mining-an overview. *International Journal of Computer Science & Communication Networks*, 5(1), 7–16.

73. URL-19] http://nlp.stanford.edu/projects/coref.shtml (Accessed 30th August).

74. Nahar, V., Unankard, S., Li, X., & Pang, C. (2012, April). *Sentiment analysis for effective detection of cyber bullying.* In *Asia-Pacific Web Conference* (pp. 767–774). Springer, Berlin, Heidelberg.

75. Dadvar, M., Trieschnigg, R. B., & de Jong, F. M. (2013a, November). *Expert knowledge for automatic detection of bullies in social networks.* In *25th Benelux Conference on Artificial Intelligence, BNAIC 2013* (pp. 57–64). Delft University of Technology.

76. Dadvar, M., Trieschnigg, D., Ordelman, R., & de Jong, F. (2013b, March). *Improving cyberbullying detection with user context.* In *European Conference on Information Retrieval* (pp. 693–696). Springer, Berlin, Heidelberg.

77. Nahar, V., Al-Maskari, S., Li, X., & Pang, C. (2014, July). *Semi-supervised learning for cyberbullying detection in social networks.* In *Australasian Database Conference* (pp. 160–171). Springer, Cham.

78. Chen, Y., Zhou, Y., Zhu, S., & Xu, H. (2012, September). *Detecting offensive language in social media to protect adolescent online safety*. In *2012 International Conference on Privacy, Security, Risk and Trust and 2012 International Conference on Social Computing* (pp. 71–80). IEEE.

79. Dadvar, M., Ordelman, R., de Jong, F., & Trieschnigg, D. (2012b). "Towards user modeling in the combat against cyberbullying," in *Proc. 17th Int. Conf. Appl. Natural Language Process. Inf. Syst., 2012b*, pp. 277–283.

80. Chavan, V. S., & Shylaja, S. S. (2015, August). *Machine learning approach for detection of cyber-aggressive comments by peers on social media network*. In *2015 International Conference on Advances in Computing, Communications and Informatics (ICACCI)* (pp. 2354–2358). IEEE.

81. Parime, S., & Suri, V. (2014, March). *Cyberbullying detection and prevention: Data mining and psychological perspective*. In *2014 International Conference on Circuits, Power and Computing Technologies [ICCPCT-2014]* (pp. 1541–1547). IEEE.

82. Pérez, P. J. C., Valdez, C. J. L., Ortiz, M. D. G. C., Barrera, J. P. S., & Pérez, P. F. (2012). *Misaac: Instant messaging tool for ciberbullying detection*. In *Proceedings on the International Conference on Artificial Intelligence (ICAI)* (p. 1). The Steering Committee of The World Congress in Computer Science, Computer Engineering and Applied Computing (WorldComp).

83. Serra, S. M., & Venter, H. S. (2011, August). *Mobile cyber-bullying: A proposal for a pre-emptive approach to risk mitigation by employing digital forensic readiness*. In *2011 Information Security for South Africa* (pp. 1–5). IEEE.

84. Huang, Q., Singh, V. K., & Atrey, P. K. (2014, November). *Cyber bullying detection using social and textual analysis*. In *Proceedings of the 3rd International Workshop on Socially-Aware Multimedia* (pp. 3–6).

85. Thu, P. P., & New, N. (2017, June). *Implementation of emotional features on satire detection*. In *2017 18th IEEE/ACIS International Conference on Software Engineering, Artificial Intelligence, Networking and Parallel/Distributed Computing (SNPD)* (pp. 149–154). IEEE.

86. Chandra, N., Khatri, S. K., & Som, S. (2018, August). *Cyberbullying Detection using Recursive Neural Network through Offline Repository*. In *2018 7th International Conference on Reliability, Infocom Technologies and Optimization (Trends and Future Directions)(ICRITO)* (pp. 748–754). IEEE.

87. Dinakar, K., Reichart, R., & Lieberman, H. (2011). *Modeling the detection of textual cyberbullying*. In *In Proceedings of the Social Mobile Web*.

88. Burn-Thornton, K., & Burman, T. (2012, November). *The use of data mining to indicate virtual (email) bullying*. In *2012 Third Global Congress on Intelligent Systems* (pp. 253–256). IEEE.

89. Squicciarini, A., Rajtmajer, S., Liu, Y., & Griffin, C. (2015, August). *Identification and characterization of cyberbullying dynamics in an online social network*. In *Proceedings of the 2015 IEEE/ACM International Conference on Advances in Social Networks Analysis and Mining 2015* (pp. 280–285).

90. Kontostathis, A., Reynolds, K., Garron, A., & Edwards, L. (2013, May). *Detecting cyberbullying: query terms and techniques*. In *Proceedings of the 5th annual acm web science conference* (pp. 195–204).

91. Del Bosque, L. P., & Garza, S. E. (2014, November). *Aggressive text detection for cyberbullying*. In *Mexican International Conference on Artificial Intelligence* (pp. 221–232). Springer, Cham.

92. Muneer, A., & Fati, S. M. (2020). A comparative analysis of machine learning techniques for cyberbullying detection on Twitter. *Future Internet*, 12(11), 187.

93. Xu, J. M., Jun, K. S., Zhu, X., & Bellmore, A. (2012a, June). *Learning from bullying traces in social media*. In *Proceedings of the 2012 Conference of the North American Chapter of the Association for Computational Linguistics: Human Language Technologies* (pp. 656–666).

94. Sheeba, J. I., & Vivekanandan, K. (2013, December). *Low frequency keyword extraction with sentiment classification and cyberbully detection using fuzzy logic technique*. In *2013 IEEE International Conference on Computational Intelligence and Computing Research* (pp. 1–5). IEEE.

95. Potha, N., & Maragoudakis, M. (2014, December). *Cyberbullying detection using time series modeling*. In *2014 IEEE International Conference on Data Mining Workshop* (pp. 373–382). IEEE.

96. Sanchez, H., & Kumar, S. (2011). Twitter bullying detection. *International Journal of Engineering Research Applications*, 12, 5–22.

97. Sintaha, M., & Mostakim, M. (2018, December). *An Empirical Study and Analysis of the Machine Learning Algorithms Used in Detecting Cyberbullying in Social Media*. In *2018 21st International Conference of Computer and Information Technology (ICCIT)* (pp. 1–6). IEEE.

98. Dadvar, M., Jong, F. D., Ordelman, R., & Trieschnigg, D. (2012a). *Improved cyberbullying detection using gender information.* In *Proceedings of the Twelfth Dutch-Belgian Information Retrieval Workshop (DIR 2012a).* University of Ghent.

99. Sood, S. O., Churchill, E. F., & Antin, J. (2012). Automatic identification of personal insults on social news sites. *Journal of the American Society for Information Science and Technology,* 63(2), 270–285.

100. Xu, J. M., Zhu, X., & Bellmore, A. (2012b, August). *Fast learning for sentiment analysis on bullying.* In *Proceedings of the First International Workshop on Issues of Sentiment Discovery and Opinion Mining* (pp. 1–6).

101. Lee, S. J., Xu, Z., Li, T., & Yang, Y. (2018). A novel bagging C4. 5 algorithm based on wrapper feature selection for supporting wise clinical decision making. *Journal of Biomedical Informatics,* 78, 144–155.

102. Ting, K. M., & Witten, I. H. (1997). Stacking bagged and dagged models.

103. Deng, L., & Yu, D. (2014). Deep learning: methods and applications. *Foundations and Trends in Signal Processing,* 7(3–4), 197–387.

104. Hssina, B., Merbouha, A., Ezzikouri, H., & Erritali, M. (2014). A comparative study of decision tree ID3 and C4. 5. *International Journal of Advanced Computer Science and Applications,* 4(2), 13–19.

105. http://www.stat.yale.edu/Courses/1997-98/101/linreg.htm (Access 10.08.2020).

106. Elhan, A. H. (1997), *Lojistik Regresyon Analizinin İncelenmesi ve Tıpta Bir Uygulaması. (Biyoistatistik Yüksek Lisans Tezi) A.Ü.,4–29,* ANKARA.

107. Zamorano, J. P., & Sancho, J. L. (2014, August). *Using maximum entropy models to discriminate between similar languages and varieties.* In *Proceedings of the First Workshop on Applying NLP Tools to Similar Languages, Varieties and Dialects* (pp. 120–128).

108. Baitharu, T. R., & Pani, S. K. (2016). Analysis of data mining techniques for healthcare decision support system using liver disorder dataset. *Procedia Computer Science,* 85, 862–870.

109. Pal, M. (2005). Random forest classifier for remote sensing classification. *International Journal of Remote Sensing,* 26(1), 217–222.

110. Lin, C. H., Liu, J. C., & Ho, C. H. (2008, April). *Anomaly detection using LibSVM training tools.* In *2008 International Conference on Information Security and Assurance (isa 2008)* (pp. 166–171). IEEE.

111. Kim, S., Hovy, E. (2004). *Determining the sentiment of opinions.* In: *Proceedings of the 20th international conference on Computational Linguistics.* Association for Computational Linguistics. p. 1367.

112. Fahrnberger, G., Nayak, D., Martha, V. S., & Ramaswamy, S. (2014, June). *SafeChat: A tool to shield children's communication from explicit messages.* In *2014 14th International Conference on Innovations for Community Services (I4CS)* (pp. 80–86). IEEE.

113. Tung A.K.H. (2009). Rule-based Classification. In: Liu L., Özsu M.T. (eds) *Encyclopedia of Database Systems.* Springer, Boston, MA. https://doi.org/10.1007/978-0-387-39940-9_559

114. Mahmud, A., Ahmed, K. Z., & Khan, M. (2008). *Detecting flames and insults in text.*

115. https://wearesocial.com/digital-2019-global (Access 19.01.2021).

116. https://wearesocial.com/digital-2020 (Access 20.01.2021).

8 Cyberbullying Severity Detection Using Deep Learning Techniques
A Multi-Class Classification over Varied Class Balance Data

Sharyar Wani, Khan Nasik Sami, and Zian Md Afique Amin
International Islamic University Malaysia, Kuala Lumpur, Malaysia

Yonis Gulzar
King Faisal University, Al-Ahsa, Saudi Arabia

CONTENTS

DOI: 10.1201/9781003134527-11

8.1   BACKGROUND

The upheaval caused by social networks has led a considerable population to embrace it as a de-facto for socializing and communicating [1]. The number of platforms is also numerous, each specializing in a particular context of interaction. The features across these social networks are also diverse, which makes the data highly heterogeneous [2]. People even use multiple platforms such as Facebook, Twitter, Instagram, WhatsApp, Tumblr, and YouTube at the same time. These social networks allow users to post text, pictures, audios, videos, comments and interact with other users without any limitation [3]. It cannot be denied that most social networks provide privacy settings, but most people are not well versed with these. While these platforms have fostered social connectivity and collaborations, they present adverse effects as well [4]. The almost unmoderated freedom of posting, commenting and communicating with the public presence of all parties has made social media a dangerous place [5]. Aggressive behavior, hate speech, racism, Islamophobia, grooming, pornography and cyberbullying are among a few of the categories of the harmful impact that many users face in the virtual world. Among these, cyberbullying is one of the severe menaces that is prevalent in almost every social network [6]. Cyberbullying has been defined as deliberate and continuous harassment aimed to harm individuals using online platforms [7]. Cyberbullying encompasses all forms of harassment, such as physical appearance, lifestyle, racism, gender, disability, stalking, social exclusion, intelligence, worldview, etc. The bullies operate both openly and anonymously. Statistics reveal that more than 20% of children and adults are cyberbullying victims. Cyberbullying leads to psychological distress, loneliness, low self-esteem to the extent of suicide [8, 9]. Given the popularity of social networks and the extreme effects of cyberbullying, research has been geared toward detecting cyberbullying. Numerous machine learning [4, 6] and deep learning models have been proposed using the data from different social networks for automated detection of cyberbullying [10]. While these efforts are commendable, most of the current work deals with cyberbullying detection as a binary classification problem. Although detection is crucial, some cyberbullying levels need immediate attention compared to others due to their life-threatening nature for the bullied person. It is tough to detect such instances due to the sheer volume of online data and its varied characteristics [11]. Minimal attention has been geared toward cyberbullying as a multi-class classification problem, detecting and classifying different severity levels of cyberbullying events. The literature investigation reveals only a few studies that deal with this problem. Either machine learning models are not very conducive to this task due to the tedious feature selection process, or deep learning models have not been appropriately documented, raising questions about their validity. Other deep learning models that are more relevant for multi-class classification in domains such as cyberbullying have also not been studied.

8.2   PROBLEM STATEMENT

Cyberbullying is a severe issue with life-threatening consequences plaguing social networks. Manual moderation methods and community-based reporting are not feasible due to the enormous amount of data generated and a considerable number of reporting per day. While the entire phenomenon of cyberbullying is a menace and requires strong regulatory policies for intervention and support, some cyberbullying events need immediate intervention and support compared to others due to their life-threatening nature for the bullied person. Most of the current work deals with cyberbullying detection as a binary classification problem. Minimal attention has been geared toward cyberbullying as a multi-class classification. There is an urgent need to detect and classify cyberbullying events according to their severity. It is tough to detect such instances due to the sheer volume of online data and its varied characteristics. Deep learning approaches have been successfully applied to numerous multi-class classification tasks but rarely used in the severity detection of cyberbullying.

8.3 MOTIVATION

Nearly 20 out of every 100 individuals have been bullied online [12]. It is necessary to detect the severity of cyberbullying events so that immediate attention and resources can be channeled by various stakeholders based on the seriousness of events. Manual methods are not feasible, and the learning process of current methods is quite cumbersome. Deep learning comes with the promise of higher performance without human supervision and a deeper contextual understanding of events. Therefore, this research proposed using some of the deep learning approaches to detect and classify severity in cyberbullying incidents.

8.4 PAPER ORGANIZATION

The remainder of the paper is structured as follows: Section 8.5 discusses some of the related work to cyberbullying detection using deep learning, Section 8.6 presents the significant contributions of this work, Section 8.7 explains the essential components of the experimental setup, Section 8.8 sheds some light on the experiment, and Section 8.9 explains the evaluation techniques used in this work. Section 8.10 presents the results from multiple perspectives, while Section 8.11 discusses the results in light of the models and datasets. Finally, the paper is concluded in Section 8.12.

8.5 RELATED WORK

This section provides an overview of different approaches for cyberbullying and severity detection based on machine learning and deep learning methods. The literature survey confirms the lack of work dedicated to severity classification, which is the main aim of this work.

8.5.1 CYBERBULLYING DETECTION: BINARY CLASSIFICATION

Binary classification or cyberbullying detection using a lexicon-based approach, logistic regression, random forest, support vector machines (SVM), GRU, CNN, bi-directional GRU, HAN, BERT, etc., using data from multiple social networks has been reported in [13]. Aggressive behavior detection focusing on cyberbullying using Word2Vec and long short-term memory (LSTM) have been used for the Indonesian language [14]. Efforts toward cyberbullying detection in the Indonesian language have also been reported using LSTM, BiLSTM, and CNN. The study reported near average accuracies of 90% throughout the models [15]. CNN and RNN have been used to detect bullying events in the Arabic language [16]. An optimized deep learning approach for detection is presented in [17]. This work avoids the standard feature extraction step from Twitter data. Instead, it represents each tweet as a set of word vectors to retain the sentence's semantic meaning or tweet. Post vector transformation, the data is fed into deep learning classifiers – CNN. However, no experimental study or result has been reported to gauge the efficiency of the proposed method. MILL-DNN was used to detect cyberbullying on a freshly curated Hinglish (Hindi & English) dataset reporting high accuracy at 0.97 [18].

A pre-trained BERT model has been used for detection performing above 80% efficiency after multiple oversampling [19]. Similarly, a classification rate of over 90% based on F1-Score using has been reported in [20]. ALBERT, a BERT variant, is reported to perform the binary classification at F1-Score of 0.95 [21]. Bi-directional LSTM is depicted to be performing better than CNN and C-LSTM for cyberbullying detection [22]. CNN was reported to detect cyberbullying incidents with over 90% accuracy on Twitter data [23]. These studies utilize datasets from various social networks such as Facebook, Twitter, Formspring, etc. Gaming platforms have seen increased interest, particularly in the last few years. The associated forums are not moderated due to the nature of the industry. Naïve Bayes yielded an accuracy of 0.92 for detection using chat logs from Dota and Ragnarok, games played using online platforms [24].

8.5.2 Severity Detection: Multi-Class Classification

Hate speech has grown exponentially in the last few years. Hate speech incidents can vary from overtly aggressive to covertly aggressive. The aggressive behavior has been classified using traditional machine learning approaches such as SVM, Logistic Regression, Convolutional Neural Networks, Attention-Based models, and BERT. The performance metrics indicate that the models are not very successful in classifying aggression properly [25]. Severity classification, particularly on cyberbullying data, is a rarely studied subject. In [26], various machine learning and deep learning models have been deployed for severity classification. Using SVM, Naïve, Bayes, Random Forest, Logistic Regression, CNN, LSTM, BLSTM – Attention and BLSTM (GloVe), over data from three social networks (Twitter, Formspring and Reddit), the research tried to address the classification issue. However, the models did not work well unless heavy oversampling was introduced, and experimental details do not seem to be very well documented. In another study, machine learning algorithms such as Naïve Bayes, KNN, Decision Tree, Random Forest, and SVM were used for detecting cyberbully severity using Twitter data. The base classifier SVM reported the highest kappa score of 0.48, which signifies the model was heavily underperforming. The study oversampled the data using SMOTE, but the kappa score almost stayed in the same range. Finally, they proposed adding various features such as SMOTE, word embedding, sentiments, lexicon, and PMO-SO before feeding it to the classifier, which helped the kappa' coefficient improvement to 0.71 [27]. The authors have presented similar work with additional features such as content features, network features, activity features, user features, personality features, and PMI – Semantic Orientation for severity classification. Random Forest performs the best with a kappa coefficient of 0.8, while the recorded F-Measure and accuracy were over 90% [28]. Thus, it becomes clear that base classifiers in machine learning approaches do not have the ability for severity classification. With the addition of numerous features, some of the base classifiers start showing improvement. Feature selection and extraction is a tedious task [29]. On the contrary, deep learning approaches are well known for their ability to perform well without human supervision. At the same time, they are also able to perform automatic feature extraction from raw data. These models and their variants can generate and learn the contextual understanding of words and sentences in natural language tasks such as text classification. Therefore, this research proposes to use different deep learning techniques for predicting severity in cyberbullying incidents, dealing with it as a multi-class classification problem.

8.6 CONTRIBUTIONS

Pursuant to the above discussion, this work mainly contributes to the following aspects:

1. The research proposes cyberbullying severity detection based on multiple deep learning approaches – CNN, HLSTM (HAN & LSTM), and RNN-BiLSTM using combined data from various social networks.
2. The research curates three new datasets of varied balance by combining data from three existing datasets using random sampling.
3. We explore multiple datasets of varied balance for cyberbullying detection using the deep learning methods and study the effect of the varying balance on the performance of the deep learning methods.
4. The research explores the area of multi-class imbalance and studies the effect of varied balances of classes for multi-class classification problem.

8.7 EXPERIMENTAL SETUP

8.7.1 DATASET

This study uses three datasets with a varied number of records. The datasets were curated using random sampling from three annotated datasets created by [26,30,31]. The authors in [27] categorized the dataset from [30] into four severity categories – low (L), medium (M), high (H), and none (N). None refers to non-cyberbully events; low refers to cyberbullying events related to intelligence; medium refers to cyberbullying events pertaining to politics and race, while sexual and appearance-based records were labeled of the highest severity. As the study sought to merge the three datasets to obtain data of varying nature and classes, it was important that the newly curated dataset followed similar rules for categorizing the records. Therefore, rules crafted in [27] were used for classifying cyberbullying events in the newly curated datasets. We curated the three datasets as follows:

1. Dataset 1: It consists of records obtained from datasets provided by [26] and [30]. The dataset from [26] has been categorized into four categories, while the dataset from [30] only consisted of H, M, and L classes. Therefore, the N class records were utilized from [26]. The medium and high categories are almost similar while none and low categories are low in number, making Dataset 1 relatively imbalanced across various classes as depicted in Table 8.1 and Figure 8.1.

TABLE 8.1
Dataset Details

	Class	Class Size	Data Size
Dataset 1	High	9022	28,551
	Medium	9107	
	Low	5537	
	None	4885	
Dataset 2	High	8874	31,817
	Medium	8874	
	Low	5184	
	None	8885	
Dataset 3	High	8874	37,313
	Medium	8874	
	Low	9680	
	None	9885	

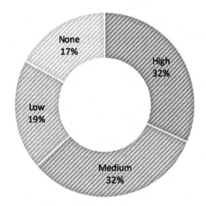

FIGURE 8.1   Class Distribution in Dataset 1.

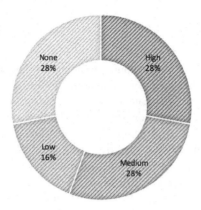

FIGURE 8.2   Class Distribution in Dataset 2.

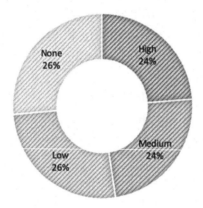

FIGURE 8.3   Class Distribution in Dataset 3.

2. Dataset 2: Dataset 2 has been relatively balanced (refer to Table 8.1 and Figure 8.2) with almost similar numbers across none, medium, and high, while the low class still remains at a lower percentage. It was curated from [26] (HMLN) [30] (HML) and [31]. Mendeley dataset only contributed to the none class.

3. Dataset 3: It can be observed that this dataset is almost balanced across all class labels; refer to Table 8.1 and Figure 8.3. In an attempt to balance the classes, none and low classes were added from the [31] while retaining the contribution of HLMN classes from [26] and [30].

Table 8.1 details the distribution of classes and the total number of records in the three curated datasets.

We categorized the three datasets as imbalanced, moderately balanced, and highly balanced, respectively. This categorization aims to study the effect of differently balanced data on deep learning models for severity classification. Real-world data is mostly imbalanced. Often researchers apply various balancing techniques such as oversampling and undersampling to address this issue. While these techniques address the problem of imbalance, they either reduce the context or generate synthetic data. It is often reported that deep learning models in multi-class classification problems such as the one addressed in this research suffer due to data imbalance. As such, this research intended to analyze the effects of various types of data balance by curating the three datasets.

8.7.2   Data Pre-Processing

Text cleaning removes unwanted or irrelevant content from the data, preparing the raw data into a machine-readable format [32]. This step involved removing unwanted characters such as HTML tags, special characters, usernames, punctuation, non-letter characters, etc. This was followed by applying lower case formatting to the text data to avoid any sparsity issues. This process is also referred to as denoising of the data in order to enhance data quality.

Tokenization is the process of splitting the data into smaller units like a document or a paragraph into sentences, sentence into words, etc. These small split units are known as tokens and include words, numbers, and punctuation marks based on word boundaries. This helps in understanding the meaning of the text by individually analyzing the tokens that constitute the entity. Tokenization can be done by split methods, using regular expressions, natural language toolkits, and other pre-built natural language processing libraries. The tokenization process of our data yielded 55,659 unique tokens.

The data needs to be divided into training and validation sets. The training set is the actual data that is used by the model to learn. The validation set provides test candidates for the model to be evaluated. The dataset was split into 80–20 proportion for training and validation, respectively. The split proportion is based on the infamous Pareto principle [33], which states that roughly 80% of outcomes come from 20% of causes given a multi-outcome situation in a real-world setting. This is a very common split in machine learning and deep learning models. However, sometimes the ratio is modified so that both parameter estimates and performance statistics do not have very high variance.

Deep learning models treat all forms of data as vectors. Therefore, it is required to vectorize the input data so that different model layers can apply geometric transformations when the data passes through them. Thus, the meaning is understood in terms of vectors and geometric spaces, which undergo incremental learning mapping one vector space to others. Global Vectors, commonly known as GloVe, is an unsupervised learning algorithm to obtain these vector representations [34]. It creates a huge word context co-occurrence matrix, where each element represents the occurrence of a particular word in a particular context. Matrix factorization helps to approximate the matrix. This provides the contextual understanding of words inside the data. A pre-trained GloVe model (GloVe 6B 100d, consisting of 4,00,000-word vectors) was used to vectorize data, producing a text matrix. By setting the max number of words, each record has a fixed length l. The word-embedding model GloVe generates a text matrix (size $l \times g$) where l is the max limit per record and g is the word-embedding dimension set in GloVe.

8.7.3   Proposed Deep Learning Techniques

8.7.3.1   CNN

Convolution is defined as a study of mathematical relationships between two objects to produce a third relationship. Convolution neural networks utilize multiple volumes of inputs compared to a neural network. Each layer attempts to extract useful patterns or embedded information in the data passed through that layer. In our case, each convolution layer will be used to extract relevant information and hidden features from the text from various social networks. The text matrix from the GloVe based embedding layer serves as an input to the convolution process. Features are extracted using a filter f, where f has the dimension of $n \times g$; n being the number of records inside the dataset, and g is similar to the text matrix's embedding dimension. The sliding filter f performs on the stride

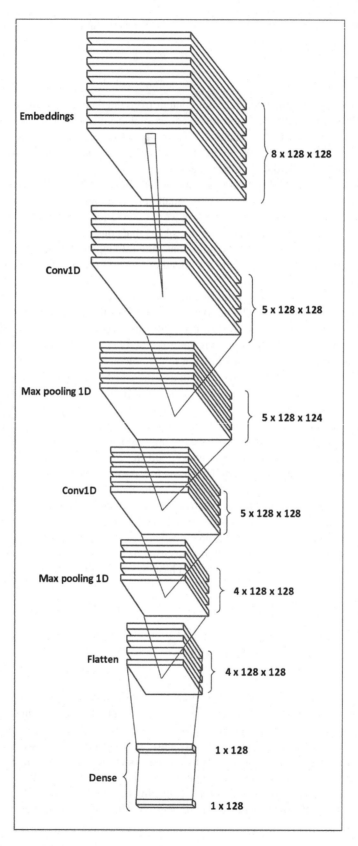

FIGURE 8.4 Proposed CNN architecture.

and filter count parameters. Stride is defined as the size of steps f moves every time toward the end of the text matrix. Filter count refers to the numbers of filters used in the process. The CNN model in this work sets various sizes for the feature extraction filter. A simplified version of the proposed CNN architecture is presented in Figure 8.4.

A max-pooling layer follows each convolution layer. Pooling extracts significant features from the set of extracted features from the preceding convolution layer. Max pooling has proven to be beneficial for text classification, especially in multi-class problems. Not all extracted features from the convolution layer using the sliding filter are relevant to the classification process. We use multiple max-pooling layers to reduce the dimensional complexity while preserving the significant output from the convolution process, avoiding any overfitting of data.

Finally, we flatten the matrices into vectors, followed by a fully connected dense layer. Flattening helps to create a single long feature vector supplied to the final classification layer. Densely connected layers have the advantage of learning features from their preceding layer compared to convolution layers that rely on consistent features within a small repetitive field. Thus, the fully connected layer analyses the pooled features and, using a SoftMax activation function, performs multi-class classification related to cyberbullying severity (none, low, medium, and high).

8.7.3.2   HLSTM – HAN & BiLSTM

Hierarchical Attention Network (HAN) is a neural architecture based on the hierarchical document structure. Words connected together make up sentences, and sentences connected together construct entire documents. At the same time, the words and sentences are distinctively informative. Simply put, not all words or sentences are equally crucial in every contextual understanding. HAN uses recurrent neural networks (bidirectional RNN – GRU) for the hierarchical document structure and an attention mechanism to extract significant words and sentences in a document. The significance extraction is based on the contextual understanding of words. The bidirectional RNN seeks the contextual meanings of words, and the attention network computes the importance of these contexts as a single vector. The same process is repeated at a sentence level where the document representation only receives a sentence vector of each sentence.

LSTM networks are recurrent neural nets that solve the problem of long-term dependencies. They tend to be successful in remembering information over longer durations of time. Unlike RNNs that have a single neural network layer inside the repeating module, LSTMs possess four layers or gates: input gate (i_t), output gate (o_t), forget gate (f_t), and memory unit (c_t). The input gate fetches the data into the model. Next, the forget layer decides to throw away the irrelevant data from the cell state. f_t is mathematically governed by the following equation:

$$f_t = \sigma \left(W_f \left[r_{t-1}, i_t \right] + b_f \right)$$

(8.1)

where W_f is the weight, r_{t-1} is the output from the previous timestamp, i_t is the new input and b_f is known as bias.

Following this, a decision is made about the new information to be stored in the cell state. The input layer decides the values to be updated, while a tanh layer generates a new vector for the new data. The aforementioned steps can be represented as follows:

$$i_t = \sigma \left(W_i \left[h_{t-1}, x_t \right] + b_i \right)$$

(8.2)

$$c_t = \tan h \left(W_c \left[h_{t-1}, x_t \right] + b_c \right)$$

(8.3)

The old cell state C_{t-1} is updated into C_t. The old state is multiplied by f_t forgetting the information decided earlier, followed by adding $i_t * c_t$. This is the new candidate value, given by

$$r_t = f_t * t_{t-1} + i_t * c_t \tag{8.4}$$

Finally, a decision is made regarding the output by the output gate o_t. The output is a two-step filtered version of the cell state – running a sigmoid layer to decide the part of cell state for output and pushing the cell state through tan$h$ for the values to be between −1 and 1, multiplying it with the output of the sigmoid gate and is given by:

$$o_t = \sigma\left(W_o\left[h_{t-1},\, x_t\right] + b_o\right) \tag{8.5}$$

$$h_t = o_t * \tan h\left(C_t\right) \tag{8.6}$$

Bidirectional LSTM (BiLSTM) comprises two LSTM models that bring together two separate inputs and forward input states. The two LSTM models are trained based on the input sequence and a reversed copy of the input sequence, providing additional context and faster learning in the network. As such, they present a very rich contextual understanding compare to the classic LSTM models.

This research uses BiLSTM based on HAN (see Figure 8.5) for the severity classification problem. While the LSTM is efficient in overcoming the long-term memory problem, HAN architecture helps to understand the social texts in the context of sentences and documents. This helps to extract significant features based on contextual understanding to predict cyberbullying events into H, L, M, and N classes.

8.7.3.3 RNN

Recurrent neural networks (RNN) are a special type of neural network that focuses not only on the current input but also on the past inputs to determine the outputs. These are recurring feed-forward neural networks where the output at each time step is determined by the last feed-forward layer's current input and output. Therefore, the same input can produce different outputs based on the hidden state vector from the previous input.

The difference between a simple feed-forward network and a recurrent network is the recurrent edges that span along time steps bringing the notion of time to the model. The functioning of basic RNNs can be conceptualized as accepting a set of input sequence $i_1, i_2, i_3, \ldots, i_n$ connected to particular time intervals. For each input, the network updates the hidden states $h_1, h_2, h_3, \ldots, h_n$ and output $o_1, o_2, o_3, \ldots, o_n$. The operational behavior as a dynamic system can be defined by the following on-linear matrix equations:

$$h_t = f_h(W_{ih}x_t + W_{hh}h_{t-1} + b_h \tag{8.7}$$

$$y_t = f_o\left(W_{oh} + b_y\right) \tag{8.8}$$

where f_h represents the hidden unit activation, f_o refers to the output unit activation, W_{ih}, W_{hh} and W_{oh} are representative weight matrices for input, hidden and output vectors, b_h is the bias associated with hidden vector while as b_y is the bias associated with the output vector. A simplified version of the proposed RNN-BiLSTM architecture is presented in Figure 8.6.

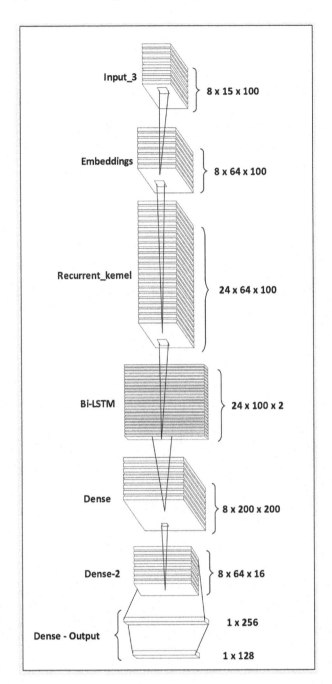

FIGURE 8.5 Proposed HLSTM architecture.

8.8 EXPERIMENTS

The experiments were conducted using Keras with Theano backend. Other libraries from the data science stack, such as Numpy, Pandas, Matplotlib, etc., were also used. As discussed earlier in the data pre-processing section, all the datasets were pre-processed before model training and testing. The pre-processed datasets were split into a 4:1 ratio utilizing four parts for training and 1 part for testing the model. The train-validate class details per dataset are detailed in Table 8.2.

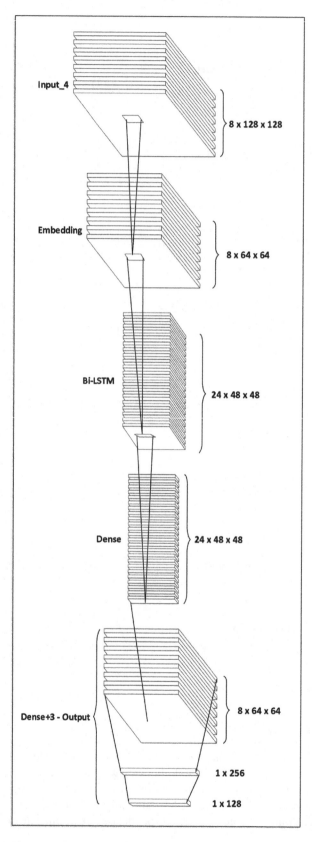

FIGURE 8.6 Proposed RNN-BiLSTM architecture.

TABLE 8.2
Train-Test Distribution

	Train	Test	Total
Dataset 1	22,841	5710	28,551
Dataset 2	25,454	6363	31,817
Dataset 3	29,851	7462	37,313

The CNN and LSTM model hyperparameters were set to 15 epochs for training with a batch size of 256 texts, while the RNN with bidirectional LSTM was set to 15 epochs with a batch size of 64. The hyperparameter values were determined based on multiple runs with different epochs and batch sizes to achieve optimal model performance. Since this research deals with multi-class classification, categorical cross-entropy, and the SoftMax activation were used as a loss function. The Rmsprop optimizer performed better in the model settings compared to Adagrad, Adam, and Adaboost optimizers.

8.9   EVALUATION TECHNIQUES

Performance metrics are essential indicators of model performance. It is essential to choose the appropriate metrics based on various characteristics such as nature of the problem, data balance, importance of false positives, false negatives, labels, etc. This research takes two main factors into consideration – classification type and balance. Severity detection is a multi-classification problem. Simultaneously, models are trained and tested over three sets of data with varied size and balance between the labels. As such, it becomes important to choose metrics that can cater to both issues, irrespective of the differences. The models were evaluated using the following metrics of measurement.

1. **Macro Average Precision & Macro Average Recall**: Precision provides information about the model's capability of identifying actual positives. It determines the trustworthiness of a model in predicting positive labels. In a binary classification problem, there exist two classes labeled as positive and negative. It is given by the fraction of True positive elements divided by the total number of positively predicted elements.

$$\text{Precision} = \frac{\text{True Positives}}{\text{True Positives} + \text{False Positives}} \qquad (8.9)$$

On the contrary, recall measures the model's ability to detect the positive elements in the dataset. It is the ratio of true positive elements to the total number of positively classified elements. Equation 8.2 reflects the recall for a binary class problem:

$$\text{Recall} = \frac{\text{True Positives}}{\text{True Positives} + \text{False Negatives}} \qquad (8.10)$$

Since multi-class classification problems present more than two classes, they are not labeled as positives and negatives. Therefore, such scenarios use macro average precision and recall instead. The macro average metrics help to determine the performance of a model across multiple classes in the data. They are computed as the arithmetic mean of the metrics for single classes given by:

$$\text{Macro Average Precision} = \frac{\sum_{c=1}^{C} \text{Precision}_c}{C} \qquad (8.11)$$

$$\text{Macro Average Recall} = \frac{\sum_{c=1}^{C} \text{Recall}_c}{C} \qquad (8.12)$$

where C represents a generic class.

2. **Accuracy**: Accuracy is the widely used indicator for measuring model performance. It intends to provide an overall measure of correct prediction given the entire set of data. Each unit in a class contributes equally to having equal weight to this indicator. Therefore, classes that have more units will contribute higher weights toward the accuracy calculation. Therefore, accuracy is most suited when determining the model performance about predicting the highest number of units in the correct class, without the effect of class distribution across the dataset. The value of accuracy ranges from 0 and 1, the distance of the obtained value from 1 provides the model's misclassification rate. Accuracy can be calculated from the confusion matrix as follows:

$$\text{Accuracy} = \frac{\text{True Positives} + \text{True Negatives}}{\text{True Positives} + \text{True Negatives} + \text{False Positives} + \text{False Negatives}} \qquad (8.13)$$

3. **Macro F1-Score**: Similar to Precision and Recall, F1-Score must encompass all classes in multi-class classification. Typically, F1-Score is determined as the aggregation Precision and Recall.

$$F1 - \text{Score} = 2 * \left(\frac{\text{Precision} * \text{Recall}}{\text{Precision} + \text{Recall}} \right) \qquad (8.14)$$

The formula represents F1-Score as a weighted average between the two metrics under the concept of harmonic mean. The harmonic mean in multi-class classification problems is an aggregation of macro average precision and macro average recall given by

$$\text{Macro } F1 - \text{Score} = 2 * \left(\frac{\text{Macro Average Precision} * \text{Macro Average Recall}}{\text{Macro Average Precision}^{-1} + \text{Macro Average Recall}^{-1}} \right) \qquad (8.15)$$

There is no particular effect of the major or the minor class while calculating the macro score. This implies that classes are treated equally, where the higher macro levels indicate well-predicted labels for the classes.

4. **Cohen's Kappa**: Although F1-scores present a quick, high-level comparison about model performance, they have a major drawback. They provide equal weight to precision and recall, which has an adverse effect on sample performance. Not all classes have necessarily the same importance in a classification problem. This problem aggravates with macro, micro, and weighted F1-scores as the domain knowledge is not taken into account in multi-class classification.

Kappa measures the agreement between the predicted labels and the true labels. These two classes are known as random categorical variables. Cohens Kappa indicates the dependence between the prediction and actual classification of a model. Generally, the coefficient value is given by:

$$k = \frac{\text{Observed Agreement} - \text{Chance Agreement}}{1 - \text{Chance Agreement}} \qquad (8.16)$$

For a multi-class classification problem such as ours, it is calculated using the following:

$$k = \frac{c \times s - \sum_{k}^{K} p_k \times t_k}{s^2 - \sum_{k}^{K} p_k \times t_k} \qquad (8.17)$$

where

$c = \sum_{k}^{K} C_{kk}$, total number of correctly predicted elements

$s = \sum_{i}^{K} \sum_{j}^{k} C_{ij}$, total number of elements

$p_k = \sum_{i}^{K} C_{ki}$, frequency of class k prediction (given by column total in a confusion matrix)

$t_k = \sum_{i}^{K} C_{ik}$, true occurrence frequency of class k (given by row total in a confusion matrix)

The value of kappa usually ranges between 0 and 1. The former indicates an agreement by complete chance, while the latter is an indication of strong agreement. The farther the value of kappa moves from 1, the lesser the model's trustworthiness in classification. If the kappa value is negative, it indicates that the model performs even worse than a complete agreement by chance. Hence, the model is deemed entirely untrustworthy.

8.10 RESULTS

Our experiments deal with the multi-class classification of predicting the cyberbullying severity into low, medium, high, and non-cyberbullying events. We conducted nine experiments involving three deep learning models over three differently balanced datasets. We present our findings from various perspectives using Confusion Matrices – Figures 8.7–8.21. All the performance scores are tabulated in Tables 8.3 and 8.4. HLSTM performs better compared to CNN and RNN throughout all the datasets. The Cohen's kappa or simply k-score is the most suitable evaluation metric and stands at 0.80, 0.81 and 0.75 for HLSTM across Dataset 1, Dataset 2 and Dataset 3, respectively. RNN performs very closely to HLSTM with only an average difference of 0.02 across the three datasets. The k scores for RNN are 0.78, 0.79 and 0.75 for the three datasets.

On the other hand, the k values for CNN lag quite far behind both HLSTM and RNN. The lowest k value for CNN is 0.63 on Dataset 3. It has performed relatively well on the other two datasets at a k value of 0.70. The average k value of HLSTM is 0.78, which demonstrates its superiority in the multi-class classification problem of predicting severity in cyberbullying incidents.

Interestingly, the increase of L classes in Dataset 3 to achieve a higher balance in the dataset affects the k value compared to Dataset 2, where classes are relatively balanced. Although not

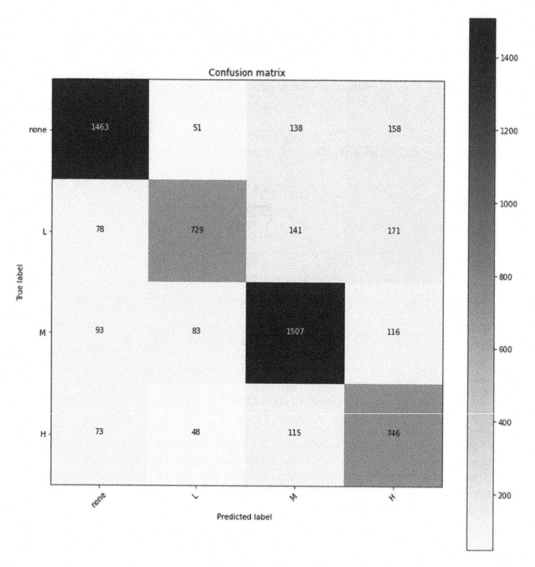

FIGURE 8.7   Confusion Matrix for CNN – Dataset 1.

substantial, a similar effect can be seen for CNN and RNN as well. Generally, the k value demonstrated by all the models is lower in Dataset 3. HLSTM and CNN perform at the same level with a k value of 0.75 in the highly balanced dataset. Across the three datasets, HLSTM, RNN, and CNN's performances are almost in the same range in Dataset 1 and Dataset 2, while all of them drop their performance on Dataset 3.

The harmonic mean metric macro F1-Score also indicates that HLSTM performs better than RNN and CNN. HLSTM demonstrates more than 80% efficiency in all three modeling experiments. The highest F1-Score for HLSTM is 0.85 for Dataset 2, while the lowest is 0.82 for Dataset 3. RNN again performs close to HLSTM with F1-scores equal to 0.82, 0.83 and 0.81 for the three datasets in sequence. CNN, on the contrary, demonstrated quite inferior performance to the other two deep learning techniques. Based on the F1-scores, all the models perform best on Dataset 2, compared to

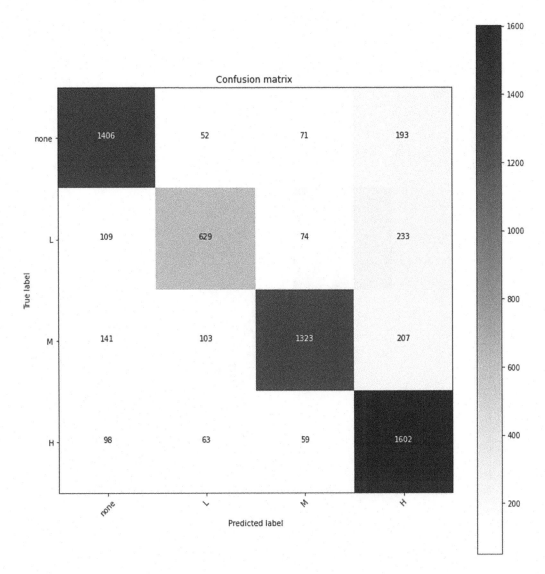

FIGURE 8.8   Confusion Matrix for CNN – Dataset 2.

less balanced and highly balanced data in the other two datasets. The individual comparative perfor-mance of models is almost identical across the three datasets used in this research.

Macro average precision and macro average recall also support HLSTM to be the strongest can-didate for prediction. In fact, both the metrics agree with each other, along with the F1-Score for HLSTM across all the datasets. The macro values and harmonic mean for HLSTM are 0.83, 0.85 and 0.82 for the three datasets in sequence. Again, RNN is right behind HLSTM, with only a small gap between the scores for the two models. However, RNN does not present absolute sync between the macro values and F1-Score as HLSTM. CNN again seems to underperform based on macro scores across all three datasets. The best performing model HLSTM generates the best macro scores for Dataset 2, presenting an 85% efficiency of the model for severity classification.

The testing accuracy indicates near equal performance for both HLSTM and RNN, while CNN's performance is again low compared to the two. The highest testing accuracy has been reported at

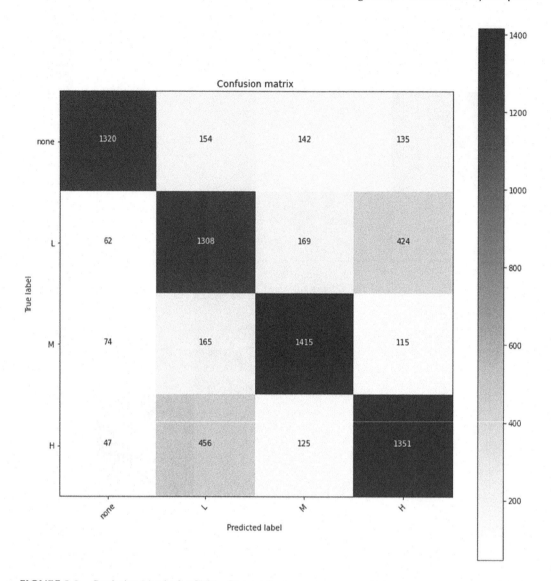

FIGURE 8.9 Confusion Matrix for CNN – Dataset 3.

86% by HLSTM on Dataset 2, while CNN recorded the lowest on Dataset 3 at 72%. Dataset 2 again represents quality data balance across the datasets, demonstrating high testing rates for all three models. The highest and lowest misclassification rate for HLSTM and RNN is 0.18 and 0.12 respectively.

It has been observed that HLSTM performs better than RNN and CNN based on all performance measurement metrics used in this research. While RNN closely follows the lead, CNN has performed less significantly for multi-class classification of severity detection in cyberbullying. At the same time, Dataset 2 has demonstrated quality balance for all the three deep learning models, whereby all classes are relatively balanced rather than a positive or negative skew among multiples classes in a multi-class classification problem.

CNN classified 83% N and 81% M classes most accurately in Dataset 1. The classification of the H class seems to be at a loss of 31%. Except for the H class, the rest of the three classes N, M, and L,

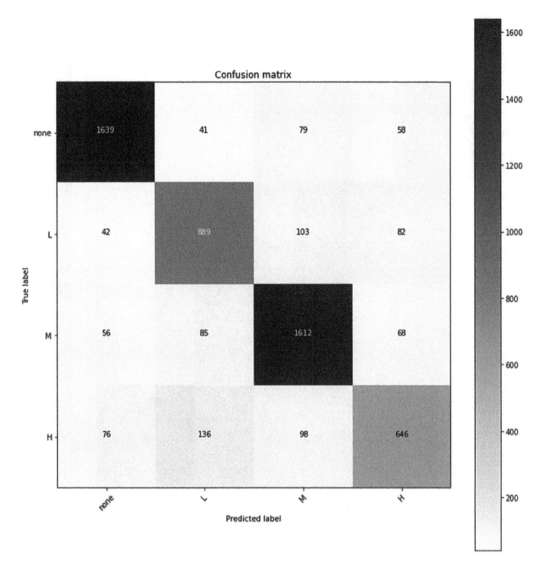

FIGURE 8.10 Confusion Matrix for RNN – Dataset 1.

seem to be classified decently. The precision values in Dataset 1 reveal that 86% of the N class unit are correctly predicted while L & M classes follow suit at 80% and 79%. The H class again seems to suffer, having a precision value of 0.63. However, the recall value presented support toward M class at 84% of relevant items being appropriately labeled. The N and H classes are appropriately labeled with 81% and 76% relevance. While the H class suffered in precision, it does significantly well with regards to recall. For Dataset 2, CNN performed almost alike as Dataset 1 for N & M classes. However, F1-scores demonstrate better classification for H labels increasing from 0.69 in Dataset 1 to 0.79 in Dataset 2. Although there is only a slight decrease of L labels in Dataset 2 compared to Dataset 1, the classification rate drops significantly from 72% to 66%. The relative relevance rate of samples has increased in Dataset 2, where all rates seem to be above 70%. M labels have the highest precision at 87%. On the contrary, a similar value is reported for recall for the H class in the dataset while the L class retrieved relevance is only 60%. F1 score for N class in Dataset 3 remains above

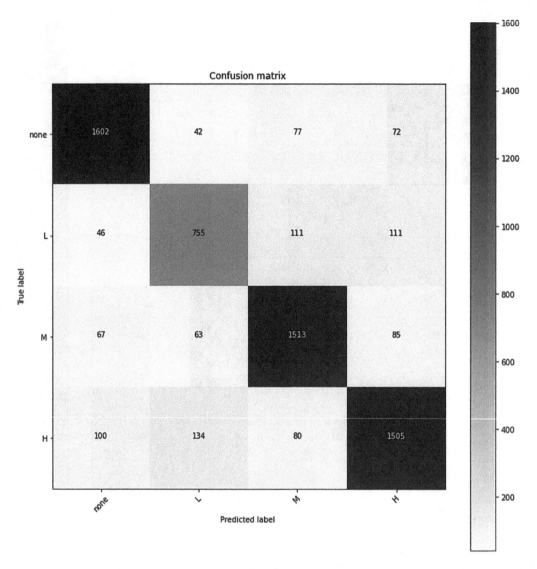

FIGURE 8.11   Confusion Matrix for RNN – Dataset 2.

80%, similar to the two previous datasets. A further decrease is reported for L and M class, while the H class almost behaves similar to other datasets. Overall, CNN predicts N class most accurately, closely followed by M class and H class. The classification of L class is at 68%, which is the lowest classification rate by the CNN model.

HLSTM, which is the best performing model for severity classification, demonstrates a high classification rate for all four classes across the three datasets. For all the class labels, the value does not drop below 70%. Most class classification rates by HLSTM are in the range of 80–90%. Although N labels are the most accurately classified, the other classes mostly follow closely. A similar observation can be made for precision and recall. The classifying accuracy and relevance of HLSTM do not drop below 0.71, while most of the values range between 0.80 and 0.90. All four classes – N, L, M, and H are predicted equally on overage with respect to the class itself across the datasets. In general, HLSTM seems to be in sync for classifying all the classes, with the class size and balance have minimum impact.

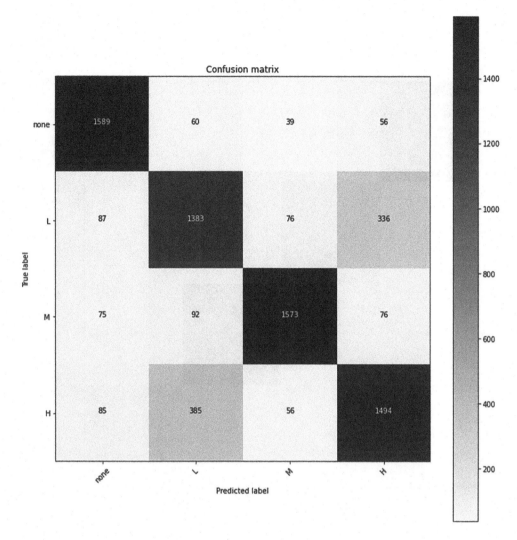

FIGURE 8.12   Confusion Matrix for RNN – Dataset 3.

RNN, which has been observed as the second-best deep learning model for severity classification, also does not drop the classification rate below 71% for all the class labels. Although the N label is again classified most accurately, the other three labels are also classified at decent accuracy rates. N and L labels in all three datasets are classified more accurately. An interesting observation for the M label in Dataset 3 is that the precision value hits 90% while the recall close behind at 87%. Overall, RNN performs equally well for all class labels in all three datasets with average classification accuracy above 80%.

In summary, the classification efficiency of HLSTM and RNN is established across all the datasets with different sizes and class balances. The size and class balance do not seem to significantly impact the performance for predicting different classes. Almost all metric values are close to each other for HLSTM and RNN with no significant fluctuations. Sharp increase and decrease across different metrics are only seen on CNN. HLSTM clearly seems to behave superior among the three models during multiple experiments conducted using the three datasets used in this research.

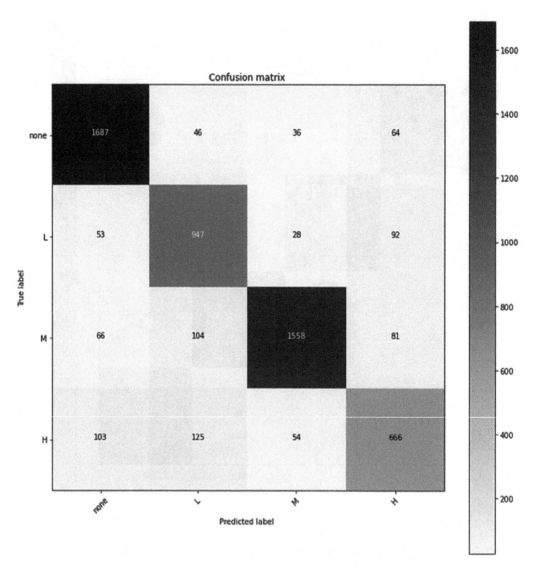

FIGURE 8.13   Confusion Matrix for HLSTM – Dataset 1.

8.11   DISCUSSION

As the results indicate, HLSTM outperforms other deep learning models for severity detection in cyberbullying. They combine efficiency from two deep learning models, HAN and LSTM. HANs have the capability of deeply understanding the context of documents. In severity classification, it is crucial to break down the structure of every text, understand the words used, construct their contextual understandings by assigning weights and rebuild the document with semantically rich understanding. Since they are bi-directional RNNs, they have a clear advantage over classical RNNs. This is because bi-directional RNNs are capable of both feed-forward and backward learning. HANs have demonstrated high performance in many language classification tasks.

LSTMs, on the other hand, are efficient at solving long short-term memory problem. They are dependent on the current input and use their past learning or understanding to make inferences.

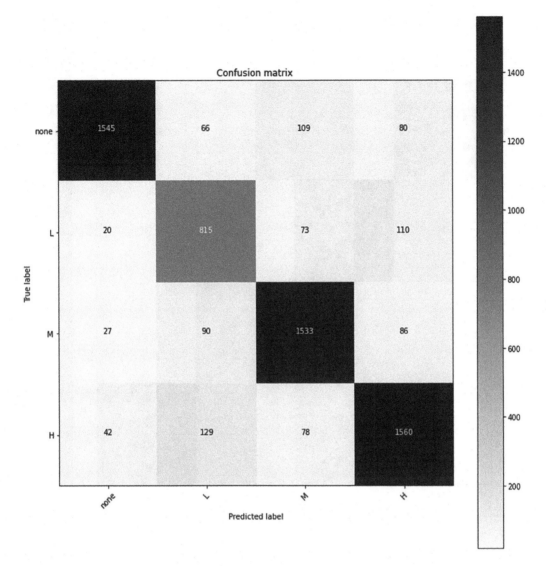

FIGURE 8.14 Confusion Matrix for HLSTM – Dataset 2.

LSTM contributes to classify each new text on the severity scale based on the result of past records that it has already classified. The combination of attention for contextual understanding and usage of experience with every input from HAN and LSTM, respectively, makes the architecture an efficient candidate for severity classification in cyberbullying.

On the other hand, RNNs with the bi-directional LSTM also perform quite well; in fact, they are very close to HLSTM in terms of performance. RNNs on their own can utilize previous learning experiences for new data. However, they suffer from long-term information retention. The bi-directional LSTMs, which are a variant of classical RNNs help to overcome this problem. As discussed in the earlier sections, RNNs can select, store, and connect related information. Since bi-directional LSTMs have two separate inputs and forward input states, this helps to enhance contextual understanding of the model for the text content and classification. For a multi-class classification problem such as ours, deep contextual understanding is of utmost importance.

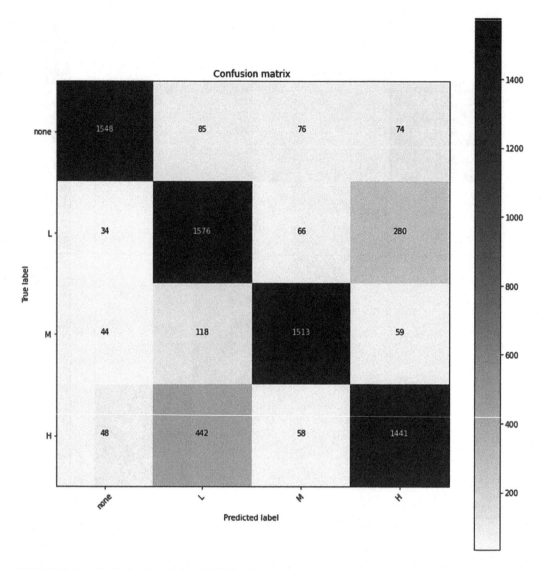

FIGURE 8.15   Confusion Matrix for HLSTM – Dataset 3.

In the context of the datasets, class size seems to have minimal impact on classification tasks. Class balance seems to be a relatively important factor affecting the performance of deep learning techniques. Dataset 2, which is considered moderately balanced or Dataset 1 that is less balanced, seems to perform better than Dataset 3, where we tried to achieve a higher balance between the classes. While deep learning models require more data than traditional machine learning models, achieving a very high balance between the class labels in multi-class classification tasks might not be necessarily important. Perhaps, more emphasis should be given to the quality of data across the labels for better severity predictions. In general, the N category seems to be efficiently predicted, followed by L, M, and H. Non-cyber bullying events are relatively easy to classify because they can be understood as general events where nothing extraordinary understanding is required. The other three labels are tricky where peculiar contexts need to be understood, and deep contextual understanding is required to determine their place in one of the severity levels. Sometimes, it is even hard

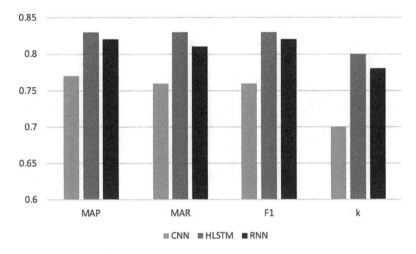

FIGURE 8.16 Overall Model Performance – Dataset 1.

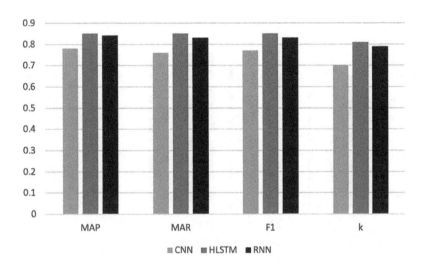

FIGURE 8.17 Overall Model Performance – Dataset 2.

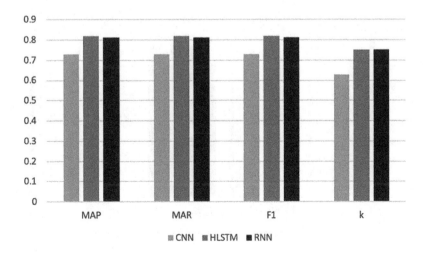

FIGURE 8.18 Overall Model Performance – Dataset 3.

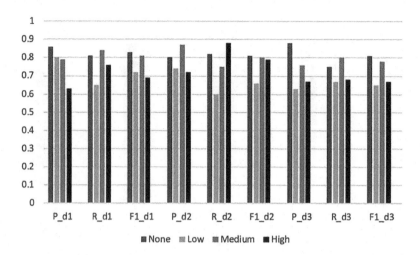

FIGURE 8.19   CNN – Class Wise Performance.

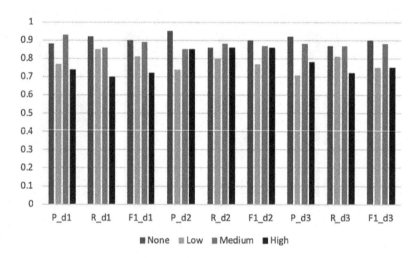

FIGURE 8.20   HLSTM – Class Wise Performance.

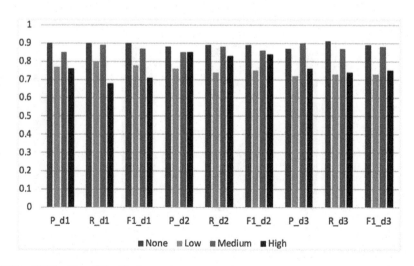

FIGURE 8.21   RNN – Class Wise Performance.

TABLE 8.3
Class Wise Model Performance

	CNN									HLSTM									RNN								
	Dataset 1			Dataset 2			Dataset 3			Dataset 1			Dataset 2			Dataset 3			Dataset 1			Dataset 2			Dataset 3		
Class	P	R	F1	P	R	F1	P	R	F1	P	R	F1	P	R	F1	P	R	F1	P	R	F1	P	R	F1	P	R	F1
None	**0.86**	0.81	**0.83**	0.82	0.80	**0.81**	**0.88**	0.75	**0.81**	0.88	**0.92**	**0.90**	**0.95**	0.86	**0.90**	**0.92**	0.87	**0.90**	**0.90**	**0.90**	**0.90**	**0.88**	**0.89**	**0.89**	0.87	**0.91**	**0.89**
Low	0.80	0.65	0.72	0.74	0.60	0.66	0.63	0.67	0.65	0.77	0.85	0.81	0.74	0.80	0.77	0.71	0.81	0.75	0.77	0.80	0.78	0.76	0.74	0.75	0.72	0.73	0.73
Medium	0.79	**0.84**	0.81	**0.87**	0.75	0.80	0.76	**0.80**	0.78	**0.93**	0.86	0.89	0.85	**0.88**	0.87	0.88	**0.87**	0.88	0.85	0.89	0.87	0.85	0.88	0.86	**0.90**	0.87	0.88
High	0.63	0.76	0.69	0.72	**0.88**	0.79	0.67	0.68	0.67	0.74	0.70	0.72	0.85	0.86	0.86	0.78	0.72	0.75	0.76	0.68	0.71	0.85	0.83	0.84	0.76	0.74	0.75

TABLE 8.4

Overall Model Performance

| Model | Dataset 1 | | | | | | | Dataset 2 | | | | | | | Dataset 3 | | | | | | |
| | Accuracy | | | | | | | Accuracy | | | | | | | Accuracy | | | | | | |
	Train	Valid.	Test	MAP	MAR	F1	k	Train	Valid.	Test	MAP	MAR	F1	k	Train	Valid.	Test	MAP	MAR	F1	k
CNN	0.97	0.78	0.78	0.77	0.76	0.76	0.70	0.96	0.79	0.78	0.78	0.76	0.77	0.70	0.96	0.73	0.72	0.73	0.73	0.73	0.63
HLSTM	0.96	0.87	**0.85**	**0.83**	**0.83**	**0.83**	**0.80**	0.96	**0.88**	**0.86**	**0.85**	**0.85**	**0.85**	**0.81**	0.91	0.83	**0.81**	**0.82**	**0.82**	**0.82**	**0.75**
RNN	**0.98**	**0.89**	0.84	0.82	0.81	0.82	0.78	**0.98**	**0.88**	0.84	0.84	0.83	0.83	0.79	**0.98**	**0.84**	**0.81**	0.81	0.81	0.81	**0.75**

TABLE 8.5
Legend – Table 1 and Table 2 Abbreviations

P	Precision
R	Recall
F1	F1-score
Valid.	Validation
MAP	Macro average precision
MAR	Macro average recall
k	Cohen's kappa

TABLE 8.6
Legend – Figure 7.9 Abbreviations

P	Precision
R	Recall
F1	F1-Score
x_d_n	n is dataset number

to distinguish the levels in a particular text because of the mixed context where some parts point to multiple levels of severity. These kinds of texts or records need understanding the words with a contextual understanding of the entire document.

8.12 CONCLUSION AND FUTURE WORK

Cyberbullying has plagued social networks, which were supposed to be tools for community transformation. It has already been declared a severe public health threat. Certain cyberbullying incidents require immediate response due to their life-threatening tendencies compared to others. This makes cyberbullying severity classification a critical task. Minimal research has been geared toward this multi-class classification task. This research proposed various deep learning-based techniques for the detection and severity classification of cyberbullying incidents. The results indicate that the proposed techniques perform well for the multi-class classification task. The research used three datasets of varying balances to study the impact of class imbalance in deep learning-based multi-class classification tasks. The results indicate that deep learning models perform well with moderately balanced class data.

These models can be deployed over streaming data in big data platforms to generate instant alerts about cyberbullying events and their severity. This will help the concerned stakeholders to take necessary action and provide instant support for the victims. Perhaps, constant monitoring might even help reduce this menace and make social networks safe places to a large extent. Immediate intervention techniques could also include exclusion of bully users and their messages. Further research also needs to be directed for obtaining higher efficiencies by experimenting with other available deep learning techniques. Deep learning models can be trained using different languages. People often used bullying words in their language of origin mixed with English. Thus, urban slang must be updated in the datasets and lexicons. Generative adversarial networks (GANs) can be used to generate data for resource-poor languages. Models need to learn from their mistakes in order to be robust and stay up-to-date. Automatic model retraining could help retrain the models based on correctly classified events while separating the falsely classified ones.

REFERENCES

1. A. Bessarab, O. Mitchuk, A. Baranetska, N. Kodatska, O. Kvasnytsia, and G. Mykytiv, "Social networks as a phenomenon of the information society," *J. Optim. Ind. Eng.*, vol. 14, no. 1, pp. 35–42, Dec. 2021, doi: 10.22094/JOIE.2020.677811.

2. S. Wani, M. R. Wahiddin, and T. M. T. Sembok, "Logico-linguistic semantic representation of documents," 2016, doi: 10.1109/DASC-PICom-DataCom-CyberSciTec.2016.135.

3. S. Wani, T. M. T. Sembok, and M. R. Wahiddin, "Rule based modeling of knowledge bases," in *Proceedings – 2017 International Conference on Computational Science and Computational Intelligence, CSCI 2017*, pp. 823–827, Dec. 2018, doi: 10.1109/CSCI.2017.142.

4. A. Muneer and S. M. Fati, "A comparative analysis of machine learning techniques for cyberbullying detection on Twitter," *Futur. Internet*, vol. 12, no. 11, p. 187, Oct. 2020, doi: 10.3390/fi12110187.

5. S. Sadiq, A. Mehmood, S. Ullah, M. Ahmad, G. S. Choi, and B. W. On, "Aggression detection through deep neural model on Twitter," *Futur. Gener. Comput. Syst.*, vol. 114, pp. 120–129, Jan. 2021, doi: 10.1016/j.future.2020.07.050.

6. Z. Zainol, S. Wani, P. Nohuddin, W. Noormanshah, and S. Marzukhi, "Association analysis of cyberbullying on social media using Apriori algorithm," *Int. J. Eng. Technol.*, 2018.

7. M. S. Nikhila, A. Bhalla, and P. Singh, "Text imbalance handling and classification for cross- platform cyber-crime detection using deep learning," Jul. 2020, doi: 10.1109/ICCCNT49239.2020.9225402.

8. K. S. Ray and R. Kusshwaha, "Detection of malicious urls using deep learning approach," in *Lecture Notes in Networks and Systems*, vol. 163, Springer Science and Business Media, Deutschland GmbH, pp. 189–212, 2021.

9. P. P. Adikara, S. Adinugroho, and S. Insani, "Detection of cyber harassment (cyberbullying) on Instagram using naïve bayes classifier with bag of words and lexicon based features," in *ACM International Conference Proceeding Series*, pp. 64–68, Nov. 2020, doi: 10.1145/3427423.3427436.

10. D. Mukhopadhyay, K. Mishra, K. Mishra, and L. Tiwari, "Cyber bullying detection based on Twitter dataset," *Lecture Notes in Networks and Systems*, vol. 141, pp. 87–94, 2021, doi: 10.1007/978-981-15-7106-0_9.

11. N. Lu, G. Wu, Z. Zhang, Y. Zheng, Y. Ren, and K. R. Choo, "Cyberbullying detection in social media text based on character-level convolutional neural network with shortcuts," *Concurr. Comput. Pract. Exp.*, vol. 32, no. 23, p. e5627, Dec. 2020, doi: 10.1002/cpe.5627.

12. "Facts About Bullying," 2021. https://www.stopbullying.gov/resources/facts.

13. E. Zinovyeva, W. K. Härdle, and S. Lessmann, "Antisocial online behavior detection using deep learning," *Decis. Support Syst.*, vol. 138, p. 113362, Nov. 2020, doi: 10.1016/j.dss.2020.113362.

14. C. Slamet, A. Krismunandar, D. S. A. Maylawati, Jumadi, A. S. Amin, and M. A. Ramdhani, "Deep learning approach for bullying classification on twitter social media with Indonesian language," Sept. 2020, doi: 10.1109/ICWT50448.2020.9243653.

15. L. Anindyati, A. Purwarianti, and A. Nursanti, "Optimizing deep learning for detection cyberbullying text in indonesian language," Sept. 2019, doi: 10.1109/ICAICTA.2019.8904108.

16. B. A. Rachid, H. Azza, and H. H. Ben Ghezala, "Classification of cyberbullying text in arabic," Jul. 2020, doi: 10.1109/IJCNN48605.2020.9206643.

17. M. A. Al-Ajlan and M. Ykhlef, "Optimized Twitter cyberbullying detection based on deep learning," Dec. 2018, doi: 10.1109/NCG.2018.8593146.

18. A. Kumar and N. Sachdeva, "Multi-input integrative learning using deep neural networks and transfer learning for cyberbullying detection in real-time code-mix data," *Multimed. Syst.*, pp. 1–15, Jul. 2020, doi: 10.1007/s00530-020-00672-7.

19. J. Yadav, D. Kumar, and D. Chauhan, "Cyberbullying detection using pre-trained BERT model," in *Proceedings of the International Conference on Electronics and Sustainable Communication Systems, ICESC 2020*, pp. 1096–1100, Jul. 2020, doi: 10.1109/ICESC48915.2020.9155700.

20. S. Paul and S. Saha, "CyberBERT: BERT for cyberbullying identification: BERT for cyberbullying identification," *Multimed. Syst.*, pp. 1–8, Nov. 2020, doi: 10.1007/s00530-020-00710-4.

21. J. K. Tripathy, S. S. Chakkaravarthy, S. C. Satapathy, M. Sahoo, and V. Vaidehi, "ALBERT-based fine-tuning model for cyberbullying analysis," *Multimed. Syst.*, pp. 1–9, Sept. 2020, doi: 10.1007/s00530-020-00690-5.

22. A. Pradhan, V. M. Yatam, and P. Bera, "Self-attention for cyberbullying detection," Jun. 2020, doi: 10.1109/CyberSA49311.2020.9139711.

23. V. Banerjee, J. Telavane, P. Gaikwad, and P. Vartak, "Detection of cyberbullying using deep neural network," in *2019 5th International Conference on Advanced Computing and Communication Systems, ICACCS 2019*, pp. 604–607, Mar. 2019, doi: 10.1109/ICACCS.2019.8728378.

24. J. A. Cornel et al., "Cyberbullying detection for online games chat logs using deep learning," Nov. 2019, doi: 10.1109/HNICEM48295.2019.9072811.

25. S. Modha, P. Majumder, T. Mandl, and C. Mandalia, "Detecting and visualizing hate speech in social media: A cyber Watchdog for surveillance," *Expert Syst. Appl.*, vol. 161, p. 113725, Dec. 2020, doi: 10.1016/j.eswa.2020.113725.

26. A. Aggarwal, K. Maurya, and A. Chaudhary, "Comparative Study for Predicting the Severity of Cyberbullying Across Multiple Social Media Platforms," in *Proceedings of the International Conference on Intelligent Computing and Control Systems, ICICCS 2020*, pp. 871–877, May 2020, doi: 10.1109/ICICCS48265.2020.9121046.

27. B. A. Talpur and D. O'Sullivan, "Cyberbullying severity detection: A machine learning approach," *PLoS One*, vol. 15, no. 10, p. e0240924, Oct. 2020, doi: 10.1371/journal.pone.0240924.

28. B. A. Talpur and D. O'Sullivan, "Multi-class imbalance in text classification: A feature engineering approach to detect cyberbullying in Twitter," *Informatics*, vol. 7, no. 4, p. 52, Nov. 2020, doi: 10.3390/informatics7040052.

29. J. Alasadi, R. Arunachalam, P. K. Atrey, and V. K. Singh, "A fairness-aware fusion framework for multimodal cyberbullying detection," in *Proceedings – 2020 IEEE 6th International Conference on Multimedia Big Data, BigMM 2020*, pp. 166–173, Sept. 2020, doi: 10.1109/BigMM50055.2020.00032.

30. M. Rezvan, K. Thirunarayan, S. Shekarpour, V. L. Shalin, L. Balasuriya, and A. Sheth, "A quality typeaware annotated corpus and lexicon for harassment research," in *WebSci 2018 – Proceedings of the 10th ACM Conference on Web Science*, pp. 33–36, May 2018, doi: 10.1145/3201064.3201103.

31. F. Elsafoury, "Cyberbullying datasets," vol. 1, 2020, doi: 10.17632/JF4PZYVNPJ.1.

32. Z. Zainol, A. M. Azahari, S. Wani, S. Marzukhi, P. N. E. Nohuddin, and O. Zakaria, "Visualizing military explicit knowledge using document clustering techniques," *Int. J. Acad. Res. Bus. Soc. Sci.*, 2018, doi: 10.6007/ijarbss/v8-i6/4307.

33. H. Kartal, A. Oztekin, A. Gunasekaran, and F. Cebi, "An integrated decision analytic framework of machine learning with multi-criteria decision making for multi-attribute inventory classification," *Comput. Ind. Eng.*, vol. 101, pp. 599–613, Nov. 2016, doi: 10.1016/j.cie.2016.06.004.

34. J. Pennington, R. Socher, and C. D. Manning, "GloVe: Global vectors for word representation," in *EMNLP 2014 - 2014 Conference on Empirical Methods in Natural Language Processing, Proceedings of the Conference*, pp. 1532–1543, 2014, doi: 10.3115/v1/d14-1162.

9 Cyberbullying among Neurodiverse Learners during Online Teaching and Learning amidst COVID-19

Mohammad Shadab Khan and Sharyar Wani
International Islamic University Malaysia, Kuala Lumpur, Malaysia

Eima Fatima
School of Pharmaceutical Education and Research (SPER), Jamia Hamdard, New Delhi, India

CONTENTS

DOI: 10.1201/9781003134527-12

9.1   BACKGROUND

The fundamental characteristics of intention, repetition, and aggression classify a bullying event. Bullying events have been directly correlated to lethal consequences ranging from anxiety to suicide. Such events take many forms, such as physical, verbal, social, and cyberbullying. Cyberbullying refers to bullying events that occur online using technology that includes verbal or physical harassment. A serious aspect of cyberbullying is the non-existence of geographical boundaries, high likelihood of chain bullying, and privilege of anonymity to the bullies. The virtual space is generally considered an expressive platform for people who cannot express themselves in face-to-face settings. This becomes more so for neurodiverse youth as they tend to establish relationships and expressiveness behind the screen, where their conditions are not exposed, providing them with an improved sense of security. Cyberbullying shatters the victim's confidence and creates an environment of mistrust among peers. This distances people from active relation-building, which is of utmost importance to most neurodiverse youth. Bullying tends to have aggravated consequences for such youth as they blame themselves for their limitations. Furthermore, many of these children are non-expressive, non-verbal, less social, thereby leading to internalization of these events and consequences without discussing and seeking support and comfort from others.

The COVID-19 pandemic has forced almost all activities into the online space. Online collaboration and coordination have been at an all-time high since the advent of the pandemic at the end of 2019. This has led to a mass digital transformation of teaching and learning. Schools and therapies for neurodiverse youth are no exception to this effect. While this is the least preferred mode for activities for such learners, the pandemic has left no option. Cyberbullying has existed pre-pandemic for both neurodiverse and neurotypical youth. Access and exposure to online platforms during the pandemic has significantly increased. The neurodiverse learners and their caretakers have no option but to conform to these new forms of interaction. While the pandemic is expected to last for a few years, it becomes essential to gain more significant cyberbullying insights during the pandemic. The investigation is more critical for neurodiverse learners as an already marginalized community. The current study aims to investigate cyberbullying among neurodiverse learners, considering the context of COVID-19. Generally, the amount of research studies concerning cyberbullying among neurodiverse learners is scarce. Therefore, this study aims to contribute to understanding the prevalence, experience, and impact of cyberbullying among neurodiverse learners. The current work focuses on gaining more in-depth insight from the caretakers, mostly parents during the pandemic, about neurodiverse learners' challenges during this online shift, especially in online teaching, learning, and therapies. The exploration leads to discussions on parents' challenges, cyberbullying types, incidents, and preventive measures from parents or other caretakers' perspectives, applicable in general but the pandemic in particular.

9.2   BULLYING

Bullying is recognized as an unwanted repetitive behavior without regard for others, depicting an imbalance of power. Its manifestations are both emotional and physical [1, 2]. Bullying rarely stops on its own, and volition bullying behaviors are repetitive [3]. The second part is the danger of using labels. There are unintended consequences of labeling someone as a bully or a victim. Labeling sends a message of unchangeable behavior – bullies cannot become better, and victims always have to suffer [4, 5].

Schools have been found to of prime hotspots for bullying as teenagers and youngsters spend most of their time together in schools. This is a common phenomenon in all schools worldwide [6]. The hallways are a frequent location for bullying. Students who are not in the class also get to interact with each other at such places. Buses are another physical avenue for bullying. School bus drivers are too busy to keep watch, and therefore students are left to fend for themselves [7]. More hotspots located within the school include the cafeteria and playground. Bullying in cafes is primarily by exclusion, where bullies segregate others from the group. Playgrounds can be lonely places for both male and female students and tend to have lesser behavioral rules [3]. It is thereby turning them into ideal bullying avenues.

There are various roles that children take on during bullying. Children who bully usually bully more than one student, and the behavior can frequently escalate. Often these students require support to change their behavior. The bullied children need help and support to overcome the trauma and deal with such situations in the future [3]. Other roles include defenders who actively comfort the bullied peers, bystanders who remain neutral, and bully helpers serving as assistants to the bullies. The bystanders neither reinforce the bullying behavior nor defend the child that is being bullied. Most children get involved in bullying incidents taking multiple roles throughout their life. However, children that are perceived as different may be at higher risk of being bullied [8].

As such, children with disabilities and other special health needs are at a higher risk of being bullied because they often cannot defend themselves. The children may be specifically targeted based on their religion; for example, Muslim girls who wear headscarves or Sikh boys who wear turbans are targeted because they are more easily identified. The students may be specifically targeted based on race or nationality. It is not clear how often kids get bullied because of their race, ethnicity, or national origin, as the research is still growing in these areas [9].

Physical bullying involves hurting a person's body or possessions. Physical bullying includes hitting, kicking, punching, pinching, spitting, and pushing. Relational bullying, a less recognized form, refers to social bullying hurting someone's reputation or relationships. It relates to exclusion, where other children are told not to be friends with someone or embarrassing someone in public. Lastly, verbal bullying includes teasing, name-calling, inappropriate sexual comments, taunting, or even threatening to harm someone [2, 4].

Bullying is not restricted to physical spaces. Bullying also takes place online. It is easier to threaten and insult someone from behind a computer compared to a face-to-face confrontation. Online bullying attracts a broader audience compared to physical bullying within the school walls [10].

Bullying indicators include the inability to sleep, nightmares, injuries, and depression due to traumatic bullying experiences. Physical bullying can manifest itself in real injuries, and long-term bullying can lead to a decline in school grades. The students who are bullied at school may deliberately miss classes to escape a bully student. Bullied students want to stay under the radar academically. Depression is a clear indicator of being bullied, and bullies can have a severe and damaging effect on a child's self-image. Another temporal indicator is missing electronics. Students who are bullied are often robbed of their electronics [1, 8].

Individuals must be on the lookout for these indicators of bullying. One must not be a bystander in any form of bullying [11]. Depending on whether the individual is an adult or a child, the community must set an excellent example to reach out, offer friendship and kindness. Bullying must be reported to a trusted adult [8]. This individual can be either a teacher, parent, school counselor, principal, or coach as long as they are deemed trustworthy [12]. The bully must not be provided with an audience at any cost. Most of the time, students bully other students because they want to make themselves look better in front of their allies. The students, being bullied need active support. Therefore, students collectively need to focus their energies to offer them help and care [10].

9.3 CHILDREN WITH SPECIAL NEEDS

The children identified as special needs require extra attention to their necessities [7]. Special needs can be defined concerning a child's widespread health condition, such as physical impairment, learning disability, and other types of terminal illnesses. These individuals with special needs might require long-term medical assistance, which can be lifelong and have an escalating cost [6]. The special needs children also require alternative ways to learn. The education mechanism is unique compared to their neurotypical counterparts [4]. Each special need child is unique, possessing their own set of strengths and weaknesses in their day-to-day activities, depending upon the disability. Most importantly, they miss out on their emotional expressional strengths compared to neurotypical children [13, 14]. Hence, it is always challenging to understand them when they are present in an unfamiliar setting like schools, therapy centers, etc., anything other than their safe spaces, i.e., their home.

Special needs children are broadly categorized into four categories. These categories are physical, developmental, behavioral/emotional, and sensory impairment [13–15]. Each of these subsections is further sub-divided, depending upon the diseases. Table 9.1 highlights the categorization:

9.3.1 PHYSICAL DISABILITY

It is classified as a long-term condition affecting the physical body structure; these physical impairments confine the physical adroitness or endurance, mobility, and functionality [16]. Physical disability corresponds to the reduction of the physical ability of a person to perform body movements. The reduced ability restricts limb movements such as the arm and legs, which results in the inability to sit, stand or walk and lesser or almost no control over the muscles [17]. This affects performing daily tasks, such as holding, moving things, or dressing, etc., taking longer than normal individuals [18]. Such disability could exist by birth or acquired because of fatal accidents, injuries, or side effects to medical conditions. Some examples of physical disabilities are cerebral palsy, epilepsy, muscular dystrophy, multiple sclerosis, chronic asthma, carpal tunnel syndrome, physical amputations, and injuries to the spinal cord.

9.3.2 DEVELOPMENTAL DISABILITY

The developmental disability affects the central nervous system, metabolism, and function of human cells. Intellectual developmental disability is closely related to genetics. It involves learning, cognition, communication, and working memory, which results in poor social communication, critical behavior, and restrictions on the emotional perspective. Intellectual disability is identified among individuals finding it hard to perform everyday activities because of their incapability to function on an intellectual level [19]. These individuals experience common problems such as talking or expressing their needs and desires, eating, reading, self-care, and using the essential tools to complete their routine tasks. It was also known as mental retardation in the earlier days, but the term is no longer in practice. Individuals with intellectual disabilities can learn in a completely different way when compared to their neurotypical counterparts. These children can have partially or totally independent lives after reaching adulthood. Such individuals can also have other physical issues

TABLE 9.1

Different Types of Special Needs

Physical	Cerebral palsy, epilepsy, muscular dystrophy, multiple sclerosis, chronic asthma, etc.
Developmental	Dyslexia, Down's syndrome, sensory processing disorder, autism, etc.
Emotional/behavioral	Bipolar disorder, attention deficit hyperactivity disorder, oppositional defiance disorder
Sensory impairment	Deaf or hearing impaired, total blindness, or partial blindness

such as speaking, hearing, seeing, and some type of seizures. A complete evaluation for the child is necessary when he/she is suspected of intellectual disability so that the parents and supporting staff have proper knowledge about the situation. Based on the special abilities, a comprehensive plan for educational learning and growth is designed and monitored.

9.3.3 EMOTIONAL/BEHAVIORAL DISABILITY

Emotional and behavioral disorders may be associated with intellectual disabilities and may interfere with the child's progress. Most children with intellectual disabilities recognize that they are behind others of their age [19]. Some may become frustrated, withdrawn, anxious, or act "bad" to get other youngsters and adults' attention. Children and teens with intellectual disabilities may be victims of bullying in school and social settings. Adolescents and young adults with intellectual disabilities may become depressed and even suicidal. Youth, teens, and young adults may not have the language skills needed to express their feelings. Their depression may be shown by recent problems in their eating, and sleeping, and behavioral patterns. It is essential to evaluate children, both medically and psychiatrically, in the event of behavioral changes, especially aggressiveness. The child may also be experiencing an underlying medical problem that they are unable to discuss.

9.3.4 SENSORY IMPAIRMENT

Sensory processing disorder is a quite baffling condition as no two children struggling with them are alike. It has been referred to as dysfunction or disorder in sensory integration, sensory needs, or sensory load. The children could be over-stimulated by the world around them or not respond to their surroundings. This causes them to seek additional sensory input, which may not be apt and socially acceptable [20]. The sensory system includes eight different types such as auditory, olfactory, oral-sensory, vestibular, proprioceptive, tactile, visual, and interoceptive works in cohesion to keep control of the body movements and spatial awareness [21]. Special needs children are sensitive to sensory needs. The difficulty in processing the incoming sensory information can be identified by measuring detection capabilities, modulation, interpretation, and organization. The interrelation within sensory processing and social factors foresees the performance of motor coordination, where the sensorimotor processing discrepancies may be partially responsible for motor learning and control difficulties. Sensory processing is the emerging result of the interaction between the neurological threshold and self-regulation [22]. The neurological threshold refers to the number of sensory stimuli needed by a person for noticing and responding. It ranges from quick to detect (low threshold) to slow to detect (high threshold). Self-regulation refers to the behavioral management of sensory input. Children with passive strategies do not counteract the stimuli, while children with active self-regulation strategies plan a reaction to counteract it.

The four sensory processing patterns emerging from the interaction of neurological threshold and self-regulation are as follows:

a) low registration or bystander (high threshold and passive self-regulation);
b) seeking or seeker (high threshold and active self-regulation);
c) sensitivity or sensor (low threshold and passive self-regulation);
d) avoiding or avoider (low threshold and active self-regulation).

A child categorized under sensory processing difficulty may experience all the mentioned stages [21].

9.4 BULLYING IN CHILDREN WITH SPECIAL NEEDS

Several definitions for special needs children have emerged within the literature, and each definition has some variations because of the child's underlying condition. These fundamental conditions include terminal illness, physical disorders, and learning disabilities classified under cognitive or psychiatric problems. Special needs children require continuous support and monitoring. This requires alternative approaches that consider their unique conditions and help them develop self-supportive measures to function independently.

Children with special needs have been reported to have a higher rate of victimization from bullying. The experiences encountered by the victims are verbal, physical, relational, and technology-based [23].

Meta-analysis-based research on 107 articles revealed that children with special needs had more chances of being the victim and suffered abuse through verbal, physical, relational, and cyberbullying approaches. It was also observed in general that the bullied victims displayed relational and physical aggression [12]. Another systematic literature review to identify poly-victimization was conducted by [24], for children and adolescents with autism spectrum disorder (ASD) and attention deficit hyperactivity disorder (ADHD). The review included studies from Asia (Hong Kong), Europe (France, Norway, and Spain), and North America (USA). Poly-victimization means experiencing different forms of violence and abuse. It was determined that the victims with ASD and ADHD were not understood by their neurotypical peers and were bullied more often in schools, public places, their homes, and neighborhood. A study by [10] concluded that both bullies and victims suffer from mental health problems, whereas the victims were on low self-esteem and displayed severe depression and anxiety. This study was conducted in Taiwan for 219 students in their adolescent age with high functioning ASD. Children with ASD have a high prevalence of bullying in comparison to standard or neurotypical children. The researchers reviewed 29 studies about school children with ASD under 18 years [6].

In summary, it can be concluded that children with disabilities are often soft targets for bullies. Bullying behaviors seem to be prevalent in schools and community places. The physical and behavioral differences between the neurodiverse and the neurotypical children create visual distinction. Children with ASD are more likely targets because of the relative problem in communication, socialization, and repeated behavioral patterns [25]. It is often misunderstood that children with ASD do not like to participate with other neurotypical children because of their behavioral fixation. This develops propensity for children with disabilities as the bullying target [26]. Children with ASD have higher chances of victimization in inclusive school settings than segregated ones [24]. The conclusions by [10] summed that both bully and victims suffer from mental health issues which need appropriate intervention. Failure to do so may result in severe depression and anxiety.

9.5 CYBERBULLYING

The advancement of technology and the increasing dependence on various technological tools make users more vulnerable to technological drawbacks. Virtual bullying or cyberbullying is one of such rampant downsides. The individuals connected to the internet come across various forms of abuse [27]. In the digital age, nearly all household members tend to be connected to the internet, especially since the outbreak of the pandemic. The tasks which required a social presence are swiftly transforming into mandatory virtual intercommunication. Examples include small or medium-scale food vendors, manufacturing, production, retail, healthcare, education, and monthly grocery shopping. This migration to the virtual interface avoids social intermingling and maintains social distancing guidelines to regulate the spread of this lethal COVID virus strain. The increasing number of online platforms has resulted in an overwhelming increase in the number of users. However, users find it hard to utilize the services efficiently and achieve their goals due to inexperience. Moreover, a lack of understanding among novice users makes them prone to bullying in cyberspace. In a study conducted by the Microsoft Corporation in 2012, it was reported that India ranks third in the world for cyberbullying victims, right behind China and Singapore (Figures 9.1 and 9.2) [28].

The study, as mentioned earlier, was conducted to understand the worldwide occurrence of cyberbullying. It was observed that cyberbullying differs based on culture and individuals. Online negative experiences related to teasing, being called by mean names, and unfriendly treatments were

53% Bullied Online

54% Bullied Offline

77 % Bullied Online and Ofline

India

Cyberbullied 53% (compared with 25 country average of 37%) of children age 8-17 who responded to the survey say they have been subjected to a range of online activities that some may consider to be online bullying or to have adverse effects:

➢ 22% - Mean or unfriendly treatment

➢ 29% - Made fun of teased

➢ 25% - Called mean names

FIGURE 9.1 Online bullying among youth 8–17 years old in India [28].

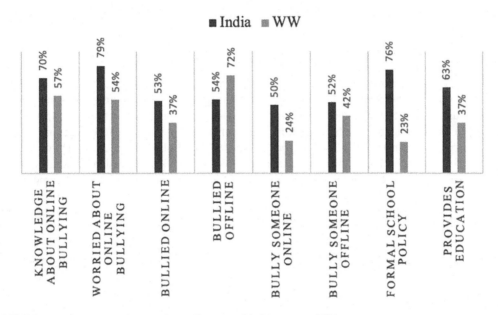

FIGURE 9.2 Online bullying metrics India vs. worldwide average [28].

recorded among children within the age group of 8–17 years. A substantial population of the respondents (79%) reported that they were worried about being victims, and 70% of the respondents had some or detailed understanding of cyberbullying. The findings also revealed that a total of 77% are being bullied online and offline, or either one; 50% of the respondents confess that they bullied others online, 52% acknowledge that they bullied others offline and children with the age group of 8–12 years have 58% chance of being bullied online.

The survey indicated no gender bias toward cyberbullying behavior, as both girls and boys were prone to be victimized, 53% and 52% respectively. The American Medical Association found that one in every four Indian teenagers have been cyberbullied at least once [29]. India is in the midst of a social media revolution. This has led to more and more youth being cyberbullied. While social media has given youth immense power but unfortunately, some have abused the same.

Although behaviors such as teasing, being called mean names, and unfriendly treatment might not directly coincide with the bullying behavior, they still have an adverse effect on the victims. As there is no clear definition of cyberbullying, the traditional aspects of bullying like intent to harm, repetition of the behavior, and power imbalance between the bully and victim, are also applied and found cyberbullying [2]. When a bully posts mean, hurtful, embarrassing, and tormenting messages on social media or other internet platforms repeatedly, it is classified as cyberbullying. It is often compared to bullying over the internet continually, except it happens in front of hundreds or thousands of familiar friends. Although it occurs in the virtual space, the impact is still long-lasting.

Unfortunately, 9 out of 10 cyberbullied victims do not share their trauma with anyone. This is the hidden scourge of cyberbullying. Victims do not admit that it exists, yet millions and millions of people worldwide suffer from it every day. The victims experience low self-esteem issues and depression. Cyberbullied youth are more likely to drop out of school, indulge in drug abuse, and in rare cases, even commit suicide [30].

9.6 CYBERBULLYING IN CHILDREN WITH SPECIAL NEEDS

The advent of COVID-19 has transformed the lives of every individual. Neurodiverse learners have also felt the effects of pandemic around them. Although these might be the best times for neurodiverse learners, as they live in their safe spaces and do not need to stimulate their sensory functions, initiate conversations, or socialize with strangers forcefully. However, the closure of schools, therapy centers, parks, and other community places have a massive drawback for this community. In present times the transformation of all social events into online meetings and webinars has given neurodiverse learners a better chance for participation in learning activities. This technological emergence using handheld devices diversifies communication into new forms like audio calls, video calls, blogging, photo sharing, tweeting, and instant message sharing. The exceeding presence of novice neurodiverse users has increased their vulnerability to encounter bullying even in their safe spaces. The bullies can hide behind the screen and victimize innocent targets without the fear of getting caught.

The surge of internet users during the pandemic is because of the extensive usage of internet facilities for communication, attending classes and lectures, and socialization. Several kinds of research have been carried out to study the impact of the pandemic on neurodiverse learners. In a recent review by [24], it was found that children with neurodiversity conditions such as ASD, ADHD, Dyslexia, and other diseases have far greater chances of getting bullied than their neurotypical counterparts. It was also reported that these bullying incidences are not reported. Another recent study by [29], pre-pandemic and during the pandemic, concludes that the pandemic has affected our susceptibility to cyberbullying. It has been growing as a social menace in developing countries, including India, and has been labeled as a sociological issue. A recent poll by Ipsos in 2018 covering 28 countries placed India on top of the list with 37% (Figure 9.3) [31].

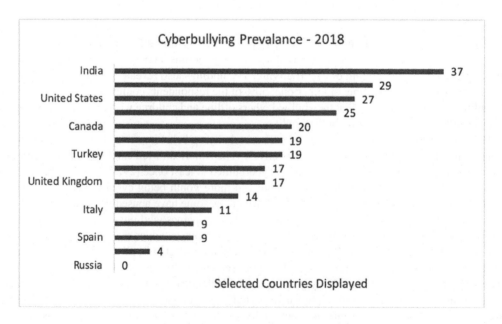

FIGURE 9.3   Ipsos cyberbullying prevalence report [32].

In the United States, over a quarter of parents said their child had also experienced the problem, numbers jumping to 27% from 15% recorded in 2011. A news report published in Forbes also stated that cyberbullying rates are much more mixed in Europe, with 17% of parents in the UK confirming it and 14% in Italy and 9% in Spain and France. Interestingly, the phenomenon seems to be virtually non-existent in Russia, with no parents citing instances of cyberbullying.

According to [33], the frequency of hurtful, embarrassing, threatening, and derogatory statements transmitted through digital platforms increases workplace embarrassment. It is easier to make hurtful, embarrassing, or threatening statements on the internet because of the comparative difficulty in detecting and identifying misbehavior. At the same time, the identity of the offending party tends to remain anonymous. Hence, children with special needs are more vulnerable to such technological drawbacks.

9.7 RELATED WORK

The current work that primarily focuses on cyberbullying studies among neurodiverse learners or special needs children seems very scarce. A study focusing on bullying awareness and knowledge among young adults with special educational needs revealed a severe lack of cyberbullying information. A group of 96 adults participated in the study. A questionnaire was distributed to measure the general bullying knowledge of all the participants. Results revealed that the participants lacked the skills, knowledge, and resources to deal with bullying. 42.7% of the participants deemed bullying as abnormal. At the same time, others tried to ignore or avoid bullying situations. Only 62.5% of the participants knew necessary steps in a bullying situation, while 63.5% reported that the reporting avenues at work or school are insufficient. A training program followed this, and a similar measurement was done post-training. The results indicated a promising improvement in the participants' awareness about the problems surrounding bullying. Post-training, only 20.5% considered bullying to be expected, while a significant increase was observed under various other categories. Almost 20% more people knew what to do when bullying occurs, and 64% had attended courses related to the prevention of disablist bullying [34]. Nearly half of the intellectual and developmental disabilities (IDD) population has experienced cyberbullying at some stage in their life. Parents of special Olympic youth were interviewed to study their exposure to cyberbullying. Around 60% reported cyberbullying experiences. The desire of having a social circle puts youth with IDD at a higher chance of cyberbullying. This study used routine activity theory (RAT) for question design and thematic analysis, measuring these youths' cyber involvement and exposure to bullying incidents [35]. It has been reported that individuals with a smaller social circle are more vulnerable to peer aggression [36–38]. Nine out of 10 students with ASD reported bullying experience in a study conducted to outline recommendations. Both the parties recommended better communication channels, pro-active teachers, and strict cyberbullying policies to be included in schools. Parents and students expressed a lack of confidence in the government. They recommended that the government revisit bullying laws and introduce harsher penalties and consequences for bullying [8]. In the era of digital citizenship, librarians need to tailor programs and services for neurodiverse youth. The nature of online platforms and interaction makes the youth susceptible to cyberbullying. The role of librarians for inclusiveness was studied in [39], to study the surrounding issues so that future librarians can be equipped with necessary inclusiveness skills. Cyberbullying victims have a higher level of post-traumatic stress (PTS) than bullying victims in school environments. Girls are more prone to PTS following cyberbullying incidents. These findings were extracted from a co-relational study on 5058 secondary school Italian students. The study focused on finding the relationship between PTS and bullying/cyberbullying in both victims and perpetrators [40]. Similarly, in another co-relational study comprising 638 undergraduate students, 57% of students had experienced cyberbullying. The results indicate that cyberbullying affects the victims' academic, social, and emotional development [41].

9.8   METHODS

This study is based on interviews conducted with ten parents with neurodiverse children in January 2021. The interviews focused on gathering parental insights about cyberbullying experiences, mainly during online teaching and learning during the first pandemic year 2020. The interviews also aimed to understand their insights about supporting and preventing such incidents for their neurodiverse children.

9.8.1   PROCEDURE

Participants were contacted through online communities of neuro-diverse parents. An open invitation to the study was disseminated through these channels with information about the current study's aims and intentions. Those who registered their interest were asked to provide some last details to ensure that they qualify for the current study. The most important criteria that were emphasized were that they must be caretakers of neurodiverse learners and attending teaching and learning classes during the pandemic. Those who acted as shadow teacher's pre-pandemic were given preference because of their field experience during the current pandemic. All interviews were conducted online due to the pandemic restrictions. The interviews were recorded and transcribed for analysis. Questions focused on the awareness, experience, prevalence, consequences, and recommendations for cyberbullying prevention to create a holistic, inclusive environment for neurodiverse learners. Anonymity and confidentiality were discussed and guaranteed before the interview process.

9.8.2   PARTICIPANTS

This study's sample was parents of children with various special needs in an urban setting from the capital city New Delhi in India. Since India has emerged as one of the most prevalent cyberbullying regions among the 28 selected countries globally, it is imperative to learn about its current prevalence rate. A total of 30 parents were contacted for online interviews, out of which 17 parents committed to the interview date and time. Later, three parents cancelled the interview because of other commitments. A total of 14 respondents were interviewed. Three of the 14 parents were not comfortable sharing information about their children's bullying experiences due to the fear of school expulsion. Post-interview, they requested to withdraw their participation. The audio from one of the participants was not recorded clearly due to internet issues and dropped from the sample. The researchers ended with interview data from 10 participants for the current study.

9.8.3   DATA ANALYSIS

This study employed thematic analysis, critically analyzing the messages contained within. The thematic analysis helps to identify common themes from the interviews. An inductive approach was chosen to identify the salient themes contained within the interview data. Our analysis used both semantic and latent approach during the theme building and discussion process. As indicated earlier, all the interview data were transcribed for analysis. Transcripts were initially analyzed only about the recurring themes. These themes were highlighted within the text and coded as necessary for the discussion section. An essential step at the first stage is to familiarize the data and a shared understanding between the authors by thoroughly discussing the responses. Coded items were further arranged into broader themes where attempts were made that each theme contained the most relevant data underneath it. However, it is hard to separate the response in every case, leading to contextual imbalance.

9.9 RESULTS

The analysis is presented under various themes to address this investigation's objectives: to determine the prevalence, experience, and impact of cyberbullying among neurodiverse children during online teaching and learning, especially in the pandemic context, based on parental perceptions. Further investigation led to finings related to intervention and recommendations from the parents.

9.9.1 THE PANDEMIC EFFECT

The interviewed parents have identified the disruption in essential support services for their neurodiverse learners to be significant during the pandemic. In essence, most parents believe that COVID-19 hurts children's overall development. The guidelines from the authorities restricted physical movement, confining the children in their homes. The closure of schools, therapy centers, parks, and other social activity places has deterred progress, making it more challenging for neurodiverse learners. The majority of parents believe that the substantial increase in screen time is inevitable, as the students need to attend their classes and therapy lessons online. The overhead load from the online classes and therapies has placed the parents under much stress. The learners who are not in terms with the developments in the physical environment are finding it difficult to adjust to the new norms. The parents' primary segment reported increased anxiety, melt-downs, aggression, and other behavioral symptoms among their children. Mood swings, irregular sleep cycles, and alteration in food habits have also been reported frequently.

> *…Yes, many new behaviors have come during the pandemic, like self-hitting behavior, breaking glass objects, running, and jumping over the furniture. Aggression and most of the time, he is upset and throwing tantrums. He has encounters of epileptic attacks too and has serious food allergies.*

All these contributing factors create a sensory imbalance, leading to an extreme behavioral change. The neurodiverse children are more dependent on their parents in comparison to their neurotypical counterparts. Irrespective of their age, a neurodiverse child needs support for necessary day to day activities. Amid COVID-19 pandemic movement restrictions and lack of social contact, parents are overstressed, finding the right balance between their personal and professional emotional quotient.

Moreover, when parents have neurodiverse children, their concern overpowers their emotional behavior. Inability to cater to the need of the children makes them overwhelmed. In continuation of this study's findings, a large segment of parents reported being overburdened, anxious, and on low energy level because of the lack of support from the partners in managing the routine for their neurodiverse child. A significant number of parents also reported a lack of support from the school, teachers, and therapists.

> *… Very much overburdened, as our family mostly was dependent on the therapies, but now when therapies are not safe due to the pandemic, it gets extremely hard for us to keep our son busy. My son gets bored too … I feel anxious as it gets difficult to leave him with the maid as I go out for work. It is an added responsibility which I find difficult to maintain. I am overly stressed as everything has come on me. My husband is less supportive.*

9.9.2 BULLYING/CYBERBULLYING PERCEPTION

According to previous studies, bullying is explained in typically developing children as a repetition of the behavior, a power imbalance between the bully and victim, and intent to harm. Based on these themes bullying behavior can be differentiated from other acts such as playing, teasing, and fighting. Several definitions exist based on these themes, but none are agreed upon [3]. Without such a definition, the effect of bullying is likely to be impacted by an individual's attitude, perception, and behavior. The understanding of bullying among the teachers and parents varies based on their experiences. In this research study, many parents who were interviewed highlighted factors such as emotional and physical harm, derogatory remarks, use of foul language, criticism in public and social spaces, and actions belittling the victim's self-esteem.

Bullying can occur in several forms. Direct bullying, bullying at a physical level that might include slapping, pushing, kicking, and damaging possession of someone.

Any physical or emotional statement made by a person that can hurt or harm the other person which might lead to suicides too ... it is a serious problem.

... taunt, negative comments, abusive language, hurting someone physically and emotionally affecting the sleep pattern and loss of appetite.

Bullying is a kind of cruelty like verbal insults or physical harassment inflicted upon someone who is either different or weak ...

All these findings were found to be in continuation of the parallel studies being conducted to classify bullying as a serious offence, with severe implications for neurodiverse individuals, especially those on the autism spectrum. The extreme cases lead to critical mental health conditions to the extent of suicidal tendencies.

A significant increase in cyberbullying has been observed during the pandemic, both in neurotypical and neurodiverse learners. This was not the case with the neurodiverse learners or the children with ASD earlier. However, the closure of schools and therapy centers and their migration on technological platforms have made cyberbullying more rampant. The fundamental three aspects of bullying are consistent with cyberbullying [2]. The themes elicited from the interview sessions among the parents of children on the autism spectrum were aligned on the same idea, and a majority of parents identified cyberbullying as bullying behavior from behind the digital screen, criticism or verbal bullying on social media platforms, in the online classrooms and therapy sessions.

I think that cyberbullying is one of the worst things that a teenager may be exposed to. But in this age, kids cannot act properly. The cyber-bullies are always not self-confident children who, in many cases, envy their victims.

Previously, bullying had been confined to the school playground, bus, or outside in the neighborhood; however, this deadly phenomenon has now entered into the digital world and is known as cyberbullying.

... social criticism on social media Facebook and Instagram, no experience while online class learning.

... negative impact on person's ability to anything can be verbal, or criticizing in social or public space; the experience can be more humiliating and rattle the confidence of an individual to the core because they are being exposed to wide number of users.

Individuals with various disabilities have a higher risk of being victimized and harassed by their peers [25], and their assessment is aligned with the findings of current research. World Health Organization (WHO) estimates that more than 5% of children aged 0–14 have a disability. The civic interest in bullying and cyberbullying among school children is focused on their mental health and wellbeing, especially for the students, who are victims with disabilities such as ASD [6]. Such students are predominantly exposed to bullying due to their social and communication difficulties. The behavioral change and disruption in emotional, sleeping, and dietary patterns were the most prominent indicators. This is in accordance with the findings in this current research, where a majority of parents have expressed that their kids were bulled before the pandemic, and a heightened prevalence has been observed during the pandemic.

> *Yes, my son gets bullied often because he is non-verbal so he often faces exclusion, and he is not included in sports, my son also likes to hear rhymes, so his classmates often make fun of him and call him a baby. Children fool him as he is unaware of reasoning and questioning. I learned this when I replaced him as a shadow teacher.*
>
> *... Verbal, body shaming, inappropriate comments, and negative remark.*
>
> *... By his physical appearance, he is verbal, so he communicated the whole incident to me.*
>
> *... Previously, bullying had been confined to the school playground, bus, or outside in the neighborhood; however, this deadly phenomenon has now entered into the digital world and is known as cyberbullying.*
>
> *She experienced verbal bullying because of her physical experience, exclusion because of the lack of physical strength and use of wheelchair, inability to perform similar action as neurotypical children.*

9.9.3 BULLYING/CYBERBULLYING EXPERIENCES

The bullying rate for students with all disabilities is between 1 and 1.5 times higher than for typically developing students, and students with ASD are at the most significant risk of bullying [25]. It has been observed that most of the interviewee children were vulnerable to bullying and cyberbullying, and it was prevalent from their behavioral changes and other habits. According to [6], a total of 5% of children worldwide at the age of 0–14 are disabled. The seniors frequently practice bullying behavior, and in some cases, the bully belongs to the same classroom. Henceforth, the victim's age is most often the same, or they are younger than the bullying student. According to the findings of this research, the average age of the victim was seven years. Some of the victims were verbal and able to speak out their concerns. However, most of the victims were non-verbal, and the effects of bullying were reflected in their day to day social and behavioral patterns [3].

It was reported by [10] that schools are the most common premises where bullying behavior can build. This is because students from different age groups assemble and have several places to come across each other. It is experienced in virtual environments in common social spaces like chat groups, live class sessions, and discussion rooms. The bully hides behind the screen and criticizes the victim, which goes viral as the sessions are recorded and shared over the platforms. The technological platforms have become a haven for the bullies because it is almost impossible to identify the miscreant's identity. This research reveals that the neurodiverse youth experienced bullied behavior both before the pandemic and during the pandemic.

> *It was happening at his school and then during online classes when he would be interacting or participating through speech, they would bully him by giggling or imitating his words and modified pronunciations.*
>
> *... playground, in classroom by the teacher on teacher's day online event, school functions, parks, restaurants, class participations.*
>
> *School, playgrounds, classroom when the teacher is not present, public spaces, malls, parks, and therapy center.*

It is important to note that during the pandemic, not just the students but some teachers were also reported to display bullying behavior. The most common themes that emerged before the pandemic about bullying practice were school buses, playgrounds, parks, cafeterias, classrooms, and therapy centers. Whereas during the pandemic, the bullying behavior was experienced during the classroom sessions online, school functions, online events, and discussion rooms. These themes were identified from the parental perception interviews and were find almost consistent with the findings in [7].

Children with intellectual and physical disabilities are more prone to be bullied than neurotypical children [25]. It is more evident for children with no verbal or social communication, as in children with ASD. As per the current research findings, it happened quite frequently, almost multiple times daily, because of many common points of interaction between the victims and bullies. However, the pandemic's onset has confined the interactive time, and traditional bullying practices have been transformed into bullying practices using technology, which is also termed cyberbullying.

> *It happened very often, and he would not want to interact during online class, as he understood they were making fun of his speech.*
> *... some occasions in pandemic, prior to pandemic often.*
> *... Often, I kept getting complaints before the pandemic/less experience during the online phase.*
> *... quite a few number of times in playground and few times during online annual day.*

Cyberbullying can include episodes that use cell phones, Internet tools, and social media [25]. Children with learning and intellectual disability, ADHD and ASD, have a higher risk of being bullied than their neurotypical peers. While children with ASD lack attention capability and struggle to create and sustain relationships among their peers, they have a higher risk of being bullied [42]. In a school environment where social interactions are exceedingly possible, neurotypical students are always at the forefront of opportunities. This leads to the development of power centric groups, and the students are classified into different categories based on their intellectual or physical ability. This creates a high likelihood of bullying by exclusion. According to the parent's perception in this study, most parents highlighted the following themes for bullies: schoolmates of the elderly age group, classmates, playmates in school, and parks. Some parents also reported bullying behavior from the therapists, neighbors, and teachers, which is uniquely observed in this study.

> *His seniors did this intentionally, although everyone in his class knows that he is allergic to wheat including the seniors too.*
> *... physical bullying, social criticism on social media, public shaming, body shaming.*
> *... Teasing was the most common, verbal harassment.*
> *... Classmates/fellow students, experience of exclusion by the teacher.*
> *Neighbors, classmates, schoolmate ... he would hit him on his head and on his private parts too. They would snatch his bag and would empty his water bottle ... ask him to run four rounds on the ground.*

A wide variety of methods used for bullying have surfaced from the current research. Most parents commonly report verbal abuse, physical harm, body-shaming, teasing, looking down, implying exclusion, theft, or damaging personal property (electronics, stationary, notebooks, schoolbags). Popular themes that were elicited in this research were in line with the observations by [8].

9.9.4 BULLYING/CYBERBULLYING IMPACT

The pandemic has reformed the lives of adults and children. It has been beneficial for neurodiverse learners, enriching their lives and limiting their social interaction and public appearance. However, it also comes with challenges such as harassment, cyberbullying, trolling, and grooming. These adverse features can disproportionately affect children and young people [43]. Individuals with disabilities are more exposed to strenuous activities, bullying, and threats than individuals without any disability [44]. In this research majority of the parents have enrolled their children in mainstream inclusive education programs. Mainstream education is typically designed for neurotypical students, where any neurodiverse learner's participation is seemingly irrelevant unless there is an understanding of inclusion among the teachers and the students. The exclusion could result in dissatisfaction, leading to symptoms of depression. This is an unruly bullying behavior toward intellectually disabled learners. Individuals with ASD who have co-morbid conditions are more prone to be victimized. Their communication inability suffers because they are pre-verbal, semi-verbal, or non-verbal, which results in extreme sensory imbalance contributing to behavioral shifts. The students with ASD with co-morbid assuming indications might end up with anxiety, disorders, and depression [1]. Aggression, tantrum, anger build-up, behavioral change, low motivation, upset, irritation, emotional and physical anxiety, mood swings, and withdrawal feelings among bullied children were observed from the interviews.

> ... aggression, tantrum, anxiety and anger build-up, behavioral changes.
>
> When it all started, he was very young, but as he is a grown-up, he has started to understand the stare and the abusive language that people use as my son has become more verbal during the past few years.
>
> He didn't want to talk in class and refused to participate through speech.
>
> He cried a lot when they hit him, although he was little. But as he grew up, he wrote a note to me in which he wrote that he doesn't want to attend school, it hurts.
>
> ... He had nightmares, would cry a lot, get angry or aggressive more than usual, had mood swings, not want to talk about what's wrong, he felt anxious, and seem withdrawn.
>
> My child got so scared that he would not step inside the center and started crying and would not do any activity. He would always want me to carry him and be with him even when he is in the session.
>
> It affected his personality, he didn't want to attend the school before the pandemic and now during the pandemic, if he finds his friends making his fun online ... he would just shut the computer.

These experimental factors are similar to other findings in the literature [1, 43, 45]. The child's reaction mechanism toward such bullying events developed a sense of insecurity, emotional exhaustion, aggression, anxiety, fear of medication, nightmares, and unfamiliar gathering. The majority of these elicited factors for neurotypical children, especially individuals with ASD, are also observed in [42].

9.9.5 ONLINE TEACHING AND LEARNING DURING THE PANDEMIC

Parents reported that sudden change in the school and therapy routine during the COVID-19 pandemic had left them with very few options. The drastic change in their children's routine had an adverse effect on their behaviors and parental mental health. Neurodiverse learners are unable to adapt to the new norm due to their intellectual disabilities. The online classes are of mainstream inclusive nature. The majority of parents voice their concerns about the teachers and therapists' lack of support and attention toward their neurodiverse learners. The virtual classrooms lack the physical touch and experience which connects the neurodiverse learners and creates an engaging experience. Online classes tend to create an additional distraction for neurodiverse youth, leading to inadequate focus on the content being taught.

> Due to pandemic, his online classes have started, which makes it a lot more difficult to make him sit at the chair table. His mental age is around seven years, so he has no understanding of what is taught, but his special educator and I modify his syllabus accordingly ... It is very tiring for me and for my son as he makes it so difficult. Moreover, the therapist's attitude is so bad that I feel drained while following her instructions ... Online experience is not helpful at all as my kid is hyperactive and cannot focus on an activity or audio-visuals for more than 5mins. He needs a more interactive environment to focus his energies.

Reference [46] explains the overlaying stress on parents during the COVID-19 pandemic. The absence of support makes the learning process more challenging for learners and their parents. Emotional burnout and overwhelming feeling are common among parents as they struggle to find a solution to their neurodiverse wards' lack of attention. Most parents believe that neurodiverse children cannot soak up the learning pressure and have lost in-person academic experience. The presence of a special needs' educator, class teacher, or therapist is significant, which is currently being substituted by the parent [19]. A feeling of overwhelming emotions seems to overpower the parents, and they feel left alone with insufficient support and guidance.

> *Highly unsatisfactory, could not find proper support, not supportive of online therapy in case of their child ...*
> *Irregular sitting time, poor attention span, and she experience sensory overload because of the breaking sound of teachers and the students because of the internet issues ...*
> *Tough, as it is so difficult to wake him up for the online class in the morning. He disconnects the video call and doesn't want to attend the online class ...*
> *He finds the class really lengthy and gets bored with too much information ...*

In addition to the inability of the neurodiverse learners to cope up and understand the new normal, factors like low attention span, irregular sitting time, lengthy sessions, and the experience of sensory overload were reported by a majority of parents. These factors were found aligned with the result summarized by [47], where they recommended that both parents and teachers working together and persistently will lead toward meaningful incentives.

9.9.6 CYBERBULLYING DURING THE PANDEMIC

The cyberbullying incidents are reported throughout the interviews. These incidents seem to have a common point of origin, i.e., online classes during the pandemic. Bullying is not restricted to students, but some teachers and therapists also seem to be a part of the problem The neurodiverse children are unable to express themselves like the neurotypical population. This aggravates during virtual interactions. Peers laugh, giggle, and use unacceptable names for neurodiverse children when they struggle or express themselves differently. Their struggles provide an avenue for these bullies for further exploitation. Some teachers have been unappreciative, rather than helping the children, and tend to blame the parents. Some cyberbullying incidents have severe consequences where one of the children needed to be admitted to a psychiatric ward for almost a month. The child was vomiting continuously and unable to eat. Other cases report spreading nasty stories about neurodiverse learners leading to chain cyberbullying. This led to depression and unwillingness to attend online classes. The most horrifying incident seems to be reported about a therapist being obscene, and suggesting to tie the child to a chair to attend therapy sessions. Among all the environments, the therapist environment should be a haven for neurodiverse kids and must act as most helpful, especially in the pandemic world. It is unfortunate to report that these avenues are not free from danger for neurodiverse children.

> *Teacher is unappreciative, excludes him, doesn't include him in the activities, asks the parent to work harder.*
> *Yes, he was cyberbullied on the internet over a period of 2 hours by his school friends ... The event was so traumatic it caused my son to have an acute psychotic break and to be hospitalized in an adolescent psychiatric ward for almost a month. He was so mu disturbed that he was vomiting all over and didn't eat any food. He is changed forever and will never be the same mentally ...*
> *Yes, my son is being cyberbullied during the pandemic when he communicates by writing and shows what he has written on the camera in his online class. The other children call him*

deaf and dumb and laugh at him. He gets irritated and shows anger by breaking everything that comes his way. He is often threatened.

But the therapist they assigned for my son is so rude, she says my son has an attitude, she asked me to tie him to a chair to make him sit in front of the computer so that he attends online sessions. She never talks to my son, politely. It is really getting too much for me and my son ...

Parents stand divided reporting cyberbullying during the pandemic. Due to the current circumstances, there is fear due to a lack of opportunities. Parents feel that their reporting might come across as nagging given the current situation. They do not report, lest the schools or other limited online avenues for such children might expel or sideline, affecting the limited interaction these children are having during the pandemic. While some of the parents reported cyberbullying to concerned in charges, no action was taken demonstrating their complete helplessness due to the current situation. Parents also tend not to report because they fear their children will be in the limelight, leading to further humiliation and exclusion in the current virtual settings due to the pandemic.

I have not reported the cyberbullying as I fear this might further humiliate my son and teacher would say that I am forever complaining.

I didn't report as I am not confident enough to report, and moreover, there are no therapy centers around my area to approach.

I complained to his teacher, but she said she could not do much.

9.9.7 Bullying/Cyberbullying Intervention

Almost all the parents have reported bullying to the immediately concerned authorities, e.g., teachers, principals, coaches, government officials. The reporting choice is mostly based on immediate in charge rather than senior officials within the same setting. Despite being reported, it has been reported throughout that the bullying did not stop. In some instances, the concerned authorities seldom took any action at all. A particular case reported that they could not report bullying because they were unaware of reporting medium and guidelines. There seems to be a division in terms of responsibility felt by the concerned authorities after bullying is reported. While some show well responsible behavior, others tend to cast off the issue without any follow-up. The action, wherever taken, is only limited to warning the bully. There seem no efforts in terms of awareness, and therefore, the bullying incidents are reported to be repeating.

I talked to the schoolteacher in parent-teacher meetings, but mostly the kids were left off with a warning, and nothing much was done regarding the problem and the bullying continued.

... to the teacher, she apologized and promised that she would keep better watch, and wouldn't happen in the future. My son was pulled of a swing in the school, and she had not noticed. She acted very thoughtfully.

... written to government authorities on several occasions. Once the office tells us to go there, they tell us to go to another one, in the end, we get tired, there is no benefit ...

Yes, I complained to the school principal, but she didn't take any serious action against the students involved ...

Many of the parents and caretakers report the events without any hesitation. They feel obliged to report because they are the voice of these children in the non-inclusive environment. However, these reports are about those not in authority, e.g., peers, students in the same school, etc. It was noted that bullying cases are not reported if the bully has some sort of authority over the child's environment, such as teachers, therapists, etc. Parents tend to be afraid as they fear the expulsion of their children. The lack of other avenues acts as a substantial barrier to report bullying in such cases. It is also noteworthy that the confidence levels eventually decline as the bullies grow in age and strength. Parents fear physical harm to their children at later stages and stop reporting altogether.

> *... feared that my child might get expelled because teacher was the bully ...*
> *yes, I was confident to report that time, but now I feel scared because those boys have grown stronger too, and I fear they might harm my son physically if I complain against them.*
> *Yes, I was quite confident because I am a mother, and if I will not complain, then who else ...*

9.9.8 Parents' Recommendations

There is a unanimous agreement that schools must play a vital role to curb bullying or cyberbullying. Parents suggest that there must be continuous education programs to help students understand the issues surrounding neurodiverse children and their challenges. The workshops must focus on the ill effects of bullying and its consequences on others, especially neurodiverse children. Attempts should be made to create an empathy-based culture to avoid such incidents altogether. Other suggestion includes the presence of a separate unit dealing with any form of bullying. They must be responsible for providing support and immediate intervention to the victims. At the same time, they must investigate the bullies and take necessary action without any pressure or bias. Schools must create safe spaces and inclusion policies for neurodiverse children, which must be brought into effect. Therapy and other support centers must strictly employ people with proper training. The expectations are much higher from these centers than schools, and any form of harassment violates the sanctity of such safe spaces and the children therein.

> *There should be a proper education program to acquaint children with disability and teach them how kindness toward special needs kid can be rewarding for the whole society.*
> *School officials must have a separate supportive department where parents can contact if they find their child has been bullied.*
> *Setting up an anti-bullying assembly program during and after school hours can help. School should have safe lunchtime options for children, like a library, chess, or gardening clubs, supervised safe places for children to go if they need to and must assign a member of staff that children know they can report bullying to, and a bully box to use if they don't want to speak to someone.*

The role of parents is equally important as the school. Parents of both neurodiverse and neurotypical children must contribute to stopping this menace. It is vital to regularly check about neurodiverse kids' wellbeing, moods, behavior, etc. Parents must be open to listening, initiate conversations when they even find the slightest hints of the possibility of such events. Hesitance to attend schools or therapies, or other events must be investigated. These are typical signs of such incidents and must be thoroughly checked because of supporting these children. Parents should not hesitate to report these incidents so that the bullying behavior remains in check. As for parents of neurotypical children, they must make an effort of educating their children. Manners to deal with others who might not look different, behave differently must be taught at home.

> *Educate everyone; parents should educate their children ...*
> *They must look deeper if the child wants to tell them something or if he denies attending the school or gets some medical issue. make sure your child is safe.*
> *Must address and report the bullying incident to the respective authority ...*

Students and peers must be empathetic toward neurodiverse learners. They should understand that these children are part of society. They need help to adjust as they are already struggling with other issues. Students can participate in awareness campaigns and not possess a bystander attitude. Bullying is not limited to neurodiverse children only. So, they must play an active role in reporting such incidents so that the bullies are strongly discouraged. More senior kids can participate in therapy centers to support their neurodiverse peers. This will hopefully create empathy and an inclusive environment.

They should try to understand the needs of a special child and be patient and willing to extend a hand of friendship toward a special kid. They should report bullies to the concerned authority.
   …But elder kids can start a project and create awareness, and they can also start a project and create awareness and they can also enroll themselves in various special education programs and can voluntarily participate in therapies at the centers, or they can obtain proper training and then can support families with special need children by giving them therapies at home.…

The respondents strongly urge the government to initiate awareness programs, create support channels, table strict laws and enforce them. There must be strict laws to deal with bullies in general and special provisions for neurodiverse children. Punishments should involve financial and legal implications so that they are taken seriously. The communication ministries must continuously and actively screen such content in the same way as other agendas. There must be a rigorous system to train and certify therapists. Constant follow-up with therapy centers about their procedures should be conducted as well.

Bullying is no longer restricted to school environments or direct physical contact; bullying can now expand from one continent to the other without the individuals involved even personally knowing each other. Govt. must give strict instructions to the Information Technology Department to keep a record of the cyberbullying cases …
   Consequences of bullying, no matter what age, a bully is a bully. Proper punishment. Raising awareness, campaigns, help in social awareness, differently-abled people need inclusion.
   Govt. Should give proper training to therapists and therapy center personnel so that they have knowledge of the disorders and disabilities and they must know how to educate parents too who find their kids newly diagnosed.

9.10   DISCUSSION

Results from this study indicate that the pandemic has harmed the children's overall development. Significant behavioral changes due to sensory imbalance among neurodiverse learners have made it very difficult for the parents. Similar outcomes have been reported while studying sensory factors and their impact on children's daily lives [22]. There is a lack of support to navigate this transformation from schools, teachers, and therapists. This makes adaptation of the new standards more difficult for neurodiverse learners. At the same time, parents also feel overstressed and emotionally overwhelmed. This study's findings align with the conclusions of [39]; that the parental stress and emotional wellbeing of parents with neurodiverse children have been unfavorably affected by the COVID-19 pandemic.

There has been a significant increase in cyberbullying incidents for neurodiverse learners during the pandemic due to increased exposure to online platforms. Cyberbullying majorly seems to originate from online classes during the pandemic. The typical notion of peer bullying has been challenged as parents reported that some teachers and therapists have also bullied children during online classes. The bullying frequency reported by parents was significantly similar to the reporting in [26, 39, 40], in the context of online meetings/classes/sessions during the pandemic. These children depict insecurity and emotional exhaustion due to these incidents. Many parents fear a lack of opportunities during the pandemic and therefore tend not to report these incidents. Social pressure seems to be another significant factor for not reporting cyberbullying. Even if the bullying has been reported, there seems no stop it.

In some cases, the concerned authorities neglected the complaints. Eventually, a decline in confidence in reporting bullying is observed due to increasing the bullies' age and physical strength. Parents fear physical harm to their children because of this. The parents strongly recommend schools and parents to educate neurotypical children and society. The schools and the government must set independent cyberbullying units to intervene in such incidents and provide immediate support to the victims. Parents strongly urge the government to introduce strict anti-cyberbullying laws with both legal and financial implications. Moreover, there must be strict enforcement of these laws.

The current results suggest an immediate study of support required by parents of neurodiverse children to tackle the changes due to the ongoing pandemic, which might last a few years. This will also help to understand the efficient use of online technologies for children with special needs. The efficacy of online and offline learning, including therapies, must be evaluated as well. Content creation for neurodiverse learners for online mode must be investigated. There is a need to study constant monitoring frameworks to protect neurodiverse children in particular and neurotypical children in general from the menace of cyberbullying. Online platforms must create safe spaces using emerging technologies such as artificial intelligence for real-time detection of cyberbullying.

Further studies are required to study the impact of cyberbullying based on age groups in neurodiverse children. This will help parents monitor children at certain points, specifically compared to others, and policies can be created based on these findings. There is an immediate need to investigate teacher–child bullying, therapist–child bullying, and bullying by any other support staff or caretaker. There is a tremendous need for awareness about neurodiverse children and training for bystander intervention. Reporting channels and their ease and effectiveness must be studied to propose best practices for creating more robust anti-bullying resources.

The pandemic made it very difficult to conduct interviews. The parents were overstressed and found it hard to dedicate time for the interviews due to increased responsibilities during this time. The interview medium could only be online because of the restrictions during the pandemic. Some parents did not have stable internet connections, which became a deterring factor for the interviews. Therefore, this study basis its conclusion on a smaller sample limiting its ability to generalize the results. Despite these limitations, the conclusions still highlight some essential details that must not be ignored. Many parents among the current sample are very well-versed with the neurodiverse community's needs and provided general and specific perspectives. Most of the reported conditions are faced across the board by such parents. Future research must be directed toward areas highlighted in this study. More importantly, policies must be enacted to help children with special needs and their families at various levels; wider family, neighborhood, community, school, therapy centers, and government, etc.

9.11 CONCLUSION

The pandemic seems to have positively affected the neurodiverse community. Cyberbullying events have been on the rise, and the entire sample of the study has experienced cyberbullying during the pandemic. This is quite worrisome and challenging for a community that is already marginalized otherwise. Although this is a social problem not limited to neurodiverse youth, there seems to be minimal to no support for the victims and their families. There seems to be non-existence of anti-cyberbullying measures or minimal consideration given to these cases by authorities. Cyberbullying victims, especially the neurodiverse community, require immediate support and intervention to tackle this social menace.

REFERENCES

1. J. Ashburner et al., "How are students on the autism spectrum affected by bullying? Perspectives of students and parents," *J. Res. Spec. Educ. Needs*, vol. 19, no. 1, pp. 27–44, Jan. 2019, doi:10.1111/1471-3802.12421.

2. M. Campbell, C. Whiteford, and J. Hooijer, "Teachers' and parents' understanding of traditional and cyber-bullying," *J. Sch. Violence*, vol. 18, no. 3, pp. 388–402, 2019, doi:10.1080/15388220.2018.1507826.

3. H. E. Morton, "Assessment of bullying in autism spectrum disorder: Systematic Review of methodologies and participant characteristics," *Rev. J. Autism Dev. Disord.*, 2021, doi:10.1007/s40489-020-00232-9.

4. E. Fink, J. Deighton, and M. Wolpert, "The development of a set of indicators to capture the incidence and experience of bullying, and well-being in children and young people with special educational needs/disabilities," *Rep. Natl. Child. Bur.*, no. March, pp. 1–84, 2014.

5. E. O. Dowd, "Inclusion and autism spectrum disorder: Relationships between teacher attitudes towards inclusion, self-efficacy, stress and experience," Dublin School of Business, School of Arts, Dublin, pp. 1–66, 2016.

6. D. Falla, S. Sánchez, and J. A. Casas, "What do we know about bullying in schoolchildren with disabilities? A systematic review of recent work," *Sustain. MDPI*, vol. 13, no. 1, p. 416, 2021, doi:10.3390/su13010416.

7. L. C. White et al., "Brief report: Impact of COVID-19 on individuals with ASD and their caregivers: A Perspective from the SPARK cohort," *J. Autism Dev. Disord.*, no. 0123456789, 2021, doi:10.1007/s10803-020-04816-6.

8. S. Carrington et al., "Recommendations of school students with autism spectrum disorder and their parents in regard to bullying and cyberbullying prevention and intervention," *Int. J. Incl. Educ.*, vol. 21, no. 10, pp. 1045–1064, 2017, doi:10.1080/13603116.2017.1331381.

9. V. Bitsika and C. F. Sharpley, "Understanding, experiences, and reactions to bullying experiences in boys with an autism spectrum disorder," *J. Dev. Phys. Disabil.*, vol. 26, no. 6, pp. 747–761, 2014, doi:10.1007/s10882-014-9393-1.

10. W. J. Chou, P. W. Wang, R. C. Hsiao, H. F. Hu, and C. F. Yen, "Role of school bullying involvement in depression, anxiety, suicidality, and low self-esteem among adolescents with high-functioning autism spectrum disorder," *Front. Psychiatry*, vol. 11, no. Jan. 2020, pp. 1–9, 2020, doi:10.3389/fpsyt.2020.00009.

11. T. Farmer, T. L. Wike, Q. R. Alexander, P. C. Rodkin, and M. Mehtaji, "Students with disabilities and involvement in peer victimization: Theory, research, and considerations for the future," *Remedial Spec. Educ.*, vol. 36, no. 5, pp. 263–274, 2015, doi:10.1177/0741932515572911.

12. M. Pinquart, "Systematic review: Bullying involvement of children with and without chronic physical illness and/or physical/sensory disability a meta-analytic comparison with healthy/ nondisabled peers," *J. Pediatr. Psychol.*, vol. 42, no. 3, pp. 245–259, 2017, doi:10.1093/jpepsy/jsw081.

13. American Psychiatric Association, "DSM-5 diagnostic and statistical manual of mental disorder," 2013.

14. American Psychiatric Association, "DSM-5 criteria," *Am. Psychiatr. Assoc.*, 2018.

15. M. S. Khan, N. A. K. Mohamadali, Z. A. Maher, S. Q. Nisa, H. Shaikh, and A. Shah, "Information technology (IT) based intervention among individuals with ASD (autism spectrum disorder): A review," *2nd IEEE Int. Conf. Innov. Res. Dev. ICIRD 2019*, pp. 2019–2021, 2019, doi:10.1109/ICIRD47319.2019.9074749.

16. M. Bloemen, L. Van Wely, J. Mollema, A. Dallmeijer, and J. de Groot, "Evidence for increasing physical activity in children with physical disabilities: A systematic review," *Developmental Medicine and Child Neurology*, vol. 59, no. 10. Blackwell Publishing Ltd, pp. 1004–1010, Oct. 2017, doi:10.1111/dmcn.13422.

17. E. L. de Hollander and K. I. Proper, "Physical activity levels of adults with various physical disabilities," *Prev. Med. Reports*, vol. 10, pp. 370–376, 2018, doi:10.1016/j.pmedr.2018.04.017.

18. C. Maher et al., "Fatigue is a major issue for children and adolescents with physical disabilities," *Dev. Med. Child Neurol.*, vol. 57, no. 8, pp. 742–747, Aug. 2015, doi:10.1111/dmcn.12736.

19. M. S. Khan, N. A. Mohamadali, and A. Shah, "Chapter 2: Special education teachers for autism spectrum disorder children: Behavioral intention and use of technology in Malaysia," *Exploring Information Systems Research Boundaries (EISRB)* – Series 3, Malaysia Association for Information Systems (MyAIS), Jan. 2021, pp. 9–18. eISBN: 978-967-17741-1-3.

20. B. Y. D. Abraham, C. Heffron, P. Braley, L. Drobnjak, and D. Abraham, *Sensory Processing*, vol. 101, LLA Media LLC, Sept. 2015.

21. L. Delgado-Lobete, S. Pértega-Díaz, S. Santos-del-Riego, and R. Montes-Montes, "Sensory processing patterns in developmental coordination disorder, attention deficit hyperactivity disorder and typical development," *Res. Dev. Disabil.*, vol. 100, no. Apr. 2019, pp. 1–8, 2020, doi:10.1016/j.ridd.2020.103608.

22. W. Dunn, L. Little, E. Dean, S. Robertson, and B. Evans, "The state of the science on sensory factors and their impact on daily life for children : A scoping review," *OTJR Occup. Particip. Heal.*, vol. 36, no. 25, pp. 3S–26S, 2016, doi:10.1177/1539449215617923.

23. C. Maïano, A. Aimé, M. C. Salvas, A. J. S. Morin, and C. L. Normand, "Prevalence and correlates of bullying perpetration and victimization among school-aged youth with intellectual disabilities: A systematic review," *Research in Developmental Disabilities*, vol. 49–50, no. 2016. pp. 181–195, 2016, doi:10.1016/j.ridd.2015.11.015.

24. L. Hellström, "A systematic review of polyvictimization among children with attention deficit hyperactivity or autism spectrum disorder," *Int. J. Environ. Res. Public Health*, vol. 16, no. 13, 2019, doi:10.3390/ijerph16132280.

25. M. Wells, K. J. Mitchell, L. M. Jones, and H. A. Turner, "Peer harassment among youths with different disabilities: Impact of harassment online, in person, and in mixed online and in-person incidents," *Child. Sch.*, vol. 41, no. 1, pp. 17–24, 2019, doi:10.1093/cs/cdy025.

26. H. E. Morton, J. M. Gillis, R. E. Mattson, and R. G. Romanczyk, "Conceptualizing bullying in children with autism spectrum disorder: Using a mixed model to differentiate behavior types and identify predictors," *Autism*, vol. 23, no. 7, pp. 1853–1864, 2019, doi:10.1177/1362361318813997.

27. Z. Zainol, S. Wani, P. Nohuddin, W. Noormanshah, and S. Marzukhi, "Association analysis of cyberbullying on social media using apriori algorithm," *Int. J. Eng. Technol.*, vol. 7, no. 4.29, pp. 72–75, 2018.

28. Microsoft Corporation, "Online bullying among 8–17 years old-worldwide Microsoft," Retrieved from https://www.microsoft.com/en-us/download/%20confirmation.aspx?id%20=30148 on April 10, 2012.

29. O. Jain, M. Gupta, S. Satam, and S. Panda, "Has the COVID-19 pandemic affected the susceptibility to cyberbullying in India?" *Comput. Hum. Behav. Reports*, vol. 2, no. Sept., p. 100029, 2020, doi:10.1016/j.chbr.2020.100029.

30. T. S. Rao, D. Bansal, and S. Chandran, "Cyberbullying: A virtual offense with real consequences," *Indian Journal of Psychiatry*, vol. 60, no. 1. pp. 3–5, 2018, doi:10.4103/psychiatry.IndianJPsychiatry_147_18.

31. M. Newall, "Global views on cyberbullying," https://www.ipsos.com/sites/default/files/ct/news/documents/2018-06/cyberbullying_june2018.pdf, 2018 (accessed Mar. 10, 2021).

32. N. McCarthy, "Chart: Where cyberbullying is most prevalent | statista," https://www.statista.com/chart/15926/the-share-of-parents-who-say-their-child-has-experienced-cyberbullying/, 2018 (accessed Mar. 10, 2021).

33. K. C. Karthikeyan, "Social and legislative issues in handling cyberbullying in India," *IGI Global.com*, 2021, doi:10.4018/978-1-7998-4912-4.ch021.

34. V. González-Calatayud, M. Roman-García, and P. Prendes-Espinosa, "Knowledge about bullying by young adults with special educational needs with or without disabilities (SEN/D)," *Front. Psychol.*, vol. 11, p. 3782, Jan. 2021, doi:10.3389/fpsyg.2020.622517.

35. M. C. McHugh and D. E. Howard, "Friendship at any cost: Parent perspectives on cyberbullying children with intellectual and developmental disabilities," *J. Ment. Health Res. Intellect. Disabil.*, vol. 10, no. 4, pp. 288–308, Oct. 2017, doi:10.1080/19315864.2017.1299268.

36. C. A. Rose, D. L. Espelage, and L. E. Monda-Amaya, "Bullying and victimisation rates among students in general and special education: A comparative analysis," *Educ. Psychol.*, vol. 29, no. 7, pp. 761–776, Dec. 2009, doi:10.1080/01443410903254864.

37. J. H. Schroeder, M. C. Cappadocia, J. M. Bebko, D. J. Pepler, and J. A. Weiss, "Shedding light on a pervasive problem: A review of research on bullying experiences among children with autism spectrum disorders," *J. Autism Dev. Disord.*, vol. 44, no. 7, pp. 1520–1534, Jan. 2014, doi:10.1007/s10803-013-2011-8.

38. E. Van Roekel, R. H. J. Scholte, and R. Didden, "Bullying among adolescents with autism spectrum disorders: Prevalence and perception," *J. Autism Dev. Disord.*, vol. 40, no. 1, pp. 63–73, Jan. 2010, doi:10.1007/s10803-009-0832-2.

39. A. L. Phillips and A. Anderson, "Cyberbullying, digital citizenship, and youth with autism: LIS education as a piece in the Puzzle," *Libr. Q.*, vol. 90, no. 3, pp. 264–282, Jul. 2020, doi:10.1086/708957.

40. A. C. Baldry, A. Sorrentino, and D. P. Farrington, "Post-traumatic stress symptoms among Italian preadolescents involved in school and cyber bullying and victimization," *J. Child Fam. Stud.*, vol. 28, no. 9, pp. 2358–2364, Sept. 2019, doi:10.1007/s10826-018-1122-4.

41. Y. Peled, "Cyberbullying and its influence on academic, social, and emotional development of undergraduate students," *Heliyon*, vol. 5, no. 3, p. e01393, Mar. 2019, doi:10.1016/j.heliyon.2019.e01393.

42. F. W. Lung, B. C. Shu, T. L. Chiang, S. J. Lin, and M. Tusconi, "Prevalence of bullying and perceived happiness in adolescents with learning disability, intellectual disability, ADHD, and autism spectrum disorder: In the Taiwan Birth Cohort Pilot Study," *Med. (United States)*, vol. 98, no. 6, pp. 1–5, 2019, doi:10.1097/MD.0000000000014483.

43. P. K. Smith, "Commentary: Ways of preventing cyberbullying and evidence-based practice," in *Reducing Cyberbullying in Schools*, vol. 42, no. 2016. Elsevier Inc., 2018.

44. Å. Borgström, K. Daneback, and M. Molin, "Young people with intellectual disabilities and social media: A literature review and thematic analysis," *Scand. J. Disabil. Res.*, vol. 21, no. 1, pp. 129–140, 2019, doi:10.16993/sjdr.549.

45. P. H. Hawley and A. Williford, "Articulating the theory of bullying intervention programs: Views from social psychology, social work, and organizational science," *J. Appl. Dev. Psychol.*, vol. 37, no. 1, pp. 3–15, 2015, doi:10.1016/j.appdev.2014.11.006.

46. T. Alhuzimi, "Stress and emotional wellbeing of parents due to change in routine for children with Autism Spectrum Disorder (ASD) at home during COVID-19 pandemic in Saudi Arabia," *Res. Dev. Disabil.*, vol. 108, p. 103822, Jan. 2021, doi:10.1016/j.ridd.2020.103822.

47. S. Saline, "Thriving in the new normal: How COVID-19 has affected alternative learners and their families and implementing effective, creative therapeutic interventions," *Smith Coll. Stud. Soc. Work*, vol. 91, no. 1, pp. 1–28, 2021, doi:10.1080/00377317.2020.1867699.

Part IV

Other Issues for Securing Social Networks and Online Profiles

10 Profiling Online Users
Emerging Approaches and Challenges

Mohammad Mamun and Muhammad Al-Digeil
National Research Council Canada, Ottawa, Canada

Sherif Saad Ahmed
University of Windsor, Windsor, Canada

CONTENTS

DOI: 10.1201/9781003134527-14

10.1 INTRODUCTION

In this chapter, we discuss the concept of user profiling as a tool to secure a network. User profiling has emerged as a useful idea in cybersecurity. It provides a way to organize the plethora of network usage data into a manageable perspective that enables more effective monitoring of potential threats. Specifically, it allows for adaptive control of a network's security policies.

Users of a network tend to exhibit specific behaviors, and their usage follows predictable or identifiable patterns. User profiling capitalizes on this idea to protect networks. If a malicious agent attempts to subvert a network, it typically does so with specific usage patterns and behavior. We will turn our attention to the methods that can be used to detect these patterns, how a user profile is used, and the challenges in generating user profiles.

Of these methods, machine learning algorithms will feature most prominently as these have taken cybersecurity by storm in the past decade and they are producing remarkable results. Before turning to specific concepts in user profiling, we discuss machine learning models generally: their concept and the process of training them and, specifically, how they can be used for user profiling.

User profiling is a broad and vibrant area of research and this chapter does not attempt to provide a comprehensive survey of the current research. Instead it focuses on key concepts, techniques, and the kinds of results one may expect from work in user profiling. Many of these results, referenced by cited research papers, are surprising and show how much information about a user can be extracted from seemingly unworkable network traffic.

We cover examples in the hopes of highlighting concrete details that come up in user profiling. For instance, we discuss feature extraction generally and then provide specific examples, from different applications, of the kinds of features that are useful in practice. And, in the case of user interest modeling, we show how an architecture may be set up to collect pertinent data and how to deal with different data types.

We hope that the reader will emerge from this chapter with a clearer notion of what is involved in user profiling, and to become primed with possibilities that are open in user profiling.

10.2 SOURCES OF ONLINE USER PROFILE DATA

The prevalence of internet technology means that user data is spread throughout enormous networks and in order to build a cohesive and useful user profile there must be some organizing principles at play in creating the profile. The necessity of a user profile stems from potential threats that a user poses to a network and this consideration should drive the framework for building the user profile. The threats are malicious in intent and result in the stealing of valuable informational resources or the disruption of network services.

The most basic technique for securing a network against threats is the blacklisting of users and websites known to cause problems. However, maintaining a blacklist requires constantly updating it with the latest threats – an impossible task to do manually given the abundance of possible threats, and, if done too cautiously, the network becomes less useful as resources and connections that would otherwise be available become inaccessible. As such, automatic techniques are needed to deal with the rapidly changing environment.

Fundamentally, there are two sources of user data: (i) information gleaned from network traffic that look at payloads or network flow and (ii) publicly accessible user data (e.g., YouTube channels, social media feeds).

Payload-based techniques (also known as deep packet inspection) rely on information that can be determined from the payload of a network packet. This can provide information such as the source of the payload, its size, service type as well other static information useful in establishing the type of payload in question. Network flow techniques attempt to determine network behavior through broader network statistics such as Inter Arrival Time (IAT), the average number of packets, network latency, jitter, flow cut-off time, packet loss, and fragmentation. Such statistics yield useful information enabling the fingerprinting of applications.

Publicly available datasets simplify the process of data collection, however, they are thoroughly anonymized when using real traffic which poses problems for user profiling.

Beyond these two basic sources of network information, other ways of obtaining information rely on the internet's infrastructure. For example, it is possible to perform lexical analysis on a URL and then to determine with reasonable certainty whether a particular URL is malicious [1].

10.3 MODELING OF USER ONLINE BEHAVIOR

Traditionally, the predominant approach to network security was rule-based. In such a scheme concrete rules are specified to filter and track network traffic. The rules, although admitting wildcards, tend to be rigid and hence specificity has to be carefully controlled so that the right level of security is achieved. As usual, the trade-off is between being so lax with the security rules that threats are not properly managed versus being so restrictive that network resources and features cannot legitimately be used.

Since the 1980s, and especially with the proliferation of Artificial Neural Networks and, more recently, Deep Learning, machine learning models have gained traction in cybersecurity. These models work on the premise of being able to detect patterns in network traffic. These patterns are higher-order than rules enumerated in a rule-based approach and thus allow for adaptive modes of filtering. This flexibility however comes at a cost of comprehensibility. Where the rules in a rule-based model can generally be read and understood, machine learning models are notoriously opaque and they tend to be weak on explainability.

The two approaches, Rule-based [2] and Machine Learning [3], can be used in unison and the hybrid approach provides powerful solutions.

10.3.1 RULE-BASED MODELS

It is possible to secure a network by specifying rules that determine access to resources. For instance, a host can be configured to reject traffic from a specific IP address. The rules can be simple ones like that or sophisticated ones that establish a context for the application of the rules. A more sophisticated rule might involve, at a certain time of day, peering into a packet and if it originates from a known host to redirect to another host if the payload contains a specific string. As such, the set of rules constitute a model that captures the knowledge of existing threats and the manner of tackling them.

Utilities such as *iptables* [4] allow the administrator to specify rules to apply to network traffic. These rules can be at various levels of granularity and in the case of *iptables* the filtering is performed at the level of the packet.

Rule-based approaches are prevalent but they suffer the same shortcoming as blacklisting: the network environment constantly changes and it is difficult to engineer flexible rules that adapt to evolving threats.

10.3.2 MACHINE LEARNING MODELS

Machine learning algorithms provide a flexible alternative to traditional approaches to implementing programs or rules. Where a software developer or system administrator might look at a problem, try to discern the patterns that would determine the solution in the form of a written program or rules for the system, a machine learning approach turns this on its head and presents data to the learning algorithm in the hopes that it will detect patterns and internally represent them in a model. Thus a machine learning model learns from experience.

Unfortunately there is no single learning algorithm that is suitable for all tasks. The typical workflow of a machine learning solution involves manipulating data and selecting an appropriate machine learning algorithm and these two steps often influence each other. There is trial-and-error involved in tuning the algorithms to obtain a solution but practitioners have built a body of knowledge about best practices and expectations for learning algorithms.

There are numerous machine learning algorithms available each with its strengths and weaknesses. Options include: Artificial Neural Networks, Support Vector Machines, Random Forest, Bayesian Networks among many more.

Learning algorithms generally work on the presumption that it is possible to construct a scheme so that the algorithm learns patterns in the provided data that it can generalize to new data. Hence a learning algorithm tries to learn a function f that given a vector $\mathbf{x} \in \mathbf{R}^n$, outputs $\mathbf{z} \in \mathbf{R}^m$ where $\mathbf{z}$ is the output expected for the given input in the problem's context. The vector $\mathbf{x}$ is called a feature vector and its individual elements (its features) play a key role in the performance of the algorithm.

There are two basic approaches in machine learning: supervised and unsupervised. The choice of approach of approach depends on the nature of the data available as well as the goal of the task to be solved. Some learning algorithms can be applied in both modes. For instance, neural networks can be implemented as a supervised learning algorithm in the form of a traditional multilayer perceptron (MLP) or unsupervised like a self-organizing map (SOM). Other learning algorithms like k-nearest neighbors (k-Means) are, specifically, unsupervised techniques.

10.3.2.1 Supervised Learning

Supervised models imply the training of the model involves a kind of "teacher" in the form of tagged data. This means that the data is labeled with the appropriate classification or target value. During training the model is fed input data without being shown the label. The result of the model's computation is compared with the label and, based on the difference between the two, a loss function is evaluated and propagated back to the model to adjust its parameters. In this way, it is hoped the model will converge to one that predicts the labels with high accuracy.

A shortcoming of this approach to machine learning is that labeled data is hard to come by. Generating the labels manually can be labor-intensive especially for large data sets. However with some ingenuity, it is possible to generate labeled data automatically. Data requirements can also be met using data augmentation techniques and also by using generative models such as Generative Adversarial Networks (GAN) [5] and Variational Encoders (VAE) [6]. Data augmentation involves modifying the existing training data with transformations that preserve the meaning of the data while qualitatively modifying its more superficial features. Generative models on the other hand attempt to learn the statistical features of the data so that meaningful new data can be obtained from latent spaces.

10.3.2.2 Unsupervised Learning

In contrast to supervised learning, in unsupervised learning the data provided is not labeled. Hence the task of the algorithm is to detect patterns inherent in the data without direct clues about the direction of learning. In practice, there are two primary methods of unsupervised learning: Clustering (e.g., K-Means Algorithm, Association Rule Mining) and dimensionality reduction (e.g., PCA or Principal Component Analysis).

In clustering, the aim is to determine types that naturally divide the data. The simplest clustering algorithm is perhaps the k-Nearest neighbor algorithm. In this algorithm, when presented with data vectors the algorithm uses Euclidean distance between the vectors to determine which data points can be considered within a predefined distance from a centroid and therefore it determines the cluster (or neighborhood).

Principal Component Analysis is a dimensionality reduction technique that is able to reduce the dimensionality of data by finding principal components with maximal explanatory power. So, for instance if your initial feature vector contains 500 features, it might turn out that the space of these features is representable using 15 principal components without significant loss of information. This is useful for data compression but also, importantly, it makes the data more manageable for isolating and detecting patterns for the machine learning models.

10.3.3 Data Collection

10.3.3.1 Pre-Processing Data

Before raw network data can be used for modeling it must be carefully filtered and sanitized. Network traffic contains extraneous data and this data has to be identified and removed from the dataset. The type of sanitization performed depends on the type of data obtained. For instance, for network data, one may choose to ignore empty payloads or packets less than a specified size by assuming that packets with less than the threshold size will lack interesting information for modeling.

At this stage, if the data is to be used in a supervised learning scheme, the data may be tagged to establish the ground truth. For example, to validate that we filter specific application data flows, a deep packet inspection tool can be used to recognize exact flows of the targeted data. With the help of flow information (source IP, destination IP, source port, destination port, protocol) and time period for any specific application runs, packets can be recognized and labeled.

An important consideration for pre-processing for supervised learning is the ratio of data to be used for training, validating, and testing. The 60%–20%–20% is a common splitting but there are other possibilities depending on the particular situation.

The determination of the learning algorithm to be used depends on the kind and quality of available data and the problem to be solved. User profile data that is useful for training a user profile model can be obtained in one of three ways, it may be: (i) sniffed from the network with a tool such as Wireshark, (ii) obtained from the host, or (iii) provided publicly by a third-party available data.

Collecting a high-quality dataset tends to be a difficult task because available datasets and the problem-at-hand rarely align perfectly. However, capturing real-life application traffic is challenging for two reasons: privacy concerns, and noise stemming from uninteresting traffic. Hence, traffic is typically either collected from trusted sources or it is captured in a controlled environment.

10.3.3.2 Network Sniffing

To automate data collection (Figure 10.1) in a simulated environment, encrypted and unencrypted applications are run at the endpoint (workstation or mobile) and application packets are captured by passive sniffing tools such as Wireshark, *tcpdump*. These are stored in files such as .pcap files and, because they usually capture more traffic data than is needed, they require further manipulation before they can be of use.

10.3.3.3 Host Data

A lot can be gleaned from the transport layer of the host [7] such as information about attempted connections to the host, including the source IP addresses, and the ports they are trying to reach. This kind of information coupled with the timings of such connections can manifest helpful behavioral information about a user. Since the host has full access to this data, it provides a valuable resource for building user profiles.

10.3.3.4 Publicly Available Datasets

Since building a dataset can be a laborious task, it is worth considering whether publicly available datasets are suitable for the problem-at-hand. Examples of sources include such sites as Security Repo [8] and the Unified Host and Network Data Set from the Advanced Research in Cyber Systems [9]. It is rare that a dataset perfectly aligns with a project goal so the effort of modifying the data to suit the purpose must be weighed against that of generating data from scratch.

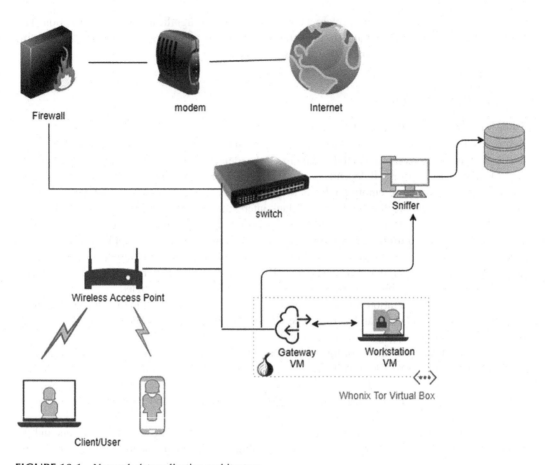

FIGURE 10.1 Network data collection architecture.

It should be noted that publicly available datasets are thoroughly anonymized which renders them tricky to use for user profile experiments.

10.3.3.5 Feature Extraction

Once a good dataset has been identified, a crucial step in determining the performance of a model is the features that are extracted from the data. These features are typically represented as the scalar elements of a feature vector. In general the smaller the feature vector the easier it is to train if each element is carefully considered. This is because the model will generally have less parameters to adjust and this will lead to faster training.

It is not always possible to limit the dimensions of the input vector and sparse inputs are fairly common in practice. There are techniques, particularly Principal Component Analysis, that can help to reduce the dimensionality of the data.

Selecting good features requires creativity, a deep understanding of the data as well as trial-and-error. The process of figuring out features is often iterative. Since feature selection plays such an important role in the performance of machine learning algorithms, in this section we give examples of how features were generated for different problems. In doing so we hope to shed light on the process of extracting features as well as the kinds of features that tend to produce good results.

Example 1:   Characterizing Tor Traffic Using Time Based Features

In a problem for characterizing Tor traffic using time-based features [10], Weka, a machine learning framework was used to run experiments. Different feature selection algorithms were applied to each dataset (10 s, 15 s, 30 s, 60 s, and 120 s) and the performance was measured in terms of weighted average precision and recall.

The best combination of features and dataset was evaluated using the corresponding validation dataset and it was determined, using this empirical evidence, that a certain combination of algorithms yielded the best feature selection (Cfs SubsetEval+BestFirst and Infogain+Ranker).

Example 2:   Characterizing Encrypted Data Using Time-Related Features

The focus of this study [11] is on time-related features for characterizing encrypted data. When choosing time-related features, two different approaches are considered. In the first approach time is measured the time, e.g., time between packets or the time that a flow remains active.

In the second approach, time is fixed and other variables are measured, e.g., bytes per second or packets per second. The features generated were the following:

- *duration*: the duration of the flow.
- *fiat* (Forward Inter Arrival Time): the time between two packets sent forward direction (mean, min, max, std).
- *biat* (Backward Inter Arrival Time): the time between two packets sent backward (mean, min, max, std).
- *flowiat* (Flow Inter Arrival Time): the time between two packets sent in either direction (mean, min, max, std).
- *active*: The amount of time a flow was active before going idle (mean, min, max, std).
- *idle*: The amount of time a flow was idle before becoming active (mean, min, max, std).
- *fb psec*: Flow bytes per second.
- *fp psec*: Flow packets per second.

An application, ISCXFlowMeter, written in Java was created to help in generating features from network flows. ISCXFlowMeter generates bidirectional flows, where the first packet determines the forward (source to destination) and backward (destination to source) directions, hence the statistical time-related features are also calculated separately in the forward and reverse direction.

Flow timeout (ftm) values with their corresponding classifier accuracy on the same dataset are studied. In particular, duration of flows are set to 15, 30, 60, and 120 seconds.

In the experiments, the classifier has a response time of (FT + FE + ML) seconds, where FT is the customized flow-time, FE is the feature extraction time and ML is the machine learning algorithm time to perform classification. It is then observed that the maximum accuracy is achieved with (FT = 15 s) for all the classifiers.

Example 3:   An Information Theoretic Approach to Encrypted Application Profiling

A study using information theoretic techniques to profile encrypted applications [3] found the following features to be useful:

- *Payload size*: The actual data of a packet. Each packet consists of a payload appended to the header for transport.
- *Entropy of the entire payload* using Shannon's conventional entropy for computation.
- *Entropy of n-length word or sliding-window* where $n = \{4, 8, 16, 32, 64, 128, 256, 512, 1024\}$.

It was observed in the study that encoding the encrypted payload accelerates the entropy discrimination significantly which in turn helps distinguishing encrypted application. These are the kinds of observations that must be made to obtain useful features.

Example 4: Detecting Malicious URLs

To detect malicious URLs [1], initially 79 features were selected from components such as URL, domain, path, file-name, and argument. A feature selection algorithm was applied on each data-set and different sets of features were eventually chosen:

- *Entropy Domain and Extension*: Malicious websites often insert additional characters in the URL to make it look legitimate. By inserting characters the entropy changes more than usual.
- *CharacterContinuityRate*: Character Continuity Rate is used to find the sum of the longest token length of each character type in the domain Malicious websites use URLs with variable numbers of character types.
- *Features related with Length Ratio*: The length ratio of the parts of URL is computed to find the abnormal parts.
- Features related to count of letters, tokens, and symbols.
- *Symbol Count Domain*: A dictionary of delimiters such as://.:/?=,;()] + are calculated from domain. Phishing URLs, e.g., have more dots compared to benign ones [12,13].
- *Domain token count*: Malicious URLs use multiple domain tokens. Number of tokens in the domains are calculated.
- *Query Digit Count*: Number of digits in the query part of the URL.
- *tld*: Some phishing URL use multiple top-level domain within a domain name.
- *Number Rate of Domain*, *DirectoryName*, *File-Name*, *URL*, *AfterPath*: Number rate calculates the proportion of digits in the URL parts of directory name, domain, file-name, URL itself and part after the path [14].
- *Features related to Length*: Length of URL gets longer due to addition of variables or redirected URL [15,16].
- *ldl getArg*: In phishing URLs masquerading is done by adding digits in the letters. For detection of these deceptive URLs, a sequence of letter-digit-letter in URL and path is calculated [14]. 3 URLs originating from pages that are written in server-side scripting languages, often have arguments [17]. The longest variable value length from arguments of URL is calculated.
- *spcharUrl*: URLs use special characters which are suspicious such as // and they have higher risk of redirection [16].

10.3.4 User Profiling Based on Web-Based Fingerprinting

User profiling based on web-based fingerprinting leverages information provided by the user's browser rather than relying on client-side accessible information. Such information may include:

- browser customizations
- user configuration
- browser family
- browser version
- language
- code-name
- plug-ins
- user's operating system
- user agent
- information about cookies such as whether they are enabled or disabled
- location (city, region, country)
- screen information (resolution, width, height, depth)

Murad et al. [18] show how browser cookies can be used even when the cookies are disabled by the user to identify returning users based on non-cookie attributes such as screen-info, the browser's name and version, the agent header, location info, the organization derived from the IP address, device information such as the type of device, e.g., smartphone, brand, e.g., HTC, model number, OS information such as the name and version, browser plug-ins installed, and the hash key by which the user is identified.

Moreover, Károly et al. [19] propose a browser-independent fingerprinting method to identify online users using a user agent string (UAS), IP address, availability of the font set, the time zone, and the screen resolution.

When a user selects to browse privately, this only disables the cache, history, cookies, and local storage, but not JavaScript, the broadcast IP address and the UAS of the browser (Figure 10.2) which they use for the profiling. Thus private browsing does not prevent passive, or implicit, profiling.

10.3.5 CREATING A USER PROFILE

In creating a user profile, we seek a representation of a user's interests, behavior, and preferences so we can match specific users with their profile and based on their behavior (malicious or not) we are able to sanction them accordingly.

The figures below (Figures 10.3 and 10.4) show a profile of a user that tells us about their network usage patterns as well as their preferences. This profile was derived from encrypted network traffic

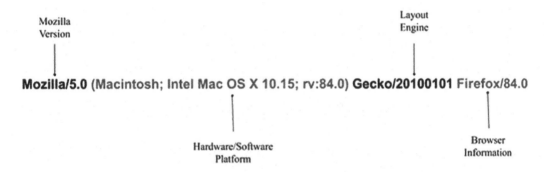

FIGURE 10.2   User agent string (UAS).

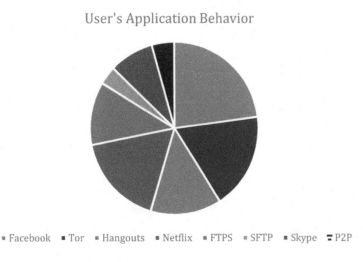

FIGURE 10.3   User profiling based on online user behavior.

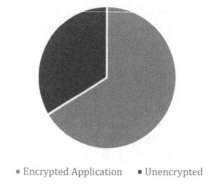

■ Encrypted Application   ■ Unencrypted

FIGURE 10.4   User profiling based on application behavior.

[3] using binary classification (to determine whether the traffic is encrypted) and multi-class classification (to determine which application is in use).

This kind of classification can be done with high accuracy which is particularly impressive because the underlying data used is encrypted. The below Tables 10.1 and 10.2 show the results of the classifiers along with the respective algorithms used to produce them.

The measures indicated (Accuracy, Precision and F-Measures) are commonly used metrics to evaluate machine learning algorithms. They are computed as follows:

$$\text{Accuracy} = \frac{\text{True Positive} + \text{True Negative}}{\text{True Positive} + \text{True Negative} + \text{False Positive} + \text{False Negative}}$$

$$\text{Precision} = \frac{\text{True Positive}}{\text{True Positive} + \text{False Positive}}$$

$$\text{F1 Score} = \frac{2 \cdot \text{Precision} \cdot \text{Recall}}{\text{Precision} + \text{Recall}}$$

TABLE 10.1

Binary Classifier: Accuracy & Precision metrics for Random Forest (RF), C5.0, Decision Table (DTable)

		Encrypted	Unencrypted
Accuracy	RF	**0.998**	**0.997**
	C5.0	0.947	0.992
	DTable	0.997	0.99
Precision	RF	0.998	0.996
	C5.0	0.995	0.906
	DTable	0.995	0.995
F-Measure	RF	0.998	0.997
	C5.0	0.97	0.947
	DTable	0.996	0.992

TABLE 10.2

Multi-class Classifier: Accuracy & Precision Metrics for Random Forest (RF), C5.0, Decision Table (DTable)

		facebook	hangout	netflix	p2p	scp	sftp	skype	tor
Accuracy	**RF**	**0.974**	**0.902**	**0.907**	**0.999**	**1.000**	**0.991**	**0.908**	**0.934**
	C5.0	0.969	0.904	0.801	0.996	0.998	0.990	0.898	0.824
	DTable	0.944	0.845	0.791	0.972	0.996	0.986	0.85	0.817
Precision	RF	0.937	0.945	0.935	0.996	1.000	0.989	0.910	0.912
	C5.0	0.935	0.933	0.816	0.995	0.999	0.985	0.911	0.808
	DTable	0.877	0.928	0.811	0.981	0.999	0.987	0.849	0.805
F-Measure	RF	0.955	0.923	0.921	0.997	1.000	0.99	0.909	0.923
	C5.0	0.952	0.918	0.806	0.995	0.999	0.988	0.905	0.816
	DTable	0.909	0.884	0.801	0.977	0.997	0.986	0.849	0.811

Another commonly used metric is recall:

$$Recall = \frac{True\ Positive}{True\ Positive + False\ Negative}$$

10.3.5.1 Case Study: An Architecture for Generating a Labeled Private Traffic Dataset

To demonstrate an example of the process involved in generating data we look at a classification example. In [10] it is shown that it is possible to classify traffic that utilizes Tor, a privacy enhancing tool. Not only that, but within this traffic it is shown that it is possible, with a high probability, to determine what application is running based on the time characteristics of the traffic.

Obtaining data to do this classification is not trivial. For one, among other problems, using real network data runs the risk of violating user privacy. But more importantly, the data obtained is encrypted and thus very opaque for the classifier to do anything useful with it. Hence it is necessary to generate such data, taking advantage of knowledge accessible at the point of data generation (so this knowledge can act as labels for the data). However, generating data has to ensure that the generated data is as diverse as real-world data. This can be done by defining a set of tasks that mimic real-world data in quantity and diversity. Accounts for users Alice and Bob are created and they use services such as Skype and Facebook. The generated dataset contains eight types of traffic that a typical user would use: browsing, chat, audio-streaming, video-streaming, mail, VOIP, P2P, and File Transfer. This is done using more than 18 representative applications.

Whonix, a Linux distribution configured to route all traffic through the Tor network, is used to stage the simulation. This distribution is composed of two virtual machines, the gateway, and the workstation. The workstation connects to the internet through the gateway virtual machine, which in turn routes all the traffic through the Tor network.

With this setup, using the Tor network at the workstation, the virtual machine is transparent. The outgoing traffic at the workstation and the gateway is captured simultaneously, collecting a set of pairs of .pcap files: one regular traffic pcap (workstation) and one Tor traffic .pcap (gateway) file. The captured traffic is labeled in two steps. First, the .pcap files captured at the workstation are processed: the flows are extracted, and it is confirmed that the majority of traffic flows were generated by a specific application – the object of the traffic capture.

Then, all flows from the Tor.pcap file are labeled X. This is done because Tor is a circuit-oriented protocol: all traffic from the gateway to the entry node will be encrypted and sent through the same connection. The flows generated from the Tor traffic captured will be indistinguishable from each other as they will have the same source IP, destination IP, source port, destination port, and protocol. But since the data is generated in a controlled environment, and one application at a time is executed, most of the Tor flows will belong to the running application. Because of the labeling process, the training and validation datasets will include some noise (flows of type X labeled as type Y) which in turn it will affect the accuracy of downstream classifiers.

At this point data has been generated but it cannot immediately be used by a classifier. The relevant features of the data must be isolated and any useless data that has been collected must be sifted out.

10.4   USER ONLINE INTEREST MODELING

A behavioral, or adaptive, profile is autogenerated in systems where user attributes and served content change over time [20]. Attempts have been made to analyze user temporal behavior for the purpose of dynamically learning user profiles, e.g., [21, 22]. Baluja et al. [23] build a recommendation system on a 3-month snapshot of live data from YouTube. Akbari et al. [21] study profiling of users' wellness in the class of event wellness by analyzing the relation that exists among different events. As part of the research on personal wellness event extraction from tweets of diabetic patients, they construct a dataset by manually labeling lifestyle and wellness related tweets of known diabetic patients as the category of wellness events. They used the contents of the tweets along with event category relation to obtain users wellness events on the timeline such as eating, exercising. They employed a dynamic user and word embedding model to track the semantic representation of the words dynamically over time that can distinguish between long-term and short-term interests. The short-term profile represents the current interest of the user while the long-term profile represents the interest over an extended period of time. Authors in [24] present and discuss experimental results of generating a set of useful profiles derived from the analysis of YouTube metadata crawled manually from the subscription network using breadth-first-search (BFS) where users are considered as nodes and connected friends as directed edges linking users.

User profiling that requires individuals or experts to manually create their user profiles by supplying personal data explicitly is considered an incomplete profile and is difficult to implement, time-consuming and cannot be extensively used for service personalization [25]. However, the automatic approach such as adaptive profiling for building a behavioral profile using machine learning techniques is more efficient and reliable. Usage of social network services such as YouTube, Twitter, and LinkedIn can be used for adaptive profile creation.

An interest model [26] can be created using methods used to gage the degree of interest demonstrated by the user. A simple approach to interest modeling directly collects the user's data on their interest such as watching sports videos, retweeting messages related to politics. Another approach to interest modeling is to consult the recorded past experience of the user as found in records such as browsing history and watched videos.

User information can be accessed directly in order to construct a user profile. The explicit method of gathering user information relies on capturing personal information by the user. The user profile can be directly accessed with the intervention of the users. The data collected may consist of demographic characteristics such as personal interests and hobbies, internet purchases or web events, or evidence regarding the user such as the categories of the most viewed video type or the most regularly visited website by the user. However, this way of gathering information is not effective because users are often hesitant to make their profile information public due to privacy concerns. Additionally, filling out forms is burdensome, and users tend to skip them. In addition to these drawbacks, this form of data collection is time-consuming for the users and depends on their cooperation. As part of users' online interest, we will focus on two most popular social networking services: YouTube and Twitter.

10.4.1 DATA COLLECTION AND PROCESSING

For YouTube, browser extensions can track a user's actual watching time of YouTube videos. These extensions can take into account in-video advertisements and text related to advertising, pauses during the viewing, and activity while playing the video to track data such as whether the user had the video in a window they were not watching. Data from these extensions can be stored in local storage and accessed from there to collect data on the user over a period of time.

In order to collect public Twitter data, the Twitter API can be used. This requires an app with consumer keys and authentication tokens. The Twitter API can provide information such as the user names or IDs of the user's followers and follows and the hashtags the user used (Table 10.3).

10.4.2 DATA COLLECTING ARCHITECTURE

An extension can be developed for browsers to collect users' data and send it to the server for further processing. A browser extension allows the request to be checked without requesting other tools before encryption. To relieve the burden on the browser, a Java server agent can be implemented that recognizes a URL (such as YouTube) and returns the associated label.

An alternative solution to collect data is by setting up a proxy server. A proxy server is a bridge between the user and internet. It's an intermediate server that divides end users from the pages they're visiting. Proxy servers have differing degrees of availability, protection, and privacy depending on the use case, requirements, or company policy. Although a proxy service can filter network requests, HTTPS requests are not readable with a normal proxy. Therefore, a third-party MITM proxy can be set up that can read requests before encryption. Given the organization policy in place, users may be bound to comply with their data to be redirected to a third-party proxy server. A browser (e.g., Firefox) extension can capture URLs and make a GET request to the proxy server for further analysis.

A basic extension can be developed that utilizes a background script to retrieve a user's watching history (e.g., on YouTube) including watching duration for each video in seconds, unique video ID, unique IDs of ads, and recommended videos loaded while watching. Watching time should consider pause and resume functions, tracking multiple windows or tabs in the browser.

Collected users' data can be forwarded to a pre-assigned proxy server. Knowing the username of the Twitter account, a proxy server can collect, for ongoing profiling, information such as the user's hashtags, retweet's hashtags, retweet account's hashtag.

TABLE 10.3

Using Twitter API [https://developer.twitter.com/en/docs/tweets/search/guides/standard-operators]

Operator	Finds Tweets...
watching now	containing both "watching" and "now." This is the default operator.
"happy hour"	containing the exact phrase "happy hour."
love OR hate	containing either "love" or "hate" (or both).
beer-root	containing "beer" but not "root."
#haiku	containing the hashtag "haiku."
from:interior	sent from Twitter account "interior."
list:NASA/astronauts-in-space-now."	sent from a Twitter account in the NASA list, "astronauts-in-space-now
to:NASA	a Tweet authored in reply to Twitter account "NASA."
@NASA	mentioning Twitter account "NASA."

Profile data obtained from social media has superfluous information. For this reason, the collected datasets need to be cleaned in such a way that the extracted features for the modeling of the profile will deliver a better output result. Some basic pre-processing methods used for this process include: tokenization, repetition elimination, term elimination, and labeling.

10.4.3 Data Source and Feature Selection

In practice, raw data contains noise and requires a clear representation of the data-by-data cleaning and pre-processing. In this section, we explore how we represent the data source for the task of user online social media interest modeling. Two data sources are defined: a textual content embedding data source such as Twitter, and a visual content embedding a data source such as YouTube (Figure 10.5). Data processing and underlying constraints vary by the type of application.

User activity characterization approaches that are focused on individual user functionality such as YouTube watching, are not suitable for web networking platforms such as Twitter. In these settings, users communicate with the web and other users through a variety of interfaces that allow them to upload and display content, rate favorite content using hashtags, subscribe to users, and engage in other interactions. A methodology for characterizing and analyzing user habits or sentiment may be built based on the interaction with online social networks. After performing sentiment analysis on the Twitter data for a targeted user, a useful profile can be extracted to classify various classes of user activity. The exponential rise in the number of YouTube videos offers viewers an

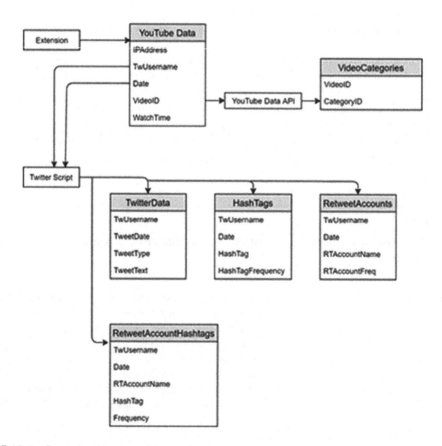

FIGURE 10.5   General architecture of data collection.

immense opportunity to discover content that is of interest to them. A browser extension can be built based on the user-video interest to create a user interest model.

To build a visual content source, a user's watching history can be combined to extract features using a browser extension. The extracted features are as follows:

- Watched video category
- Number of sessions and session duration per category
  - Session: time users spend on specific YouTube video category
- Recommended videos category
- Recommended ads URLs on the page
- Player ads unique IDs
- YouTube features that are available through APIs
  - Subscribers
  - Video categories
  - Channels
  - Following
  - Video likes or dislikes
  - Uploads
  - Posted videos

To represent users with video categories they watch, an unsupervised deep neural network (DNN) approach can be trained using a relational graph as in [27]. This model represents users with the video category they like most and this can be used to find similar users. Consider a matrix where each row in the model portrays a user and columns represent the video category the user watched. The value of each matrix entry is the number of videos or the total watch time in that category, otherwise it is zero. In this way Big-N ($N = 3, 4, 5$) personality traits can be predicted for each user.

To build a textual content source, a user's Twitter updates can be combined in the dataset into one document per day. Each user can be represented with the following linguistic aspects consisting of features related to standard count, psychological attachments, personal affairs, and other linguistic dimensions [28]:

- number of user's followers and following
- number of hashtags and their category (such as psychological process, e.g., hate, anger, joy, etc.)
- number of tweets per topic
- polarity of the Tweet topic
- subjectivity of the Tweet
- number of retweets and their categories
- number of verbs in tenses (future, past)
- number of words refer to personal affairs such as family, job, politics, etc.
- n-grams of tweets

Integrating data from several sources such as YouTube, Twitter, LinkedIn makes the profiling framework robust and accurate. This type of model leverages multiple sources of a user's data and integrates the association between models by mapping all data sources into shared representations.

To accomplish this, we target some active user's Twitter data in order: (i) to train a Latent Dirichlet Allocation (LDA) model using their daily tweets over a month for topic modeling and (ii) to predict personality traits of the user. For evaluation, we choose a user's top five words from the topic chosen by the hashtags used in a day to use as a YouTube query. Based on the query results suggested by YouTube, we choose the three most frequent video categories to see if they align with the topic model chosen by Twitter. At the same time, we collect the video IDs watched by the user in a day and choose their favorite video categories based on frequency and watched duration, aiming to evaluate the user interest profiling model for the tasks of predicting the user's interests.

10.4.4 MACHINE LEARNING MODELS

A user model is a distinguishing aspect of the adaptive scheme. It represents user information in an adaptive framework for efficient adaptation. For example, when searching for relevant content, it helps to prioritize an adaptive collection of relevant behaviors of users.

We apply the EGADS (Extensible Generic Anomaly Detection System) Java Library [29] to automatically detect anomalies in large scale time-series data. EGADS automatically calculates thresholds and outputs the most likely anomalies. The EGADS library can be used in a wide range of contexts to identify outliers and time-series shift points that may have different seasonal, pattern, and noise components. Anomaly detection in time-series data using Long Short-Term Memory (LSTMs) and automatic thresholding can be applied to users' YouTube watching history. LSTMs are trained to learn normal behaviors of the users using a user's prior watched videos category and duration. Predictions are generated at each time step (a day) and the errors in predictions represent deviations from expected behavior. Telemanom [30], a nonparametric and unsupervised anomaly detection tool in time-series data using LSTMs and automatic thresholding can also be used for automatic thresholding the errors and identifying anomalous sequences of user behaviors.

10.4.5 NATURAL LANGUAGE PROCESSING

LDA, a form of generative unsupervised natural language processing model, is used to expose the hidden structure of a set of texts. In terms of clustering, this can be considered a set of words instead of numerical features that we want to group together in such a manner that each group represents a subject.

Topical modeling is used in a range of applications such as news flow aggregation and recommender systems aiming at discovering the hidden thematic structure in the text. The underlying assumptions is that any composed text, whether a tweet, post, or blogs, fits into an identifiable theme such as politics, science, aerospace. This model can be used on a user's Twitter data such as hashtags and tweets [31].

Sentiment Analysis is a method of knowledge analysis using a number of techniques to extract individual clusters of information from the test data generated. This is an automated method of evaluating and organizing text data by user's emotion (positive, negative, or neutral). By using LDA and a sentiment analysis algorithm on a user's Twitter data, it is possible to profile the user's views on different topics [32].

As well, IBM Watson's Tone Analyzer is used for emotion recognition, expression recognition, and sentiment analysis in human behavior based on how humans interact with the world. They simplified this through the Big Five personality traits: fear, disgust, anger, joy, and sadness. Users' Twitter data can be used to profile users based on their average score for each personality trait per day [33].

10.4.6 PROFILING GROUPS OF USERS

A group-level profile complements a user profile focused on an individual. A group profile allows for the consolidation of user profiles exhibiting similar network behavior. Specifically, group profiling is a user profiling methodology that exploits the target users' interests and preferences in order to profile user groups. This type of profiling enables capturing major patterns or trends in the behavior of a small but relevant number of user classes and to compare user activity within and between groups. Combining multiple users profiling as a group profile has been proven effective in some user profiling applications such as recommender systems. By integrating the social, historical, behavioral, geographical, and categorical knowledge available from the social media and relationships within a group of the target users, authors in [34] introduce a behavior-induced hybrid personalized recommender framework for aggregating recommendations for travel applications from multiple recommenders. In [35], the authors compare user behavior from three online social networks such as Facebook, Twitter, and Google based on user connectivity, activity, and reactions.

10.5 PRIVACY ISSUES

Despite the usefulness of user profiling in securing networked systems, profiling users is ethically a thorny issue due to the hazards of abuse of the information gleaned from profiling. This is especially so when the user profiling violates civil liberties. To counteract some of the negative effects of user profiling nations around the world have instituted legislation targeting the use of personal information.

Profiling users exposes a conflict at the core of two fundamentally different views of ethics: deontological ethics versus utilitarianism. Deontological ethics places emphasis on actions themselves and argues that whether an action is justifiable or not should be based on principles and not the consequences of those actions. On this view, profiling a user, in general, is ethically indefensible no matter the outcome as it violates established ethical principles such as the respect of privacy.

The utilitarian view does not presuppose an abstract set of ethical principles that determine the ethical merit of an action, instead focuses more on the consequences of the action. As such it places emphasis on the public good. An action is justifiable if it provides benefit to the majority in society. As such, profiling users can be justified if it leads, for example, to society being safer.

The arguments for and against each view are more nuanced and the above discussion is a cursory sketch meant to highlight the essence of the ethical issues at stake. In practice, most of the issues related to the use of personal information (and by extension, user profiling) that come up in practice are governed by legislation. Some of the main laws governing personal information are the General Data Protection Regulation (GDPR) in Europe and the Personal Information Protection and Electronic Documents Act (PIPEDA) in Canada. Other regions, like the United States, do not have an overarching law governing personal information but provisions can be found in various legislations such as the Health Insurance Portability and Accountability Act (HIPAA). User profiling, and privacy in general, pose an interesting challenge in international law since privacy laws can have interjurisdictional force meaning that if profiling occurs across borders it is important to be aware of legal considerations in all jurisdictions where data can come from or be used.

User profiling discussed in this chapter relates to the kind of profiling performed with the intent of securing a network. In this context, the owner of the network (a corporation, government, or a university) has more power over the monitoring of the resources they own and what happens on their networks. As such, as long as any personal information is not illegally obtained and also not exposed to the public, the network owner is generally given more facility within the perspective of the law to protect their network by collecting information it deems useful for this purpose. Despite the extra leeway for network monitoring afforded to owners of networks, legislation must be consulted for the use and storage of personal information. When such information is to be shared for further analysis, it should be anonymized to prevent personal information, especially of innocent users, as well as sensitive information from being leaked.

It is worth mentioning that the kind of profiling discussed here relates to behavioral profiling and must be distinguished from more politically-charged kinds of user profiling that relate the user to the groups they identify with. None of the features mentioned in this chapter are interested in the user's personal identity but rather the focus is on their behaviors as they pertain to the network.

10.6   FUTURE WORK

Machine Learning models are notorious for their opacity. Although model performance can be measured to gain confidence of the model's quality, detecting bias is very difficult. This bias often originates from biases in the data or from assumptions the designer has. It would therefore be useful if a neural network, for example, could provide an explanation about how it arrived at an output and this is the subject of recent work in machine learning. This work has gained traction in applications of machine learning to areas such as finance and healthcare. Explainable artificial intelligence (AI) for user profiling also has obvious benefits as it allows us to see if a model is subject to bias and this is a developing research area.

Human-Centric Cybersecurity goes beyond our existing conception of cybersecurity as a purely technological concern. It realizes that modern communities have become so reliant on online digital technology that security vulnerabilities in these technologies amount to destructive social and political consequences that can only be resolved by an interdisciplinary approach with a focus on the social sciences. Such an approach emphasizes the role of the human element in cybersecurity.

Interactions between humans and online platforms, the dynamics of online risks as well as malicious interactions need to be studied more to enable better profiling of online users. The term "online user" applies to a vast range of varying users including cyber-victims, offenders as well as ordinary users who all present particular risks.

Along with individual human behaviors, social structures such as collective action by groups and communities, and the types of public and private interventions that shape societal responses, have tremendous impact on modern cybersecurity defense. Therefore, interdisciplinary research across the social and computer sciences is necessary to address a range of complex cybersecurity problems. The abundance of social media data that's generated captures an extensive span of people's activities, both including both regular and irregular behaviors. From the perspective of the social sciences, and also for such tasks as identifying social bots, the substantial amount of information is worth exploring.

In contrast to machine learning approaches, visual analytics that focuses on collusive anomalous behavior can be used to identify anomalous or normal behavior, for example, to detect a social Sybil attack using a social trust graph, or inference of personal information relevant to the posting behavior. There is opportunity for further attempts to discover anomalous activities of online users in a collusive way.

Research thrust in the area of user behavioral anomaly detection using network communication has remained relatively consistent – classical studies were published nearly two decades ago. Research trends in this area includes – identifying suspicious activities from data produced by multiple endpoints in real-time manifested by the realization of streaming data processing, cyber threat hunting using machine intelligence and dynamic and interactive visualization with the help of near-real-time streaming Kafka, etc. These stems from the need for prompt malicious attack identification. However, with the improvement in computing power, we continue to see more applications emerging that can manage streaming.

With the rise of social networking, inaccurate or fake profiling is a major challenge. This is because: (i) recommender systems based on user profiling may perform sub-optimally when they are created from multiple sources such as Twitter and LinkedIn due to the user's different, and often incongruent, preferences and personalization, (ii) the integrity of the user information is compromised by sharing false information on social media, and (iii) adversarial attacks using generated fake user profile, especially behavioral profiles, make other users vulnerable to these attackers due to the lack of information secrecy.

In the age of information sharing where securing individual privacy is a formidable challenge. There is no effective method in most situations to discern fake information or to distinguish between a fake profile from a real one. While some studies have been carried out to determine how trustworthy a user profile is, privacy preserving user profiling techniques will remain a very active area of research in the near future. More in-depth analysis toward the process of false profile detection would alleviate many problems in cybersecurity.

Regulatory measures can be explored that enhance cybersecurity. Specifically, regulatory policies surrounding such issues as privacy, openness, accountability, responsibility – often considered important concerns in governance – need to be investigated in order to develop effective cybersecurity strategies at the regulatory level.

10.7   CONCLUSION

In this chapter we discussed the concept of user profiling as a tool to secure a network. User profiling allows for finer grained control of network traffic that enables flexible network policing. It is an intelligent alternative to such methods as blacklisting.

We examined how features are selected, and the kinds of features that tend to be useful in practice. As well, we discussed an architecture for online user online interest modeling and the kinds of choices that present themselves depending on the type of profiling that is intended.

Inevitably, network technologies advance and with these, new advancements challenges emerge. Some challenges such as increased data obfuscation in traffic as well as developments in cryptography – techniques intended to protect user and user information – could make the task of user profiling more difficult but these developments go hand-in-hand with new advances in machine learning and other supporting fields that user profiling harnesses. Now and in the future, the idea of user profiling provides a clean concept for navigating the complexities of network security.

REFERENCES

1. Mamun, Mohammad, et al. "Detecting malicious urls using lexical analysis." *International Conference on Network and System Security*. Springer, Cham, 2016.
2. Eyharabide, Victoria, and Analía Amandi. "Ontology-based user profile learning." *Applied Intelligence*, vol. 36, no. 4, pp. 857–869, 2012.
3. Mamun, Mohammad, Rongxing Lu, and Manon Gaudet. "Tell them from me: An encrypted application profiler." *International Conference on Network and System Security*. Springer, Cham, 2019.
4. "The Netfilter.org project." *Netfilter/Iptables Project Homepage – The Netfilter.org Project*, Retrieved Jan. 31, 2021, from https://www.netfilter.org/.
5. Ring, Markus, et al. "Flow-based network traffic generation using generative adversarial networks." *Computers & Security*, vol. 82, pp. 156–172, 2019.
6. Wan, Zhiqiang, Yazhou Zhang, and Haibo He. "Variational autoencoder based synthetic data generation for imbalanced learning." *2017 IEEE Symposium Series on Computational Intelligence (SSCI)*. IEEE, 2017.
7. Karagiannis, Thomas, et al. "Profiling the end host." *International Conference on Passive and Active Network Measurement*. Springer, Berlin, Heidelberg, 2007.
8. Sconzo, Mike. "Samples of security related data." *SecRepo*, Retrieved Jan. 31, 2021, from https://www.secrepo.com/.
9. Turcotte, Melissa JM, Alexander D. Kent, and Curtis Hash. "'Unified host and network data set." *arXiv preprint arXiv:1708.07518*, 2017.
10. Lashkari, Arash Habibi, Gerard Draper-Gil, Mohammad Mamun, and Ali A. Ghorbani. "Characterization of tor traffic using time based features." *ICISSP*, pp. 253–262, 2017.
11. Draper-Gil, Gerard, et al. "Characterization of encrypted and VPN traffic using time-related." *Proceedings of the 2nd International Conference on Information Systems Security and Privacy (ICISSP)*, 2016.
12. Xiang, Guang, et al. "Cantina+ a feature-rich machine learning framework for detecting phishing web sites." *ACM Transactions on Information and System Security (TISSEC)*, vol. 14, no. 2, pp. 1–28, 2011.
13. Ma, Justin, et al. "Beyond blacklists: Learning to detect malicious web sites from suspicious URLs." *Proceedings of the 15th ACM SIGKDD International Conference on Knowledge Discovery and Data Mining*, 2009.

14. Lin, Min-Sheng, et al. "Malicious URL filtering – A big data application." *2013 IEEE International Conference on Big Data*. IEEE, 2013.
15. Abdelhamid, Neda, Aladdin Ayesh, and Fadi Thabtah. "Phishing detection based associative classification data mining." *Expert Systems with Applications*, vol. 41, no. 13, 5948–5959, 2014.
16. Xu, Li, et al. "Cross-layer detection of malicious websites." *Proceedings of the Third ACM Conference on Data and Application Security and Privacy*, 2013.
17. Le, Anh, Athina Markopoulou, and Michalis Faloutsos. "Phishdef: URL names say it all." *INFOCOM, 2011 Proceedings IEEE*. IEEE, 2011.
18. Ali, Murad, et al. "User profiling through browser finger printing." *International Conference on Recent Advances in Computer Systems*. Atlantis Press, 2015.
19. Boda, Károly, et al. "User tracking on the web via cross-browser fingerprinting." *Nordic Conference on Secure It Systems*. Springer, Berlin, Heidelberg, 2011.
20. S. Kanoje, S. Girase, and D. Mukhopadhyay. "User proling trends, techniques and applications." *arXiv:1503.07474*, Mar. 2015.
21. M. Akbari, X. Hu, N. Liqiang, and T.-S. Chua. "From tweets to wellness: Wellness event detection from Twitter streams." *Proc. 13th AAAI Conf. Artif. Intell.*, pp. 87–93, Feb. 2016.
22. S. Liang, X. Zhang, Z. Ren, and E. Kanoulas. "Dynamic embeddings for user profiling in Twitter." *Proc. 24th ACM SIGKDD Int. Conf. Knowl. Discovery Data Mining*, pp. 1764–1773, Aug. 2018.
23. Baluja, Shumeet, et al. "Video suggestion and discovery for YouTube: Taking random walks through the view graph." *Proceedings of the 17th International Conference on World Wide Web*, 2008.
24. Maia, Marcelo, Jussara Almeida, and Virgílio Almeida. "Identifying user behavior in online social networks." *Proceedings of the 1st Workshop on Social Network Systems*, 2008.
25. A. A. Barforoush, H. Shirazi, and H. Emami. "A new classification framework to evaluate the entity proling on theWeb: Past, present and future." *ACM Comput. Surv.*, vol. 50, no. 3, p. 39, Jun. 2017.
26. M. Gao, K. Liu, and Z. Wu. "Personalisation in Web computing and informatics: Theories, techniques, applications, and future research." *Inf. Syst. Frontiers*, vol. 12, no. 5, pp. 607–629, Nov. 2010.
27. A. Grover and J. Leskovec. "Node2Vec: Scalable feature learning for networks." *Proc. of the 22nd ACM SIGKDD International Conference on Knowledge Discovery and Data Mining*, ACM Press, pp. 855–864, 2016.
28. J. Pennington, R. Socher, and C. Manning. "Glove: Global vectors for word representation." *Conference on Empirical Methods in Natural Language Processing (EMNLP)*, vol. 14, pp. 1532–1543, 2014.
29. EGADS. "Extensible generic anomaly detection system." Retrieved Jan. 31, 2021, from https://github.com/yahoo/egads
30. Hundman, Kyle, et al. "Detecting spacecraft anomalies using lstms and nonparametric dynamic thresholding." *Proceedings of the 24th ACM SIGKDD International Conference on Knowledge Discovery & Data Mining*, 2018.
31. Resnik, Philip, et al. "Beyond LDA: Exploring supervised topic modeling for depression-related language in Twitter." *Proceedings of the 2nd Workshop on Computational Linguistics and Clinical Psychology: From Linguistic Signal to Clinical Reality*, 2015.
32. Agarwal, Apoorv, et al. "Sentiment analysis of twitter data." *Proceedings of the Workshop on Language in Social Media (LSM 2011)*, 2011.
33. Golbeck, Jennifer, et al. "Predicting personality from twitter." *2011 IEEE Third International Conference on Privacy, Security, Risk and Trust and 2011 IEEE Third International Conference on Social Computing*. IEEE, 2011.
34. Logesh, R., et al. "Efficient user profiling based intelligent travel recommender system for individual and group of users." *Mobile Networks and Applications*, vol. 24, no. 3, pp. 1018–1033, 2019.
35. Motamedi, Reza, Roberto Gonzalez, Reza Farahbakhsh, A. Cuevas, R. Cuevas, and R. Rejaie. "Characterizing group-level user behavior in major online social networks." *Tech. Rep.*, 2014.

11 Securing Mobile Social Networks

Robert Gordon

American Public University System, Hollywood, California, USA

CONTENTS

11.1 INTRODUCTION

Social networking has become more global than ever before. In addition to this worldwide reach of social networking, there has been a growing penetration of social networking users on mobile phones. In 2020 there were 5.1 billion mobile phone users, 3.8 billion social media users, and 89% of mobile phone users report having a social networking app on their phone [1]. Social networking

DOI: 10.1201/9781003134527-15

is the highest represented application on mobile phones today, being tied with messaging apps (89% of phones), which many are connected to a social networking app [1]. In 2020, mobile phones became the predominant technology for people to access the internet [1]. The use of mobile phones had grown 8.6% by the end of 2019 over 2018 to achieve a level of 53.3% of the web traffic by device, eclipsing the next closes device of desktops and laptops that fell 6.8% to 44% of the traffic during the same period [1]. This change in user preference will continue to fuel the growth of mobile phones. More organizations are moving to app-based programs and technology rather than computer/laptop web-based technology. This change in preferences has changed how people access social media and, hence, is changing the public's security needs.

Wireless phone technology continues to evolve, and with increased usage, the greater the potential of security risks. As a social media user on a mobile device, three important areas need to be examined. First, there is the topic of mobile security and the importance of securing a mobile device. Second, a mobile user needs to be aware of security risks and specific security risks using social media on a mobile device. Third, any person using social media on a mobile device needs to understand the laws, risks, and challenges that directly impact their security and privacy to avoid becoming a cybercrime victim.

11.2 MOBILE SECURITY

Social network users need to understand that a mobile device can be less secure than other devices because people have the misconception that mobile devices are safer. This misguided belief has been part of the reason for the increase in cybercrime. There is no doubt that cybercrime is increasing, so wireless and cellular technology must become more secure. Users sometimes believe that since a wireless device is connected to a network that the user is paying to access, the network provider will protect the individual. This idea in for the most part incorrect, however, some providers will be moving to secure their network better. Wireless technology will continue to expand, and carriers' recent thinking move to 5G will only speed up the need for greater security [2]. 5G Wireless technology will transmit and receive at 100–1000 4G LTE [3]. At this expected speed, one could expect to download a full-length movie in seconds. 6G wireless technology, which is already being discussed, is expected to stream at one-hundred gigabytes per second [2]. At these speeds, it would be dangerous to operate without greater security. Consider that one of all cellular networks' elements cryptography [4]. Given the rise of artificial intelligence uses, new programs could be developed to benefit from cellular phones' faster transmission speeds [5].

New cryptographic applications could be designed to cut through older security measures in seconds [3]. Increased speeds would allow encryption without perceivable delays. Additional encryption could certainly help, but it seems that phone providers have been focusing on the hardware and not considering the security implications. Furthermore, 6G will come hot on the heels of 5G. As we are already on the cusp of nations implementing full 5G networks, one has to wonder what the next generation of technology will bring [2]. 6G is already forecasting download speeds like never before [2]. No longer will individuals have to wait to download a full feature film, but 6G will allow the simultaneous download of several movies.

Social media users need to understand that just because they are operating within a social media app, that malware can attempt to deceive people into downloading other apps that could be malicious. In some cases, innocent-looking postings on social networks can redirect people to malware or other apps. These external apps could just be trying to steal data about the user, or they could be more malign and attempt to decisive people to submit secure information to insecure sites. Although there are technically no known viruses for cellular phones, there is undoubtedly a lot of malware out there. People often feel that postings to a social network are safe, but people need to use common sense and avoid downloading unknown apps. Some may contain malware that can cause the mobile phone user a lot of problems. People should understand that just because something is posted to a social network does not make the posting safe. Social networks monitor and protect their interests first, and once complaints start coming in, they will take action about potentially malicious postings.

Also, keep in mind that opening malware outside of the social network is not their concern, and the user needs to be careful when handling information of that nature. It is all too easy to click a link on one's feed to take the person to an insecure place.

11.3 BEING SECURE MEANS REMAINING SKEPTICAL

Although there are some tools out there to help secure your mobile phone, the best protection is to be careful about what apps you download and always use a trusted source. Keep in mind that even sites like the App Store or Google Play might have malicious apps. Although these storefronts try to keep users safe, there is no guarantee that they are safe. Being mindful about what you download is a good start but wary that many seemingly innocent apps are designed with a malicious payload. One should avoid downloading apps from unknown or lesser-known retails. One should avoid being one of the first to download a new app. One needs to consider using a safe browsing app like Lookout premium for Android.

As a general rule, one needs to be skeptical of all available apps before downloading. Just because an app has a high rating by people you do not know does not mean that these apps are safe. Also, keep in mind that apps might perform as advertised, but that does not mean that they are not selling your private information or harvesting your credit card information for malicious intent. One needs to be skeptical whenever anyone or any app asks for sensitive and security information. Keep in mind that there are no known viruses for mobile phones that spread like computer viruses. However, that does not mean we will not see this in the future.

Social engineering attacks are often most successful when they are socially engineered to target a specific target or targets. One needs to always think about the source of information before blindly clicking away. Even seemingly innocuous apps like FaceApp might not be seen as an attack. It certainly has some unusual terms and conditions about keeping all uploaded data for their uses, even after being deleted [6]. FaceApp might not seem like a wireless attack. Still, it could be coupled with artificial intelligence (AI) to access mobile devices that are more commonly being unlocked with facial recognition. In addition, compiling a database of facial data could be used to create fake personas on social media that would be hard to detect as being fake accounts Of course, this sounds a little farfetched, but why is a Russian company interested in keeping facial records of so many people under the guise of a free app. Beyond FaceApp, there have been significant security concerns about TikTok, which has already been banned by the US military and India [7]. And even if they are entirely above board and are doing it for other reasons, the data is out there for someone to steal one day and do what they are afraid of [6]. The risk is real because whenever data is put on the web, that data needs to be protected, but not all organizations prioritize cybersecurity. What has become clear is that personal data needs to be protected by the individual and to remain skeptical whenever that data is passed to another organization to hold secure.

Security is no small matter, and people must remain skeptical, and they must take steps to protect themselves and your device from bad actors with ill intent. Figure 11.1 below offers a means to prioritize your security whenever using your mobile device. In particular, when accessing social networks, personal information could be exposed that others might use.

Whenever using social networks, start by securing your device. An excellent way to remember is to use the acronym S-R-P. First, one should only use secure networks to access social media. One must make sure that one is accessing social media through a secure app and not through a third party. Second, the risks of accessing and revealing personal information must be kept in mind. Whenever a mobile device is signing into a social media site, personal data is being transported through the network. If the network is not secure, then there is a risk that someone might be seeing private information. Third, always protect personal information. Different social media surveys may seem harmless enough, such as a survey to ask about a person's favorite book or movie, but others could use that information. Keep in mind that two-factor authentication might ask for that information, which in the wrong hands could allow them access to personal accounts. By remaining vigilant, a person can avoid becoming a target by bad actors looking to steal and sell personal information.

FIGURE 11.1 Mobile security – risks – personal information.

11.4   SOCIAL NETWORKING USERS ARE BEING TARGETED FOR CYBERCRIME

Cybercrime continues to threaten users in a variety of manners. Cybercrime has become an elevated threat worldwide, and many nations are already working together to combat this threat, along with the threat to privacy [8]. Furthermore, the stakes are high as organized crime rings have developed to exploit as many targets as possible [8]. The risks are real, and many are known, so there is no reason that individuals and organizations should not take steps immediately to protect their data and their interests. Keep in mind that as a social network user, one is putting a lot of information about oneself on public display. One might feel they are just highlighting their achievements but placing information on social media gives cybercriminals more information to work with. Giving criminals information that can be used against social networking users is a risk that needs to be balanced against rewards. A person needs to understand the dangers of social networking and cybercrime and balance them against potential rewards. People need to recognize the risks with mobile devices and social media, and they must take steps to protect their personal information.

11.5   MOBILE DEVICE RISKS AND SOCIAL MEDIA RISKS

Once a person decides to put their information on display on social media, there are certain inherent risks that a person must understand. Not understanding these risks exposes a person to being exploited by bad actors. Understanding and learning about these risks can help mitigate and reduce these risks. The first type of risk will be called social engineering risk. The second will be called risks due to security protocols. The third is referred to as other cyber threats.

11.5.1 Social Engineering Risk

Social engineering has been one of the most common manners of compromising a mobile device. Social engineering attacks are designed to influence individuals to take a particular prompt action due to scarcity [9]. The classic social engineering case is the used car salesperson mentioning that a specific car being examined is desired by someone else who might buy it very soon [9].

A common type of social engineering attack on cellular devices is the SMS variant of a phishing attack known as SMiShing. A SMiShing attack uses a fraudulent SMS to get people to download something like a malicious app or possibly to give the attacker a credit card or other secure information that could be used against the victim. Although one would think that people might be more skeptical about their mobile devices, people are often less suspicious because the attacker appears to know who they are [9]. That veil of fake trust can often put people off their guard.

11.5.1.1 Security Options for Mobile Social Networking

Social networking on mobile devices exposes a person to the challenges of navigating safety. It also opens a person up to security risks associated with sharing data across a cellular network. Cellular phone owners are growing as targets by many different bad actors. No longer can a person expect that the mobile company will, in some way, protect them from harm. Cellular providers refute liability of security issues, and the user needs to protect themselves from harm. The first line of defense for anyone using a mobile device is to have regular backups of all data [10]. Beyond this type of security, mobile device owners should also look at cellular protection services and cellular protection programs. Both will be discussed and can help keep cellular users safe from many different attacks.

11.5.1.2 Cellular Protection Services

Two types of services will be discussed, internal and external. Internal protection services are what a user can do, such as keeping a current back up to keep data safe. External protection services are those services that can be bought from external vendors to monitor or otherwise keep cellular phones safe for an organization. Two internal controls that can be implemented are using stronger passwords and keeping all your software up to date [10]. Both of these should be implemented organizationally to make sure that everyone is up to date.

Other internal protections that a person can take would be to activate all two-factor authentication and activate Face ID wherever possible on a mobile device. Two-factor authentication may seem like a pain, and there are limitations, such as when one is accessing the internet on a plane, one will not be able to use two-factor authentication via phone. Two-factor authentication is to keep people from accessing one's account. Besides, Face ID can keep people out who might otherwise be able to access your account. Again, Face ID has particular challenges in the pandemic world as there are times and places that a person might not remove a mask to activate Face ID. A mobile user of social networking needs to activate as many additional security protocols as possible. There is no substitution for actively trying to keep one's information and access safe.

External protection is when an external company monitors devices, such as Keeper security or Lookout [11]. Keeper security can secure mobile software for business, family, and personal use [11]. The use of multi-factor authentication, deep level encryption, and a robust password management system can keep mobile users safe [11]. Lookout offers post-perimeter security to provide mobile endpoint security [11]. There are other external providers; however, an organization needs to determine their need and price point when shopping for these protection services.

11.5.2 Cellular Protection Programs

In addition to the internal factors that an organization can take, several mobile programs are available to help protect mobile users. Two good examples safeguard users from malicious apps, while the other protects against payment fraud. NowSecureffers a service to a security test app before a company phone downloading them [11]. By allowing a security firm to vet app, it keeps users from downloading a malicious app. Sometimes it is better to have someone checking an app before allowing it on the phone. Second, Payfone reduces risk by confirming digital identities and verifies customer information to avoid account takeovers [11]. Payfone offers an extra layer of security to ensure that mobile users have a safe and secure transaction experience.

11.5.2.1 Security Protocol Risk

Although individuals might not realize it, there is also a risk associated with cellular network data. A social networking user will be sending secure information that others can exploit by monitoring a mobile network. Also, one must remain careful whenever attaching to a public Wi-Fi network and accessing social networking apps. Although individuals might feel safer that data is encrypted, keep in mind that the faster the network and the quicker the information moves in a public network, the faster that bad actors can scan and decipher data.

Two known security protocol risks are the Wired Equivalent Piracy (WEP) and the Wi-Fi Protected Access (WPA) attacks. WEP uses a security key for security management, but WEP lacks key management [12]. If the key is being used in a public network such as a coffeehouse or airport, if the intruder can learn the security key, they could have access to many potential victims [12]. The security risk here is due to the increased computing power that has made deciphering cryptographic algorithms easier for attackers.

WPA attacks focus on tracking packets; just like the cybersecurity professional can monitor packet traffic to keep a network safe from attack, bad actors can use that same information to focus on the traffic in an attempt to use that information for mal intent. Note that WPA2 has more robust security protocols, but it is still susceptible to tracking network traffic [12].

11.5.3 OTHER CYBER THREATS

Several other cyber threats continue to cast a long shadow upon users of mobile devices. However, three have started to take on more relevance than before. The first is mobile ransomware. The second is the growing threat posed by botnets. The third is the proliferation of malicious apps.

11.5.3.1 Mobile Ransomware

Ransomware became a well-known threat when the *WannaCry* virus impacted thousands of companies. There are already reports of mobile ransomware attacks where people are being extorted by their data for either denial or threatened release [9]. Bad actors might be interested in cellular users' data and potentially blackmail people. Keep in mind that the *WannaCry* virus was based upon a known vulnerability with an active security patch available [9]. Yet, many people did not implement the patch and were infected with *WannaCry* [9]. This attack led to more companies taking an active interest in patch management, whereas before, it was considered one of those tasks that companies would get to later. Something like this will likely happen in the near future with regards to wireless systems and devices.

11.5.3.2 Botnets

Botnets happen with computers where a bad actor gains control of the device to use it for some nefarious purpose [11]. Sometimes the purpose is more of an annoyance than something that cripples the device. Botnets are like parasites that slow down a system to the benefit of others. For example, a botnet might take control of a computer to mine bitcoin in the background to benefit the attacker at the victim's expense.

11.5.3.3 Malicious Apps

Malicious apps are growing in popularity as they can make fraudulent charges on the victim's credit card [11]. One needs to be careful to download apps from known sources and to avoid things that might be too good to be true. For example, an app that offers free unlimited music for three months, and one can cancel at any time. One might remove the app, but the criminals will continue to charge the credit card.

11.5.3.4 Password Risk

Researchers and manufacturers are already looking at new methods to circumvent the ubiquitous password. After all, having a password is always an active link because when a person gains access to a password, they have access or are close to having access to any system [13]. Microsoft is already discussing the discontinuation of all passwords in the future, which would mean that they would have to move to some other biometric validation system such as facial recognition or fingerprint recognition [13]. Furthermore, mobile users need to send a password through the mobile network and the app to gain validation. As long as this data needs to pass through an app and the mobile network, there is the potential that others will be able to read this data and utilize it with bad intent. Social networking users are often asked to supply credentials. The more information is passed, the greater the risk that bad actors monitoring the network will decipher the encrypted data to access social networking accounts.

Society could expect to see the expanded use of implants to validate identity. In 2020, one person took the plunge and implanted a key chip and antenna into their arm to allow them to open their Tesla with a wave of their arm [13]. Although unusual, there are already companies, such as Vivokey, that specialize in implanted keys [13]. One might think that the future is far in the distant future, but it is already happening. The future certainly seems to point toward implants. However, implants might not catch on like wearables, which was touted in the recent past as the next big thing. Furthermore, the growth of virtual private networks (VPN) has been sparked by growing security concerns. One can expect that there will be mobile VPNs to secure wireless transmissions and secure personal data.

11.6 THE FUTURE RISKS ASSOCIATED WITH SOCIAL NETWORKING ON MOBILE DEVICES

The future of wireless technology is far from being written, and society can expect more significant innovation than ever before in this field. Yet, this does not mean that this brave new world will be secure. Cybercrime is on the rise and getting more organized to exploit more people than ever before. Wireless technology is inherently risky as anytime one is transmitting over the air, there is the potential of information being intercepted, jammed, or otherwise compromised. People continue to struggle with known security risks as people need to move past the belief that they are impervious to attack because they are a good person. Security will continue to grow and expand, and just as there are identify monitoring services, one can expect to have wireless monitoring for everyone soon. 5G and 6G mobile networks offer great benefits, but there are risks. Service providers need to be held accountable to add new protection layers to avoid massive hacks into their systems. All this turmoil is being driven by people's need to have faster download speeds. In closing, technology will continue to grow and make our lives easier. Still, the price for security and privacy needs to be mitigated by the manufacturers, service providers, and individuals interested in their data security.

11.6.1 Mobile Devices and Privacy

Cybercrime continues to make headlines in the news as more and more incidents are being more widely reported. As cybercrime grows, cybersecurity professionals need to be more diligent in using evidence to prosecute bad actors. However, the social networking user needs to understand that there are clear challenges regarding privacy with the social networking host and the cellular service provider and possibly with the Wi-Fi provider. Social networking programs require having access to the internet to function effectively. As such, mobile social networking users will be governed by many different groups with varying degrees of responsibility for the individual's privacy. One also needs to understand the relationship of the social networking user to these other groups.

Most social networking programs are being offered to the end-user for free. Along with this free license, the individual carries more risk and must protect their privacy. Free programs can limit their potential liability to the individual because the user accepts the program 'as is' and carries individual liability and will often be indemnifying the social networking owner. The user needs to understand this privacy risk and understand that other potential criminal actors are looking to exploit fewer savvy individuals.

Individuals need to accept that cybercrime is happening daily. Not only is cybercrime happening, but it is expanding and growing because of the development of new and creative ways to cheat people. To better protect the individual, they must understand how data will be handled in the event of a crime. Furthermore, privacy concerns can depend not only on the program being used but the Wi-Fi or mobile network being accessed.

A person will need to understand their rights if they are accessing social networking via a corporate network. Different organizations will have additional security and computer use policies to control cyber incidents better. Techniques of data evidence recovery from computers and the internet will be examined. All these challenges are daily concerns of the cyber professional, and all need to be understood and complied with during an investigation. Failure to follow procedure and protocol might jeopardize evidence being entered into court. Cyber investigations must be conducted properly and properly documented to ensure that the court accepts all evidence.

11.6.2   Electronic Evidence in Court

As different nations handle the admissibility of electronic evidence into court, only the United States' court system will be discussed for the sake of this discussion. The electronic evidence in court needs to follow specific steps to be admissible in court.

However, the judge presiding over the case will make the ultimate determination whether or not evidence can be admissible into court [14].

Although there are many approaches to entering evidence into court, two important questions need to be answered to attempt to enter electronic evidence into court. As outlined by the US Department of Justice:

1. Can all reasonable alternative explanations be disproved?
2. Is it necessary to disprove all alternative explanations?

It cannot be understated how important these questions are to entering evidence. As stated, it is critically important to ensure that all possible reasons regarding evidence are examined.

In Norwich, Connecticut, a case underscores the importance of reviewing all possibilities before deciding the evidence at hand. A conviction of pornography being exposed to children at a school was thrown out by a higher New London court. However, the forensic evidence showed that the accused was actively viewing pornography before the incident [14]. Web browser records were examined and found that other pornography had been considered before the incident [14]. However, further investigation by the higher court discovered that a computer virus had hijacked the computer before the viewing of pornography. Based on this additional evidence, the courts threw out the conviction and fined the defendant on a much lesser charge [14]. Given that the expert witness and investigator felt the accused was guilty, this incident shows the importance of reviewing all possibilities before jumping to judgment.

This example shows the importance of understanding what one accesses via a social network is not considered private and could be admissible in court. One might feel that the access that one has through a social network is deemed confidential. There are many different layers of access. First, the social network has laws that govern the interactions and information being shared. Most professional social networks will restrict pornography and violence; however, the social network might not always police everyone. However, all the data and logs could be requested as part of legal action, and the social network would be compelled to surrender that information to the courts.

Social networks often feature privacy settings to keep prying eyes away from information. However, the individual is not protected if requested as part of legal action. As such, a person needs to be very mindful of what data is presented on any social network.

Second, as discussed in the example, the network provider or Internet Service Provider (ISP) could also be requested to turn over browser information. Although many internet browsers offer 'private' browser access, that only refers to the local logs. The ISP or network provider will still know the browser activity of the individual.

The social network individual might try to access pages privately. However, the local logs might be deleted; the ISP will maintain records for much longer. Individuals accessing social networks through a mobile device will also contend with the mobile carrier's cellular data and logs. Although one might think that a person has greater protections with a mobile carrier as the user is a paying customer, the courts have made it clear that mobile carriers are a utility and must surrender information as part of a court case when requested. This information might be presented to the user as part of the user agreement. Many users fail to read or understand the limited privacy rights that they have. Keeping this in mind, users should realize forensic information and electronic forensic investigations to know how data will be handled in a crime.

11.6.3 CRIMES AND INCIDENTS INVOLVED WITH ELECTRONIC FORENSIC INVESTIGATIONS

Various crimes and incidents are involved in electronic forensic investigations. Almost every crime will likely involve electronic forensic evidence. Given that most people in the US are heavily connected, there will probably need to be a review of the accused computer and phone to review the digital logs to determine the individual's mindset at the time of the crime. Besides, since phones are connected to a GPS, a person's phone location can also show that the accused was in the area at the time of the crime. Furthermore, social networking encourages people to share location information, tracked and logged by the social networking company for use in the future.

11.6.4 US PATRIOT ACT OF 2001

Computer forensics continues to grow in importance in both the public and private sectors. Since more organizations rely upon electronic communication, there needs to be more excellent protection of this data to avoid it being accessed by bad actors will mal intent [14]. The passing of the US Patriot Act of 2001 ushered in a new era where electronic crimes were recognized as a national threat and created new laws and taskforces to deal with the nation's growing threat [14]. A social networking user needs to understand that all electronic communication can be accessed, and privacy is trumped by national security. Although most social networking users are not going to be posting matters of national security, one needs to understand potential national security implications.

In 2019, a health and workout app allowed users to share locations to enable individuals to find other like-minded users. It turned out that the US military individuals started to extensively use the app so that military personnel could find workout partners. The app seemed safe enough; however, the app would allow people to find partners worldwide.

One savvy individual started mapping individuals' movement using the app and found large clusters of individuals in seemingly uninhabited parts of the globe. It became clear that these clusters of individuals were US military personnel at classified bases. What seemed to be a social networking app to link up people who had similar interests in health and fitness became an issue of national security. The US military quickly took steps to ensure that military personnel would avoid offering their location public, but the damage had been done.

11.6.5 THE ELECTRONIC COMMUNICATION PRIVACY ACT (ECPA)

The Electronic Communication Privacy Act (ECPA) is a set of laws governing how intellectual property must be respected and maintained by individuals who work with sensitive, private, or proprietary information. The ECPA was developed to protect individuals from acquiring information and detailed knowledge from one company. Although one intent of the law was to avoid illegal wiretaps, it has also been successfully used to keep an employee from taking and gathering proprietary information from one company and then using it at a new company. The ECPA is designed to punish those that perform illegal intelligence gathering or illicit corporate espionage.

The ECPA was initially crafted to restrict private electronic communications [15]. The ECPA intended to keep the government from utilizing unauthorized wiretapping. However, it would also be used to protect against and potentially prosecute individuals that attained proprietary information confidentially to pass along to a new employer in hopes of gaining a competitive advantage. Since people are apt to share data in social networks related to work accomplishments, one would be well served to understand what one should be sharing and what they should be avoiding.

Although the ECPA was never intended to restrict employees from gaining new employment, this law has been successfully applied to keep ex-employees from walking away with a treasure trove of electronic knowledge [15]. Brent describes a case where an employee utilized an email 'rule' to covertly have emails sent to their boss to be routed to the employee without their boss's knowledge [15]. The employee continued to collect, monitor, and save these emails for future use. The employee was eventually caught and prosecuted under the law. During the case, it was disclosed that the employee had been doing this for some time, and without permission, the jury found the employee guilty.

Although the sample case seemed to be clear, what was interesting is that the jury could have believed the other party had the employer not been meticulous and careful about gathering the evidence in the case [15]. Keep in mind that had this information been shared on social networking and found elsewhere, the case might have turned out differently. In this case, the individual was purposefully trying to steal sensitive information; it could have turned out differently. The importance of gathering information cannot be understated. Other cases have found the employee innocent due to the company making errors during the information gathering or while addressing the situation internally. Since electronic data theft can be difficult to prove at times, particularly the intent, the company must be meticulous when gathering information to build the case.

The law and an actual case where an individual gathered corporate knowledge for future use outside the company showed mal intent by the employee [15]. The systematic gathering and saving of emails that were not sent to the employee made it clear that the employee was not just receiving emails by mistake. Still, they were receiving them for far more malicious reasons. The employee was eventually found guilty of violating the ECPA.

11.6.6 SECURITY AND COMPUTER POLICY USE

Many people access social networking throughout the day; however, an individual would be advised to understand their company's security and computer use policy. Every organization needs to have a security policy and a computer use policy to ensure that employees know what acceptable and unacceptable behavior is and the company's items. The security and computer use policy needs to be uniformly applied and individually acknowledged. Keeping this documentation is critical in the event; there is an incident where the individual was involved. Although no policy can protect against all incidents, the policy needs to explain responsible behavior and address important behavior.

The intent of a security policy and a computer use policy should be to punish those who act against the company's good. However, in some cases, the policy can be applied to those unintentionally against the company. For example, a recent incident where the City of Burlington had sent $503,000 to a fraudulent company [16]. Had there been a security policy regarding the handling of secure client information, the incident might have been avoided, and the loss of $503,000 would never have happened.

Social networking users would be best to keep all company information secure unless directly advised the information is available for disclosure. Some individuals enjoy being the first to report on breaking news. However, individuals should avoid this urge. One might not think that information is classified. However, corporate espionage can be a real issue. The old adage of loose lips sink ships is as true today as when a nation is at war. Keep in mind that cybercriminals and corporate criminals are often trying to piece together information from various sources.

In most cases, the computers reviewed will be owned by the organization, and there would be no expectation of privacy, as outlined in the computer use policy. But information that passes through the company Wi-Fi should also have no expectation of privacy. Keep in mind that even a guest Wi-Fi can be monitored, and data can be revealed in the event of a crime.

11.6.7 TYPES OF ELECTRONIC EVIDENCE

Several types of computer and electronic evidence will be discussed to give a broader understanding of the use of this type of evidence. There will be three types of evidence that will be addressed to understand better how evidence should be handled and reviewed. First, the internet logs offer a lot of information regarding what sites had been visited and by whom. Second, the network logs show what programs were running and what data was being accessed at different times of the event. Third, there would need to be a review of the data and data logs of what data might have been deleted to determine what data might be useful evidence regarding the crime.

11.6.8 INTERNET LOGS

Understanding who had been visiting different websites, intentionally or unintentionally, can offer some important clues to surround the cyber incident. The core of understanding log files is to understand the purpose of log files. A log file tracks the actions that a particular computer takes to identify the who, what, when, and where of actions one specific computer took. Although log files are an excellent way to monitor against intrusion, they are also instrumental in a cyber investigation. XPLICO is an important tool that can extract application data from internet logs [17]. This tool could be used as part of an investigation to understand who was doing what and what applications were running at the time of the incident.

11.6.9 NETWORK LOGS

Reviewing and analyzing log files is important to work for a cyber incident. Given the importance of log files to investigations, NIST released Special Publication 800-92 to outline a guide of computer log files [18]. Some important security matters related to log files, such as log files, need to be accessed by a limited number of people, avoid non-essential recording information, such as passwords, protect the access log, and secure the process that generates log files [17]. If these important security matters are not managed, then it opens up the network to intruders.

Given how important network logs are to the overall safety of a network, it is important to make log files as difficult to access as possible. However, if an incident does occur, then one using a tool such as LastActivityView can help determine what activity was happening in the log files at the time of the incident [17]. Understanding network activity at a particular time can be important information in an investigation.

11.6.10 DATA LOGS

There will be an attempt to obfuscate or otherwise obliterate evidence of the buildup before the attack in most cyber incidents. Once the payload has been delivered, there will likely be an attempt for the criminal to cover their tracks. This situation makes it important to review what data was being used or deleted at the time of the incident. A tool that could be helpful in an investigation would be FTK Imager [17]. FTK Imager could be used to examine deleted files to try to recover them [17]. Investigating this type of evidence can help better explain what happened and how it happened.

11.7 EXAMINING THE FUTURE

As mobile technology continues to infiltrate everyone's daily lives, there needs to be a greater under-standing of the risks that come with this greater connectivity. Although some worry about their personal liberties being compromised by too much connectivity, the more considerable concern should be personal security. As more data is available about everyone electronically, keeping information secure from prying eyes becomes even more difficult. At any given time, an individual could have dozens and dozens of essential passwords and use biometric data. Because of the necessity to have password information electronically to validate, more and more data will be held electronically.

Looking forward, one can expect to have more electronic information available somewhere on the web. The more information housed with different organizations; the likelihood of some data breach becomes increasingly likely. Although changing passwords and using different secret infor-mation can be helpful, a person can only keep track of so much information without making some type of copy. In addition, in 2020, FireEye was hacked by a suspected nation-state, showing that even the organizations that protect against cybersecurity attacks are not immune to attack. If a com-pany entrusted to keep companies and national data safe can be breached, can a person with limited resources remain immune from a cyber-attack?

The future of security will become more prominent and more significant business, and organiza-tions and nations seek to keep specific data safe from prying eyes. The more money that organiza-tions are willing to put toward security, the more complex security they will become to secure information. Cybersecurity will soon eclipse the amount spent upon physical security due to more data being held somewhere on the web. The much-heralded Internet of Things (IoT) will become the IoT of cybersecurity because the more technology is connected, the more crucial cybersecurity becomes.

However, all is not doom in gloom for the future because as technology continues to change, companies are already moving to eliminate all forms of passwords to create other unique methods of validation. As these technologies evolve, other means of unique identification may be developed. Just as wearables will be able to monitor blood glucose without drawing blood, new technologies may find a way to uniquely identify each person to avoid hackers from gaining access to individuals' personal data.

11.8 CONCLUSION

In closing, this chapter hopes to allow individuals to make better choices when accessing social networking through a mobile device. Accessing social networks has become increasingly popular with mobile devices users, understanding the risks and privacy issues has become more important than ever. Social networking users might understand some of the issues with joining a social net-work. Still, most do not understand or recognize the multiple layers of privacy issues that come with accessing a social network through a mobile device. One might be subject to different laws and dif-ferent rules depending on how one accesses social networking. Since many of these layers might be outside the individual user's realm of control, it becomes vital that the individual take a more active role in protecting their information and privacy. The individual needs to takes steps to understand the risks and take the necessary steps and precautions to remain safe. Everyone needs to realize that cybercriminals are looking for ways to exploit naïve individuals who believe that others are handling security and safety.

REFERENCES

1. Kemp, S. (2020, January 30). *Digital 2020 special report.* Retrieved from Wear Social https://wearesocial.com/blog/2020/01/digital-2020-3-8-billion-people-use-social-media. Accessed February 7, 2021.

2. Nelson, P. (2018, June 28). *Get ready for upcoming 6G wireless, too.* Retrieved from Network World: https://www.networkworld.com/article/3285112/get-ready-for-upcoming-6g-wireless-too.html. Accessed February 7, 2021.

3. Freedman, A. E., & McGarry, C. (2019, June 11). *What is 5G? The definitive guide to 5G networking.* Retrieved from Tom's Guide: https://www.tomsguide.com/us/5g-networking-faq,news-20629.html. Accessed February 7, 2021.

4. Traymor, P., McDaniel, P., & La Porta, T. (2008). *Security for telecommunications networks.* New York: Springer.

5. Business World. (2018). 5G and GDPR can be a boon to cyber criminals. *Business World.*

6. Webb, K. (2019, July 18). *The Russian photo app that makes you look old is probably keeping your data.* Retrieved from Science Alert: https://www.sciencealert.com/viral-russian-app-that-makes-you-look-old-is-probably-keeping-your-data. Accessed February 7, 2021.

7. Cox, M. (2019, December 30). *Army follows pentagon guidance, bans Chinese-owned tiktok app.* Retrieved from Military News: https://www.military.com/daily-news/2019/12/30/army-follows-pentagon-guidance-bans-chinese-owned-tiktok-app.html. Accessed February 7, 2021.

8. Kahn, J., Abbas, H., & Al-Muhtad, J. (2015). *International workshop on cyber security and digital investigation (CSDI 2015) survey on mobile user's data privacy threats and defense mechanisms.* Retrieved from Elsevier.com: https://reader.elsevier.com/reader/sd/pii/S1877050915017044?token=62A6F62B330 639F09F39AD2FB852BE2B33B58D78240190983DF4952B4EB7CBD086F2BAF87BC8669B51 ACCE8E65ED2C9B. Accessed February 7, 2021.

9. Tanner, N. H. (2019). *Cybersecurity blue team toolkit.* Indianapolis: Wiley.

10. Siciliano, R. (2019, June 25). *Keeping your mobile devices safe from cyber threats.* Retrieved from The Balance: https://www.thebalance.com/keeping-mobile-devices-safe-from-cyber-threats-4122471. Accessed December 12, 2020.

11. Schroer, A. (2019, April 30). *Guardians of the gadgetry: 9 mobile security companies safeguarding our devices.* Retrieved from Built In: https://builtin.com/cybersecurity/mobile-cybersecurity-companies. Accessed December 12, 2020.

12. Geeks for Geeks. (n.d.). *Types of wireless and mobile device attacks.* Retrieved from Geeks for Geeks: https://www.geeksforgeeks.org/types-of-wireless-and-mobile-device-attacks/. Accessed December 12, 2020.

13. Rapier, G. (2019, August 13). *Tesla owner gets key implanted into her arm.* Retrieved from Business Insider: https://www.businessinsider.com/tesla-owner-gets-key-implanted-into-her-arm-2019-8. Accessed February 7, 2021.

14. Hayes, D. (2015). *A practical guide to computer forensic investigations.* Indianapolis: Pearson.

15. Brent, C. (2010). *Departing employees and the stored communications act: Employers beware.* Retrieved from Fisher Phillips: https://www.fisherphillips.com/Non-Compete-and-Trade-Secrets/Departing-Employees-and-the-Stored-Communications-Act-Employers-Beware. Accessed December 12, 2021.

16. The Canadian Press. (2019, June 13). *Burlington falls for $503K phishing scam: Investigations underway.* Retrieved from CityNews: https://toronto.citynews.ca/2019/06/13/burlington-falls-for-503k-phishing-scam-investigations-underway/. Accessed December 12, 2020.

17. Tabona, A. (2018, July 10). Retrieved from TechTalk: https://techtalk.gfi.com/top-20-free-digital-forensic-investigation-tools-for-sysadmins/. Accessed December 12, 2020.

18. Kent, K., & Souppaya, M. (2006). *Guide to computer security.* Retrieved from NIST Special Publication 800-92: https://nvlpubs.nist.gov/nistpubs/Legacy/SP/nistspecialpublication800-92.pdf. Accessed December 12, 2020.

12 Protecting Regular and Social Network Users in a Wireless Network by Detecting Rogue Access Point
Limitations and Countermeasures

Md. Tanvir Hasan and Md. Redwan Hossain
Southeast University, Dhaka, Bangladesh

Al-Sakib Khan Pathan
Independent University, Dhaka, Bangladesh

CONTENTS

DOI: 10.1201/9781003134527-16

12.1   INTRODUCTION

Today's internet users, especially the social network users are no strangers to wireless networks that do not need any wire or cable to connect their devices with the internet. Wi-Fi networks are often found in almost all cities in the world while the rural areas are also well-covered wirelessly in many geographical regions. This mode of communication has allowed the growth of internet users, many of whom today often use online social networks for interacting with friends, relatives, colleagues, and others [1]. The wireless networks make it easy for the users to connect their devices with the internet anytime via radio signal frequency. For such a connection, there is an access point (AP) that links to a wireless router which transmits signals over the air. Everyone within the range of wireless signals of the AP can access to the internet.

There are several kinds of wireless networks: WLAN (Wireless Local Area Network), WPAN (Wireless Personal Area Network), WMAN (Wireless Metropolitan Area Network), and WWAN (Wireless Wide Area Network). A typical wireless network setting is shown in Figure 12.1. Here, a wireless router can be a basic router with an added feature on an inbuilt AP. WLAN covers a small range of exposure areas across a university campus or library, hospital, airport, etc. to create a network or to gain access to the internet. The advantages of WLAN are the sufficient range and maximum data transfer rate with IEEE 802.11 standard [2]. Mobility is an important consideration in WLANs [3, 4]. WPANs are small-scale networks that interconnect between individuals. The two existing technologies for wireless personal area networks are Infra-Red (IR) and Bluetooth (IEEE 802.15). WPAN provides a connected communication to the various types of end users such as computers, smartphones, laptops, tablets, smart TV, etc. within the user's personal range. WPAN provides average performance with low cost [2]. WMANs allow the creation of wireless network connections in metropolitan areas. WMAN provides a connection between several wireless LANs. The advantages of WMAN networks are high performance with IEEE 802.16, HiperMAN (High Performance Radio Metropolitan Area Network), and HiperACCESS (High Performance Radio Access) standards [5]. A WWAN (Wireless Wide Area Network) [2] can cover a large geographic area compared to WLAN. For example, city, countries through satellites. Installing WLAN card in a laptop is the simplest way to allow connectivity from anywhere within the regional boundaries of cellular service. At present, WWAN is used for mobile access to the internet from outside areas which is offered by cellular service companies.

While wireless network can bind us together with its rapid growth, complexities also increase in such setting very fast. In some cases, there could be rogue devices using the wireless AP without any authorization or by violating the authentication and authorization processes. Rogue devices can then

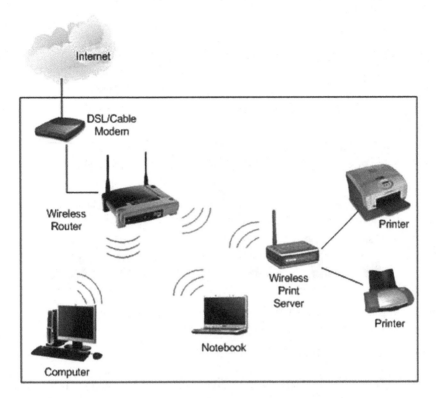

FIGURE 12.1   Wireless network.

compromise confidentiality, integrity, and availability by undermining trust between systems and intercepting or corrupting valuable data in the network. Again, although not technically considered rogue devices, personal smartphones and tablets can often invade into corporate networks creating unique risks and challenges. When social networks or social media are used via such wireless setting, multiple real-life challenges can appear to threaten the security of the communications. There are in fact, a number of threats that exist in wireless LANS, which include: RAP (rogue access point), DoS (denial of service), Unauthorized Client Access, MITM, Evil Twin, IP Spoofing, Honey Spot Access Point attack, Jamming Signal attack, and so on.

In this chapter, we focus on RAP, as this is a very dangerous threat for business organizations as well as for personal networks. We classify different detection techniques of RAP and suggest how an organization can overcome the known threats. We also suggest some prevention techniques for ensuring a secure network.

12.2   ROGUE ACCESS POINT (RAP)

RAP is an unauthorized AP which is installed on a secure network without any awareness of authorized network administrator. Since it is an unauthorized AP, anyone can get access to that network via this very easily. Once the rogue AP is deployed, it becomes easier for the eavesdroppers to launch various types of security attacks (as mentioned earlier). A RAP could be a serious security threat to a lot of large organizations or even one's home network. Why? Because anyone accessing that RAP can be monitored – everything can be recorded like what the user is browsing, which websites one is searching, what types of files someone is downloading, and so on. Even personal data can be explored in this setting by other intruders [6]. The key concern about RAP is that this whole process can be done without any consent of the network's actual owner. To protect one's network

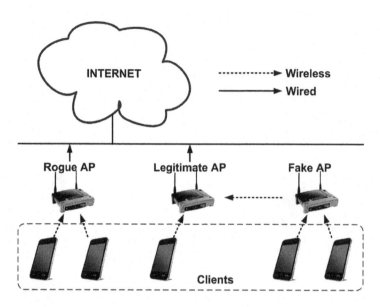

FIGURE 12.2   Rogue AP, Legitimate AP, and Fake AP.

against unauthorized AP, the IEEE 802.11i [7] has some authentication mechanisms which one needs to follow.

For better understanding, we discuss here two types of unauthorized APs – I) Rogue AP and II) Fake AP. Figure 12.2 shows a scenario.

There are four different categories of rogue APs. They are:

- Evil Twin
- Improperly Configured
- Unauthorized
- Compromised AP

An Evil Twin is a kind of man-in-the-middle attack where attacker sets up a fake AP so that the attacker steals end user's information. An intruder or attacker can usually deploy an Evil Twin using a laptop or PC (personal computer), smartphone, or other electronic devices. The attacker is able to enter the system to capture traffic or install malware. The Evil Twins appear as valid APs by cloning the MAC (Medium/Media Access Control) address and network name or Service Set Identifier (SSID). The user enters this network considering it as a valid AP. The victim will have no idea that the hacker might be intercepting communications like bank transactions. The attacker easily manages his activities on free public Wi-Fi such as airports, bus stations, shopping malls, and other zones. After getting the access to the users, attacker sends radio signal as a legitimate AP. In addition to using the same network name and settings to attack the end user, the attacker also physically places itself so that its signal could be the strongest within the range. The strong signal manually connects the end user to two people from different places for internet access and gives the attacker the ability to intercept sensitive data. To protect sensitive information from attacker, user (or, say, the social network user) should not log in via public Wi-Fi and avoid insecure Wi-Fi hotspots. It is a fact that often the free services like these are already unreliable. For such cases, one way of better protection is to use two-factor-authentication for all sensitive accounts and log ins. If user uses public Wi-Fi, VPN (Virtual Private Network) is a good option to protect the privacy and security [8]. This is because it would encrypt traffic before it leaves the user device.

Improperly configured AP refers to lack of proper knowledge of network configuration which consists of inappropriate encryption (WPA – Wi-Fi Protected Access, WEP – Wired Equivalent Privacy), physically misconfigured, or corrupted AP driver. Improperly configured AP can pose security threats if used by opponents [9]. Some wireless devices like smartphones, laptops and tablets may have remote configuration features, unauthorized APIs (Application Programming Interface), or software bugs that can open the door for fake APs.

A wireless network should be carefully configured by skilled people and the system or network administrator should use WPA II or WPA III encryption to protect the network from fake APs. Without proper configuration, there would always be some kind of loophole for the attackers to work within the wireless network.

An unauthorized AP acts like a valid AP, but in reality it is not. It is launched in a network without any permission of network administrator. For example, unauthorized access can happen by guessing the username and password or with repeated trials. Network administrators should create an alarm system, if someone wants to get an attempt to unauthorized access, so they can investigate the cause and work for it [10].

A compromised AP is a rogue AP, where intruders crack the encryption mechanism of the network system and establish their accessibility to the network. It is considered the most dangerous rogue AP because hackers gain access to network by obtaining for instance, WPA-PSK (WPA pre-shared key) and WEP's shared keys. Security credentials will be at risk if a compromised AP is established. Such an AP allows unauthorized users to access the WLAN, to invalidate billing information, causes loss of privacy of a legitimate user, and unauthorized use of QoS (Quality of Service), if supported.

In should be mentioned for clarification that a fake AP is also a rogue AP that has different characteristics than other APs. Fake AP is installed by false users for malicious behaviors like-eavesdropping, falsification, and others. Since fake AP looks like a legitimate AP, if any legal user communicates with a fake AP, eavesdroppers can easily read the messages in transit and other confidential information that should not be read or seen by unauthorized party. Once a rogue AP is installed without any security features, an intruder can gain illegal access to the entire network. Thus, a rogue AP can cause serious damage to a network's normal functions.

12.3 ROGUE ACCESS POINT DETECTION APPROACHES

In this section, RAP discovery approaches will be discussed. We can classify the approaches into four categories. They are: i) Traditional approach, ii) Client-side approach, iii) Server-side approach, and iv) Hybrid approach. Table 12.1 shows various approaches at a glance. The traditional approach is almost obsolete today. Some of the most efficient solutions can be found for the hybrid approach. Let us know these one by one.

TABLE 12.1
RAP Detection Approaches

RAP Detection Approaches			
A) Traditional Approach	B) Client-Side Approach ↓	C) Server-Side Approach ↓	D) Hybrid Approach ↓
	i. Round trip time	i. Temporal characteristics	i. Covert channel
	ii. Received signal strength and sequence hypothesis	ii. Hidden Markov model	ii. Multi-agent sourcing
		iii. Clock skew	
		iv. Hybrid framework	

12.3.1 Traditional Approach

To construct a *whitelist*, the traditional approach uses some parameters like – SSID, MAC, and other parameters of legal AP. It inspects the MAC address and SSID. This process declares an AP as a valid AP, only if all parameters (MAC, SSID) match. Just to clarify here, *whitelisting* is the practice of explicitly allowing some identified entities access to a particular privilege, service, mobility, access, or recognition. A whitelist records the identities of all the legitimate entities in the network (who are considered acceptable and trustworthy). After creating a *whitelist*, the traditional approach captures 802.11 frames and filters out MAC addresses to detect rogue AP. This approach is a simple and efficient process, but invading spot can violate this method by changing the MAC address of the AP [11]. There are tools like NetStumbler and AirMagnet being used to detect rogue AP by scanning the RF (Radio Frequency) signals. However, these tools need a large number of sensors and it could be sometimes quite costly for users [10].

12.3.2 Client-Side Approach

Client side means that the action takes place on the user's (the clients) side. Client-based RAP detection method uses the client computers or nodes to apply the detection of the rogue AP [12, 13]. Unauthorized APs are difficult to find on client-based networks due to the lack of network information. Sometimes clients have no idea about a valid AP list and there are no efficient software tools at the nodes. There are many methods to secure nodes on a wireless network. Some vendors have pre-installed software on their own devices for network monitoring and before connecting to an AP, it observes all the traffic of the AP to determine whether the AP is authorized or not [14].

In most organizations, the employees (client or node) are connected to the switches, so the activities between the client and the network are not easily visible to other clients. Switches transmit traffic to administrative routers that are externally connected to other routers in some external networks. In wireless networking, other people can sniff traffic or packets over corporate networks. It is like solving a problem with an encrypted channel between the client and the AP [15]. On the other hand, mobile networks require client-side solutions that do not require authorization or AP and no information about users. In [16], the authors propose a client-side method to detect mobile RAP using three phases: RTT (Round Trip Time) measurement, preprocessing, and classification.

Evil Twin attack can appear on client-side in the network. This is an AP that pretends to be a valid AP with the same SSID. The attacker serves as an MITM attacker on a network, as mentioned before. For this, the work in [17] suggests a client-side solution to detect Evil Twin attack.

There are a few strategies to consider under the client-side approaches. Let us discuss these in the subsequent paragraphs.

12.3.2.1 Round Trip Time

We all know how data is transferred from one place to another place over the internet. Suppose a user living in Dhaka wants to communicate with another user who lives in Berlin. When requested by a client in Dhaka, network traffic is transferred across different routers located in different geographical locations before ending up on the server in Singapore (for instance). The Singapore server then transmits a response across the internet to a Berlin location. Once the request is over in Berlin, the amount of time it takes to make a round trip between the two locations can be roughly assumed. This RTT can be a valuable measurement for this case.

Han et al. [18] in their work use RTT between the client and local DNS (Domain Name System) server to distinguish whether the AP is rogue or legitimate. The client will request a DNS for a hostname with a non-repeating option and wait for the answer from the local DNS server and calculate the RTT. Users continue this system using various hostnames for each time by scanning AP. They also measure the differences between RTT and calculate threshold value to determine whether it is fake AP or not. Instead of one hop, the connection between the user and the RAP will take two hops to reach the DNS server, and measuring the RTT will delay the time to reach the WLAN. They calculate the 802.11 based delay process for sending packets. The effects of network traffic will be determined using search requests and responses. For channel traffic collisions, both investigations will take a long time to send a response message and the signals will be re-sent after the conflict. Again the AP's workload search response message will have to wait in a queue for packets to be sent.

12.3.2.2 Received Signal Strength and Sequential Hypothesis Testing

RSSI (Received Signal Strength Indicator) is the amount of power for the client device that is obtained by the physical layer of the antenna. Typically, RSS stays close to the physical location. Here, dBm and RSSI units are two ways to measure the values of RSS where dBm gives better results for finding RF signal strength [19]. While client-side systems may provide dynamics for secure communication, existing client-side systems have a complex mechanism for detecting fake APs. It should be however mentioned that overall client-based approach is less effective in case of mobile technology [20].

In [3], the authors try to solve the client-side problems through the measurement of received signal strengths. They use three stages: first stage is collection of RSS; second stage is classifications of RSS, and finally, normalization of signal strength. For easy understanding, let us know about the stages one by one in brief.

a) **Collection of received signal strengths**: In this stage, the RSSI is obtained in the IEEE 802.11 infrastructure to quantify the power present in the radio signals obtained using beacons from close APs.

   To establish associations, a wireless device uses one of two scanning methods to search for APs. These two methods are: 1) active scanning and 2) passive scanning. Active scanning means starting the wireless device/client search effort. In active scanning, a wireless device transmits a probe in the frequency range of each channel; a special type of frame, and waits for an AP to respond. In passive scanning, the user does not initiate device search efforts; instead, it just sits back and listens to all available channels within a frequency range for available APs. An AP regularly broadcasts a beacon frame in its service area. This special frame of beacon contains AP information such as SSID.

   A series of received signal strength expressed as:

   $$s_i = \left[s_1^i, \cdots, s_i^t \right]^T$$

   where s_i^t is the received signal strength from i_{th} AP at time t. Then, express k sequences as:

   $$S = \left[s_1, s_2 \ldots s_k \right] T \tag{12.1}$$

b) **Normalization of signal strengths**: In this phase, the collection of received signal data are tested and normalized for detecting the fake AP(s). Signals can be lost due to some features of WLAN such as wind conditions, obstructions, household items and noisiness or other causes; and the signal strength can become zero. In normalization method, the provided equation converts the received signal strength within a limit of [0, 1].

c) **Classification of RSS**: By measuring the classification process in this step, RSS classifies multiple signals that are highly connected to each other and determines the threshold values that are generated from the fake AP. If the calculated value is not multiple signals AP, then it will be legitimate APs.

12.3.3 SERVER-SIDE APPROACH

In the server-side approach, network administrators monitor the entire network by installing software on the server. This particular software detects which AP is valid or rogue by considering various parameters. If it detects suspicious behavior at the AP, it prepares the barrage for access to the network. The advantage of this method is that the users do not need to do anything different to keep his network protected. The drawback of this method is that the client has no idea which access point is valid and which is fake AP. Once hackers crack the password and enter, they can easily deploy numerous attacks like MITM, DoS (Denial of Service) through rogue AP, and so on. The network can be protected from these types of attacks if security credentials are made and maintained more strictly [12].

12.3.3.1 Using Temporal Characteristics

The work in [21] suggests using temporal traffic characteristics to find rogue AP in wired and wireless technologies (IEEE 802.11). The authors performed an experiment considering a central location which was set up by a switch and other wired and wireless devices. By observing the curves of inter-packet spacing between wired and wireless packets, the authors noticed that the area of the wireless network is less compared to wired network. When transferring packets, they consider both forward and reverse path between wired and wireless network. According to the test results, it can be estimated that 80% of the inter-packet spacing was less than 1 ms for the wired link, while for wireless traffic, the authors found 90% of the inter-packet spacing of more than 1 ms. The work in [12] talks about inter-packet intervals to detect rogue APs in wireless network. With the addition of extra hop, inter-packet spacing continues to grow in the network and this could be something useful in this case.

12.3.3.2 Hidden Markov Model

The authors in [22] propose a mechanism named HMM (Hidden Markov Model) to detect a rogue AP in WLAN. The HMM model is applied to the router at the entrance (gateway) of a network where packets are received and explored. There are two levels to their approach. The number one level is HMM training and level two is RAP identification based on trained HMM. At the second level, the Viterbi algorithm is used to detect rogue APs. The three states of security of the HMM model are shown in Figure 12.3.

The AP has three safety measures – good, probed, and compromised. At good state, it specifies that the AP is not probed or compromised; it is in a secure condition. The AP's probe state specifies that it has been probed and may be attacked. Finally, compromised AP refers to unknown access by the attacker.

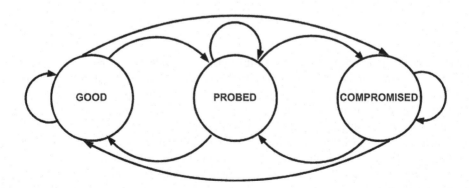

FIGURE 12.3 Three security states of HMM model.

12.3.3.3   Clock Skew

The authors in [23] use Time Synchronization Function (TSF) timestamps in the IEEE 802.11 network to compute clock skew of an access point and detect rogue AP in WLAN. Clock skew is a physical feature commonly used in real-time networking by an AP. Authors have estimated the clock skew using TSF, which is sent continuously with the help of beacon/probe response frames. The two methods used by the authors for this process are linear programming and least-square fit. Their measurements show that the clock skew remains the same over time in the case of same AP. In this way, someone can trace a clock skew extremely fast by increasing the resolution of the timestamp obtained from frames. This method defines unexpected transformations and distinguishes the data collected from beacons which are obtained from several APs in the wireless network.

12.3.3.4   Hybrid Framework

The authors in [9] create a hybrid structure to protect both wired and wireless network identification and localization from rogue APs. This structure improves network flexibility from rogue AP. The described method does not require any specialized hardware or software. The hybrid structure is made up of two pieces; first one is Distribution Detection Module (DDM) and the last one is Centralized Detection Module (CDM). DDM APs integrate as small coverage areas and are responsible for collecting wireless traffic. The CDM is located on the local area network gateway router to check all traffic coming in and out of the network. DDM is implemented through three components; wireless frame collector, preemption engine, and detection engine. Clients can easily detect rogue AP using fingerprint technique. Fingerprint functional detection engines are: user-specific traffic fingerprinting, OS (Operating System) fingerprinting, wireless network interface card (NIC) driver fingerprinting, and client location fingerprinting. CDM is created by scrutinizing and filtering on gateway routers. The hybrid framework can operate on security protocols such as WEP, WPA, and under various network settings. Figure 12.4 shows the CDM and DDM models.

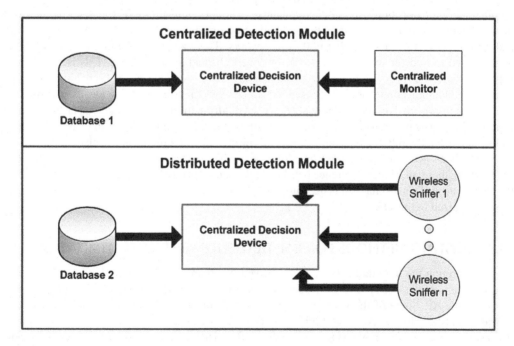

FIGURE 12.4   CDM and DDM models.

12.3.4 HYBRID APPROACH

The hybrid approach is an important and effective way to detect rouge AP. In this approach, the server side and the client side have proper roles to play in bringing out the rogue AP. A dedicated server will constantly transmit the packets received and the client will be notified each time the rogue AP is present in that network [24]. Many methods have been used before to defend against unwanted APs. However, the desirability and prevalence from the hybrid approach is higher than other methods. Here, we discuss mechanisms that may be used for hybrid approaches.

12.3.4.1 Multi-Agent Sourcing

Multi-Agent based methodology is very effective. The proposed algorithm in [25] does not need to manually scan to identify and remove unauthorized AP. This saves time and it is also cost-effective. There is no need to spend extra amount for specialized software or hardware.

This automated method automatically detects and eliminates unauthorized APs by applying the mobile multi-agents to the network. Mobile agents have features like local network monitors that can reduce network delays and network loads. Mobile agents are used across more regions than traditional RF and SSID scans.

There are two different levels of mobile agents: Master and Slave mobile agents. A master agent is generated in this mechanism which is responsible to regulate all the authorization processes of the network. This master agent generates slave agents depending upon the number of active APs connected to the server at a particular time. The next step is to dispatch the slave agents on the respective APs. Again, the slave ages are cloned on every AP to client systems. When a clone slave agent at the client system detects any new AP, it automatically builds and sends an INFO packet which has the information about the SSID, MAC address, Vendor Name, and Channel used. Any unauthorized AP is caught in this way as this information is sent to the master agent on the server. Then, the suspected AP is identified and matched against other information stored in the repository of all APs.

12.3.4.2 Covert Channel

Using covert channel for avoiding rogue AP is proposed in [26]. The authors propose the concept of terminal AP authentication using a covert channel. The mechanism uses IEEE 802.11 timestamp field of the beacon frame for sending the authentication string to each client AP within the network and creating covert channels in IEEE802.11 networks. This can be performed by modifying the module used to transfer subsequent frames for covert channel authentication. This is an effective method because it does not require any additional hardware. Covert data channels are hidden through legitimate communication channels. These kinds of channels interfere with the means of communication in an unexpected or unconventional way to send information in an anonymous fashion. Cover channels [27] basically transmit small quantities of confidential information using vast amounts of valid channel bandwidth. Such covert channels allow one-way communication only.

AP sends an additional covert set of information which is received by all stations. Using this information, they can tell the difference between legitimate AP and a rogue one that will not transmit the covert string. This mechanism is used in both the AP and client station. The station and AP must be synchronized in this case.

12.4 EXISTING METHODS FOR RAP DETECTION AND THEIR LIMITATIONS

After performing the literature survey, it is observed that there is quite a long list of works in this area, but many of the works have used a single parameter like SSID or MAC address for the detection of rogue AP. Some of the researchers used the temporary traffic characteristics, inter-packet arrival time, RSS, clock skew, or multiple parameters. However, because of the environmental conditions, these parameters may change their values often. Hence, there would be always some possibility of false positives for those works.

TABLE 12.2
RAP Detection Methods and Their Limitations

RAP Detection Method	Description	Limitations
Brute force attack	Equip age 5. workers with wireless packet analyzer equipment (e.g., sniffers) on laptops and scan the network traffic.	- Ineffective and time-consuming and decreases throughput. - RAP can be easily plugged in when the scan is performed. - IT workers need to upgrade their detection tools to defend different frequencies.
Enterprise extensive area from the initial location	This can be done using sensors.	- Expensive due to use of sensors. - Useless if a corrupt employee uses a directive antenna or lowers the signal strength.
RF monitoring	Exploiting additional information gathered at routers and switches.	- It depends extremely on a few features of IEEE 802.11, which can be easily stopped.
RAP detection through temporal characteristics	The arrival time of inter-packets is more random for wireless traffic than wired traffic.	- Direct connection to the WAP is mandatory. - This only works when the wireless host uploads the data.
Wired approaches	Detect APs by querying routers and switches for company MAC address assignments.	- It can fail because it can be easily spoofed or turned off by any RAP.
Mobile agent	Mobile Agent code is installed on all authorized nodes in the network.	- Mobile Agent code cannot be deployed without the agent's permission.

Some of the early methods use the Brute Force approach, where specific vulnerable AP detection software is installed on the laptop and admin would travel or roam around the company territory to detect the RAP. But it is more time-consuming and not always possible in a big company premises. Another way like enterprise-wide scan from a central location (where the central server receives data from the sensors that are assigned to the companies) is expensive. Again, radio frequency monitoring expects additional information involved in routers and switches. RAP then is detected through temporal characteristics and this requires inter-packet arrival time which is not static. Depending on the wired or wireless state, the state of the environment, and the number of nodes in that situation, the method can be complex or relatively easy. For wired approaches, APs are detected by querying the routers and switches for their company given MAC addresses. Table 12.2 shows some key RAP detection methods along with their limitations.

12.5 THE PARAMETERS

In this section, we discuss the parameters considered for our theoretical experiment to identify the rogue AP. To understand the parameters, we have described each one in separate sub-sections.

12.5.1 SSID

SSID stands for "*Service Set IDentifier*" [28]. SSID is the single identifier used to identify network names by a wireless AP. It is used as a very basic security measure. When more than one wireless network overlaps at a specific location, SSID ensures that the data have been transferred to the correct destination. For example, the owner of a wireless network can name the router or base station "TECNO." Users will see this name when browsing the available wireless networks in the area. It is basically a distinct 32-character string that ensures that network names are different from those of other close networks. Each packet sent via a wireless network contains an SSID, which ensures that the information transmitted via the air reaches the right destination. If there is no SSID, data would be transmitted and received anywhere by any wireless network in a completely haphazard or disorganized way.

12.5.2   MAC Address

MAC stands for *"Medium Access Control"* or *"Media Access Control"* [29]. A MAC address is a 48-bit hardware identification number that uniquely identifies every device on a network. MAC addresses are created on each network card, namely an Ethernet card or Wi-Fi card and it cannot be transferred. As there are billions of devices capable of networking from so many vendors, and each device has a single MAC address, there must be an extensive range of available addresses. For this, it is composed of hexadecimal number system and separated by colon. With MAC address filtering, only identified devices will be able to connect to the correct AP. The problem with enabling MAC address is that it increases the work on the user's part. Fortunately, the user does not need to memorize or know this address, as it is set by default on most networks.

12.5.3   Wi-Fi Scanner

The main function of a Wi-Fi scanner is to easily identify data from all nearby Wi-Fi networks. It is in two parts; one is hardware and the other is software scanner. For optimal signal quality, the user needs to find the AP of the *in-house* wireless network. Users can retrieve valuable information using Wi-Fi scanner tools such as SSID, bands, channels, security, and signals. To use a Wi-Fi scanner, there are a few things to consider like choosing the right time, measuring from the right location, and focusing on the scan to get the right results. Wi-Fi scanner supports IEEE 802.11 ac and IEEE 802.11a/b/g/n and detects security standards such as WEP, WPA, or WPA2 for wireless networks.

12.5.4   Beacon Frames

Beacon frame is used for announcing the availability of the network and maintenance of tasks. It is transmitted periodically at a time called Target Beacon Transmission Time (TBTT). Beacons are designed to allow a station to find out everything it needs to match parameters with the Basic Service Set (BSS) and begin communications. The beacon's frame body resides between the header and the CRC (Cyclic Redundancy Check) field and constitutes the other half of the beacon frame. Each beacon frame carries the following information in the frame body: Timestamp, Beacon Interval, Capability Information, SSID, FH parameter set, DS parameter set, CF parameter set, IBSS (Independent BSS) parameter set, and TIM (Traffic Indication Map). Beacon frame informs SSID and also has the TIM Information element used by the stations which are in power saving mode, to retrieve buffered frames at AP. AP announces its capabilities to wireless stations around it.

12.5.5   Channel and Frequency

A channel is used to deliver useful signals from one or more transmitters to one or more receivers. A channel can transmit maximum rate of information which is measured in bits per second (bps). Now, for every channel, the particular frequencies are fixed; hence, if we set our particular access point with channel one, then if any other access point with a different channel comes in that area, we can easily recognize that the other AP is working on different channel and frequency.

12.5.6   RSSI (Received Signal Strength Indicator)

RSSI stands for Received Signal Strength Indicator. The unit of RSSI value is indicated by power ratio measured by dB (Decibels). The higher the RSSI value, the stronger the signal. When measured in negative numbers, the number that is closer to zero usually means better signal. For instance, −50 is a pretty good signal, −75 – is fairly reasonable, and − 100 is no signal at all. Table 12.3 shows a chart with some values.

TABLE 12.3
RSSI Range and Signal Quality

RSSI Range	Signal Quality
Better than –40 dB	Exceptional
–40 dB to –55 dB	Very Good
–55 dB to –70 dB	Good
–70 dB to –80 dB	Marginal
–80 dB and beyond	Intermittent to no operation

12.5.7 AUTHENTICATION TYPE

Authentication refers the user security on a network. This mechanism helps user communicate without any vulnerability with the other end. It allows only the authenticated or verified user on a network to perform the intended task. For this, a system control matches the credentials of a user with the database credentials of a user. Three types of authenticate mechanisms are: 1) WEP 2) WEP I 3) WEP II. We use the Wi-Fi internet connection at office, home, and places where they are installed providing the security of the mobile phone. WPA II is the latest one for the authentication mechanism. We can choose that provided by our ISP (Internet Service Provider) and then make our communication secure.

12.5.8 RADIO TYPE

Wi-Fi works through the radio. Data could be transmitted and received through antennas on all Wi-Fi enabled devices. Radio is used on all devices to communicate via Wi-Fi, e.g., Wi-Fi-talkie, Mobile phone, etc. Radio signals are electromagnetic signals and a radio wave works like an ocean wave. Devices transmit and receive radio waves converted by 1 s and 0 s and converted back into 1 s and 0 s. Wi-Fi Radio uses IEEE 802.11 standard and there are different types of 802.11 networking standards. 802.11a, 802.11n, and 802.11 ac use the more heavily regulated 4.915–5.825 GHz band. These are commonly referred to as the "2.4 GHz and 5 GHz bands." Again, 802.11b, 802.11g, and 802.11n-2.4 utilize the 2.400–2.500 GHz spectrum.

12.6 SYSTEM ARCHITECTURE

The process of identifying rogue APs works in two ways:

1. **User Mode**: User mode is used to display authorized APs and RAPs on the network. In user mode, the particular user will be able to see only the list of authorized and unauthorized APs.
2. **Administrative Mode**: Administrative mode is used for giving authorization to an AP within a network. Using this mode, a number of nodes can be added to the network or unauthorized AP can be authorized, if need be.

Figure 12.5 shows an architecture of an application which could help a user see the output (directly as the authorized or unauthorized or RAP) once the application is launched. In this case, the administrative body would use a Wi-Fi scanner (AP scanner) that would scan the number of access points in that region/range. It would then capture the beacon frame from the AP that is broadcast frequently. To work, like scanning certain Wi-Fi signals, the beacon frame would capture different parameters. Especially, the parameters that would be extracted from the adopted beacon frame

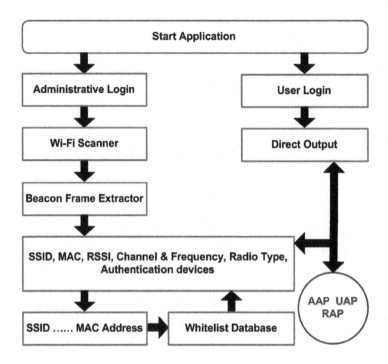

FIGURE 12.5   System architecture. Here (AAP, authorized AP; UAP, unauthorized AP; RAP, rogue access point).

are – SSID, MAC address, RSSI, Channel & Frequency, radio type, and authentication of the entire authorized node in the network.

All this information about that AP could be saved on the whitelist, which is referred to as a database. After around 10–20 milliseconds, this process would be repeated again (for identification). After that, we will be relearning the particular model in order to shake the number of parameters available at that time instance. Then, we will check the newly entered parameters for the AP which are authorized parameter; that are already stored in the whitelist database. Based on any discrepancy, our tool will declare it as an Authorized, Unauthorized, or RAP. The working mechanism of the system could be written as:

1. Beginning of the Application.
2. Enter (Log in) Application.
3. Enable Wi-Fi Scanner.
4. Take the title information of scanned Wi-Fi AP.
5. Extract the packet information from the title information.
6. Get a list of APs with details (properties).
7. Identify the RAP from the list of APs.
8. Supply a whitelist for identification.
9. Get the output.
10. Completion of Application.

From this Figure 12.5, we can see that user mode can automatically define which are Authorized, Unauthorized, or RAPs. But in administrative mode, there is a Wi-Fi scanner which would scan the APs in that area and then it will capture the Beacon Frames from that APs that they are frequently broadcasting. If any mismatch is found, our tool will declare the status of that AP accordingly.

12.7 EXPERIMENTAL SETTING

12.7.1 THE SETTING

We have created an experimental setup to assess how our mechanism works in real-life (see Figure 12.5). The AP/Wi-Fi Scanner is the server center where the admin will control and examine the system. AP scanner is a software that will be installed on a computer to test RAP on a network. The node can be PC, laptop, or any kind of device. Each individual node has a separate SSID, MAC address, and RSSI. All the parameters mentioned earlier will be scanned by AP scanner.

To identify the RAP(s), the algorithm that is applied is mentioned here:

Algorithm – RAP Identifying

Input:

H^* ← Whitelist of access points in the network.

A_t ← Legitimate access point.

B_N ← Beacon fames captured from the network N.

Output:

A_{AAP} ← Authorized access point list.

R_{AP} ← Rogue access point list.

A_{UAP} ← Unauthorized access point list.

Begin:

Step 1:

B_N, beacon frame captured by the system.

H^*, read whitelist of the access points in the network.

Step 2:

B_{mac} ← B_N, Extract MAC address of the sender AP from the beacon frame.

B_{ch} ← B_N, Extract Channel Number of the sender AP from the beacon frame.

B_{ssid} ← B_N, Extract SSID of the sender AP from the beacon frame.

B_{enc} ← B_N, Extract encryption configuration of the sender AP from the beacon frame.

B_{rst} ← B_N, Extract receives signal strength of the sender AP from the beacon frame.

Step 3: Compare B_{ssid} with H^*_{ssid}

If not matched, then add to rogue AP list and go to step 1.
Step 4: Compare B_{mac} with H^*_{mac}

If not matched, then add to rogue AP list and go to step 1.
Step 5: Compare B_{ch} with H^*_{ch}

If not matched, then add to rogue AP list and go to step 1.
Step 6: Compare B_{enc} with H^*_{enc}

If not matched, then add to rogue AP list and go to step 1.
Step 7: Compare B_{rst} with H^*_{rst}

If not matched, then add to rogue AP list and go to step 1.

If any discrepancies are found, our tool will declare that AP as a rogue AP.

Based on any mismatch found during the scan, our tool will declare whether the AP is a RAP, an authorized AP or an unauthorized AP. This is a theoretical concept for RAP identification. The detection process would be easier if this tool can be created and installed on the system. Such an algorithm is proposed in the work presented in [30]. The algorithm describes the working procedure of AP scanner tool where initially the admin panel would declare which APs are authorized and which are unauthorized in a particular network. Then the AP scanner will work to find out the authorized and unauthorized access points further in every 10 seconds for the network. For this process, new AP will be captured by the Beacon Frames and the new AP will be compared with whitelist database that has initially declared which are authorized. New AP will be compared with MAC address, Channel Number, SSID, Encryption, and Received Signal Strength of the sender AP. If any mismatch is found with whitelist database, our tool will declare it as an RAP.

Let us do an experiment – let the admin panel initially have declared some APs to be authorized and some unauthorized as in Table 12.4. Now, if we look into Table 12.5, we can see an entry with the same SSID with same name that is (Akil with MAC Address EF … D3). Its authorization type is *open* and that has similarity but for the MAC Address, our tool found some dissimilarity (a different MAC address with same SSID). That is why our tool declared it as a RAP.

On the other hand, for Table 12.6, every parameter got similarities except the authorization type (that is "*WPA personal*") but initially the admin panel declared it of '*Open*' type (Table 12.4). Hence, AP scanner tool declared it as a RAP with SSID, Akil. Finally, if we have a look into Table 12.7, the dissimilarity is found also with the RSSI (in addition to the mismatch for authorization type) that was initially set −30 but for this time, it is found −60; that is the reason it has been declared as a RAP. For all the parameters, this system will check and do comparison with all APs with the aid of a whitelist database, and it will decide the status. Figure 12.6 shows an AP scanner and some nodes that are scanned (thematic image).

TABLE 12.4
Table of Authorized and Unauthorized APs Existing in Network

ID	SSID	Authorization	MAC Address	RSSI	Channel	Frequency	Radio Type	AP Type
1.	Akil	Open	EF..........D3	−30	6	243.7 MHz	802.11a	Authorized
2.	Parsa	WPA Personal	5E..........67	−35	11	246.2 MHz	802.11g	Unauthorized
3.	TecIQ	WPA Personal	6E..........26	−26	6	243.7 MHz	802.11a	Unauthorized
4.	Tec123	WPA Personal	5C..........6E	−20	9	245.2 MHz	802.11g	Authorized

TABLE 12.5
Rogue AP Found with a Suspicious Entry for MAC Address

ID	SSID	Authorization	MAC Address	RSSI	Channel	Frequency	Radio Type	AP Type
1.	Akil	Open	EF.......D3	−30	6	243.7 MHz	802.11a	Authorized
2.	Parsa	WPA Personal	5E.......67	−35	11	246.2 MHz	802.11g	Unauthorized
3.	Akil	Open	EF.......76	−30	6	243.7 MHz	802.11a	Rogue AP
4.	Tec123	WPA Personal	5C.......6E	−20	9	245.2 MHz	802.11g	Authorized

TABLE 12.6
Rogue AP Found with a Suspicious Entry for Authorization Type

ID	SSID	Authorization	MAC Address	RSSI	Channel	Frequency	Radio Type	AP Type
1.	Akil	Open	EF....D3	−30	6	243.7 MHz	802.11a	Authorized
2.	Parsa	WPA Personal	5E....67	−35	11	246.2 MHz	802.11g	Unauthorized
3.	Akil	WPA Personal	EF....D3	−30	6	243.7 MHz	802.11g	Rogue AP
4.	Tec123	WPA Personal	5C....6E	−20	9	245.2 MHz	802.11a	Unauthorized

TABLE 12.7
Rogue AP Found with Suspicious Entries for RSSI and Authorization Type

ID	SSID	Authorization	MAC Address	RSSI	Channel	Frequency	Radio Type	AP Type
1.	Akil	Open	E5.....D3	−30	6	243.7 MHz	802.11a	Authorized
2.	Parsa123	WPA Personal	5C.....67	−35	11	246.2 MHz	802.11g	Unauthorized
3.	Akil	WPA Personal	E5.....D3	−60	6	243.7 MHz	802.11g	Rogue AP
4.	Tec123	WPA Personal	5C.....6E	−20	9	245.2 MHz	802.11a	Authorized

This procedure can be effective for a small organization, but for large companies, we need to adopt more effective and specialized strategies for detecting rogue AP. Plenty of proprietary solutions are available from various reputable vendors. Many of these systems can be established for per square meter. We have to keep in mind that walls and other barriers can further reduce Wi-Fi signals that can stop or hinder the tracking process. Rogue APs can also be on different floors or hide in some inaccessible area. In this situation, it is the best to shrink the space as much as possible and

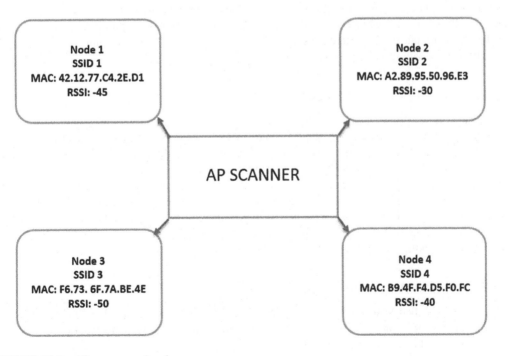

FIGURE 12.6 AP scanner and nodes.

then, go to another floor or get proper permission to check the locked rooms to determine exactly where the rogue device is. We need to monitor the entire management process of individual department within an organization and control network access by operating from a single centralized platform. In this way, the entire method can be made more effective to find and purge out rogue APs and then also, rogue users entering the network.

12.7.2 Discussion on the Results

From our experiments, it has been observed that if we consider all the parameters for rogue AP detection, it will be more efficient for the companies. Intruders always try to find easy vulnerabilities to gain access to the network so that they can capture information with little effort. Most of the time, intruders try to gain access using these parameters that we tested. The network will be much more secure if the admin can ensure the security of the proposed parameters. For this, we have tried to provide users with a solution on how to keep their networks and data secure. Currently, most vendors use their tools to provide some kind of solution where one can find the best solution but it is expensive for users and small organizations. Our effort was to find a simple and affordable solution for them. In the future, our plan is to develop a software tool for the organization using this concept so that users can easily secure their network from outsiders or unauthorized APs. Just running this tool would be enough to secure the connection while using it for any social or other networking activities.

12.8 SOME COUNTERMEASURES FOR RAP

As we noted before, a RAP is a wireless AP that has been established on a network without the administrator's approval. Several types of attacks can be launched with RAP. There are a few general network protection mechanisms that could prevent unauthorized access to the wireless network and protect the data.

Of course, the best way to secure the wireless data in such network is to use encryption or cryptography with wireless password. When the network encryption is enabled, the wireless communications will be undisclosed or encrypted, so the data would not be read or published by anyone else except the legitimate entities. Here are some other mechanisms that could be employed for ensuring security in such setting to keep away inclusion or use of RAP.

12.8.1 Implement Physical Security Controls

Physical protection plays a big role in the entire security setting of a network. Without physical protection, many of the security principles can be violated. Keycard locks and biometric locks can be used to secure the server room. Biometric locks are apparently a key solution, but they seem expensive. Moreover, most of the biometric technology is still new and comparatively unapproved. There are different types of keycard locks, but the magnetic stripe of most of their cards encodes the card owner's unity. The card readers are connected to a core computer that tracks card scans. Therefore, if someone is not allowed to access the computer closet and tries to drive his card anyway, then the computer informs the authorities that someone is trying to get access. It is also a good idea to detach unutilized network jacks [31].

12.8.2 Identify Authorized Devices

This process is called MAC address filtering. Each device has its own unique identification number which includes Medium/Media Access Control, including filtering MAC addresses; only authorized devices will be able to connect to the APs.

12.8.3 Build and Use Network Access Control

This is really important because most wireless APs come with a default username and a default password or without a password to access the wireless AP configuration utility. Each wireless AP lets one set up a password so that he can authenticate any changes to the wireless AP. If one does not change this, some external entity or someone from outside the network could potentially access the wireless AP configuration utility and change all of the settings to grant further access to the malicious or other rogue users.

12.8.4 Actively Monitor Network-Connected Devices

The admin should actively monitor which devices have access to or are involved with the network. Otherwise, intruders can easily enter the network. Once intruders gain access to the network, they can create attacks from within the network to compromise more of the other users.

12.8.5 Enable the Web Firewall

Most wireless APs come with a built-in firewall. They are designed to connect the wireless network to any other network, whether it is a DSL (Digital Subscriber Line) internet connection or just a modem internet connection or a corporate Ethernet network. One can enable a firewall in the wireless AP that prevents traffic from the wired network to the wireless network unless it is authorized and similarly, does not control the traffic from the wireless access point on the wired network. Again, this is a security measure that would prevent anyone from accessing the wireless network illegitimately.

12.8.6 Advanced Switch Port Monitoring Tool

Monitoring tools are used to monitor the state of the system in regular use, so the greatest warning is found, errors or problems can be identified and fixed to improve the system. There are a good number of surveillance equipment and tools available for servers, networks, databases, websites, and applications to ensure security and expected performance from them. Nagios XI, ManageEngine OpManager are the examples of such types of tools.

12.8.7 Corporate Policy and User Awareness

Employees who install APs often do not realize the safety hazards of their activities. To make them aware of the consequences and encourage the safety principles, the wireless safety policy should be clearly declared. Anybody who uses the network needs to at least skim through the policies and terms and conditions. This can be provided when connecting to a network and the IT (information technology) department can manage this.

12.8.8 Mutual Authentication

Mutual authentication of the customer and the authenticator diminishes the possibility of a corporate user to get authenticated by a RAP; which can prevent an invader from hijacking another user's authenticity.

12.8.9 Sniffers and WIDS

Sniffer equipment and a wireless intrusion detection system (WIDS) could be used to see continuous wind for any wireless signals and to go through the data. Then comparisons can be performed for the signals marked against the list of potential wireless devices for allocation if a RAP is present.

12.9 CONCLUSIONS

If not configured correctly, wireless network could be insecure and then, it can expose the users of it to various types of security attacks and especially, while using social networks, can make the user's personal information available to unauthorized entities. RAPs can be used by the attackers to infiltrate a network and do serious harm. Hence, as a part of efficient strategy of any type of users in a network and especially those who use the network frequently to connect with the world via social networks, we need to identify and tackle RAPs in such settings. In this work, we have discussed some generic information to address this issue and then presented some simple yet effective method to secure such wireless network from unwanted APs. Also, we have brought the other issues and measures that can be used for successful handling of RAPs.

REFERENCES

1. Hamid, A., Alam, M., Sheherin, H., and Pathan, A.-S. K. "Cyber Security Concerns in Social Networking Service," *International Journal of Communication Networks and Information Security*, vol. 12, no. 2, 2020, pp. 198–212.
2. Pathan, A.-S. K. *Security of Self-Organizing Networks: MANET, WSN, WMN, VANET*. New York: Auerbach Publications, CRC Press, Taylor & Francis Group, 2010. ISBN: 978-1-4398-1919-7.
3. Kim, T., Park, H., Jung, H., and Lee, H. "Online Detection of Fake Access Points Using Received Signal Strengths," *2012 IEEE 75th Vehicular Technology Conference (VTC Spring)*, 6–9 May 2012, Yokohama, Japan, 2012. doi:10.1109/VETECS.2012.6240312.
4. "Types of Wireless Network Explained with Standards," *CCNA Study Guide*, available at: https://www.computernetworkingnotes.com/ccna-study-guide/types-of-wireless-network-explained-with-standards.html (last accessed: 6 Nov. 2020)
5. "Wireless Network," *Techopedia*, Nov. 14, 2016, available at: https://www.techopedia.com/definition/26186/wireless-network (last accessed: 6 Nov. 2020).
6. Jadhav, S., Vanjale, S. B., and Mane, P. B. "Illegal Access Point Detection Using Clock Skews Method in Wireless LAN," *2014 International Conference on Computing for Sustainable Global Development (INDIACom)*, New Delhi, India, 2014.
7. "802.11I Overview," Feb. 2005, available at: https://ieee802.org/16/liaison/docs/80211-05_0123r1.pdf (last accessed: 7 Nov. 2020).
8. Yang, C., Song, Y., and Gu, G. "Active User-Side Evil Twin Access Point Detection Using Statistical Techniques," *IEEE Transactions on Information Forensics and Security*, vol. 7, no. 5, Oct. 2012, pp. 1638–1651.
9. Ma, L., Teymorian, A. Y., and Cheng, X. "A Hybrid Rogue Access Point Protection Framework for Commodity Wi-Fi Networks," *IEEE INFOCOM 2008 – The 27th Conference on Computer Communications*, 13–18 Apr. 2008, Phoenix, AZ, USA, 2008. doi:10.1109/INFOCOM.2008.178.
10. Pathan, A.-S. K. *The State of the Art in Intrusion Prevention and Detection*. New York: CRC Press, Taylor & Francis Group, Jan. 2014. ISBN: 9781482203516.
11. Wu, W., Gu, X., Dong, K., Shi, X., and Yang, M. "PRAPD: A Novel Received Signal Strength–Based Approach for Practical Rogue Access Point Detection," *International Journal of Distributed Sensor Networks*, vol. 14, no. 8, SAGE Publishing, 2018. doi:10.1177/1550147718795838.
12. Anmulwar, S., Srivastava, S., Mahajan, S. P., Gupta, A. K., and Kumar, V. "Rogue Access Point Detection Methods: A Review," *International Conference on Information Communication and Embedded Systems (ICICES2014)*, 27–28 Feb. 2014, Chennai, India, 2014. doi:10.1109/ICICES.2014.7034106.
13. Nakhila, O. and Zou, C. "User-Side Wi-Fi Evil Twin Attack Detection Using Random Wireless Channel Monitoring," *MILCOM 2016 – 2016 IEEE Military Communications Conference*, 1–3 Nov. 2016, Baltimore, MD, USA, 2016. doi:10.1109/MILCOM.2016.7795501.
14. Vanjale, S. and Mane, P. B. "A Novel Approach for Elimination of Rogue Access Point in Wireless Network," *2014 Annual IEEE India Conference (INDICON)*, 11–13 Dec. 2014, Pune, India, 2014. doi:10.1109/INDICON.2014.7030418.

15. Godber, A. and Dasgupta, P. "Countering Rogues in Wireless Networks," *Proceedings of 2003 International Conference on Parallel Processing Workshops*, 6–9 Oct. 2003, Kaohsiung, Taiwan, Taiwan, 2003. doi:10.1109/ICPPW.2003.1240398.

16. Kim, I., Seo, J., Shon, T., and Moon, J. "A Novel Approach to Detection of Mobile Rogue Access Points," *Security and Communication Networks*, Wiley, vol. 7, no. 10, Oct. 2014, pp. 1510–1516.

17. Lu, Q., Qu, H., Zhuang, Y., Lin, X.-J., and Ouyang, Y. "Client-Side Evil Twin Attacks Detection Using Statistical Characteristics of 802.11 Data Frames," *IEICE Transactions on Information and Systems*, vol. E101-D, no. 10, 2018, pp. 2465–2473.

18. Han, H., Sheng, B., Tan, C. C., Lin, Q., and Lu, S. "A Timing-Based Scheme for Rogue AP Detection," *IEEE Transactions on Parallel and Distributed Systems*, vol. 22, no. 11, Nov. 2011, pp. 1912–1925.

19. Ahmad, N. M., Amin, A. H. M., Kannan, S., Abdollah, M. F., and Yusof, R. "Detecting Access Point Spoofing Attacks Using Partitioning-Based Clustering," *Journal of Networks*, vol. 9, no. 12, 2014, pp. 3470–3477.

20. Gill, R., Smith, J., Looi, M., and Clark, A. "Passive Techniques for Detecting Session Hijacking Attacks in IEEE 802.11 Wireless Networks," In Kerr, K, Clark, A, & Mohay, G (Eds.), *AusCERT: Asia Pacific Information Technology Security Conference: Refereed R&D Stream: Proceedings.* University of Queensland [CD ROM], pp. 26–38.

21. Beyah, R., Kangude, S., Yu, G., Strickland, B., and Copeland, J. "Rogue Access Point Detection Using Temporal Traffic Characteristics," *IEEE Global Telecommunications Conference, 2004. GLOBECOM'04*, 29 Nov.–3 Dec. 2004, Dallas, TX, USA, 2004.

22. Shivaraj, G. Song, M., and Shetty, S. "Using Hidden Markov Model to Detect Rogue Access Points," *Security and Communication Networks*, vol. 3, no. 5, Wiley, 2010, pp. 394–407.

23. Jana, S. and Kasera, S. K. "On Fast and Accurate Detection of Unauthorized Wireless Access Points Using Clock Skews," *IEEE Transactions on Mobile Computing*, vol. 9, no. 3, Mar. 2010, pp. 449–462.

24. Alotaibi, B. and Elleithy, K. "Rogue Access Point Detection: Taxonomy, Challenges, and Future Directions," *Wireless Personal Communications*, vol. 90, Springer, 2016, pp. 1261–1290.

25. Sriram, V. S. S., Sahoo, G., and Agrawal, K. K. "Detecting and eliminating Rogue Access Points in IEEE-802.11 WLAN – A Multi-Agent Sourcing Methodology," *2010 IEEE 2nd International Advance Computing Conference (IACC)*, 19–20 Feb. 2010, Patiala, India, 2010. doi:10.1109/IADCC.2010.5422999.

26. Sawicki, K. and Piotrowski, Z. "The Proposal of IEEE 802.11 Network Access Point Authentication Mechanism Using a Covert Channel," *2012 19th International Conference on Microwaves, Radar & Wireless Communications*, 21–23 May 2012, Warsaw, Poland, 2012. doi:10.1109/MIKON.2012.6233587.

27. Thyer, J. "Covert Data Storage Channel Using IP Packet Header," *SANS Technology Institute* [Whitepaper], 2008, available at: https://www.sans.org/reading-room/whitepapers/covert/paper/2093 (last accessed: 24 Nov. 2020)

28. "SSID," *TechTerms*, available at: https://techterms.com/definition/ssid (last accessed: 30 Nov. 2020)

29. "MAC Address," *TechTerms*, available at: https://techterms.com/definition/macaddress (last accessed: 30 Nov. 2020).

30. Vanjale, S. and Mane, P. B. "Detection of Rogue Access Point Using Various Parameters," in *Advances in Intelligent Systems and Computing book series (AISC)*, vol. 468, Springer, 2016, pp. 699–710.

31. Bogue, R. L. "Lock IT Down: Don't Overlook Physical Security on Your Network," *TechRepublic*, available at: https://www.techrepublic.com/article/lock-it-down-dont-overlook-physical-security-on-your-network/ (last accessed: 28 Dec. 2020)

13 A Tutorial on Cross-Site Scripting Attack
Defense against Online Social Networks

Vassilis Papaspirou
University of Thessaly, Lamia, Greece

Leandros Maglaras
De Montfort University, Leicester, UK

Mohamed Amine Ferrag
Guelma University, Guelma, Algeria

CONTENTS

13.1 INTRODUCTION

Nowadays the World Wide Web (WWW) has been changed to a multifaceted system by incorporating a wide assortment of parts and advancements including client-side advances [1], server-side advances [2], HTTPs protocol, and wide assortment of different innovations. Web applications created on these stages try to cope with a wide range of clients, offering to them rich highlights of these cutting-edge innovations. Existing vulnerabilities among these advances present the challenge of applying those protective safety methods for the improvement of web applications. Albeit, current protective measures offer limited support to modern web applications [3].

Accordingly, a high number of internet-based web applications are defenseless against many vulnerabilities. White Hat Security's Website Security Statistics Report [4] offers a sort of

DOI: 10.1201/9781003134527-17

recognition on the present issues of security of web applications and worries that enterprises should bargain for playing out the online business in a protected manner. This website has been circulating the security bits of knowledge report on the WWW since year 2006. They have examined vulnerabilities on popular applications: Managing an account, Monetary Administrations, Wellbeing Care, Protections, and Retail. They have broken down the vulnerabilities of those independently. In light with some parameters they set up a score card for these spaces:

- Always Vulnerable
- Frequently Vulnerable
- Regularly Vulnerable
- Occasionally Vulnerable
- Rarely Vulnerable

Common Weakness Enumeration (CWE™) is a view to the top most dangerous software errors – weaknesses (CWE). The CWE list is maintained by MITRE Corporation [5] and it has XSS attack as the top widespread and critical weakness that can be discovered and exploited as software vulnerabilities. XSS attacks are simple attacks, since it's very simple to find exploitable vulnerabilities on modern websites. In general, viably anticipating XSS vulnerabilities is likely to include a combination of several measures including static testing, code audits, and dynamic testing along with applying secure coding techniques.

XSS Worm, identified also as a cross-site scripting virus, is a malicious code that instantly propagates itself to visitors to a website that tries to infect other visitors gradually. Cross-site scripting worms are a variation of one of the oldest security challenges in a web browser, cross-site scripting, which is a virus of new age flaws. A version of the stored XSS attack is the web server worm. This form of worm replicates itself using the current XSS vulnerability of web applications in other areas of web pages [6].

Previous research work reveals that XSS worms can be planted in specific places in a Social Networking Service [7, 8] in order to hijack the user's account. The attacker tries to lure a user to click on the infected link or even visit an infected web page in order to execute the malicious script at the browser side. Social networks are in fact an easy target for such attacks since many users click on links without much thought maybe out of curiosity or due to trust of their peers.

Smartphone user authentication is vital to many everyday uses, such as social networks, shopping, and banking. The compromise between protection and convenience is the secret to user authentication. A solution, though simple to use, must be safe. A variety of attempts have been undertaken to tackle this issue. PIN number, the most simple and conventional form, has both convenience (e.g., user lost pass code) and protection concerns (e.g., shoulder-surfing attacks). Authentication dependent on facial recognition may be spoofed by the user's photographs or videos quickly. Easy twists are vulnerable to video, threats, such as needing eye blinks. The most safe approach is potentially to check the iris, but it needs specific sensors not found on most mobile devices.

Although handy for authentication, fingerprint sensors face the challenge presented by the trend of ever – screen size, leaving little space for fingerprint sensors. Apple's Face ID, the new attempt, packs a dot projector, a flood illuminator, and an infrared depth sensor to detect the 3D form of the face in a small area, thereby achieving high protection while saving space. Special sensors, however, also take precious frontal space and cost extra (around 5% of their bill of materials).

In this chapter we present tutorials of two XSS attacks (JavaScript attack [9] and SQL injection [10]). JavaScript injection is a process by which we can insert and use our own JavaScript code in a page, either by entering the code into the address bar, or by finding an XSS vulnerability in a website. SQL infusion may be a web security helplessness that permits an assailant to meddle with the questions that an application makes to its database. It permits an attacker to see information that they are not regularly able to recover. This may be information that has a location for other customers, or any other information that can be used through the application itself. In numerous instances, this knowledge may be changed or deleted by an aggressor, creating tireless modifications to the substance or actions of the application. An aggressor may lift a SQL infusion attack in a few situations to compromise the simple server or other back-end configuration or execute a denial-of-service attack.

The contributions of the chapter are:

- It presents theoretical and technical information about XSS vulnerabilities and attacks
- It analytically presents simple scenarios of XSS attacks in form of JavaScript and SQL attacks
- It is accompanied by code that is uploaded on GitHub at the following dedicated link: https://github.com/vapapaspirou/javascript-and-sqlinjection
- It can be used as a self-learning or teaching tool for security students or professionals

The rest of the chapter is structured as follows. Section 13.2 includes basic information about XSS attacks. Section 13.3 presents the different types of XSS attacks. Section 13.4 presents the JavaScript attack-defense tutorial. Section 13.5 presents the SQL injection attack-defense tutorial. Finally, Section 13.6 concludes the chapter.

13.2   WHAT IS XXS

Cross-scripts (also called XSS) [11] are internet protection vulnerabilities that enable an attacker to use users' interactions with an application. It allows an attacker to ignore the security policy, which is meant to differentiate distinct websites from one another. Typically, inter-site script vulnerabilities permit an attacker to hide himself as a user, operate any moves that the consumer might also perform, and get right of entry to any of the information of the user. Although there is no single, standardized classification for XSS attacks they may be classified in three types. At least two primary sectors of XSS flaws may be distinguished: non-persistent and persistent [11]. Some sources further divide these two groups into traditional (caused by server-side code flaws) and DOM-based (in client-side code).

Non-persistent XSS vulnerabilities in a web application seem to permit malevolent destinations to attack its clients who are utilizing the app while being logged within. The non-persistent cross-site scripting vulnerability is by far the foremost fundamental sort of web vulnerability. These gaps appear up when the information is given by a web client, most commonly in HTTP inquiry parameters (e.g., HTML shape submission), and have impacts instantly in the event that the server-side of the net app parses and shows a page to the client, without properly sanitizing it.

Since HTML archives have a level, serial structure that blends control statements, formatting, and the genuine substance, any non-validated user-supplied information included within the resulting page without legitimate HTML encoding, may lead to mark up injection [12]. A reflected attack is typically conveyed through e-mail or an impartial web location. The trap is an innocent-looking URL, pointing to a trusted location but containing the XSS vector. In the event that the trusted location is defenseless to the vector, clicking the interface can cause the victim's browser to execute the infused script.

The determined (or put away) XSS vulnerability could be a more annihilating variation of a cross-site scripting imperfection: it happens when the information given by the aggressor is spared by the server, and then permanently shown on "normal" pages returned to other clients within the course of regular browsing. A classic illustration is on online message boards where clients are permitted to post HTML designed messages for other clients to read. Persistent XSS vulnerabilities can be more critical than other sorts since an attacker's malicious script is rendered naturally, without the goal to independently target victims or bait them to a third-party site [13]. Especially within social networks, the code would self-propagate over accounts, making a sort of client-side worm [7].

The strategies of injection can shift an awesome bargain; in a few cases, the aggressor may not even need to specifically associate with the vulnerability itself to misuse such a hole. Any data received by the net application (by means of e-mail, framework logs, IM, etc.) that can be controlled by an attacker may become an attack vector.

Cross-Site Scripting (XSS) attacks occur when:

1. Data enters a web application through an untrusted source, most frequently a web request.
2. The data is included in dynamic content that is sent to a web user without being validated for malicious content.

The noxious substance sent to the internet browser frequently appears as a portion of JavaScript, however, may likewise incorporate HTML, Flash, or some other sort of code that the program may execute. The spectrum of XSS-dependent attacks is virtually unlimited, but they typically include sending private information, equivalent to treatments or other meeting details, to the victim, diverting the victim to web content restricted by the attacker, or executing various malevolent procedures on the computer of the client under the appearance of the legal website. It is also possible to divide XSS attacks into two groups: stored and mirrored. There is a third, much less well-known XSS attack form called DOM-based XSS [14].

13.3　TYPES OF ATTACK

13.3.1　Stored XSS Attacks

As mentioned in the previous section, in stored attacks the injected script is stored permanently on the target. This can be a database, a forum, a visitor log, several comment fields among other. The victim that visits the infected target and requests some information, retrieves the malicious scripts from the server. Stored XSS is referred as persistent threats.

13.3.2　Reflected XSS Attacks

Reflected assaults are those where the implanted substance is reflected off the net server as a response that consolidates some of the data sent to the server. Reflected attacks are passed on to casualties using other routes, for example, in an e-mail message. At the point when a client is tricked into tapping on a malignant link or indeed basically examining to a pernicious site, the embedded code mirrors the attack back to the client's program (see Figure 13.1). The program at that point executes the code since it originated from a "trusted" server. Reflected XSS to boot a few of the time implied to as non-persistent or type-II XSS.

13.3.3　DOM-Based XSS

DOM-based XSS (or because it is called in a few writings, "type-0 XSS") is an XSS assault wherein the payload is executed as a result of modifying the DOM "environment" within the victim's browser utilized by the first client-side script, so that the client-side code runs in an "unexpected" way. That's, the

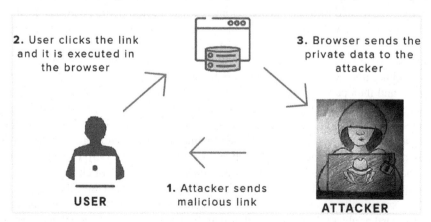

2. User clicks the link and it is executed in the browser

3. Browser sends the private data to the attacker

1. Attacker sends malicious link

USER

ATTACKER

FIGURE 13.1 Reflected attack XSS.

page itself does not alter, but the client-side code contained within the page executes in an unexpected way due to the malevolent adjustments that have happened within the DOM environment. This is in differentiate to other XSS assaults, wherein the payload is set within the page (due to a server-side attack).

Example

Suppose the following code is used to create a form to let the user choose his/her preferred language (see Figure 13.2). A default language is also provided in the query string, as the parameter "default."

The URL for the page is: http://www.some.site/page.html?default=French

If we send the following URL to a victim, then an attack (DOM-based XSS) can be executed to the page.

http://www.some.site/page.html?default=<script>alert(document.cookie)</script>.

The browser sends a request for a page which has an alert (document cookie) in the URL. This happens the moment the victim clicks on the link.

/page.html?default = <script>alert(document.cookie)</script>.

After the above move takes action, the server responds with the JavaScript code which is in the page. A DOM object is created by the browser for the page, where the document.location object contains the URL: http://www.some.site/page.html?default=<script>alert(document.cookie)</script>

The initial JavaScript code within the page does not anticipate the default parameter to contain HTML markup, and as such it essentially echoes it into the page (DOM) at runtime. The browser at that point executes the attacker's script.

The default parameter which contains HTML markup is not expected from the original JavaScript code which is in the page, so it returns it into the page (DOM) at runtime. The resulting page finally executes the script from the attacker.

alert(document.cookie).

Preventing cross-site scripting is trivial in some instances can be difficult depending on the complexity of the application and the ways it handles user-controllable data. In general, successfully preventing XSS vulnerabilities is probable to contain a combination of the following measures:

- Filter enters on arrival. At the point where consumer input is received, filter as strictly as feasible based on what is predicted or legitimate input.
- Encode information on output. At the point where user-controllable records are output in HTTP responses, encode the output to stop it from being interpreted as energetic content. Depending on the output context, this would possibly require making use of combos of HTML, URL, JavaScript, and CSS encoding.
- Use gorgeous response headers. To stop XSS in HTTP responses that don't seem to be meant to contain any HTML or JavaScript, you can use the Content-Type and X-Content-Type-Options headers to make sure that browsers interpret the responses in the way you intend.
- Content Security Policy. As a last line of defense, you can use content security policy (CSP) to reduce the severity of any XSS vulnerabilities that still occur.

```
…
Select your language:

<select><script>

document.write("<OPTION
value=1>"+document.location.href.substring(document.location.href.indexOf("default=")+8)+"</OPTION>");

document.write("<OPTION value=2>English</OPTION>");

</script></select>
…
```

FIGURE 13.2 Example Code for creation a form.

Encode data on output

Before client-controllable information is kept in touch with a website, encoding can be implemented easily, on the basis that the environment you are writing examines what kind of encoding you need to use. Values interior a JavaScript string, for instance, require a choice of getting away from those in an HTML environment. In an HTML context, you convert non-whitelisted values into HTML entities:

<*convertsto*: <

>*convertsto*: >

In a JavaScript string context, non-alphanumeric values should be Unicode-escaped:

<*convertsto*: \u003c

>*convertsto*: \u003e

You'll have to add different layers of encoding at the right request. For instance, you have to manage both the JavaScript setting and the HTML setting to securely include client contribution within an occasion handler. So, you have to get Unicode-away from the data first, and then HTML-encode it:

<a href = "#" onclick = "x" = "This string requires two layers of escaping" > test</a>

Validate entry on arrival

Encoding is probably the most critical XSS barrier line, but it is not sufficient in each particular situation to avoid XSS vulnerabilities. You should also authorize the input as carefully as possible, specifically when it is first obtained from a client. Input validation examples include:

- If a user submits a URL that is returned in a reply, verify that it starts off evolved with a tightly closed protocol such as HTTP and HTTPS. Otherwise, someone may use a malicious program to hack your website online.
- Validating that the value actually includes an integer, if a user presents a value that was supposed to be binary.
- The validation of the input requires only the expected character collection. Input validation by way of blocking off invalid enter ought to preferably work. An alternative method is extra inclined to error, attempting to easy invalid input to make it valid, and be avoided where feasible.

Whitelisting vs. blacklisting

Validation of inputs should usually use whitelists rather than blacklists. For example, just make a list of secure protocols (HTTP, HTTPS) instead of trying to make a list of all harmful protocols (JavaScript, info, etc.), and disallow anything not on the list. When new harmful protocols emerge, this will ensure that your protection does not break and make it less vulnerable to attacks that attempt to obfuscate invalid values to evade a blacklist.

Allowing "safe" HTML

Permitting clients to post HTML markup ought to be maintained a strategic distance from at every possible opportunity, yet now and then it's a business prerequisite. For instance, a blog website may permit remarks to be posted containing some constrained HTML markup. The exemplary methodology is to attempt to sift through conceivably unsafe labels and JavaScript. You can attempt to execute this utilizing a whitelist of safe labels and characteristics, yet because of errors in program parsing motors and peculiarities like transformation XSS, this methodology is incredibly hard to actualize safely. The least awful alternative is to utilize a JavaScript library that performs sifting and encoding in the client's program, for example, DOMPurify. Different libraries permit clients to give content in markdown organization and convert the markdown into HTML. Sadly, every one of these libraries have XSS vulnerabilities occasionally, so this is certifiably not an ideal arrangement. On the off chance that you do utilize one you should screen intently for security refreshes.

How to prevent XSS using a template engine server-side template engine such as Twig and Free Marker are used by many modern websites to embed complex content into HTML. These usually describe their own system of escaping. For instance, you can use the e) filter in Twig, with an argument that defines the context:

> user.firstname | e('html')

Some other template engines, such as Jinja and React, by contrast, avoid dynamic content, effectively preventing most XSS occurrences. When you decide whether to use a given template engine or system, we suggest carefully checking escape features.

How to stop XSS in PHP

There is a built-in encoding feature in PHP for entities called html entities. When within an HTML background, you can call this feature to escape your input. With three arguments, the function should be called:

- Your input strings.
- ENT_QUOTES, which is a flag that specifies all quotes should be encoded.
- The character set, which in most cases should be UTF-8.

For example: <?php echo htmlentities($input, ENT_QUOTES, 'UTF-8');?>.

When in a JavaScript string context, you need to Unicode-escape input as already described. Unfortunately, PHP doesn't provide an API to Unicode-escape a string. Here is some code to do that in PHP:

```php
<?php
function jsEscape($str) {
$output = ";"
$str = str_split($str); for($i=0;$i<count($str);$i++) {
$chrNum = ord($str[$i]);
$chr = $str[$i]; if($chrNum === 226) {
if(isset($str[$i+1]) &&ord($str[$i+1]) === 128) { if(isset($str[$i+2]) &&ord($str[$i+2]) === 168) {
$output.= '\u2028';
$i += 2; continue;
}
if(isset($str[$i+2]) &&ord($str[$i+2]) === 169) {
$output.= '\u2029';
$i += 2; continue;
```

```
}
}
}
switch($chr) { case " ":
case " ":
case "\n";
case "\r";
case "&";
case "\\";
case "<";
case ">";
$output.= sprintf("\\u%04x", $chrNum); break;
default:
$output.= $str[$i]; break;
}
}
return $output;
}
?>
```

Here we see how to use the jsEscape function in PHP:

```
<script>x =' <?php echo jsEscape($_GET['x'])?>';</script>
```
Alternatively, we could use a template engine.

How to prevent XSS client-side in JavaScript

You need your own HTML encoder to prevent user feedback in an HTML context in JavaScript. Here are several instances of JavaScript code that translates a string to HTML.:

```
function htmlEncode(str)
returnString(str).replace(/[^\w.]/gi, function(c)
return'&#' + c.charCodeAt(0)+';';
);
```

We would use then this function as follows:

```
<script>document.body.innerHTML = htmlEncode(untrustedValue)</script>
```

If your input is inside a JavaScript string, you need an encoder that performs Unicode escaping.

Here is a sample Unicode-encoder: function jsEscape(str)

```
returnString(str).replace(/[^\w.]/gi, function(c)
return'\\u' + ('0000' + c.charCodeAt(0).toString(16)).slice(-4);
);
```

You would then use this function as follows:

```
<script> document.write(I <script> x = "I + j sEscape(untrustedValue) + I"; <∨script> I) <
/script>
```

How to prevent XSS in jQuery

The foremost broadly recognized sort of XSS in jQuery is the point at which you pass client request to a jQuery selector. Web engineers would regularly utilize location.hash and pass it to the selector which would cause XSS as jQuery would render the HTML. jQuery seen this issue and settled their selector method of reasoning to check at whatever point input begins with a hash. Directly jQuery will conceivably render HTML if the principal character could be a <. On the off chance merely pass untrusted data to the jQuery selector, ensure you viably escape this value by using the jsEscape command.

Content security approach (CSP) is the final line of defense against cross-site scripting. In case that your XSS counteractions fail, you'll be able to utilize CSP to stop XSS by limiting what an attacker can do. CSP lets you control diverse things, for instance, notwithstanding of whether exterior substance can be stacked and whether inline substance will be executed. To communicate CSP you've got to consolidate a HTTP response header called content security policy. An example CSP is as follows: default-src 'self'; script-src 'self'; object-src 'none'; frame-src 'none'; base-uri 'none';

This approach indicates that assets such as pictures and scripts can be stacked as a page. So indeed, in case an attacker can effectively infuse an XSS payload they are counted as stack assets from the same root. This enormously decreases the chance that an attacker can misuse the XSS vulnerability. If you require stacking of external assets, guarantee you simply permit scripts that don't allow an attacker to take control of your webpage. For example, in case your whitelist certain spaces at that point an attacker can stack any script from those spaces. Where conceivable, attempt to have assets on your possessed space. On the off chance that that's not possible at that point you'll utilize hash- or nonce-based policy to allow scripts on different domains. A nonce could be an arbitrary string that's included as a quality of a script or asset, which can as it were be executed in case the irregular string matches the server-generated one. An attacker is incapable to figure the randomized string and so cannot conjure a script or asset with a substantial nonce and so the asset will not be executed.

13.4   TUTORIAL ON JAVASCRIPT ATTACK

First of all, we need some knowledge of PHP, HTML, and JavaScript. We need HTML to write our code and we need JavaScript to make our webpage more dynamic and add more effects. In our example we used CSS to make our webpage more beautiful and friendly to human eye.

HTML code

First of all, we must write the code, for the webpage we want. We constructed a simple one, with a button and a cell which we can write in it. The button will show us what we wrote in the cell. Quick and simple example for our cause, to show the attack. The code for the page is:

```
<!DOCTYPE html>
<html>
<head>
<title>JavaScript Attack</title>
<link href = "% static 'javascript/css/attack.css' %" rel = "stylesheet">
</head> <body>
<h1 class = "search-form-header"> JavaScript Attack</h1>
<form class = "search-form" autocomplete = "off">
<input class = "search-input" id = "query-input" type = "text" name = "query" />
<button class = "search-button" type = "submit" role = "button"> Hit it</button>
```

```
</form>
<h3 class = "search-query"> You texted: <span id = "query-output" class = "query"> </span></h3>
</li>
<script src = "% static 'javascript/js/jqValidation.js' %"> </script>
</body>
</html>
```

We will analyze the code later after we construct the JavaScript file. We make a new file and call it "static." In there we will put the JavaScript and the CSS file (optional). Inside the static file we make 1 new file named JavaScript. Next, inside JavaScript file we make 2 new files called js and css. In the js file we will make the JavaScript file and in the css file, the css.

JS file

The code for the JavaScript file is:
```
1. document.cookie = "username = vasilis"
2. document.cookie = "password = 123456"
3. if (document.readyState == 'loading')
4. document.addEventListener('DOMContentLoaded', ready)
5. else
6. ready()
7. function ready()
8. var. query = new URL(window.location).searchParams.get('query')
9. document.getElementById('query-input').value = query
10. document.getElementById('query-output').innerHTML = query
```

In the first line we see the document.cookie, which we need it to read and write cookies in our webpage. We insert our username and our password for example. The other command that we must give attention is the document.getElementById. This method returns an Element object representing the element whose id property matches the specified string. At the last row we use this method with innerHTML. This returns what we wrote in the box in our page. The innerHTML property sets or returns the HTML content (inner HTML) of an element.

13.4.1 How the Attack Works

The attack works with some lines of code, that need to be entered in the input box of our website. First, we present a simple example to see how our page works (see Figure 13.3). For this example, we put the word "hello."

Next, we initiate the attack procedure. First, we will try a line of code for understanding the existing vulnerability. The code we can insert is "<img src onerror = 'alert('hi')'>" and the webpage will return the message as shown in Figure 13.4:

Now that the attacker knows the vulnerability that exists in the code, he can try and steal our cookies by filling the input box with the line "<img src onerror = 'alert(document.cookie)'>." With this line the page executes the code and the result is to bring up in the alert box the cookies we have, in our case username and password (see Figure 13.5).

Javascript Attack

| hello | Hit it |

You texted: <u>hello</u>

FIGURE 13.3   Example of hello world.

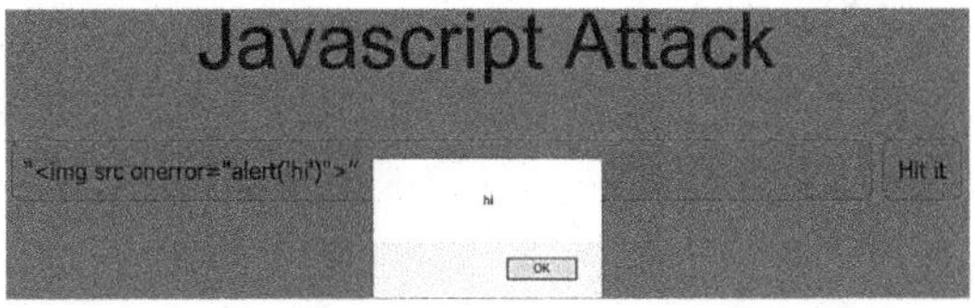

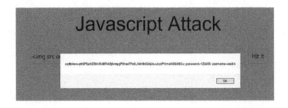

FIGURE 13.4   Our page when we input the command <img src onerror = "alert('hi')">.

Javascript Attack

FIGURE 13.5   <img src onerror = "alert(document.cookie)"> code and display.

13.4.2   MITIGATION OF THE ATTACK

Why this happens? Because the page executes the code as it's on the inner code. But why it read it and executed it like it's in the code? The answer is in the JavaScript code, in line 12 "document. getElementById('query-output').innerHTML = query." The innerHTML is the one which gives us the perforation of our page. The innerHTML property sets or returns the HTML content (inner HTML) of an element. This means that what we write in our box the page will understand as HTML code and it executes it. How to prevent it? We must change the code. We change innerHTML with innerText. With inner text whatever we write in the box will be interpreted as plain text, even if it includes code.

Now the attacker can't give any instruction-command to our system and cannot bypass the input page (see Figure 13.6).

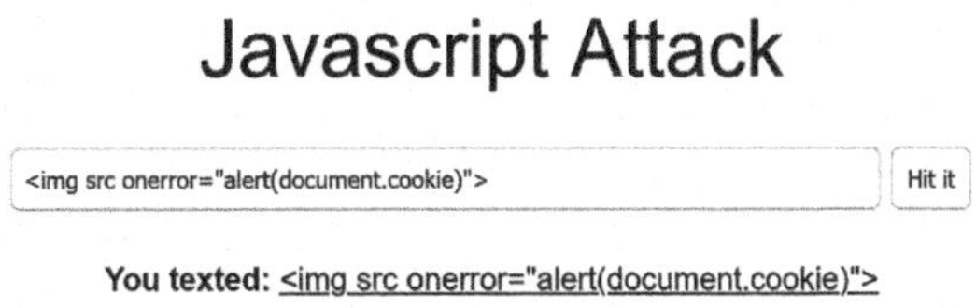

Javascript Attack

| <img src onerror="alert(document.cookie)"> | Hit it |

You texted: <u><img src onerror="alert(document.cookie)"></u>

FIGURE 13.6   Webpage after mitigation.

13.5 TUTORIAL ON SQL INJECTION ATTACK

We open a new file and we name the file sqlinjection.php. We need to name with the php at the end since we will put php code in and sql code also. Then we have to make our database before we continue. We use phpMyAdmin, and we must ensure that when we want to go to our virtual environment, WampServer is already running (down right, at the task bar). We write http://localhost/phpmyadmin at our browser (see Figure 13.7).

We fill at username the word "root" and at password we leave it blanc. At server choice we choose what server we want, we picked MariaDB. We hit go and we will enter our main page of phpMyAdmin (see Figure 13.8).

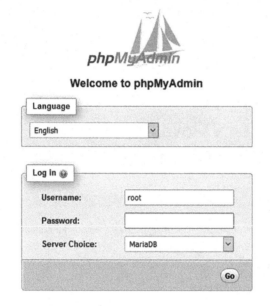

FIGURE 13.7   Initial screen.

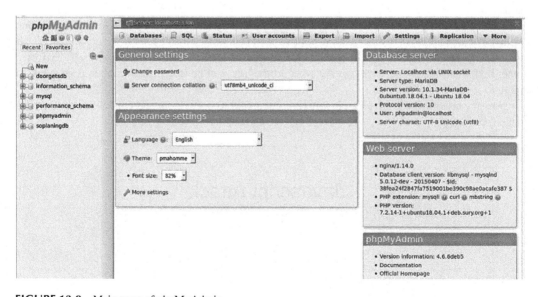

FIGURE 13.8   Main page of phpMyAdmin.

Now we can start building our database. We need to build a database with one name and one password for the login page we want to make. We choose new and write a name for the database. We give the name "sql injection" and in the box next to it we can choose freely since it doesn't have any impact. Finally, we hit the button create (see Figure 13.9).

Then we need to create our table which will have our name and password. At 'create table' we name the table, with our example we named it $_1admin_l ogin$ and at number of columns we select 3. Then we push the go button (see Figure 13.10).

Now we must write our parameters for each column. At first column we put at name the "id," because we need an id parameter which will increase each time one password is saved. We wrote for id = 1, for name = Vasilis and for password = 123456 as shown in Figure 13.11.

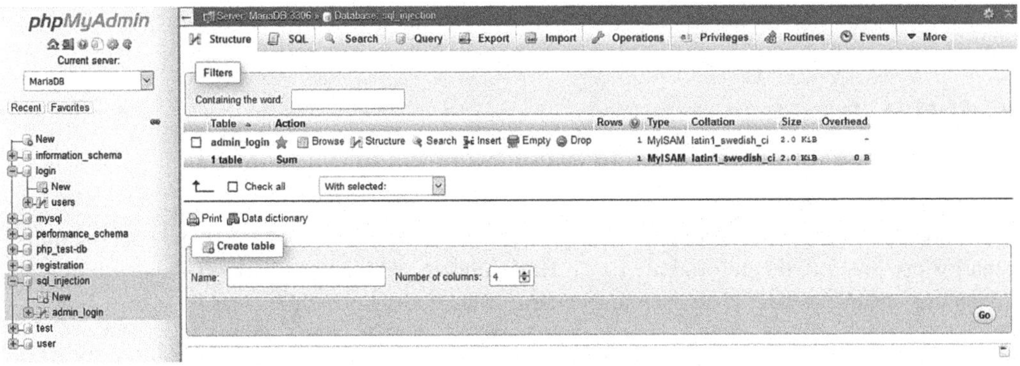

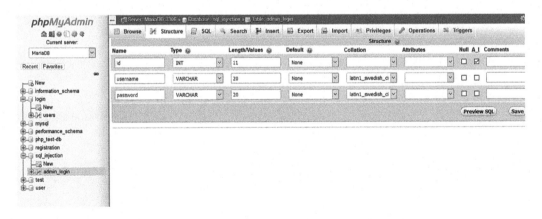

FIGURE 13.9 The database is created.

FIGURE 13.10 A snapshot of the table.

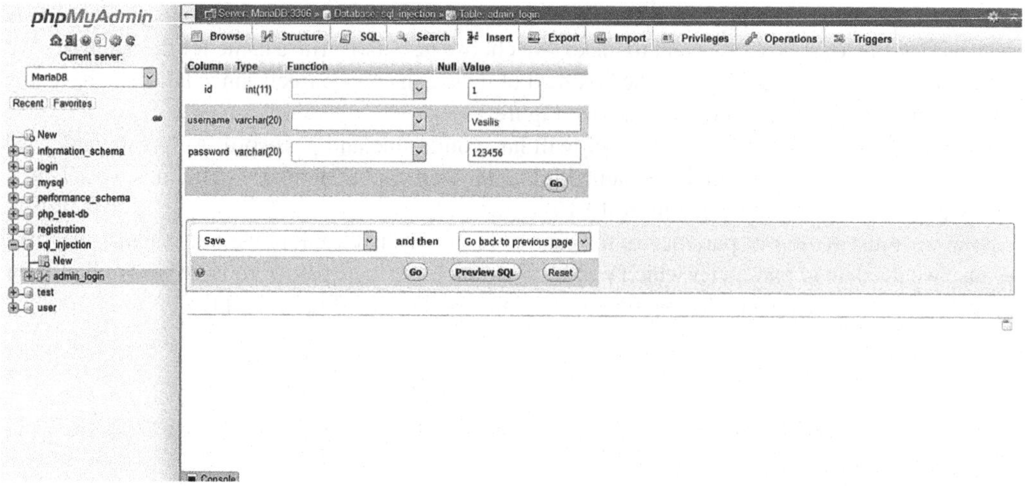

FIGURE 13.11 Inputs to the database tables.

The code that we use for executing the SQL injection is presented here. Also, the code for all the scenarios presented in this tutorial are on GitHub (https://github.com/vapapaspirou/javascript-and-sqlinjection) and the reader is advised to use them when going through the article.

1. <?php
2. if(isset(\$_POST['submit']))
3. {
4. $\$conn = mysqli_connect("localhost," "root," "sql_injection");$
5. $\$name = \$_POST['user'];$
6. $\$pwd = \$_POST['password'];$
7. $echo \$sql = "select * from admin_login where username = '\$name' and password = '\$pwd'";$
8. echo "<br/>";
9. $\$res = mysqli\_query(\$conn,\$sql);$
10. $if (mysqli\_num_rows(\$res)>0)$ {
11. echo "Login ok";
12. }
13. else
14. {
15. echo "Login failed";
16. }
17. }
18. ?>
19. <!DOCTYPE html>
20. <html>
21. <head>
22. <meta charset = "utf-8">
23. <title></title>
24. <link rel = "stylesheet" href = " ">
25. </head>
26. <style type = "text/css">

27. box input[type = "text"]{
28. border: none;
29. border-radius: 3px;
30. outline:none;
31. padding: 3px;
32. }
33. </style>
34. <body>
35. <div class = "box">
36. <center> <form method = "post">
37. <table>
38. <h1>SQL INJECTION</h1>
39. <tr>
40. <td>Name:-</td>
41. <td> <input type = "text" name = "user" value = "style" = "border: 0.5px solid \#111111">
42. </td>
43. </tr>
44. <tr>
45. <td>Password:-</td>
46. <td> <input type = "text" name = "password" value = "style" = "border: 0.5px solid
    \#111"> </td>
47. </tr>
48. <tr>
49. <td> <input type = "submit" name = "submit" value = "Login"> </td>
50. </tr>
51. </table>
52. </form></center>
53. </div>
54. </body>
55. </html>

13.5.1 How the Attack Works

Firstly, we must ensure we run WampServer; at the right bottom we will see the WampServer icon turned green. The next step is going to our browser and type ergasia.com. That's because we had created the virtual environment with that name. If we hadn't created a new environment, then we should type in the url box, localhost. With that we go to our environment and select the sql injection file and after sql injection php file. The webpage must now be in our browser. Now we write the name and password we have. If the code was correctly inserted, the page must write login ok as shown in Figure 13.12.

Now let's try and put wrong name and password. Login failed as shown in Figure 13.13.

Now we will write the line which bypasses our code. At the name we can write anything we want (although some restrictions like the size is considerable) and in password we write the line 'or'1 = 1 and we bypass authentication as shown in Figure 13.14.

The reason of this weakness is our code. It's in the meaning what conditions must be true to activate the rest of the code. The "password=" or $^1 1^1 = ^1 1^1$ condition is always true, so the password verification never happens. It can also be said that the above statement is more or less equal to, and provided that the condition is true then the system will tell, it must continue. Lines 7 and 8 are the ones that must change to prevent those attacks. $name = $_POST['user']; and $pass = $_POST['password']; The $_POST variable is an array of variable names and values sent by the HTTP POST method. The $_POST variable is used to collect values from a form with method = "post."

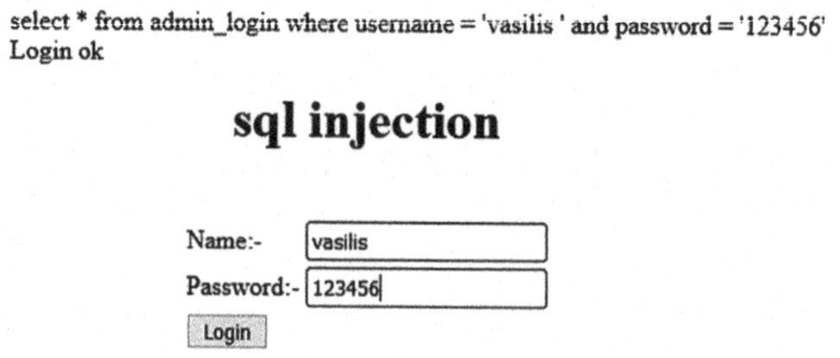

select * from admin_login where username = 'vasilis ' and password = '123456'
Login ok

sql injection

Name:- vasilis

Password:- 123456

Login

FIGURE 13.12 Successful login.

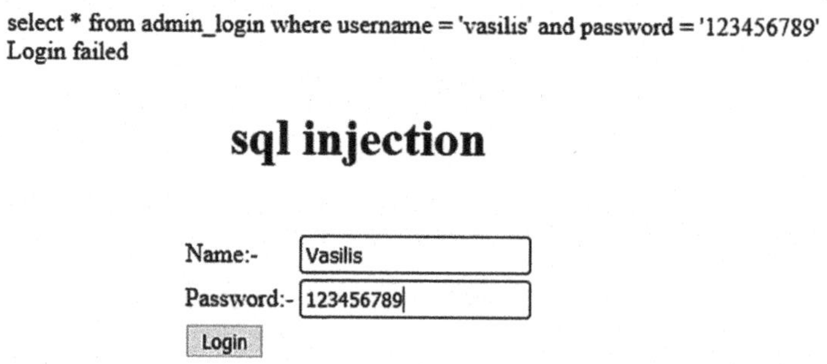

select * from admin_login where username = 'vasilis' and password = '123456789'
Login failed

sql injection

Name:- Vasilis

Password:- 123456789

Login

FIGURE 13.13 Login failed.

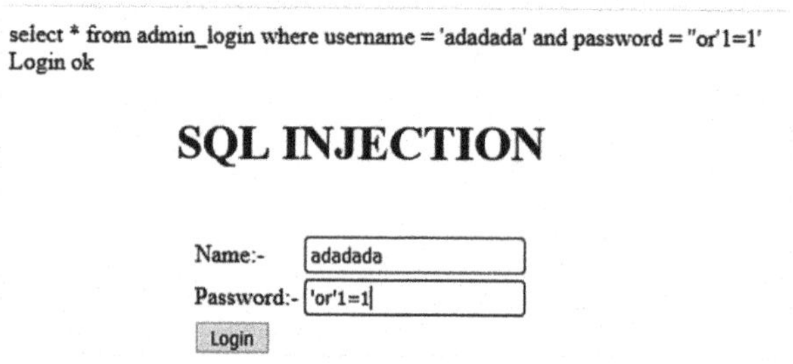

select * from admin_login where username = 'adadada' and password = "or'1=1'
Login ok

SQL INJECTION

Name:- adadada

Password:- 'or'1=1

Login

FIGURE 13.14 SQL injection successful attack.

Information sent from a form with the POST method is invisible to others and has no limits on the amount of information to send. So, our code only tests if the password variable is meeting the true condition. With the 'or' 1 = 1 the condition is always true and so it bypass any check (see Figure 13.15).

13.5.2 MITIGATION OF THE ATTACK

In order to stop the attack from taking place, we must change how the program test the values inserted. We can change lines 7 and 8 to a secure code. The new code will be:

$name = mysqli_real_escape_string($conn, $_POST ['user ']);
$pass = mysqli_real_escape_string($conn, $_POST ['password[1]]);

The real_escape_string() / mysqli_real_escape_string() function escapes special characters to a string for use in an SQL query, taking into account the current character set of the connection. This function is used to create a legal SQL string that can be used in an SQL statement. It

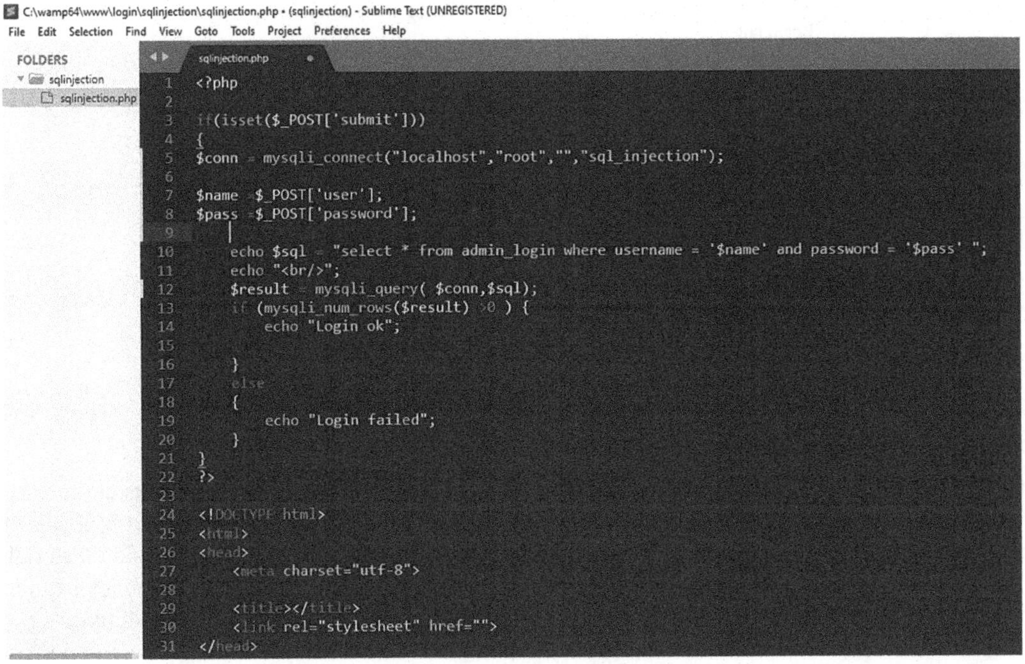

```
C:\wamp64\www\login\sqlinjection\sqlinjection.php • (sqlinjection) - Sublime Text (UNREGISTERED)
File Edit Selection Find View Goto Tools Project Preferences Help
FOLDERS
  sqlinjection
    sqlinjection.php

<?php

if(isset($_POST['submit']))
{
$conn = mysqli_connect("localhost","root","","sql_injection");

$name = $_POST['user'];
$pass = $_POST['password'];

    echo $sql = "select * from admin_login where username = '$name' and password = '$pass' ";
    echo "<br/>";
    $result = mysqli_query( $conn,$sql);
    if (mysqli_num_rows($result) >0 ) {
        echo "Login ok";

    }
    else
    {
        echo "Login failed";
    }
}
?>

<!DOCTYPE html>
<html>
<head>
    <meta charset="utf-8">

    <title></title>
    <link rel="stylesheet" href="">
</head>
```

FIGURE 13.15 Code of our page where sql injection succeeded.

prepends backslashes to the following characters: "\x00, \n, \r, \, ", and "\x1a." This function must always (with few exceptions) be used to make data safe before sending a query to MySQL (see Figure 13.16).

With that change the attacker cannot use the 'or'1 = 1 line in order to penetrate our system as shown in Figure 13.17.

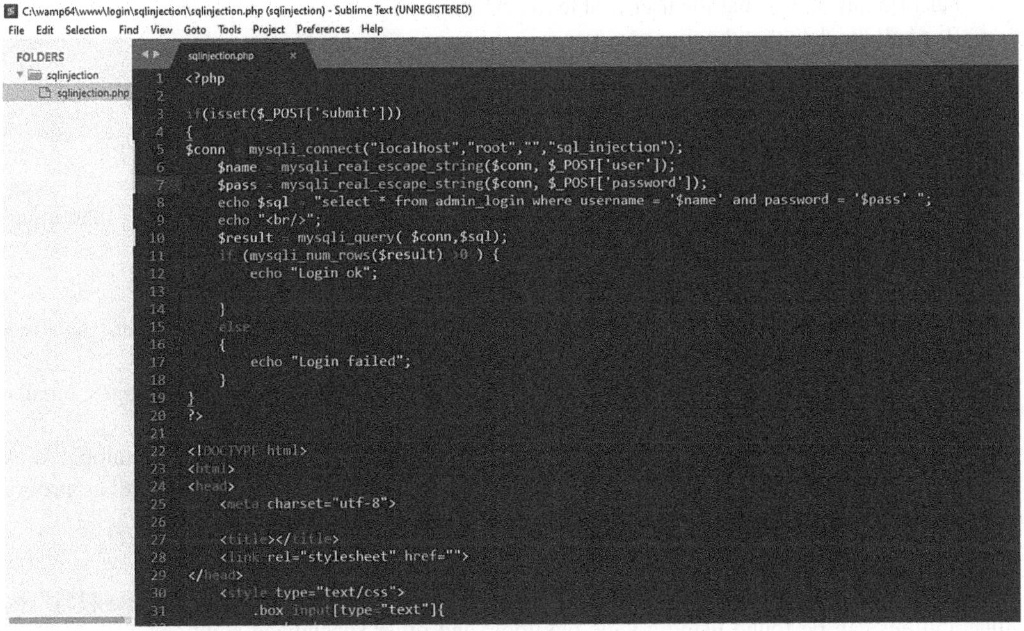

```
C:\wamp64\www\login\sqlinjection\sqlinjection.php (sqlinjection) - Sublime Text (UNREGISTERED)
File Edit Selection Find View Goto Tools Project Preferences Help
FOLDERS
  sqlinjection
    sqlinjection.php

<?php

if(isset($_POST['submit']))
{
$conn = mysqli_connect("localhost","root","","sql_injection");
    $name = mysqli_real_escape_string($conn, $_POST['user']);
    $pass = mysqli_real_escape_string($conn, $_POST['password']);
    echo $sql = "select * from admin_login where username = '$name' and password = '$pass' ";
    echo "<br/>";
    $result = mysqli_query( $conn,$sql);
    if (mysqli_num_rows($result) >0 ) {
        echo "Login ok";

    }
    else
    {
        echo "Login failed";
    }
}
?>

<!DOCTYPE html>
<html>
<head>
    <meta charset="utf-8">

    <title></title>
    <link rel="stylesheet" href="">
</head>
    <style type="text/css">
        .box input[type="text"]{
```

FIGURE 13.16 Our code after the mitigation.

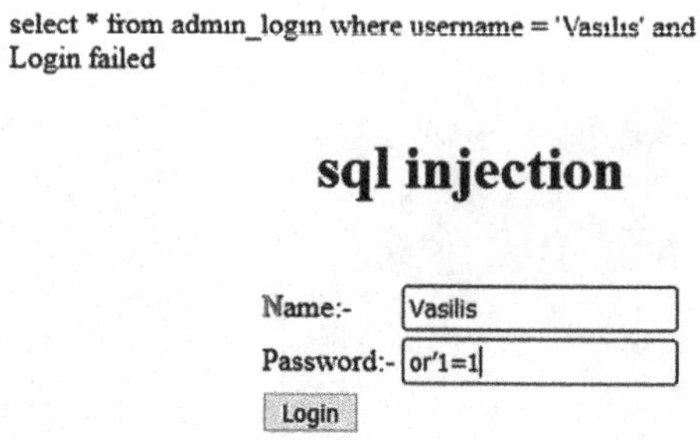

select * from admin_login where username = 'Vasilis' and password = 'or'1=1 '
Login failed

sql injection

Name:-   [Vasilis   ]
Password:- [or'1=1|]
[Login]

FIGURE 13.17   SQL injection is unsuccessful.

13.6   DISCUSSION: CONCLUSIONS

Cross-Site Scripting (XSS) assaults are a sort of injection, wherein malignant contents are infused into in any case amiable and confided in sites. XSS attacks occur where an aggressor uses a web application to send vindictive code to an alternative end recipient, often as program side material. Imperfections that cause these attacks to work are very wide and exist wherever a web application uses a customer's contribution within the output it creates without authorizing or encoding it.

In order to deliver vindictive content to a recipient, an attacker may use XSS. There is no real means for the end client software to know that the content cannot be trusted, and that the content will be executed. Because it assumes the information came from a reputable source, any treatments, meeting tokens, or other confidential data kept by the software and used for that site can be accessed by the dangerous content. These contents can even modify the substance of the HTML page. For additional subtleties on the various kinds of XSS imperfections.

An attacker who exploits a cross-site scripting vulnerability is usually able to:

- Pretend to be the victim user
- Perform any action that the user is able to perform
- Read all the data that the user can access
- Capture user credentials
- Perform the virtual deployment of the website
- Inject the Trojan's functionality into your website

The real effect of an XSS assault usually depends on the nature of the application, its functionality and information, and the status of the compromised client. For case:

- In a web-based application, where all clients are self-contained and all data is open, the affect will regularly be negligible
- In an application holding touchy information, such as managing account exchanges, emails, or healthcare records, the affect will be important
- In case the compromised client has lifted benefits inside the application (for example is an admin), at that point the effect will be large, permitting the attacker to require full control of the application and compromise all clients' information

XSS attacks are the most popular attacks since they exploit a variety of vulnerabilities [15]. The vulnerabilities can be found using google dev tools and other specialized solutions such as Burp Suite's web vulnerability scanner. The most simple way to prevent any vulnerability is to "escape" the characters a user can input and to sanitize any HTML that appears in the inputs of the web app. The manual testing step of a web application can also search for mirrored and stored XSS witch normally involves sending simple single entries (such as a short alphanumeric string) to each entry point in the application; identifying each location where the sent entry is returned in HTTP responses; and testing each location individually to determine if properly made entries can be used to execute arbitrary JavaScript [16].

Physically testing for DOM-based XSS emerging from URL parameters includes a similar process: setting a few basic interesting inputs, utilizing the browser's designer tools to look the DOM for this input, and testing each area to decide whether it is exploitable [14]. However, other sorts of DOM XSS are harder to identify. To discover DOM-based vulnerabilities in non-URL-based input (such as document.cookie) or non-HTML-based sinks (like setTimeout), there is no substitute for investigating JavaScript code, which can be amazingly time-consuming. Here dev tools can help by showing all scripts loaded on a page and a tester can ensure that all required scripts are loaded only at the end of the document (this usually prevents the attacker from using some jQuery features for example Ajax malevolent requests of the attacker).

In common, viably anticipating XSS vulnerabilities is likely to include several measures:

- At the point where client input is received, use basic input rules
- When client content arrives in HTTP reactions it ought to be encoded to avoid it from being translated as dynamic content. Depending on the settings, this might require applying combinations of HTML, URL, JavaScript, and CSS encoding
- To avoid XSS in HTTP reactions that aren't expecting to contain any HTML or JavaScript, headers can be utilized such as Content-Type and X-Content-Type-Options headers to guarantee that browsers translate the reactions correctly. As a final line of defense, CSP can be utilized to decrease the severity of any XSS vulnerabilities that still happen, XSS vulnerabilities are difficult to anticipate basically since there are so numerous vectors where an XSS assault can be utilized in most applications. As opposed to other vulnerabilities, such as SQL injection or OS command injection, XSS influences the client of the site, making it more difficult to capture and indeed harder to settle. Moreover, not at all like SQL injection, which can be dispensed with the right utilize of arranged articulations, there's no single standard or technique to prevent cross-site scripting assaults. Whereas utilizing the security layers just like the ones said over, it's a great way to avoid most XSS attacks, it is fundamental to note that whereas those avoidance strategies would cover most of the XSS attack vectors, they cannot cover everything. It is pivotal to utilize a combination of programmed static testing, code audit, and dynamic testing along with applying secure coding techniques. If these measures are not deployed and run frequently along with other security measures like intrusion detection systems [17] the attackers can take control of essential services and sensitive data.

As cyber-attacks on critical systems continue to rise, awareness and training of the appropriate personnel is very important and for that reason technical solutions should be combined with those [18]. The danger is still very large from cross-site scripting attacks that can lead to data breaches. As long as users tend to browse the internet even more than before they are exposed to several threats. When designing a web application. We must follow as much as we can security and privacy preservation rules and try not to leave any loopholes to programs. Experience is a great factor for programmers to know these attacks and articles that present simple attack defense scripts are of great need especially for junior programmers and students. This article presents simple scenario where XSS scripting attacks take place and proposes several defense actions. The presented tutorial examples are accompanied by the respective code that allows readers to experiment and learn.

REFERENCES

1. Flanagan, D. and Like, W. S. *JavaScript: The Definitive Guide*, 5th ed. O'Reilly Media, Inc., 2006.
2. MacDonald, M., Szpuszta, M., Lair, R., and Lefebvre, J. *Pro Asp. net 2.0 in C# 2005*. Springer, 2005.
3. Rahman, R. U., Wadhwa, D., Bali, A., and Tomar, D. S. "The emerging threats of web scrapping to web applications security and their defense mechanism." In *Encyclopedia of Criminal Activities and the Deep Web*. IGI Global, 2020, pp. 788–809.
4. Security, W. "Threat reports," 2020. [Online]. Available at: https://www.whitehatsec.com/resources-category/threat-reports/. [Last Accessed 1 Jul. 2020].
5. MITRE. "Common weakness enumeration," 2020. [Online]. Available at: http://cwe.mitre.org/top25/archive/2020/2020_cwe_top25.html. [Last Accessed 1 Jul. 2020].
6. Faghani, M. R. and Saidi, H. "Social networks' XSS worms." *2009 International Conference on Computational Science and Engineering*, vol. 4. IEEE, 2009.
7. Chaudhary, P., Gupta, B., and Gupta, S. "Cross-site scripting (XSS) worms in online social network (OSN): taxonomy and defensive mechanisms." *2016 3rd International Conference on Computing for Sustainable Global Development (INDIACom)*. IEEE, 2016, pp. 2131–2136.
8. Hamid, A., Alam, M., Sheherin, H., and Pathan, A. S. K. "Cyber security concerns in social networking service." *International Journal of Communication Networks and Information Security*, vol. 12, no. 2, 2020, pp. 198–212.
9. Gupta, S. and Gupta, B. B. "Cross-site scripting (XSS) attacks and defense mechanisms: classification and state-of-the-art." *International Journal of System Assurance Engineering and Management*, vol. 8, no. 1, 2017. pp. 512–530.
10. Abikoye, O. C., Abubakar, A., Dokoro, A. H., Akande, O. N., and Kayode, A. A. "A novel technique to prevent SQL injection and cross-site scripting attacks using Knuth-Morris-Pratt string match algorithm." *EURASIP Journal on Information Security*, vol. 2020, no. 1, 2020, pp. 1–14.
11. Rodríguez, G. E., Torres, J. G., Flores, P., and Benavides, D. E. "Cross-site scripting (XSS) attacks and mitigation: a survey." *Computer Networks*, vol. 166, 2020, p. 106960.
12. Al-Khurafi, O. B. and Al-Ahmad, M. A. "Survey of web application vulnerability attacks." *2015 4th International Conference on Advanced Computer Science Applications and Technologies (ACSAT)*. IEEE, 2015, pp. 154–158.
13. Tripathi, P. and Thingla, R. "Cross site scripting (XSS) and SQL-injection attack detection in web application." *Proceedings of International Conference on Sustainable Computing in Science, Technology and Management (SUSCOM)*, Amity University Rajasthan, Jaipur, India, 2019.
14. Gupta, S., Gupta, B. B., and Chaudhary, P. "Hunting for DOM-based XSS vulnerabilities in mobile cloud-based online social network." *Future Generation Computer Systems*, vol. 79, 2018, pp. 319–336.
15. Nagar, N. and Suman, U. "Analyzing virtualization vulnerabilities and design a secure cloud environment to prevent from XSS attack." *International Journal of Cloud Applications and Computing (IJCAC)*, vol. 6, 2016, pp. 1–14.
16. Sarmah, U., Bhattacharyya, D., and Kalita, J. K. "A survey of detection methods for XSS attacks." *Journal of Network and Computer Applications*, vol. 118, 2018, pp. 113–143.
17. Stewart, B., Rosa, L., Maglaras, L. A., Cruz, T. J., Ferrag, M. A., Simoes, P., and Janicke, H. "A novel intrusion detection mechanism for scada systems which automatically adapts to network topology changes." *EAI Endorsed Transactions on Industrial Networks and Intelligent Systems*, vol. 4, 2017.
18. Cook, A., Smith, R., Maglaras, L., and Janicke, H. "Using gamification to raise awareness of cyber threats to critical national infrastructure." *BCS*, 2016.

Index